THE
JOURNEY
OF YOUR
SOUL

A CHANNEL EXPLORES CHANNELING
AND THE MICHAEL TEACHINGS

SHEPHERD HOODWIN

Summerjoy Press
LAGUNA BEACH, CALIFORNIA
Revised Edition, 1999

THE JOURNEY OF YOUR SOUL:
A Channel Explores Channeling and the Michael Teachings

PUBLISHED BY:
Summerjoy Press
31423 S Coast Hwy #84
Laguna Beach CA 92651-6998
949-499-3197
877-SUMMERJoy (877-786-6375)

publisher@summerjoy.com
http://summerjoy.com

Printed in the United States of America.

ISBN 1-885469-07-1
Library of Congress Catalog Card Number 98-90138

05 04 03 02 01 00 99

15 14 13 12 11 10 9 8 7 6 5 4 3 2 1

Cover design by Melody Cassen.
Cover art copyright © 1995 by Kathleen Fowler Anderson.
Photograph of Shepherd Hoodwin by John Graves.

Dedicated to My Father

Frederick G. Hoodwin

———◦◉◦———

ACKNOWLEDGMENTS

My clients, for their questions and the use of session material.

Leslie-Anne Skolnik, Kent Babcock, and Ed Hamerstrom, for editing.

Tony Rullo, Emily Baumbach, Donna Stirling, John Friedlander, Phil Wittmeyer, Kathy Anderson, Bill Getman, Michael Grossberg, Uma Berliner, Kathy Lew, Deborah Bloom, and Mayo Gray, for proofing and feedback.

Linda Scheurle, Barry Gross and Kent Babcock, for transcribing.

Kent Babcock and Kathy Anderson, for the idea for the diagram, "3/7/5 Casting."

The other Michael channels and authors, for all their contributions to the Michael teachings.

ABOUT THE COVER ART

The painting shown on the cover, "Michael Mandala," was inspired by Shepherd Hoodwin's channeling of the Michael entity. Six intersecting circles with a seventh in the center make a larger circle, a mandala representing the tables of seven so central to the structure of the Michael teachings. Six of the roles and overleaves are represented by three sets of complementary colors to show their cardinality or ordinality. The seventh, middle circle corresponds to the scholar role, all the neutral overleaves, and the akashic plane; it has no complement, but partakes of all the other six circles. The transparency of the mandala shows the affinity between the spiritual and the physical, and illustrates that the energies represented by each circle's color are inherent to perception.

The artist, Kathleen Fowler Anderson, is a Michael student living and working in upstate New York. She painted this four-foot-by-four-foot oil on canvas during the summer of 1991. It can be viewed at the Bearsville Gallery near Woodstock, New York. To speak with the artist, call 914-679-9541.

CONTENTS

FOREWORD

Shepherd Hoodwin states that "as humanity has progressed over the last number of years, there has been an increase of spiritual consciousness, and it has become easier to channel—there is less 'stuff' in the way." In addition, "we are in the midst of planetary transformation. There are many nonphysical beings who are assisting with it, whether we know it or not. Channeling is a means of consciously working with them." Many of us are aware of this increase in channeling in its role as part of an increase in spiritual consciousness and planetary transformation.

Overall, I think that Shepherd Hoodwin has given us one of the best books to date about the phenomenon of channeling. In particular, he has given us a meticulous presentation of the information channeled from the source known as Michael, which is especially interesting.

Three things make the Michael material very unusual within the annals of channeling. First, there are a number of people claiming to be channeling this same source. Second, Michael is virtually unique with regard to the degree of consistent and elegant structure and highly elaborated detail of the system of thought they communicate within and across their individual channels. Third, as with the Edgar Cayce and Seth material before it, a whole subculture has grown up around Michael and their teachings in the last thirteen years, represented by at least a dozen books on the subject. It would seem, therefore, that the field of "Michael Studies" is becoming well established. Shepherd Hoodwin's *The Journey of Your Soul* may well be the best book of them all due to its clarity, thoroughness, and detail, and thanks to the fact that the author, an exceptionally clear-headed Michael channel himself, brings real integrity and authenticity to our understanding of Michael in particular and to the channeling process in general.

Above all, the Michael material is a precise, extremely elaborated system for thinking about personality characteristics and the process of personality or essence development both within and across lifetimes. It certainly deserves to be included alongside the best of the other major systems of this kind.

People have long been interested in personality typologies, systems that depict the kinds of personality types we possess or, in fact, are. A few hundred years ago, people's character and disposition were divided according to the dominant "humors" in their systems. With even older roots, astrology has long provided us with perhaps the best known of all systems for typing personality.

In this century, Carl Jung came up with a system, which included an introvert/extrovert scale, with two basic modes for how we tend to take in information, sensing and intuiting, and two modes for how we tend to make judgments based on such information, feeling and thinking. A socially oriented engineer, for example, might be classified as an extroverted sensing thinking type, while a poet, very much caught up in his own work, might be an introverted feeling intuitive type. One could then begin to think about the poet-type personality or way of being in the world versus its opposite, the engineer-type.

The popular typology system known as the enneagram has recently spawned a number of book-length treatments. We seem to have a fascination with such systems, including enjoying playing the game of finding out which type we each are and field-testing it against our own experience of ourselves in this lifetime: Does it seem accurate and true? Does it really fit us? Among the different systems we learn about, which one seems to best capture who we really think we are, our characteristics, traits, dispositions—the very way we tend to carry out our existence?

One of the classic college psychology textbooks, *Theories of Personality,* by Calvin Hall and Gardner Lindsay, contains a number of systems for thinking about and typing personality that comprise a central part of mainstream psychological thinking. A more forward-looking text, *Personality and Personal Growth,* by James Fadiman and Robert Frager, also includes such typology systems as the Vedantic and Buddhist, as well as perspectives drawn from consciousness studies, where the personality type in a given lifetime is set within a larger multilived, multileveled metaphysical context. But, except for this textbook, and for the fairly recent and as yet still largely unaccepted field of transpersonal psychology, which the Fadiman and Frager textbook at least partly represents, there is still a complete absence in the mainstream psychological literature of the more inclusive, metaphysical kinds of personality typology.

I am bringing up this subject because I know of no system of personality typology that is more elaborate and intrinsically interesting than that shared with us by the Michael source. According to Michael, we each begin as a spark cast from the Tao,[1] which is the source of all that is. Each of us sparks takes on a soul or essence and then begins a grand cycle, which is the long process of reincarnational integration back into the Tao, a "reabsorption process (that) drives the evolution of universes." All comes from and returns to the Tao, and "ultimately, our identity is that of the Tao itself."

---

[1]*Tao* is a Chinese word pronounced *dow*.

Using the analogy of the cross-sectional annual rings in a tree trunk, each lifetime lived puts a ring around our essence, and each grand cycle of lifetimes lived, in turn, puts a ring around the spark, the spark being "the ultimate 'I' who experiences." According to the author, "the point is...to expand the Tao through the expression of love through our uniqueness."

Hoodwin spends more than two-thirds of this book articulating in great detail the structure of Michael's teachings. The finely grained, elegant system of classification comes in sevens: Each essence goes through seven ages, from infant to infinite soul (five of them on the physical plane). We choose one of seven roles as our dominant way of being through a cycle's series of lifetimes. There are agreements we enter into in each lifetime as part of our specific life plan, as well as a life task to tackle as part of the slow reincarnational, reintegrating, evolutionary process. And there are more sevens. In each lifetime, the essence in its chosen role takes on a set of traits called "overleaves": we choose one of seven *goals*, as well as one of seven *modes, attitudes, centers, chief features,* and *body types* to work with.

When Hoodwin consciously channels what he calls a Michael Reading chart, he provides for the individual the specific designation within each of these many interknit parameters of the Michael system. This can be very helpful in looking at one's life. In that this book presents the entire framework of the system, reading it can be very helpful even without the benefit of a Michael channel's reading.

I am particularly interested in the Michael teachings about how most of us currently on earth have already experienced cycles that have involved going through sets of reincarnational lifetimes on planets other than earth, as well as going through the various nonphysical planes associated with physical level planets, earth and otherwise, that one must evolve through in the gradual integration back into the Tao. This fits well for me with the growing body of information from close encounters of the fourth kind—UFO/ET contactee and abductee experiences—and from the channeling of extraterrestrial and interdimensional sources not of our local earth lineage. I think as we progress through what I call our second Copernican revolution, currently in progress, we will develop an ever-clearer cross-cultural, extraterrestrial, and interdimensional understanding of who else is out there, or in there, and we will learn how we all have arisen from and are on our way back to the one Tao, much as Michael describes the process.

Another area that I find exciting about the Michael material as it is presented by Hoodwin is the concept of the increasing integration that occurs at each level of advancement through a cycle back into the Tao. A spark goes from its essence or soul individuation to re-uniting first with its seven-essence cadence, then with consecutively larger groupings: its greater cadence, its entity consisting of about a thousand essences (Michael being one of these), its cadre, its cadre group, its greater cadre group (which can number over half-a-million essences), and so forth. This system of Michael's, so clearly presented by Hoodwin, emphasizes continual integration at ever-higher passes of inclusiveness as one nears the ultimate act of integration, which is reuniting with the Tao, that supreme, final act pictured by all major world religions and spiritual movements and described by all mystics.

For years I have been trying to clarify for myself a system of understanding that uses the psychological concept of dissociation, as in multiple personality disorder (MPD), but which is essentially non-pathological and natural or God-given in nature and which is taken beyond psychology to transpersonal and cosmological proportions. Dissociation for me means a lack of connectedness or flow with regard to consciousness, control, or volition within or across individuals and between an individual being and its own parental ground of being from which it takes, or is given, its being.

I personally find the Michael material meaningful in light of my own attempts to understand why and how the one Being, which Michael terms the Tao, became what I call dissociated so that existence becomes a process of dissociated fragments or offspring of the One—like an MPD's subpersonalities—slowly learning to overcome what I call this cosmological dissociation and integrate back into unity: 1) to achieve integration within the individual, intrapsychically; 2) to achieve integration between individuals, interpersonally; and 3) to achieve the ultimate integration back into the source of All That Is.

I can see that by working with Michael's terms and concepts, I can clarify my own evolving understanding of individualization, dissociation, and integration, first expressed by me as "A Concluding Metaphor" at the end of Chapter Eight of my book *Channeling: Investigations on Receiving Information from Paranormal Sources* (Jeremy P. Tarcher, Inc., Los Angeles, 1987). For Michael, the process of integration begins with a spark cast from the all-containing Tao. This becomes a role-taking essence experiencing repeated existence through its own complexities of overleaves. This is followed by eventual integration with other essences into cadences, entities, and cadres, until the eventual integration back into the Tao, finishing a grand cycle. All of this very much jibes with my own intuited scheme of things.

Thus I have done what I think Michael and its channel Shepherd Hoodwin would have each of us do. "The best way to self-validate channeling is to see if it rings true and aids your growth in specific ways"; that is, field-test all channeled teachings against the right-feeling, right-thinking, right-intuiting, and right-living of one's own life. We are reminded by channel and source alike that we are responsible for our own lives and what we do with what we receive and experience. Therefore, test the material that the author provides for you in this book. I think it will be helpful to you. It has been to me.

Jon Klimo, Ph.D.
Rosebridge Graduate School
of Integrative Psychology

Concord, California
Oct. 11, 1993

PREFACE

C*hanneling* is a modern word for a means of accessing intelligence not in human form, something people have been doing in virtually every culture since perhaps the beginning of human civilization. In the past, such access was the domain of priestesses and priests, shamans, oracles, seers, and so on, who contacted "gods," "ancestors," or "spirits." Today, channels are from many walks of life and communicate with many different kinds of beings.

Michael is the name of a group or "entity" of one thousand fifty souls (also referred to as "essences" or "fragments" in the Michael teachings). For this reason, they refer to themselves as "we." The name *Michael* was chosen somewhat arbitrarily:[1] the last soul in the entity to finish its cycle of physical plane lifetimes had the name *Michael* (or its equivalent) in its last lifetime, which, according to Michael through the channel known as Jessica Lansing, was about fifteen hundred years ago.

Michael's teachings provide a unique and fascinating vocabulary identifying the building blocks we use to create our lives. They offer a context for understanding what is occurring and why, helping us be more relaxed and accepting. They also offer tools for making positive changes.

With any teaching, it is easy for beginning students to oversimplify or jump to conclusions about it. If a teaching is substantial, it is worthy of in-depth study, with attention paid to nuances and distinctions. This book is dedicated to a serious study of the Michael teachings, as well as of channeling itself. These two subjects are complementary: in seeking answers to questions about the teachings, we come to understand more about how channeling works, and vice versa.

---

[1]Names are conveniences that we humans use on the physical plane. A physical plane name for a channeled entity may have some relationship to that entity's vibration or to a name assumed in a past life, but names are always at least somewhat arbitrary. When nonphysical entities are first channeled, they sometimes resist their listeners' requests to assign themselves names—they can find that limiting.

On the lower astral plane, souls who are still reincarnating and those who work with them may, like us, also use names for convenience, but they usually use them flexibly, with the understanding that alternate names (such as from other past lives) are available and could be equally valid. Above the astral plane [*see Glossary*], names are not used. Like all words, names are representations, and higher plane entities do not use representations; they communicate their thoughts directly. (Thoughts precede words, and do not require words to exist.)

The Michael I work with is not the same as the archangel Michael, or other Michaels who are channeled. There are several people, however, who channel this particular Michael. The majority of them are in the San Francisco area. For the most part, they each draw on different members of the entity.[2]

The first book on the Michael teachings was *Messages from Michael* by Chelsea Quinn Yarbro.[3] It chronicled the experiences of a small, anonymous group that developed around a woman who channeled Michael at a Ouija board. The channeling in *Messages* (and in Yarbro's subsequent Michael books) laid the foundation for later Michael channels and groups. For this reason, I frequently refer to the Yarbro books. I am not a member of any of the groups portrayed in the Yarbro books, although I became friends with the first Michael channel (now deceased) and have spoken with others who were involved. (See Appendix A, "Interview with Former *Messages* Group Member.")[4] What I have learned from them accounts for some of the revisions in this edition. I also communicate with other Michael channels and refer to some of them throughout this book. In particular, JP Van Hulle and Aaron Christeaan channeled some fundamental concepts covered here, and I owe them a great debt. My own contributions to the basic Michael teachings are mostly limited to the concepts of cadre groups, greater cadre groups, and so forth, covered in Chapter Ten, "Cadres and Entities."[5]

Shortly after I began channeling, I was invited to write a chapter for a book project on the Michael teachings. Because I wanted to better understand channeling itself, I decided to research and write about that. The book project never materialized, and the chapter became an article, "The Nature of Channeling," which was instead published in a now-defunct magazine called *The Michael Connection*.

I continued to write articles for the *Connection*. This book contains those and other articles, greatly revised and expanded. It also includes direct quotes from Michael channeling I have done over the

---

[2]See Chapter Four, "Different Michael Fragments."

[3]Berkley Books, 1983. See Bibliography.

[4]Yarbro's account implies one continuous group, but there actually have been several. Yarbro wrote about the true original group after it had largely disbanded in 1976, although some special sessions were conducted. She and others later formed new groups. However, for sake of convenience, I refer to all the groups touched upon by the Yarbro books as the "Yarbro group," since that is how they are commonly known. The interview in Appendix A refers only to the first group.

[5]Also, see the subchapter "Number of Past Lifetimes" in Chapter Twenty-Five, "Reincarnation," for material on clusters, greater clusters, and segments.

years in both private and group sessions. These are italicized and indented; questions preceding them are also indented but not italicized. Double spacing between channeled passages indicates that they were channeled at different times. I did not channel specifically for this book, other than for the "Introduction by Michael," and to clarify material I already had.

This book is not intended to provide a comprehensive treatment of any aspect of the Michael teachings. It instead offers my personal and somewhat subjective introduction and supplement to what is provided so well by almost twenty books by other authors. A list of these books is in the Bibliography at the back.[6] Other than to provide clarity and continuity, I have avoided repeating material available elsewhere. I have sought to make this book accessible to those without knowledge of the Michael teachings, and have provided an extensive glossary to aid beginning as well as more advanced students, but you might also find it enriching to do other reading.

I have allowed what I have to say to dictate the length of my treatment of specific subjects. For example, I have more to say about scholars than about servers because I see far more scholars in my practice. Each Michael channel has areas of emphasis based on what he has an affinity for, can channel well, and has found to be useful. What his clients happen to ask about is another factor. For instance, I am interested in "Michael math,"[7] whereas some channels aren't. On the other hand, some channels get a lot of information about configurations such as sextants, quadrates and support circles (see Glossary). These subjects have rarely come up in my channeling, at least so far, so I do not cover them here, and discuss other topics, such as monads, only briefly.

There are some discussions in this book that will appeal to those who are passionate about the fine points of the Michael teachings, but may seem like hairsplitting to others. For example, you might not be interested in the discussion of how body types fit on the Michael

---

[6]I also have channeled the "Summerjoy Michael" series of books, which are of more general interest. The first is titled *Loving from Your Soul—Creating Powerful Relationships*. Upcoming titles include *Opening to Healing Energy, Growing Through Joy,* and *Being in the World.* These books are not specifically about Michael's technical teachings, although they contain Michael's perspectives. Another book, channeled from my essence, is called *Meditations for Self-Discovery—Guided Journeys for Communicating with Your Inner Self.* All in-print Michael and Summerjoy Press books can be ordered through any bookstore or from Summerjoy Press, http://summerjoy.com, 31423 S Coast Hwy #84, Laguna Beach CA 92651-6998, 877-SUMMERJoy (877-786-6375). See Bibliography.

[7]See Chapter Eleven, "Cadences and Numbers."

axes, or whether chakras correlate with roles. I have separated much of this kind of material into individual subchapters, and you may wish to skim over some of it.

In my channeling practice, I frequently give what I call Michael Readings, in which I channel and explain charts of Michael information for a person. I refer to these readings throughout this book, noting some of the trends and oddities I've found in them. (A blank chart follows Chapter Six.)

Every channel, channeling practice, and location is unique, so other Michael channels and students may have had different experiences than I have. Also, they may not agree with some of my views, or may have received channeling that seems to disagree with what I present here. No doubt my experiences and perceptions will continue to change over time, and perhaps some of what I present here will prove inaccurate. I discuss inaccuracies and discrepancies, apparent and real, at length throughout the book. For now, let it suffice to say that although no channel is one hundred percent accurate, often what seems wrong is just incomplete. There is sometimes what I call "bridge information" that explains how apparently opposing ideas can both be true, or at least partly true.

When we work to find bridge information, which is largely a matter of asking the right questions, our knowledge is expanded in ways that are not possible when we stick with one source. I don't believe that any one source, channeled or otherwise, can bring forth the complete picture of reality—we each have a piece of the whole picture. So although some disagreement is inevitable, one of the values of there being several Michael channels is the wide range of material that can come through. Each channel has a unique "instrument" to offer. I present this material not as the "final word" on any subject but as starting points for thought and discussion. Michael constantly reminds us of the need to self-validate information, no matter what its source. In writing this book, I was reminded of the saying, "The more I know, the more I realize I do not know."

For me, self-validation means that I don't assume that new information I read or hear is true or not true; I "file" it under "possibly true." I may then play with it as part of one of my "working models" of reality, seeing how well it works. The process of letting ideas about reality prove themselves out one way or the other is ongoing. Models of reality are always imperfect, and I am constantly refining mine as I receive new and better information. In this spirit, I encourage you to enjoy and make use of the ideas on these pages without assuming them to be perfect renderings of reality. Maybe they are close, but whether they are or not, they are meaningless to you if you do not make them your own.

Even if the Michael teachings provide amazing and extremely helpful models of reality, as I think they do, models are not the same as reality. Reality is far more complex *and* simple than models, including the Michael teachings, could ever fully convey. If models are reasonable facsimiles of reality, they can promote understanding by putting reality in terms to which we can relate. Hopefully, that assists us to experience reality more fully. The point is reality, not the models.

It's important not to take models too seriously. Debating models might be interesting and useful, but there are ideas in the Michael models, as in most other models of reality, that we ultimately will never be able to prove conclusively. For example, one could probably not prove Michael's concept that the universe has seven planes of creation, even if the number seven makes sense in light of other teachings; what if there were six planes, or eight? Although it may be useful to have a sense of our larger context, what cannot be proven is probably not essential to a model's function in our lives. The measure of an idea's worth is the extent to which it expands us and helps us live more fully, which is to say, helps us experience greater reality.

In a sense, every Michael student is using at least a slightly different model, because every Michael student understands the teachings at least slightly differently even while using the same or similar terms. (This could be said of adherents to any body of thought.) The Michael teachings are malleable enough to lend themselves to somewhat different models without losing their integrity. There are some relatively minor differences between the way the Michael teachings are presented in the Yarbro books and by the various authors from what I call the "Orinda group," (which includes JP Van Hulle, Aaron Christeaan, and those who trained with them). These two "camps," along with various scattered individuals, could be considered the mainstream of Michael thought. When major differences from it arise, often they stem simply from misunderstanding; however, they are not necessarily invalid. If the model works for the person using it, that may be the most important thing, even when, strictly speaking, it is no longer Michael's model. (When communicating with someone who uses Michael's vocabulary in significantly different ways, the "shorthand" of a common vocabulary is somewhat lost, and a defining of terms can be called for: "What do *you* mean when you say...?")

I channel consciously. That means that I am awake and fully present during the process. Although the material does not originate with me, Michael makes use of the contents of my consciousness, and to some degree is limited by my limitations. Transmitting information that is foreign to a channel is difficult. Channeling is a collaborative art as well as a science, involving translation through many levels of the channel. Although the material I channel is generally well beyond what I could produce on my own, in a real way it is mine, and I take full responsibility for it.

Some channeled passages needed little or no editing, while others required extensive revision, for various reasons. One is that much of it was originally spoken, and what is clear orally may not be clear when it is transcribed, because speaking and writing are different media. Some editing was necessary simply due to my imperfections as a channel and the difficulties inherent in extemporaneously translating complex concepts from the invisible to the visible. I felt guided through the writing and editing process, and I asked Michael for clarification as needed.

I am concerned about sexism in language, but constantly using "s/he," "he or she," or alternating "he" and "she" all seemed awkward, so I decided just to stick with "he" in most cases. *The Elements of Style* states that over time, "'he' has lost all suggestion of maleness in these circumstances." I hope that no one is offended by this choice.

I changed the names of all clients who are used as illustrations.

I welcome hearing from readers. You can e-mail me at shepherd@summerjoy.com or write to me in care of the publisher.[8] There is a wealth of material supplementing this book, including links to other Michael teachings sites, at http://summerjoy.com.

This is a book that can never be finished. I'm certain that even before it "rolls off the presses," I will have thought of numerous changes and additions. Nonetheless, here it is. I hope that the insights and information in it are not only interesting, but support you on the journey of your soul.

Shepherd Hoodwin
Revised April 10, 1999
Laguna Beach, California

---

[8]You can also contact me for a brochure about my professional services, such as private sessions, channeling Michael Reading charts, and workshops, and if you would like to be on my mailing list so that you are notified when new books and other offerings are available.

INTRODUCTION BY MICHAEL

This book will be a helpful clarification, we feel, not only of many points in the Michael teachings, but also of fundamental truths of life. We appreciate the care that the author has taken to be specific so as to illuminate important distinctions, which tend to get lost when too much understanding is presumed. As we have overseen the preparation of this manuscript, we have not felt it to be warranted for us to intervene too much. The author has been engaged in his own process of discovery, asking questions that he might not have asked had we guided him with too strong a hand.

As you read, we expect that questions will also arise in you. Questions are the beginning of knowledge. It is a good idea to learn to be as content with questions as you are with answers. As the author states, nothing in this book is the final word on any subject. But we are confident that if you appreciate the Michael teachings, a lively interchange with this volume will lead you to a deeper and more productive knowledge of it. Your self-validation is your best ally in this.

We support our students in further establishing a direct connection with us, whether or not they channel. In reading a Michael book, your thoughts are naturally with us. Opening to an energetic connection through those thoughts can increase your intuitive ability to use this material in your life.

Michael

HOW I BEGAN CHANNELING MICHAEL

Many of us have experienced synchronistic strings of "coincidences" leading to something new in our lives that was unexpected but that we later knew was "meant to be." In 1986, I had that type of experience which led to my channeling Michael. Previously, I had known little about channeling, although I had been receiving inner guidance for many years, and had recently attended a workshop that had enhanced my ability to receive images and thoughts from my spirit guides[1] and other discarnate[2] friends. (This is a little different from channeling, in which another soul speaks *through* one.)

I first encountered channeling early that year when a friend's girlfriend told me that she channeled an extraterrestrial. She played me a tape of one of her transmissions. I heard much truth in her words, although I was unsure whether I believed that an extraterrestrial was actually speaking through her. I decided to keep an open mind, and thought little more about it afterward.

That June, I met with another friend, who I knew gave "psychic readings" nonprofessionally, although I hadn't experienced them and didn't know what they entailed. He told me that there was a message "floating around me," and would I mind if he gave me a reading? He began channeling someone who called himself Michael. The material was quite loving, if a little general. I thought it might have been coming from my friend's own consciousness, but then he called me by the name "Shalom." This got my attention, because my grandmother used to say I was named after her father, Shalom. I had never told anyone this, partly because I wasn't sure I believed it. I later learned that in the Jewish tradition, someone could be considered to be named after someone else if he had the same first initial.

Three weeks later, the first friend's *new* girlfriend told me about something she had studied called the Michael teachings. She knew several people in and around Orinda, California, who were studying this channeled material. She told me, for example, that she thought

---

[1]Spirit guides support our growth, help us complete our life tasks, and in general provide the nonphysical assistance we need. Often we are spirit guides to others when we are not incarnate. Incidentally, these are usually not deceased relatives or friends. See Chapter Eight, "Working with Spirit Guides," in my upcoming Summerjoy Michael book *Growing Through Joy.*

[2]To be incarnate is to live in a physical body. We are discarnate souls before birth and after death. Souls who have completed their cycle of experience on the physical plane and those who have never been physical are also discarnate.

that I was probably a sage with a goal of acceptance (which turned out to be correct), and she briefly explained what that meant. Again, this made little impression on me. It didn't occur to me that there might be a relationship between the Michael she was referring to and the Michael who had called me "Shalom."[3]

About three weeks after *that*, while I was visiting Colorado, a close friend who lived there rushed out to meet me where I was staying. She could hardly wait to share a collection of teachings that had changed the way she looked at the world. They were from the book *Messages from Michael*, and we discussed them at length. After I realized that this was the same Michael who had called me "Shalom" and whose teachings my friend's girlfriend was studying, I decided that I would like to find a regular Michael channel so that I could ask some questions about the Michael teachings. Back in New York, on a quiet afternoon at work (I was a stockbroker with a discount brokerage at the time), I decided to write down my questions before I forgot them. When I finished the questions, my pencil kept moving, and answers flowed out of me. (Incidentally, that was the only time I channeled Michael through automatic writing.)

Since I had already had experience communicating with discarnate beings, I was not shocked by this; my response was something like "Oh, that's interesting." I mailed the channeling to my Colorado friend, since one of the questions was for her. She has a master's degree in linguistics from Yale; she felt that the channeling was linguistically similar to the channeling in *Messages*, and that I wasn't a good enough linguist to copy Michael's language style (I had not yet found the book anyway, although she had read some excerpts to me), so she felt the channeling was authentic.[4] She asked more questions. Soon, a mutual friend also started asking questions, and then others. I began to offer channeling and what I now call Michael Readings for other friends and acquaintances. In this way, I got started as a Michael channel.

I got in touch with Aaron Christeaan at the Michael Educational Foundation in Orinda. He answered many questions, and those at the Foundation have continued to be helpful. I realized that the previous events had been orchestrated, and later came to understand

---

[3]For my friend, having two girlfriends in a row with an interest in channeling also proved synchronous; he later channeled a book himself, although at the time, he didn't particularly approve of channeling. Furthermore, he married the second girlfriend, and they later owned the company that originally distributed this book.

[4]I have since learned that a channeled source can use different linguistics through different channels, and my channeling has evolved to be somewhat different in style from the channeling in the Yarbro books.

that I was "keeping a date" or fulfilling an agreement I had made with Michael before this lifetime began. In hindsight, it is remarkable that I don't remember ever actually deciding to channel professionally; I just started doing it. I had no conscious idea that Michael would come to play such a major role in my life. It happened gently and gracefully, with a sense of inevitability, like many of the most "right" things in my life.

By nature, I am a question-asker, and from the start, my experience of channeling raised many questions, both about the Michael teachings and about channeling itself. This book is a result of my quest to answer those questions.

"WHAT'S YOUR ROLE?"
An Introduction to the Michael Teachings

The cliché icebreaker used to be, "What's your sign?" In the near future, someone attractive might glide up to you and say something like, "Hi! I'm a young warrior in passion mode. What's your role?"

Role, mode, and soul age are part of the Michael teachings, a fascinating channeled body of information. According to Michael, each of us is an eternal being or *spark* journeying from the Tao[1] and back again in an adventure of exploration and creativity. At each step along the way, we make choices that shape our experience. After committing to a series of lifetimes on a planet, we choose a *role*, which is our primary style, or way of being. There are seven roles:

Warriors are persuasive, single-minded doers, often with a hearty sense of humor, and sometimes, the subtlety (and strength) of a Mack truck. They seek challenge.

Kings are warriors' large-picture counterparts. They are charismatic leaders, organizing others to action, sometimes in a tyrannical manner. They seek mastery.

Scholars, rather than being oriented toward doing, are a resource for others. They study and assimilate, intellectually or otherwise. Sometimes, they are overly theoretical and distanced from life. They seek knowledge.

Artisans create what is new, whether in art, hairstyles, or carburetors. They are often warm and playful, sometimes self-deceptive and artificial. They seek originality.

Sages express and communicate. They are witty, friendly, entertaining, and sometimes loud and verbose. They seek insight.

Priests inspire others through their compassion and vision. They sometimes get carried away and take too much on faith or try to force their beliefs on others. They seek what is highest.

And *servers* support and nurture others, sometimes in a self-denying and victimized way. They seek the well-being of all.

Our role is an attribute of our *essence*, or soul, and therefore characterizes us in every lifetime we have on earth. Our essence has several other attributes, such as *frequency* (speed of vibration) and *male/female energy ratio*. (All the terms mentioned in this introduction will be explored at length in later chapters, and are defined in the Glossary.) We also form permanent relationships such as that of

---

[1]The Tao is the dimensionless ground of all being. See Chapter Twenty-Seven, "Planes of Creation," or the Glossary.

essence twin (twin soul) and *task companion,* and join into larger groupings such as *entities* and *cadres.*

When planning an individual lifetime, we also choose several personality attributes, called *overleaves,* that overlay our essence. They include our *goal* (primary motivator), *mode* (dominant way of operating), *attitude* (way we tend to view life), and *center* (part of self from which we generally react). We change our set of overleaves from lifetime to lifetime in order to give us a variety of experiences. Just as there are seven roles, there are seven of each of the overleaves.[2]

The young warrior mentioned at the beginning was in passion mode. Therefore, his *modus operandi* was to act passionately, since *passion mode* pours itself out. On the other hand, *reserve mode,* its opposite, pulls itself in. *Power mode* exudes authority, while *caution mode* moves with deliberation. *Aggression mode* is dynamic, while *perseverance mode* is persistent. *Observation mode* is neutral.

Our overleaves are part of a comprehensive *life plan* we create for each lifetime. Our life plan also includes *agreements* with other souls to help us carry out that plan, and a *life task,* which is our plan's centerpiece, the most important thing we want to accomplish.

As we progress from lifetime to lifetime, we experience a developmental process that takes us through five *soul ages,* each of which has seven *levels. Infant souls* focus on survival. *Baby souls* are learning about structure, discipline, and rules. *Young souls* are interested in having maximum impact on the outer world. *Mature souls* are working on relationships and emotions. *Old souls* look at things in terms of their larger context. Mature and old souls are those most likely to be drawn to the spiritual path.

No soul age is "better" than any other, just as a forty-year-old isn't better than a twenty-five-year-old; a forty-year-old simply has different needs and perspectives than a twenty-five-year-old. To develop, we need all the steps.

In fact, nothing in the Michael teachings is, of itself, good or bad. Everything can be used either positively or negatively, and Michael defines *positive* and *negative poles* for each role and overleaf. Having names for them can help us stay in the positive poles. Furthermore, understanding soul ages and the rest of the Michael teachings can help us understand where people are "coming from" and foster greater acceptance. This is an important step toward having unconditional love for ourselves and others, which is the highest goal of life, according to Michael.

---

[2]The number seven comes up often in the Michael teachings and in metaphysical teachings in general. See Chapter Seven, "The Seven Fundamental Vibrations."

Let's look at the young warrior in passion mode. Being a young soul, this person is oriented toward worldly achievement and doesn't tend to be introspective. Being a warrior, he (or she) is a fighter, blunt, protective, and productive. Passion mode tells us that he pulls out all the stops and goes to the nth degree. In short, he is a power-house and is probably both a successful achiever and quite sexual.

Suppose you're a mature scholar in reserve mode. In some ways, the person just described is your opposite, and opposites usually at-tract, or at least carry a certain fascination. However, being a mature soul, your emphasis is relationships rather than worldly achieve-ment. You wonder how much you would be able to share with this young warrior. You take your time studying the situation, like any good scholar, as you fend off his advances. (You explain that since you are in reserve mode, you appreciate self-control, and your new friend is impressed by your class.) However, he looks like too much fun to pass up, and you decide to investigate him further—that is, until a good-looking old sage in observation mode ambles by.[3]

Obviously, this is a light way of looking at the Michael teachings, but this material can bring profound insights and be highly useful.

The most definitive way to find out your role and other Michael information is to have your Michael chart channeled by a Michael channel,[4] but you can also study the teachings through this and sev-eral other books, and try to discern your Michael traits yourself.

As we move into unprecedented changes in our world, new and better tools for dealing with it are needed. The Michael teachings are one such tool.

---

[3]Incidentally, I am an old sage in observation mode. (See "About the Author" after the Index for a more complete Michael teachings profile on me.)

[4]As mentioned, you can contact me in care of the publisher if you are inte-rested in having me channel your Michael Reading chart.

Part I

ABOUT CHANNELING

Chapter 1

THE NATURE OF CHANNELING

WHAT IS CHANNELING?

C hanneling is a means of communicating with any consciousness that is not in human form by allowing that consciousness
to express itself through the channel (or channeler).

We live in a multidimensional universe. Michael teaches
that the physical plane is only the first (and most dense) of seven
planes. The next plane is the astral; we dwell on the lower astral
plane before birth and after death. The other planes are the causal,
akashic, mental, messianic, and buddhaic. The planes will be discussed in detail in Chapter Twenty-Seven, "Planes of Creation." For
now, let's just say that these planes aren't really separate from our
lives here on the physical plane. Through channeling, we can make
conscious contact with higher planes. We can also communicate with
beings who are physical but nonhuman, such as devas (nature spirits), dolphins and whales, and extraterrestrials.

Most commonly, the term *channeling* refers to communication
with spirit guides, who are astral, and with high-plane teachers, such
as Michael, who are on planes above the astral. (Michael is on the
causal plane.) Although the universe contains an infinite variety of
consciousness that could theoretically be channeled, in practice
channels usually tune in to that with which they have a meaningful
connection and which is well-suited to the channeling process.

The most common form of communication with nonphysical consciousness is with people who have passed on, but that is usually
referred to as "mediumship" rather than channeling. (The Whoopi
Goldberg character in the movie *Ghost* was a medium.) Although
there is overlap, channeling usually refers to accessing higher knowledge in order to support spiritual growth and to gain greater clarity
about one's life. For instance, my clients often ask Michael about
what's going on "behind the scenes" in a problematic relationship.
Michael may give information about past-life connections, karmas,
agreements, and larger issues being worked on by both parties, providing a "soul's-eye" view of that relationship's dynamic. This can be
very useful, and is not the sort of information normally available from
a therapist or counselor, although if a person is seeing a therapist,
working with Michael as well can be complementary. A medium, as
defined here, might also provide this kind of information, but the intent in seeing a medium is usually to communicate with a specific

2

person who has passed on who would not necessarily be expert in accessing such information. Although those on the astral plane are generally more objective about physical experience than we are here on the physical plane, being nonphysical doesn't automatically make someone skillful, knowledgeable, wise, or loving; every consciousness must earn its "enlightenment."

There is much about the process of channeling that is unknown or difficult to put into words, and each experience of it is unique, but some generalizations can be made. Channeling occurs through what Michael calls the "higher centers," which are dormant in most of us but which can be opened with practice. Higher centers are the parts of us that can connect with universal love, truth, and kinetic energy.[1] They are like radios that can be tuned in to the frequency of the channeled entity. The "signal" is generally received first by the crown chakra.[2] In verbal channeling, it then stimulates the sixth chakra (the third eye) and the brain, searching the subconscious for correlating words. Either the entity, the channel, or both, working together in cooperation, select the specific words that seem to best express the thoughts. Even if the entity selects the words, the channel doesn't usually experience this as hearing external voices; it has the sound of his own thoughts, since channeled entities do not have physical voices. This is not unlike the process by which we translate our own thoughts into words, except that it is more difficult, because someone else's thoughts are being translated through the channel.

By definition, teachers from higher planes work more with the invisible aspects of things, and come at information differently than we do. They often seem to "spiral in" to core insights, gradually unveiling one layer after another, like peeling an onion, rather than coming up with an instant analysis of what is occurring. This is a delicate process, an art as well as a science.

---

[1]See also Chapter Twenty-Two, "Centers."

[2]The physical body has seven main chakras, which are focus points of energy; the crown chakra is the seventh, or highest. It is located near the crown of the head.

Incidentally, an "occupational hazard" afflicting some channels and psychics is that their pineal gland, the physical seat of the crown chakra, becomes exhausted and does not produce enough melatonin. Melatonin regulates the diurnal/nocturnal cycle, and a deficiency of it can cause various problems, such as sleep disorders. Melatonin supplements are now widely available. Sunlight, and pineal and tryptophan (5-HTP) supplements also support the pineal and stimulate the production of melatonin. Main food sources of tryptophan include dairy products (which is why warm milk before bed can help people sleep) and meat, especially white turkey meat, which also tends to make people sleepy (such as after a Thanksgiving dinner).

Some people channel or at least "tune in" to higher sources without being aware of it. They assume that the thoughts they are having are their own when that is not totally the case. This can account for several people coming up with a similar invention or song, for instance, at the same time—a higher-plane source is trying to get his idea to the physical plane and works with several people simultaneously, perhaps hoping that at least one of them will make it available to others. Not all inspiration comes from channeling, since we are each creative beings in our own right, but most creation involves some kind of collaboration. We receive more help than we realize.

My original impression was that channeling is a simple matter of dictation—that if Michael wishes to communicate something, it should sound the same no matter who the channel is. However, experience has taught me that channeling is a much more complex phenomenon. I now see it as a collaboration, with many variables.

Being physical, we lack the "equipment" to fully and truly understand what is not physical. We necessarily work with "two-dimensional" intellectual models. They can be helpful, but they cannot replace direct, "three-dimensional" experience, and some direct experience is simply not available to us now. Until we ourselves are nonphysical, we will not be able to fully comprehend how channeling really works, who or what Michael actually is, and many other things. Even regarding physical phenomena, science purports to explain many things that are not truly understood. Do we really comprehend photosynthesis, for example? We may appreciate an explanation of the mechanics, which may or may not be fairly accurate—science is always changing its mind—but surely that is not the whole picture. It is good to maintain a healthy appreciation of mystery. I am not suggesting blind faith or belief, but an awareness of the vastness of life.

WAYS TO CHANNEL

There are various ways to channel, each with potential advantages and disadvantages. Some material is channeled through a Ouija board one letter at a time. This technique was used by the channels in the first two Michael books by Quinn Yarbro. *Michael's People*, her third Michael book, indicated that they were no longer using it; one passage described a channel using writing. I understand that the channel known in the books as Milly later began channeling orally, like most of the channels I know. Using the Ouija board is laborious, but it can lessen the possibility of the channel editing (interfering with) the material. This can make it a particularly good technique for a beginner. I have sometimes wished that I could channel with a

Ouija board in order to get material spelled out that I couldn't otherwise get. However, Michael has told me that that isn't my path. When I first began channeling, I tried using a Ouija board with a friend. Nothing happened for a long ten minutes or so; then I heard a loud voice from within—it was my spirit guide Fred—saying, "Idiot! Open your mouth!" I haven't tried the Ouija board since.

The Ouija board has gotten a bad reputation because it supposedly attracts malevolent or mischievous spirits. The Ouija board itself is not at fault—it is merely a tool, after all. It's just that most people who casually attempt some contact with "the other side," without a higher motivation than entertainment, do so through a Ouija board. They would have similar results through any other technique, but generally, they don't know about them. If someone attempts channeling simply because he has "nothing better to do," he is likely to attract an entity who has "nothing better to do." When "Jessica Lansing" in *Messages from Michael* decided, for whatever reason, to experiment with the Ouija board, she didn't contact a low-level entity because, no doubt, she had made an agreement to channel before her life began; this was an opportunity for her essence to start her on her path.[3]

Automatic writing is a popular way to channel, in which the channel allows the channeled source to write through him, without the channel thinking. It usually happens quite quickly. There may be a sensation of "someone else" moving the pen or one's fingers. A psychic once used automatic writing to channel my mother, who passed over when I was a child. The psychic was conducting a workshop about getting in touch with one's spirit guides. We were sitting around a table, and I was trying to contact my mother, but wasn't able to. At that point, the psychic's right arm began to vibrate. When I requested that the psychic ask my mother a particular question, the psychic began to write frenetically and emphatically. I thought that the handwriting even looked like my mother's. The brief message from my mother was amazing and profound—although it revealed a perspective and insight she didn't have when she was alive, it could only have been written by her. It was also clear that she had desperately wanted to get through to me. The psychic later told me that she hadn't realized until I had spoken up that my mother was trying to write through her when her arm began vibrating. The psychic had

---

[3]The account in the Yarbro books is somewhat fictionalized (although the channeling is not). "Jessica Lansing" (and others in her group) actually first channeled a soul from the astral plane rather than Michael. Michael's energy is intense, and many Michael channels "cut their teeth" on less-intense entities.

long before decided that she would never allow a discarnate soul to use any part of her body other than her right arm, so that was how it came through.

As I mentioned, I have not channeled through automatic writing since my first experience of channeling Michael. However, I sometimes channel through what I call "conscious writing." Conscious writing is like conscious spoken channeling in that the words are formed in the consciousness of the channel in *oneness with* the channel rather than mindlessly coming *through* the channel. Conscious writing is generally slower than automatic writing, and may therefore be more precise and penetrating. On the other hand, automatic writing can establish a relatively rapid flow that may allow material to get through that would otherwise not be able to. In either case, when I channel in conscious writing, I write or type the words myself—I doubt that Michael took any typing or word processing classes in Atlantis! However, Michael is still causing the words to be formed in my mind.

Since writing, either automatic or conscious, tends to be slower and more deliberate than even slow speaking, it can be a more accurate and precise means of channeling than oral channeling. On the other hand, oral channeling has the potential of greater speed and fluidity. It also allows the entity to express himself through facial expression, movement, tone of voice, and so on, in addition to the words. However, it is important to realize that an entity such as Michael no longer has a personality, as we think of it, and hence "borrows" traits from the channel's storehouse of possibilities. That is partly why Michael sounds different through different channels, although there are common threads.

Whether the channel is speaking, writing, using the Ouija board, or using any other method, the integrity, talent, and skill of the channel is far more important than the method used. It is possible to be both accurate and fluid, both free and precise, using any method. Experience, clarity, and balance can facilitate this.

Some channels experience channeling as being like taking dictation; they maintain a clear separation between themselves and the channeled entity. It is like that for me when I channel Michael Reading charts. Unless they are already fully in my body, I usually bring Michael into only my top three chakras (the crown, "third eye," and throat energy centers). Basically, I go down lists of possibilities and Michael gives me "yes"s and "no"s, often nodding my head to reinforce those impulses.

At the other extreme from taking dictation is full trance channeling, in which there is little separation between the channel and the channeled entity. The channeled entity has the channel's body mostly to itself for the time being, since full trance channels leave their bodies, often remembering little or nothing when they return.

Between these two extremes are varying degrees of collaboration and trance, in which the channel stays conscious, fully or partially, and moves responsively with the entity. When I channel aloud (rather than through writing) for clients who are present or on the telephone, Michael is fully in my body, yet I am fully conscious. My energies support Michael's. I also operate the tape recorder, and sometimes help them find a word they are looking for, if it isn't coming right up. I might see an image, or sense the thought they are seeking to bring through, and "parade" a number of possible words before them. If I hit upon the right one, it is instantly out of my mouth before I can think about it. In general when I channel, I don't hear the word ahead of time and then speak it—Michael uses my body and mind to speak it *through* me; therefore, I hear it at the same time those listening hear it.

I once attended a group channeling with JP Van Hulle, an old warrior, and asked Michael through her to double-check something for me in the akashic records. Evidently, the fragments of the Michael entity who work with her (mostly warriors as well, I think) don't normally go to the akashic records for information. They said that it would be distracting for them at that time—although it might seem to us to take merely a moment, they might experience it as the equivalent of a much longer period of time, because of the energy expended. [4] However, they said that they would do it later, and that I should ask JP in the morning what they got. The next morning, JP surprised me by telling me that she didn't remember anything about that interchange. I had thought that all Michael channels work consciously, but obviously, there are varying degrees of how conscious they remain. She told me that warriors, the most "earthy" of the seven roles, can find it disorienting to be fully conscious during channeling and more often go into a deeper trance, whereas sages tend to not want to "miss a word," and more often stay fully conscious. The channels in *Michael's People*[5] also discuss sometimes not remembering later what they said while channeling, although they, too, are not full trance channels. Through me, Michael said:

---

[4] If I channel a Michael Reading chart during a private session, and Michael therefore needs to go to the akashic records, I, too, notice that they seem to go into a different "mode."

[5] P. 256.

Deeper trance can occur when the channel is not distracted, and there is a rhythm established.[6]

I am a fully conscious channel, and therefore remember what Michael says right after channeling, although my memory of it does become hazy with time, more so than with ordinary memories. Perhaps the fact that they are Michael's words and not mine, and that their language and thought style is a little different from my own causes what they say to not lodge in my memory as deeply as do words that are fully my own.

As when channeling charts, I do not need to bring Michael fully into my body for written channeling, although, as when channeling orally, we are still collaborating rather than my just taking dictation. Since energetic healing work is generally not a major factor in written channeling, Michael does not need the full use of my body. However, sometimes I find that not bringing them in fully can slow down the transmission; I can get stuck for longer periods of time trying to find the words they want. Therefore, I generally take the time in the beginning to bring them in adequately to establish a good flow.

When I channel in writing, most of my focus is on choosing words, since Michael isn't doing much energy work, so it tends to be more precise and "elegant." The material for my books that was channeled in writing normally needed less editing than that which was originally spoken and was accompanied by substantial energy work. Another factor is that written words are inherently designed to be read, whereas spoken words are intended to be heard and can look awkward on paper. (To verify this, you could record and transcribe some of your conversations, or read an unedited lecture.) Also, when listeners don't need to be taken into account, there is the "luxury" of more time to "go after" specific words—it is awkward to have long pauses when other people are listening. Finding the optimal words is another reason conscious written channeling can be slow and occasionally stalled (and even tedious), but can seem more profound when read later.

Full trance channeling doesn't allow the channel the tremendous education available from remaining conscious during the proceedings. On the other hand, if the channel isn't conscious, he cannot consciously interfere with or block the transmission. This can facilitate transmitting difficult material, although there can still be some interference from other levels of self. With practice and dedication, a conscious channel should be able to move with anything an entity

---

[6]A reminder: indented, italicized text is a quote from my channeling of Michael.

wishes to communicate, provided he has adequate raw material in his subconscious mind. The fact that someone is channeling a particular entity or energy usually indicates that they're already on the "same wavelength" anyway.

As humanity has progressed over the last number of years, there has been an increase of spiritual consciousness, and it has become easier to channel—there is less of a "veil" in the way. Therefore, the trend toward conscious channeling is growing. A generation or two ago, human consciousness was more dense, less responsive to higher energies, and it was generally necessary to get the channel's consciousness completely out of the way. That's why most of the "old school" channels and mediums go into a full trance.

There are many kinds of channeling besides the channeling of thoughts through words. Healers sometimes channel energies, while inspirational teachers may channel emotions. Music, images, and movement (in athletics or dance) can all be channeled. Channeling is often a combination of such things. For instance, as mentioned, I channel both words and healing energy for clients.

There is more physical fatigue in channeling from a higher plane than from the astral or physical planes, since the vibration is faster and is more foreign to the physical body. The amount of physical fatigue also partly depends on the amount of energy being channeled though the body; some channels transmit a lot of energy, and some transmit little or virtually none, although some has to come into the body in order for channeling to occur.

Mental fatigue can add to a sense of physical fatigue, and can occur in any verbal channeling. It is work for the mind to find the words to correlate with the thoughts being brought in, whether the channel, the channeled entity, or both are choosing the words. The amount of mental fatigue largely depends on the technique used, the difficulty of the material, and the precision of word choices, not on the source's plane of existence.

Conscious channeling is more mentally tiring for the channel than full trance channeling, although it is more work for the trance-channeled entity not to have the conscious help of the channel. It's a little like the difference between having one and two cooks in a kitchen—with two cooks, preparing a meal is more complex, probably dirtying more dishes and counter space, and it takes added energy to coordinate their efforts. Perhaps that is why some cooks do not want anyone else in their kitchen. Nonetheless, with two cooks, it is still less work for each of them than with just one cook. In trance channeling, the channel is out-of-body and therefore not there, so the channeled entity works more than in conscious channeling.

Many trance channels report awakening from trance feeling refreshed—they have been someplace usually described as restful—whereas I feel tired after channeling. A trance channel's mind is used while he is gone—I doubt that a source could channel verbally through someone without a mental capacity for language—so conceivably, he could return to find his mind tired, but generally there is less "wear and tear" on the mind than in conscious channeling. As the kitchen analogy illustrates, accommodating one consciousness instead of two creates less stress for the mind. Also, since the channel has left his body, the mind is more relaxed—it is simply a passive tool; as in certain stages of sleep, it has been temporarily "relieved" of some of its normal duties. Nevertheless, in spite of feeling physically refreshed, I suspect that a trance channel would not want to do heavy mental work after a long channeling session.

Certain kinds of information can be more difficult, and therefore tiring, than others for a particular channel to transmit. For example, a channel might find transmitting information about a person's life task less tiring than getting past-life information, or vice versa. Particularly complex or foreign material is also more tiring to channel.

Whether channeling or not, choosing words deliberately and precisely is more work mentally than going with whatever words come up first, so this, too, can add to mental fatigue.

INTERVIEW WITH A FULL TRANCE CHANNEL

Michael Morgan, of New Jersey, trance channels Yokar, a spirit guide and former Atlantean who specializes in information about Atlantean technology. Since Morgan's background is in engineering, it's a good match of channel and entity.

When Morgan channels, he goes to a "blue field," a restful, infinite horizon of only blue. He is conscious there, but he is not conscious of where his body is, although he is within "calling distance." He is never tired from channeling (I'm envious!)—on the contrary, he can be so energized afterward that he has to "nail his foot to the floor." After channeling for ninety minutes or so, he takes a fifteen-minute break, not to rest, but to cool down, because his body heats up. His spine can feel like a red-hot poker so that he can't move.

It takes Morgan a couple of minutes to go into full trance, but when he first began, it took twenty to thirty minutes. The first time that Yokar was fully in his body, he thought he might throw up. Coming back into his body is "a little rough." It takes him five to seven minutes to "animate" it, and it used to take much longer. In fact, when he first began channeling, he could only go two or three minutes, and then needed to rest two or three hours. Becoming a vegetarian and cutting out alcohol and sweets have helped him, as have martial arts (to balance and ground his energy) and psycho-spiritual counseling. He also says that Yokar has adjusted his body. "Some trance channels become ill after a number of years because they can't distill and process the energy into their physical bodies. Respiratory illness is especially common, because it can be hard to reactivate the lungs after channeling."

Morgan cautions that channeling is a one-way street—one can't undo the physical changes in one's body. For instance, he now finds that even a sip of wine feels like being stabbed with an ice pick. (Although I usually don't drink, I don't find that alcohol affects me in that way. Also, I am not a vegetarian. Many channels and psychics feel that a vegetarian diet is necessary in order to be a "clear recep-tor." Meat is the densest of foods, and a healthy vegetarian diet can lighten a person's vibration. However, my vibration tends to be too light and ungrounded, and I find I need some meat in my diet to stay balanced. I also seem to have a genetic need for it.)

When Morgan is "on the road," he sometimes channels as much as nine hours a day, sleeping as little as three hours a night.

Morgan is the second channel who has told me that his weight increases when he channels. (Jeff Sonnenburg, of Tucson, Arizona, told me that he gains seventy pounds when the entity he channels enters his body, and that medical researchers have documented this! He has to take his belt off before channeling, although he doesn't look much different.)

I've heard many stories about tape recorders not working nor-mally when recording channeling.[7] Some people have reported making tapes in which every voice other than the channel's is re-corded. Morgan found that until Yokar adjusted his vibration, he would get high distortion when recording Yokar—the meters would peak to the right, even with suppression circuitry, and there was a background buzz. Sometimes, while Morgan was going into trance, there would be a number of voices on the tape that were not heard at the time the recording was made.

Sometimes people report seeing what Yokar looked like when he was incarnate while Morgan is channeling him.[8]

---

[7] I haven't had much trouble recording the Michael entity, in spite of the in-tensity of the energy work, although I have ongoing problems with the machines in my life in general.

[8] See Chapter Three, "Sessions," for experiences my clients have had of seeing other faces while I channel.

When Morgan began channeling, he was fully conscious. He would hear Yokar, and repeat his words.[9] Morgan found that he was editing Yokar, preventing him from saying all that he wanted to, so Morgan agreed to become a full trance channel. It took a year to make that shift.

Morgan reports that other trance channels he knows feel that they've given up their lives for channeling, and some are quitting for that reason. Although trance channeling has some advantages, conscious channeling has the benefit of allowing the channel to experience what's happening, rather than constantly having to leave and then later listen to the tapes if he wants to know what was said.

Michael Morgan points out that every experience of channeling is unique. What I've reported here (and throughout this book) should not be assumed to be universal.

SHOULD CHANNELS CHARGE MONEY?

Some people are of the opinion that channels should not charge for channeling, and that, in fact, there should be no charge for any spiritual service, such as healing. Edgar Cayce apparently felt this way, and perhaps this has influenced many who have read his books. However, I understand that his not charging for his work put him in poverty and an early grave; he simply did not have enough money to support his family and live healthily, and because he did not wish to turn anyone away who wanted his free service, he exhausted himself. The channels in the Yarbro books originally did not charge, but theirs was a closed group, so only those who somehow found out about it and were admitted to it could have channeling. I imagine that since the publication of her books, Yarbro has received thousands of requests for channeling; according to the books, she does not respond to them. The channel known as Milly did eventually form a private practice, in which she charges for channeling, but she sees people by referral only.

Those who have access to a channel without charge must feel torn between their desire for the information and their wish not to impose, since the channel personally gains little or nothing from doing it, and channeling takes a good deal of energy. Also, channels are likely to be busy people who have many other things they might enjoy doing with their time. If people can pay, they can have as much

---

[9]I understand that Pat Rodegast, who channels Emmanual, works this way. When I channel, Michael speaks *through* me rather than *to* me.

channeling as they wish without imposing; there is an exchange of energy agreeable to both.

When I first asked Michael about charging, they had no trouble with it. (Michael doesn't tell people what they should do anyway.) They reminded me that there is no right or wrong with such things—if someone wants to charge something, and someone else wants to pay it, that is between them; it is a matter of their own free choice. But they recommended that if I did begin to charge, I not undervalue my work and undercharge for it, which would have been my tendency.

In my view, when you are paying for channeling or healing, you are paying for the channel's or healer's time and energy, which is obviously worth something, and not for the information or healing itself. If I did not charge, I simply could not afford to do it. If someone is well-to-do or has another means of income, perhaps he can afford not to charge; he might view his channeling as a sort of volunteer work or hobby, or as an opportunity to polish his skills.

There seems to be a double standard regarding spiritual things; in my view, everything is ultimately spiritual. One could make the argument that the healing that medical doctors offer comes from "God," and therefore should not be charged for either, but we do pay for the doctor's time, training, and overhead. And artists' inspiration could also be said to come from a higher source, but if we want to own their work, we pay for their "perspiration." Taking the analogy further, everything on earth is provided freely by the universe, yet we do not expect to be given clothing, automobiles, etc. without giving something in return—usually money. Although greed for money can distort what is offered in any field, money itself is neutral—neither good nor bad, but necessary in this world.

WHO CAN CHANNEL?

Channeling is similar to playing piano: almost anyone who applies himself can probably learn to do it, at least a little, and even a casual study of it can be enriching. However, learning to do it well requires a lot of energy and commitment, and obviously, it comes more easily to some people than to others. Furthering our skills in this lifetime, whatever they are, can lead to being born with more "talent" in those areas in future lifetimes.

We plan each lifetime before it begins.[10] If we desire to channel during that lifetime, we usually make agreements to do so with the

---

[10]See Chapter Sixteen, "Life Plan."

particular source(s) we wish to channel, and plan the timing and the form of the channeling we will do so that it supports our life task. We can design our overleaves and even our body to facilitate channeling. Some channels have idiosyncratic bodies for this reason.[11] Not everyone who channels planned to do so before his lifetime began, but someone is not likely to be motivated to invest the energy to learn to channel well unless channeling fits somehow in his life plan. Channeling is usually not of strong interest to the soul until the mature and old soul ages, because before that, our lessons emphasize external factors. If channeling is part of someone's life plan, much preparation may occur on both conscious and unconscious levels during the channel's lifetime before he begins to channel. Not coincidentally, I began channeling shortly after completing a year of intense emotional catharsis and healing, working with someone who was both a therapist and a psychic—I needed to empty my "vessel" of old baggage before I could become a clear channel.

According to my channeling, the channels who first brought the basics of the Michael teachings to the public through the Yarbro books studied extensively with Michael on the astral plane to prepare themselves before incarnating. They also set up their lifetimes to do a particular kind of channeling, focused in the intellectual center,[12] allowing them to bring through highly concentrated, precise material. In addition, several members of the first Michael group[13] had previously studied the Gurdjieff teachings, which use some ideas and terminology similar to some of those in the Michael teachings. (Michael has been channeled as saying that Gurdjieff was also one of their channels, although he was likely channeling unconsciously.) However, the majority of the material was wholly original, and even when Michael "recycled" from Gurdjieff, they often altered the material and used it in new ways.

The work of the first Michael channels was remarkable—I doubt that I could have done what they did. Of course, because they did it, I don't have to; I can have a channeling practice suited to my life task, and still have the benefit of the material they generated.

I am what has been called a "heart channel"—the heart is where integration occurs. I set it up in my life plan to do channeling that in-

---

[11]One highly psychic channel I know can spontaneously start to channel when a certain point on her neck is touched. Another seems to have "electrical wiring" different from most people's, and can be made ill by techniques that are usually healing for others. I myself have always had a sensitive body, which is a mixed blessing—it can be finicky.

[12]See Chapter Twenty-Two, "Centers."

[13]See Appendix A, "Interview with Former *Messages* Group Member."

corporates words, energy, and sometimes emotion to help others not only have intellectual clarity, but to integrate what is being discussed into all levels of self. My practice is not so much informational as experiential.

Every approach to channeling has pros and cons. Even though I am careful to allow through the precise words Michael wants, the intellectual side of my channeling is probably somewhat diluted because of the other elements coming through me at the same time, particularly the energy work.

The question arises as to who can channel Michael. In *Messages from Michael*,[14] Michael was quoted as saying, "We are an ancient entity that comes to all who ask." However, *Michael's People* states that Michael is not being channeled by priests, and lists a few locations as those of the sole Michael groups. I believe that this referred only to the particular fragments of Michael working with that group, not to the whole of Michael. No doubt there have been priests and people in other locations who have "asked." (I know a couple of priests who channel or have channeled Michael.) Yarbro also mentioned certain factors that facilitate channeling, such as particular overleaves, being an old soul, and being in six or seven cadence positions (discussed in the following subchapter). However, none of these things are "required." Michael might be able to penetrate more deeply and powerfully, with a larger perspective, through a channel more ideally suited for channeling them. However, the quote above from *Messages* suggests that they would welcome anyone who sincerely desires to make conscious contact with them. In the elegant way the universe works, someone who is not suited for channeling Michael will probably not be strongly interested in doing it anyway.

I offer a service I call "channeling coaching" for those who are learning to channel and need support and encouragement. In most cases, they don't really need me—they are already making the connection, but they don't trust it. I help them validate it. I also guide them through the process a step at a time, offering pointers and telling them what I'm seeing or being told by their guides. When beginning, I suggest that they ask for the highest, most appropriate source for them to channel now. It may be Michael, but often it isn't—it may be easier to channel their essence or an astral spirit guide first. They may find that channeling from the astral plane is their "niche," what they agreed to do, or what is most appropriate and comfortable for them. They may also eventually channel a higher-plane source other than Michael.

---

[14]P. 21.

The key for those learning to channel is simply to practice a lot, taking everything they get with a grain of salt without worrying too much about accuracy. It's like sketching in an art class, not being concerned about a final product at that stage.[15]

SIXES AND SEVENS

We are each a member of a permanent group of seven souls, called a "cadence," or "primary cadence," in which we have a particular numerical position, one through seven. (This will be covered in depth in Chapter Eleven, "Cadences and Numbers.") Our cadence, in turn, has a particular numerical position within its group of seven cadences, which is called a "greater cadence." Each of the numbers has certain attributes, and resonates with a particular role and particular overleaves. The "Michael-Math" chapter of *More Messages from Michael*[16] said that being in six or seven cadence or greater cadence positions facilitates channeling and other psychic work. The six connects one with the astral plane, and the seven, with the causal plane. However, I am in the fifth position of a cadence that is fourth in its greater cadence—no sixes or sevens. Overleaves with a six or seven vibration (which include those on the cardinal side of the inspiration and action axes, respectively[17]) can also be useful. However, I also do not have any overleaves in that position, other than my chief feature (primary stumbling block),[18] and I don't think that counts! The only seven I have is my soul age, seventh-level old.[19]

> *The vibration of the six or seven is strong for someone at the sixth or seventh level of their soul age, but it is not as significant as, say, the attitude of spiritualist (a six), or more importantly, being in a six or seven cadence position. Sixes and sevens give a "natural" connection with the higher planes.*

Having a strong six and/or seven vibration is rather like having cable television: the "signal" comes through a built-in connection. Nonetheless, there are ways around a lack of six and seven vibrations. My channeling largely comes through my psyche, which is like receiving

---

[15]I recommend *Opening to Channel* by Sanaya Roman and Duane Packer (H J Kramer, 1987), itself a channeled book, as a text.

[16]Pp. 203-204.

[17]See Chapter Seven, "The Seven Fundamental Vibrations."

[18]See Chapter Twenty-Three, "Chief Features."

[19]See Chapter Fifteen, "Soul Age."

the television signal through an antenna. Once I receive Michael's "signal," their energy can fill my whole body, just the same as if I had received it through "cable." However, it's more work.

> *Channeling through sixes and sevens tends to come "up" through the channel's whole being. Another way is to bring the channeling "down" through the channel's mind. This requires a lot of mental power, and is more cut off from the rest of the channel's self. In some channels, it happens both ways—that is the easiest. Neither way of channeling is "better," but having sixes and sevens gives more endurance.*

Priest is the six-position role, and king is the seven-position role. Despite the fact that six and seven cadence positions facilitate channeling for the other five roles, *Michael's People*[20] says, "Very few priests and kings make good channels because it is necessary for a channel to be able to 'ground' and the nature of six-ness and seven-ness at role level makes such grounding difficult." This is a matter of "too much of a good thing." Priests and kings already have a particular concentration of energy in their sixth and seventh chakras, respectively. Channeling, which brings more intensity to these chakras, can make priests and kings "top heavy." Priests, by nature, tend to be attracted to spiritual practices such as channeling, and I know some priests who channel successfully (I can't think of any kings who channel). The above quote shouldn't discourage priests and kings who are drawn to channel; they just need to be especially careful to ground themselves.

Michael's People[21] also discusses priests and kings getting headaches even in the presence of another person who is channeling. In my own practice, it is much more common for kings than for priests, and more common in group sessions than in private sessions; in a private session, Michael is able to tailor the energy work so that discomfort and disorientation is minimized, unless the person has a lot of resistance. In either a group or private session, if a person says something to Michael about his discomfort, Michael can usually help alleviate it.

---

[20]P. 271.
[21]Pp. 224-225.

PATHWAYS THROUGH THE MIND

Finding "raw" information is relatively easy for channeled entities. What can be difficult is properly interpreting it, and then translating it through the channel, given the limitations of language, the channels, and those listening. Over time, an entity can develop numerous "pathways" through the mind of a channel, making the translation easier. It is rather like a violinist and violin getting acclimated to each other. Music flows more easily when there is a well-developed "relationship" between the musician and the instrument. It also matters, of course, whether the violinist is a great artist or an amateur, and whether the violin is a Stradivarius or a Sears. Great artists tend to have fine instruments, and high-caliber entities tend to work with channels capable of complexity and precision.[22]

In addition, equally adept channels and channeled sources may have differing strengths and weaknesses. For example, one channel may be able to get highly complex material about health, but be limited regarding relationships, or vice versa. Although the Yarbro books contain fascinating, specific historical material, the channel called "Milly" said in *Michael's People*[23] that she's not good at getting it (neither am I), so evidently, most of the historical material in the books came through other channels. In *Messages from Michael*, much of it came through the very well-read old scholar, "Jessica Lansing." Scholars usually develop a huge storehouse of information over their span of lifetimes. Much of it may not be readily accessible to their conscious mind, but it might be accessible when channeling. Similarly, a soul who has had many lifetimes working in the healing arts would probably be able to channel more specific health information than someone lacking that experience, not just because of the knowledge accumulated, but because of having a resonance with that field.

When I began channeling body types[24] for my Michael Reading charts, it was laborious, hard work, requiring much concentration— there was no pathway through my mind for body types. Gradually, with practice, it was established, and now I usually channel them as quickly as other chart material. Because I have channeled thousands of Michael Reading charts over the years, I don't need a lot of prepa-

---

[22]I define a high-caliber entity as one with a highly developed and refined spiritual consciousness. As mentioned earlier, one could theoretically channel any consciousness—for example, the reincarnational personality of Joseph Stalin—but, obviously, we want to make intelligent choices about whom we listen to and work with.

[23]P. 264.

[24]See Chapter Twenty-Four, "Body Types."

ration to channel them, and they are now easy for me to do; that wasn't the case when I began. [25]

Sometimes when channels are going to channel a lecture on a subject new to them, they "pre-channel"—that is, they prepare by doing some channeling ahead of time to "get out the kinks." Pre-channeling is done in a situation in which channels can take as much time as they need in order to transmit complex ideas and new terminology. That allows the channeling during the lecture to flow more easily. I don't normally announce a topic ahead of time when I channel "Michael Speaks" lectures, so that Michael is free to address whatever seems most valuable in the moment. But I once announced the topic "Finding Your Mate and Developing Intimacy" (which is now a chapter in my book *Loving from Your Soul—Creating Powerful Relationships*). In doing written pre-channeling on it, Michael at a certain point wanted to distill into one affirmation everything needed to attract a healthy, happy mate relationship. It took me ten minutes to get one simple sentence, but I think that it was worth it. The affirmation is: "I am now attracting to myself a mate who is a joy to be with, and to whom I bring joy."

If channeling were simply a matter of taking verbatim dictation, I would have gotten that affirmation quickly. But in the process of channeling it, Michael was creating and refining it in my psyche, and that took time and work. Michael may have known ahead of time what thought they wanted to transmit, but they needed the resources of my psyche to translate it into language. It is like an artist needing the tools of his studio in order to paint. Michael no doubt could have more quickly said something through me that would have amounted to the same thing, but they were working through me with the human craft of writing. I have never seen a channeled poem or song lyric with a complex, accurate structure and rhyme scheme, but it conceivably could be done through a channel who himself has such skills. However, it would not likely come through as dictation, unless the channeled entity had been working it out in the channel's psyche "after hours," such as in the dream state. Such a poem or lyric would be different than if the channel had written it himself, but it would necessarily make use of his talents.

The more a channel knows about a subject, the easier it is to channel fluently about it. It's like having adequate software to do what we want to do on a computer, or being able to speak a language well before writing a novel in it—the channeled source must have raw material to work with. The knowledge may be conscious, or it may be

---

[25]As of late 1994, I had channeled about three thousand full or partial charts.

19

on deeper levels (for example, from past lives), but if a channel has no connection with certain material, it can be difficult, if not impossible, for him to move responsively with it.

It is valuable for a channel to be well-read and otherwise well-educated. I suspect that, in general, scholars have an advantage when it comes to channeling purely informational material, because knowledge is at the core of their being. When I gain new knowledge, it sometimes quickly finds its way into my channeling, although it is frequently used differently than in its original context. I sometimes feel that I am guided to information so that it can be used in channeling. For example, one day I "happened" to learn about the herb echinacea, and Michael recommended it to someone the next day. Otherwise, they might have simply directed the person to research herbs recommended for her condition, or to go to an herbalist. Similarly, a friend of mine, who is talented at channeling health information, used to get answers suggesting that clients see a homeopath. Now she is a homeopath, and she is able to channel specifically what her clients need, although she usually works it out herself. Before she had the homeopathic vocabulary, she was still sometimes able to get words not consciously known to her, because she has a general affinity for health information, being a natural healer, but it was difficult and laborious; sometimes, it made more sense for her source to simply suggest seeing a homeopath.

Lack of raw material is also why most channels have trouble getting names unfamiliar to them—there is no point of reference. The channels whose work is represented in *More Messages from Michael* said that they never or rarely got names. Michael then discussed other reasons that transmitting names is problematic. [26]

Channeling without certain knowledge is like playing a synthesizer and wanting a sound not in its memory—it can be programmed or "sampled" in, but that can be a lot of trouble; a musician might decide that it's more efficient to make do with a sound already in memory. Higher-plane beings generally practice an economy of energy—they do things in the easiest possible way that gets the job done. Therefore, they tend to use words, expressions, and insights native to the channel, recomposing them as needed, rather than trying to bring in something totally new. This can be educational for the channel, allowing him to see how a higher-plane entity focuses and expands his perceptions. This can also lead to the charge that the channeling sounds suspiciously like the channel himself talking. To aid validation, we can look for something in the channeling, either explicit or subtle, that couldn't have been known by the channel. But

---

[26]P. 221.

even without such "proof," we can learn to recognize a less tangible but unmistakable ring of authenticity. In any case, if what is said is helpful, it may not really matter where it came from. "Authentic" or not, it still must stand on its own merits.

INTUITION

A dictionary definition of intuition is "the act or faculty of knowing or sensing without the use of rational processes." Our conscious mind accounts for only a small part of our total self. Through intuition, we can access the full range of our inner knowledge, especially that of our essence, our "higher self." In addition, we can access the consciousness of our past- and parallel-life selves, subpersonalities, male and female energies, creative core, physical body (and specific aspects of it), and so forth. For example, I have asked the consciousness of my shoulders why they are tight, what they are carrying for me; in response, I have gotten pictures and/or words that have indicated the changes I need to make to release the tension. (An intuition is usually thought of as an uncannily accurate impulse that comes unbidden, but we can also ask for intuitive information.)

We cannot assume, of course, that every impulse we feel is valid and should be obeyed. The valid impulses have a deep, substantial feeling about them. Impulses arising from the surface of self are worth examining—for example, the impulse to hit someone—but not necessarily worth acting upon. If we have a sense that someone is lying to us or that things aren't as they appear to be, for example, this may be a valid intuition or it may simply be fear or suspicion based on past experience. We cannot fully trust our intuition until we have no "ax to grind." Whether or not we are having a valid intuition, we can use such a sensing to make us more alert and careful.

Although intuition is typically viewed as accessing the deeper reaches of oneself, we are also all deeply connected to other souls, and sometimes intuition comes from our spirit guides or other nonphysical souls. It may not be obvious exactly where an intuitive impulse is coming from (although we can ask within what the source is). Intuition is more informal than channeling, in which another consciousness speaks or works directly *through* the channel—the channel is a vehicle. With intuition, what usually arises are more generalized impulses rather than specific words or actions. People then translate and act on those impulses in their own way (or choose not to).

A hard-and-fast distinction cannot always be made between channeling and intuition. For instance, some people say they are channeling when an entity is not actually speaking *through* them, but is communicating *with* them in some way; the "channel" then repeats what was communicated in his own words, like someone doing simultaneous translation of a foreign language.

Channeling is usually thought of as accessing an outside source. For that reason, some people feel that it is incorrect to speak of channeling our essence; they would define that as intuition, or as simply speaking from who we really are. However, that is not cut-and-dried either. It is true that our personality is an offshoot of our essence, but the consciousness of our essence, which also includes our reincarnational selves (see Glossary), is much larger than the consciousness of our personality. It speaks with a "different voice" than that of our personality,[27] and can be formally channeled, choosing its words specifically and deliberately. Information not known to our usual waking consciousness can come through, just as it can when channeling a different entity. My essence channeling is often similar in character if not in exact content to my Michael channeling—not surprising, since my essence has been Michael's student for a long time, and both sources are using the same instrument. Although they do not always agree, what my essence has to say can be as useful as Michael's insights (depending on the subject). However, channeling another entity usually feels like a different, perhaps more intense energy coming in, whereas channeling our essence feels like a setting free of our own energy. Although I find channeling Michael physically tiring, channeling my essence can be refreshing, like meditation, if I don't do it too long, since my essence is part of me and is therefore energetically complementary to my body. If it is tiring, it is more due to the mental work involved in any verbal channeling than to the physical energy expended.

Even if we define intuition strictly, as using our deeper faculties to access only our own inner knowledge and not any outside sources, it is still extremely valuable. In fact, a person would probably not be able to channel well if he wasn't intuitive. We are vast beings and already know a great deal. Nonetheless, we are still limited in understanding to what we have experienced, so interchange with other beings is valuable. If one individual being knew everything, there would be no need for everyone else. In addition, we have some limitations simply by reason of being in bodies, so we have various

---

[27]Our higher self, or essence, can have different ways of looking at things than our personality. It is up to us, as the consciousness that bridges both, to reconcile them and make the best possible decisions. Michael addresses this topic in the chapters "Essence" and "Working with Spirit Guides" in my upcoming Summerjoy Michael book *Growing Through Joy*.

teachers and guides who are not in bodies. They are like coaches—they can give us pointers, since they are able to observe us objectively from the sidelines, but we must still play the game ourselves.

THE QUALITY AND PLANE OF THE SOURCE

When a person opens to channel, various unconscious parts of himself needing release or healing may come to the surface under the guise of channeling, especially if he hasn't already given them a chance to come up. A clear channel knows the difference between his own "stuff" and valid channeling, and keeps his subconscious "processed." Once someone is reasonably "caught up" with processing, unfinished business becomes less demanding of attention and hence easier to put out of the way, which facilitates channeling. However much unfinished emotional and mental business remains, every channel must be able to set aside his conditioned consciousness—not only his unfinished business, but his entire belief structure—in order to be effective. The more he knows himself, the easier this is.

Even if an outside source is accurately contacted, many entities are not worth channeling. One might be able to channel Jack the Ripper, but it probably wouldn't be very spiritually enlightening! Channels are wise to stay clear of unloving or immature entities. If they "come around," channels can simply tell them firmly to leave, just as you might tell a pesky person to leave. Usually, they leave quickly when they can see that the channels aren't going to work with them. In general, like attracts like. The more developed the entity's consciousness, the more powerful and refined the energy, and the clearer the channel must be to accommodate it. A person lacking in integrity or depth would be unlikely to be channeling a font of great wisdom (although some crude power could still come through).

The astral plane, being the nearest to the physical, is the easiest other plane from which to channel. Hence, there are many who channel astral entities, but relatively few who channel entities from the higher planes. There are also distinctions between channeling from the lower, middle, and upper levels of planes, particularly the astral plane. We are on the lower astral plane between lifetimes and during out-of-body experiences, so it is especially accessible.[28] Cycled-off entity mates[29] are on the middle astral plane, and they are

---

[28]When someone channels his higher self (or essence), he is usually accessing the lower astral aspect of it.

[29]Those who are cycled off have completed their cycle of lifetimes on the physical plane of a particular planet. Entity mates are members of the same

likewise quite accessible. The upper astral plane is populated by fully cycled-off entities that are recombining,[30] and is less accessible. The higher the plane or level of plane, the faster its vibration, and the more it "stretches" (and tires) the channel's body. Therefore, someone who can channel a middle-astral plane source for, say, six hours in a day might only be able to handle a middle-causal plane source for two or three hours. The type of channeling and the depth of penetration of the channeled source into the channel also make a difference. The more profound the penetration, the more tiring it can be for the channel, and the more impact the source has.

No plane is "better" than another. There is a wide variety of experience and understanding within each plane. There are a number of extraordinary teachers even on the physical plane, so quality is not a matter of the plane. Some of the best channeled material comes from those on the astral plane. They are closer to the physical plane than higher-plane teachers, and may have more knowledge of the details of our lives and of the physical plane itself. On the other hand, their knowledge and scope may be more narrow than that of higher-plane teachers. Also, on the astral plane, there can still be remnants of personality in those sentient souls who were previously incarnate; that can make them seem easier to relate to, but they can also sometimes be rather opinionated, and rigid opinions can get in the way of objectivity and accuracy. Higher-plane sources have little in the way of opinions or personality, as we generally think of them, although, as mentioned, they may "borrow" personality traits from the channel.

No source is an "all-purpose" entity. If we are interested in knowing the causal, underlying factors in a particular situation, we might go to a causal-plane teacher who "specializes" in such information. On the other hand, for more mundane information we might go to a psychic or someone who channels an astral entity. Of course, a psychic or an astral entity might also offer a higher perspective on our situation, just as a causal entity might also be helpful with more mundane information—the distinctions are not cut-and-dried, but there are areas of emphasis. If, for example, I were trying to find a kidnapped child and needed a lot of specific facts, such as descriptions of the kidnapper and possible addresses to check out, I would go to a psychic (or channel) who specializes in this area before going to Michael, although Michael could, no doubt, give some helpful guidance. If I were interested in having an in-depth conversation with

---

spiritual family. See Chapter Ten, "Cadres and Entities."

[30]When all members of an entity complete the physical plane, the entity begins to recombine so that it can work together more as a unit, rather than as individual "fragments" pursuing separate lifetimes.

someone who had recently died, I would go to a medium who specializes in that. If I were looking for vivid pictures of future probabilities coming up for me—for example, what was likely to happen in a particular relationship—I would go to someone who is especially sensitive to that type of information.

No guide or teacher can take us further spiritually than it has gone itself. However, there is more to spiritual maturity than progression through the planes of creation, just as there is more to a person's "spiritual resumé" than his soul age. Every channeled source, like every person, is the unique sum of all it has experienced.

You are getting our opinions, views, and experiences. Other equally valid entities have different slants and points of view.

THE AKASHIC RECORDS

A great deal of information is available from the akashic records. Those familiar with the akashic records tend to think of them as a place, like the reference library of the cosmos. However, the akashic records are everywhere, part of the fabric of all things. Everything that occurs is recorded there. Anyone can learn to access this information, at least to some degree. However, the records are quite complex and require a great deal of practice to use skillfully.

The core of the akashic records is the akashic plane, the neutral plane.[31] It is the overall record for the universe. The akashic plane interpenetrates the other six planes through their "local" akashic records. For example, our physical body has an akashic record of all that it has experienced; that record will ultimately be distilled[32] and integrated into the akashic plane. Since the vibration of the akashic plane is closest to those of the causal and mental planes, essences focused on those planes can access it most easily.

Some psychics directly access at least the surface of the akashic plane. However, from the physical plane, it is not possible to go very deeply into it. Accessing the akashic plane is not really what your lessons are about on the physical plane, and you are not designed for it. This is one reason you find it useful to channel sources such as ourselves. It is germane to

---

[31]See Chapter Twenty-Seven, "Planes of Creation."

[32]By "distilled," I mean that the raw material of experience will be studied, organized, and understood; it will be reduced to its essential component—what was learned from it.

*our lessons to delve into the akashic plane. We are learning to
do this, and we can access information that might be inacces-
sible to you. We are not discouraging you from trying to access
it yourselves, but we can help in this way.*

Although psychics may have limited access to the akashic plane, they
can have full access to the physical plane akashic records, which are
not yet fully distilled.

The instinctive (neutral) center[33] is the location of a person's individual akashic records; it interpenetrates the other centers and
stores their memories there; it is the seat of the subconscious. The
individual instinctive center is, in turn, connected to larger
"storehouses," such as the collective consciousness of humanity. Ultimately, it is connected to the whole, so when we clarify our
instinctive center through self-knowledge and healing, we are contributing to the clarification of the whole physical universe. Also, as
our essence integrates the reincarnational self we are in this lifetime,
our akashic records become more accessible to our whole essence,
and ultimately, our records will be distilled into the akashic plane,
contributing to the knowledge of all the planes and the Tao. Scholars,
being the neutral role, play a special part in this distillation process.
So the integration simultaneously moves outward, from the individual to the whole physical plane, and upward, through the astral and
causal planes to the akashic plane.

The instinctive center, and the akashic records in general, store
memories in whatever way they were experienced and understood, ir-
respective of any "ultimate truth." If information in it is organized and
clear, it is because the experience that it records was clear, or was
later clarified; the information doesn't necessarily naturally occur
that way. For instance, some types of information, such as traumatic
past lives, may be difficult to get clearly if the original confusion
around them is still there. On the other hand, the Michael traits are
usually clear because they consist of specific choices made by our
essence.

*There is no distillation of the akashic records except through
the evolution of those who had the experiences those records
record. If you had a traumatic experience in the past and you
dealt with it—if you evolved your experience of that trauma—
that, too, goes into the records. What ultimately remains on the
akashic plane is the distillation, what was learned, which is
what is relevant for the universe to carry forward into the fu-*

---

[33]See Chapter Twenty-Two, "Centers."

ture. The rest is compost, breaking down into its component parts. This distillation is constantly occurring as you continue to grow. It happens within you as a personality, and within your essence, entity, cadre, and so forth. When you pick up unfinished pieces from the past and see them with more clarity and understanding, you evolve the experience.

The akashic records appear to you as a literal record of things exactly as they occurred that can be replayed and looked at from different angles: each person experiences an event differently, and all those experiences are recorded. Everything that ever was is recorded, including the smallest minutiae—the falling of a tree in a forest is recorded.

However, it is not that a very extensive supply of VHS tape running through all reality is constantly being imprinted. The real explanation lies in the nature of time itself: the akashic records are actually windows into the past; they go into the neutral space directly above the time-space continuum and allow one to look into another time without actually going into that time—it is strictly a window, a place from which to view.

Since there is an infinitely long past, this could be overwhelming, but what you end up attracting to your vision is what has some relevance to you, some reason for you to see. Your being on a particular piece of land, for instance, automatically biases your looking into the akashic records to the records of that land, unless you specifically ask for something else. And why would someone see a particular event that occurred on that land, and not one of a million others back to the time it was ocean or even gas? A particular story is attracted in your presence because of something in it that resonates with you.

In Yarbro, Michael refers to the akashic plane as a "*photographic* record."[34] In fact, all akashic records could be thought of as photographic, or perhaps holographic, since they are not merely visual, but multidimensional—when we look through the "window" the records provide, we see the total experience. We could think of it as being in a "code" similar to the digital information on compact disks and CD-ROMs (which are all zeros and ones), rather than in language as we know it. Therefore, as with photographs or videos, when the code of a particular event is accessed and "played back," there are many ways it can be translated into language and interpreted. Also, there is far more in the code than is readily communicated in lan-

---

[34]*Messages from Michael*, p. 42. The italics are mine.

guage, so it is wise not to take any translation of the akashic records as the final word.

Different channeled entities sometimes give conflicting, or at least apparently conflicting, versions of everything from how the universe operates and the history of the earth, to what we are meant to eat. To illustrate why, let's look at one example: a hypothetical car accident. As is well known, if you ask twenty bystanders what happened, you are likely to get twenty at least slightly differing accounts, as well as those from the people who were in the accident. Journalists are supposedly trained to be objective, and if one is present, you would expect that he could tell you what really happened, but different journalists can also give conflicting accounts. However, you can probably piece together a good idea of what happened if you compare enough accounts and see where the common threads are.

Let's say that fifty years later, a nonphysical entity is researching that accident in order to answer a question about it at a channeling session. The "pictures" of everyone's subjective experience of that accident are in the akashic records. Whose account will the entity rely on? It might be useful for the entity to consult several. Even if many of those accounts show pictures of the accident itself with reasonable objectivity, these are also subject to interpretation, and may not completely show the factors that led to the accident. The Los Angeles Rodney King beating was on videotape, but a jury in the first trial still found the police officers innocent—they interpreted the pictures differently than most people did (which led to riots). What is the ultimate truth about the beating? Were the officers justified under the circumstances? We have to decide for ourselves, and to do so fairly would require a good deal of research and mature judgment. Our court system is supposed to provide this kind of research and mature judgment, but we all know that it often fails to do this. Similarly, nonphysical entities must research and exercise wise judgment, based on deep understanding, in order to accurately interpret akashic records.

There is no absolute version of reality and no ultimate source of information that can rightly say, "No, this is how it *really* happened—guaranteed." Everything in the akashic records was recorded by a consciousness with a particular point of view, and the records are vast. That's why it's worthwhile to explore a variety of points of view. It is true that the Tao as a whole is the ultimate source for the universe, but it is concerned with the large picture, just as the CEO of a major corporation would not be the one to tell you exactly what went on in a sales meeting in the field somewhere.

Channeled entities are in a process of growth and evolution, just as we are. And just as reading books and working with teachers and groups may assist our growth, it is similar for them. They have their teachers, groups, and "books," only their books are nonphysical—they are in the akashic records. And channeled entities, like us, are not all reading the same books. The information they give us depends on what they've been reading. Everything in the records was someone's experience of what happened; therefore, none of it can be said to be "wrong." A challenge for a channeled entity is to interpret the records from the highest and most inclusive point of view. The highest truth is the synthesis of all elements of truth in every point of view.

The akashic records, then, do not provide instant knowledge. Information must be gathered and interpreted; this is an art as well as a science.

"READING" INFORMATION PSYCHICALLY

There are many kinds of psychic skills, and not all psychics have the same ones. Most skills customarily considered psychic are outwardly directed, such as the ability to read auras, or to locate missing persons or objects. The ability to channel is also a kind of psychic gift, but it is directed "upward" rather than outward.

Entities channeled by those who are also psychically gifted in outward perception may use those gifts to read information from "around" the client. It is similar to what the channel would do if he were giving a psychic reading rather than channeling. The difference is that the channeled entity is gathering and interpreting the information, not the channel. Presumably, the channeled entity has greater knowledge and scope with which to interpret what is seen; otherwise, the channel wouldn't bother to work with the entity. Also, psychic skills tend to be heightened when channeling; the entity channeled may have greater skill in using them, and tends to bring a greater intensity of power to apply to them.

Reading information directly from the individual usually requires less energy for the channeled entity than looking it up in the akashic records, and is usually fairly accurate. Those with eyes to see can tell much just by looking. Reading through the channel can also help the channel increase his perceptive abilities; in time, he may be able to read certain information himself, freeing the entity to teach new things. On the other hand, getting information directly from the akashic records avoids some possible pitfalls. (This will be discussed later.)

Looking up information about an individual in the akashic records is going to its source. Reading it directly from the individual is

THE JOURNEY OF YOUR SOUL ✦

seeing the expression of the source, the form it takes. For example, looking up someone's role is finding the "code" for it in his record. Reading it is observing what his role looks like in his aura.

> *Roles, overleaves, and so forth manifest in people's auras in manifold ways: color, pattern, texture, shape, feeling, etc.—in fact, in all the ways that you normally recognize individual human beings, and more. But it is not so simple as to say that every time you see a particular color, for instance, in someone's aura, you are seeing a particular role. For one thing, overleaves modify the appearance of the essence. All factors interact.*
>
> *Among those who are psychic, some people's perceptions emphasize color, for instance, while others pick up more on feeling. In addition, you can tune in to different levels of an individual; what you perceive on one level is different than on others. It takes practice to fully know what you are seeing.*
>
> *As human beings evolve, they will have more and more perception of such things. People in general are perceptive now in ways they were not ten or twenty years ago.*

Michael has always given me the information on Michael Reading charts from the akashic records, perhaps partly because I'm not a particularly gifted psychic. Now that I know that there is an alternative, I'm still more comfortable doing it that way—it feels "safer" to me. I'm usually able to validate what I channel once I observe someone. However, it would be nice to be able to share Michael's psychic perception of a person's aura as another means of validation, especially if there is a discrepancy, either between me and another channel, or between what I channeled and what the person seems like to me. On the other hand, although I don't see auras, after years of practice I do have a feel for what some of the Michael traits tend to look and feel like, so that offers me some means of validation.[35]

When, through some other channels, Michael psychically reads a person's Michael traits, the person must either be with the channel (which is preferable), or the channel must have good, recent photographs, with the person's eyes showing. In the way I work, the photograph doesn't need to be recent, since its purpose is simply to verify who the soul is; Michael isn't reading the information from the photograph. I channel charts without photographs when I've met the subject, or heard his voice on the telephone or a recording. It doesn't

---

[35]See the subchapter "How Roles Appear Physically and Energetically" in Chapter Nine, "Roles."

matter if I can't consciously remember people I had spoken with earlier; my guides keep track of them and help Michael identify them.

Before visiting the California Michael group in Orinda (near Berkeley), where Michael through various channels routinely reads information psychically from photographs, it never occurred to me to ask for pictures at all in any of my channeling, and I seemed to be getting accurate results. I now ask for photographs, to be on the safe side. If a client requests a chart of a person he doesn't know well and therefore has little connection with, Michael may not be certain that they're tuning in to the right person without a photograph, which can reinforce the "signal" they're picking up energetically. In addition, I like having photographs so I can try to guess the role before channeling the chart. This is fun, and I'm getting better at it, although I'm still wrong fairly often. I also ask clients to bring photographs of people whom they want to discuss in question-and-answer sessions with Michael, both for identification and possibly to read psychically some information other than Michael Reading chart material, although even then, the photograph is mainly for identification; Michael psychically tunes in more through the client's connection with the person. Without a photograph, if Michael has any doubt that they're tuning in to the right person, they might describe characteristics they're picking up, to see if they jibe with the client's experience of that person.

Michael does psychically read past-life and other information through me. Past lives that relate to our current one are present in our aura like folders from our files open on our desk—we are drawing from their "stories" and dealing with their issues, so the information is "right there" to be read. Michael may then draw from my knowledge to translate them into words. For example, they may find the word in my mind for a farm implement they see being used; if that word isn't in my mind, they might just describe it. To explain the historical context of the lifetime, they may also draw from my knowledge, to whatever degree of specificity it will allow, in order to "match" their own (which is mostly not in language per se). If I have a languaged version but it doesn't match theirs, they may check it in the akashic records. I don't usually get the exquisite historical detail found in the Yarbro books, but the issues and basic circumstances are usually clearly illuminated.

OTHER SOURCES OF INFORMATION

Besides referring to the akashic records and reading auras psychically, channeled entities also draw from their own experience, observation, and memory (just as we would), as well as from their teachers and friends. Logically, it makes a difference if the entities are acquainted with their listeners. If they aren't, they can contact the listeners' guides or teachers for more information. However, Michael tends to challenge themselves to get the information without outside help, at least at first. This is characteristic of kings and warriors in general—they like to be self-reliant.

A client may have a strong connection with Michael from having worked with members of their entity in previous lifetimes, between lives, or in earlier sessions through me or other Michael channels. When that is the case, the material often flows more easily and is richer. When I first began channeling, a friend had gathered several people in her living room, and everyone had a chance to ask a personal question. The first person who spoke showed Michael a picture of her boyfriend (who was not present), and asked what her connection was with him. Michael said that they were essence mates (former essence twins), and then said, "We want to call him 'Jon.'"[36] She turned white, and said, "His name is Jonathan." Then Michael said that they have musical agreements, and she replied that he was teaching her guitar. Those answers sure got everyone's attention!

I would never consciously stop Michael from saying anything they wished to, but I was nervous as I sensed that they were about to say that her boyfriend's name was Jon. They had never said anything like that before, and I felt that if they were wrong, it would destroy my credibility (which is especially hard on a sage with a goal of acceptance). Out of consideration for me, they softened their statement to "We want to call him..." rather than something as direct as "His name is...."

I didn't know that woman at all, or anything about her. My friend had met her earlier that day, and had found her to be negatively skeptical. Apparently, she needed a dramatic validation that what was happening was genuine, although, as I will discuss shortly, Michael doesn't give such validations on demand.

But it was more than that. At the next group meeting, she brought Jon, and Michael said that he was an old student of theirs. They joked with him about how, in past lives, he often played, at the expense of paying attention to his lessons. Jon laughed and confirmed that he was still doing that.

So in spite of how difficult it is to get names, in that one instance, a specific name came through, because the Michael fragments I was working with had a strong connection with the person (and it was a common name). I also imagine that Jon has a

---

[36]As throughout the book, I changed the name.

strong connection with me as well, since we're in the same cadre (see Glossary). I find that when someone has a strong connection with me, that also facilitates my channeling for him. I have had some particularly powerful experiences channeling for entity mates of mine.

WHAT DO SPIRIT GUIDES KNOW ABOUT CONSUMER ELECTRONICS?

Channeled entities can provide detailed and specific information, but they are not meant to replace physical resources. I went through a phase in which I "asked within" about everything. After buying an expensive computer program and a compact disk player that I had gotten "yes" answers on and was later unhappy with (and couldn't return), I finally realized that spirit guides don't know much about consumer electronics. They've been dead for years! Unless we have a spirit guide who happens to be a recently deceased techno-nerd, which is highly unlikely, reading *Consumer Reports* and doing our own research is probably smarter than asking for spiritual guidance when planning such a purchase.

In fairness to my guides, I must say that I got weak "yes"s, as if to say, "I guess that's all right. It looks okay to me." Later, it was explained that the only thing found in the akashic records about my Discman was that metal cases are sturdier than plastic, and this one had a metal case. They found nothing in the records about the irritating hum that this particular model had.

The lesson, other than not to make important purchases where we can't take them back, is that we're here partly to learn to make choices, not to have "higher" sources make them for us. Spiritual guidance cannot "save" us from all the hassles of living on the physical plane. In a similar vein, I would not use channeled information in place of a reliable and readily available medical test, although I might use it as a supplement. Sometimes we have to do some physical plane research before higher plane sources can assist us further— they need more information that is easier for us to get than for them.

Incidentally, "yes" and "no" answers are very limited; detailed answers are usually more useful. Sometimes a "yes" just indicates support for moving forward in that general direction, rather than wholesale approval. When working with "yes" and "no" answers, it is important to be careful how we word our questions, and to ask further if we are unclear about what is meant.

Some people view channeling as an all-purpose resource. However, in the spirit of doing things in the easiest and most direct way, I would recommend a library for general reference (or being friends with a lot of scholars!).

WHAT CHANNELED ENTITIES SEE

Einstein taught that physical matter cannot be destroyed, only transformed into energy, just as energy can be transformed into matter. I would take that further and say that matter, and, in fact, everything in the universe, on every plane of existence, *is* energy. We perceive matter as such because it vibrates in the same portion of the energy spectrum we do. Channeled entities do not perceive physical matter in the same way we do except when they are being channeled and have the use of physical eyes, ears, and so forth. Otherwise, they perceive energy in the way they normally would on their plane of existence, just as psychics see higher planes in terms of the physical plane, since human beings have no means to directly perceive higher planes.

The substance of physical life is matter, the substance of astral life is emotion, and the substance of causal life is intellect. Although this is an oversimplification, it could be said that those on the astral plane perceive the physical plane in terms of its emotional substance, and those on the causal plane, in terms of its intellectual substance.

I feel a bond with the soul who was George Gershwin. (We are in the same entity.) I saw *Porgy and Bess* at the Metropolitan Opera a few years ago, and mentally communicated with him about it. I thought that it was a poor production, and was surprised when he said that it was exactly what he had had in mind. Later, I realized that he was mainly perceiving the astral (or emotional energy) component of it. From his vantage point, he could probably not tell too much about the acting or the appropriateness of the casting. Therefore, he probably wasn't in a position to critically appraise the production, although what he was able to perceive—perhaps including the feeling of the music if not the precise physical sound—pleased him. (Also, he had originally planned for the Met to premiere it, and decided on a Broadway run instead in order to give it more exposure, so a Met production was probably gratifying.) Now, when I see a theatrical production with his music, I usually channel him so that he can see it physically rather than astrally. When I "took him" to the Broadway musical *Crazy for You*, he told me to get better seats next time—he would pay for them! (I was in the balcony.)

In 1983, I wrote narration for, directed, and sang in a musical review for the local community theater in Loveland, Colorado, where I was living at the time. A friend who is metaphysically inclined came to see it. She is normally unemotional and objective, but she cried throughout it, and thought that everything I did was absolutely wonderful (which was probably not objectively the case!). At the end, she heard herself thinking, "Now I can pass on." She realized that she had been channeling my mother, who had continued to feel responsible for raising me. Being channeled, she could more directly look in on my physical well-being and see that I was safely on my path. This freed her to go on to other things. I was twenty-eight at the time, which astrologically is the time of the "Saturn return," in a sense the beginning of adulthood. In terms of the Michael teachings, I was also moving in soul age from sixth- to seventh-level old, and I had just begun a career as a stockbroker (after substitute teaching and operating my own singing telegram business), so it was a time of major transition for me. It makes sense that my mother would have felt that she could relinquish responsibility for my well-being at that juncture. She didn't actually need to be channeled in order to "see" me, but what she saw from the astral plane when she wasn't being channeled was an astral rendering, a fluid astral "picture" of my feelings and thoughts, rather than a precise view of the details of my day-to-day life.[37] Had she tried to stay close enough to my physical reality to continually perceive it in a physical-like way, it would have kept her earthbound, a prisoner of the life she needed to leave behind.

Certainly she had been aware of me, and had offered whatever help she could, ever since her passing. A few months after it, I was at summer camp (I was eight), lying in my bunk trying to go to sleep, but I couldn't. Bedtime was eight p.m., and it was already eleven. My main thought was how tired I would be the next day. Then she appeared to me in a vision that reminded me in its vividness of looking through a View-Master (a toy through which one looked at intensely colored slides). With her was someone who I thought was Moses, but who was probably one of her guides (or one of mine). When I blinked, they were still there. I didn't hear any words, but she made a gesture that communicated that everything would be all right. This kind of transmission takes a great deal of effort; the reason I couldn't sleep for those three hours was probably that they were trying to get through all that time.

Incidentally, before she passed on, when she unconsciously knew that she was dying, she painted a painting with a symbolic message to me about her death; the canvas was found unfinished in the trunk of her car after her death. She was also a singer, and left behind a tape recording of herself singing a lullaby with the words, "Don't you cry. Mama won't go away....Even when you're a great big man, Mama won't go away."[38]

---

[37]Sometimes our pets channel our departed loved ones so that they can physically look in on us.

[38]In Michael's terms, my mother was a sage, which was demonstrated by her

ACCURACY AND SELF-VALIDATION

One of the most confusing issues in channeling is that of accuracy. As with any human endeavor, there are many reasons errors crop up. Errors can originate with both the channel and the channeled entity. Many channels say that the information through a good channel is perhaps seventy to eighty percent accurate. Of course, it depends on what kind of information it is, and how we are measuring accuracy.[39]

One channel claimed in his newsletter ninety-eight percent accuracy for a series of political and economic predictions he had made. I compared his lists of what he had said with what had actually happened. I would have interpreted the same data in maybe the forty percent range of accuracy (which still is pretty good for predictions). In my opinion, he was stretching the truth when he gave himself full credit for accuracy when he was only "in the right neighborhood," sometimes vaguely so.

In any case, there is no one hundred percent accurate and complete source of all information anywhere, no final arbiter of truth. It is well, then, to view channeling as one of many possibly valuable resources, rather than the ultimate source of guidance for our lives. In my opinion, it is unwise to make decisions based solely on channeled or psychic information, just as it is unwise to make decisions based solely on what another person says. It can be useful to gather information and points of view, but our choices are our own responsibility, and they should look and feel right and sensible to us. Learning to make wise choices is a major lesson of physical-plane existence. Those who feel that they cannot make a decision without first consulting a channel, psychic, astrologer, therapist, parent, or anyone else are letting their choice-making "muscles" atrophy. In the final analysis, we ourselves are our own ultimate source. Although mistakes and contradictions in channeled information, apparent or real, can be frustrating, they do keep us on our toes. They force us to decide for ourselves what we wish to accept.

There are several possible pitfalls in channeling. Excessively skeptical or cynical people can create self-fulfilling prophecies by not opening to the process. A chaotic vibration, such as in an unfocused crowd, can cloud psychic perception. Some people don't want to be read, and put up smoke screens.

Also, even strong and clear psychic impressions can be attributed to various factors, so interpretations can be faulty. For example, someone who habitually feels taken advantage of may have a chief

---

communicating with me and my brothers through art and music.

[39]See also Chapter Five, "Channeling Michael Information More than Once."

feature of martyrdom, may be in the negative pole of the goal of submission, subservience, or may be a server in the negative pole, bondage. These traits can look and feel similar.

Using more examples from the Michael teachings, some people slide between overleaves.[40] A person in observation mode sliding to passion may be read as being in passion mode if he happens to be there at the time of the reading. Each role has a set of "natural overleaves," those on the same side of the same axis.[41] For instance, sage is the cardinal expression-axis role; its natural overleaves are those also on the cardinal side of the expression axis, such as idealist, so a sage can feel somewhat like an idealist even when that is not his chosen attitude for that lifetime. Also, various factors can inhibit a person's natural tendencies: A sage raised by warriors may not look very sage-like, especially earlier in life. A high-male-energy woman might emphasize her female energy in order to fit in. Frequency is sometimes expressed higher or lower due to stress or depression.

Mistakes can occur simply because the source being channeled has inaccurate or incomplete information. No source is omnipotent, and passing to the astral or a higher plane doesn't necessarily make someone wiser or better informed, although there is new knowledge available which he can make use of if he chooses.

Some channels are better than others at putting aside their conditioned consciousness; it is a good idea for channels to deliberately ask within to do this. Unless a channel is scrupulous about disengaging his prejudices and opinions, subtle or not-so-subtle "editing" can creep in, especially when the channel has charged feelings about the specific material being channeled or the people involved. Since channeling comes through the channel's essence as well as his personality, subtle belief structures in the essence can also interfere. In addition, channeling and psychic work can be very risky, continually putting oneself out on a limb, so channels might "play it safe" and not let through material they aren't certain is correct.

Various other factors can interfere with the clear reception of channeling: a headache, an illness, or just a weakened or tired physical state; excessive alcohol, medication, drugs, caffeine, or sugar; and a confused or conflicted mental/emotional state. Of course, this primarily applies to the channel himself, but the atmosphere of the listener(s) also has an effect. Some people are easy to channel for; the words seem to leap out. With others, it's difficult or even impossible.

---

[40]*Sliding* means temporarily moving to another overleaf. See the subchapter "Neutral Overleaves" in Chapter Eighteen, "Comments on Overleaves," or the Glossary.

[41]See Chapter Seven, "The Seven Fundamental Vibrations," or the Glossary.

It is also easier to channel in some places than in others. When channeling on St. Maarten in the Caribbean, I found that I was able to bring Michael fully into my body more quickly and that the energy work was easier—clients seemed to be "lit up" with Michael's energy almost instantly, rather than having to build up to that. There was also less psychic debris to remove from their auras. In addition, the information generally came more easily. Why? Some people say that psychic skills are enhanced around water, and not only is this small island surrounded by ocean, but it has a lagoon internally. Manhattan, where I used to live, is an island, too, surrounded by the Hudson and East rivers, but obviously it is very different. Just across both rivers are millions more people, and Manhattan itself has a very intense, jangled vibration. It is almost all covered with layers of concrete. It has polluted air and water, and an extremely dense population. St. Maarten has a relatively natural environment, with clean air and water, and a small population. In Manhattan, many creative and intuitive people prefer to work at night, when the vibration is relatively quiet. There is no such necessity in a place where the vibration is already pretty quiet. (Interestingly, some psychics feel that St. Maarten has a "negative vibration." I did find some of the native vendors surly and dishonest—I perceived a "chip on their shoulder"—and heard stories about the use of voodoo to attack others, but my dominant perception was of the natural beauty. Of course, New York is also full of people with negative intent, far more of them concentrated into a small place.)

Sometimes, what appears to be an error or a discrepancy actually is not. It can be useful to carefully examine the exact wording of both the question and the answer. Faulty question-asking can bring not only misunderstandings but inferior results in general. We usually get answers only to the questions we actually ask, not what we meant to ask or thought we asked. If we haven't clarified our questions, our answers may not be what we are really looking for. The more our questions deeply and clearly zero in on exactly what we want to know, the richer the material tends to be. Vague or general questions tend to yield vague or general answers, even though the entity may be trying to be as helpful as possible, which I find to be always true of Michael. Learning to ask the right questions is an important life lesson in general. The act of formulating a question actually sets in motion the dynamic of receiving the answer—it is a case of cause and effect. Some clients report that in working on their questions before their session,[42] the answers that had previously

---

[42]I require that clients write out their questions before private sessions with me, prioritizing and clarifying them.

eluded them start to well up from within them, perhaps from Michael, their essence, or both.

Here's an anecdote illustrating another kind of apparently wrong information: I have curly hair and over the years, I have found it difficult to get a good haircut. When someone who had been cutting my hair well moved away, I needed to find someone new. My inner guidance said that I would find someone soon. I asked where this person worked; the answer was, "nearby." Since I wanted to find him and wasn't getting an address, I began a process of elimination: Is he on 62nd St.? No. 63rd? No. I got a "yes" on 64th between 2nd and 3rd Avenues. To my chagrin, when I went there I found that there was no salon on that block. Perhaps a year later, I channeled for a group and met someone I resonated with strongly. It turned out that he worked for a salon about three blocks from there. He began cutting my hair (although he came to my apartment) and we became good friends. What I hadn't understood was that we had needed to meet through the group. Even if I had walked into his salon, I might not have connected with him, and I wouldn't have been able to afford the salon price anyway. Furthermore, my guides knew who he was but not his exact work address—that wasn't relevant information. Although the address they had given me wasn't exactly correct, it was the best they could do, and it was quite close. They also knew that our essences were planning a meeting soon, but didn't know exactly when or how it would work out.

What looks like "soon" to those who are nonphysical often turns out to take longer than we might like. There can be many obstacles in the way of our meeting someone, for example, whom our essence wants us to meet. There first may be many unsuccessful attempts to work it out. Also, we experience time rigidly on the physical plane because our bodies need to sleep at regular intervals, and we adhere to work and meal schedules, etc., all based on the earth's physical rotation around the sun. Our culture feels particularly "pressed" for time and also tends to demand instant gratification. In some cultures, people feel that they have "all the time in the world," so they might define the word *soon* more broadly than we do. Those without physical bodies experience time more fluidly still. Time is relative, anyway; against the backdrop of infinity, what's a few million years?

Here is another anecdote about accuracy: I received a call from a woman in Virginia whose brother-in-law was coming from India. His young wife had died unexpectedly, and he was devastated. He wanted to talk to her directly and understand what had happened. I explained that mediumship is not my specialty, and surely she could find someone close by who could bring through his wife. However, she wasn't able to find anyone. I said that I was willing to try, but offered no guarantees.

When her brother-in-law arrived in the U.S., they drove him to New York to see me. He brought some items that had belonged to her so that I could tune in to her vibration. I invited her to come into my body and began to feel her distinct presence. Her husband could feel it, too. Being channeled was very difficult for her, since she was relatively recently departed, and hence not totally adjusted to her new surroundings. She also had had no experience being channeled, so the words came with great difficulty.

To validate that it was her, he asked her to tell him about something they used to share. She told a long, painstaking story about how they used to go to another city and stay with her mother to celebrate a holiday. Her mother made brown, triangular-shaped pastries with nuts in them (which I could see in my mind as she discussed them). However, he was very fond of these pastries and would eat them all the night before the celebration.

When she was done telling the story, he simply said, "I don't understand." My heart sank—I thought that the story wasn't true. I didn't know what had gone wrong, since I had done everything I could to be "out of the way" and to let her come through accurately.

She then said that this was too difficult for her and that she could not continue. Michael then came in and explained that the two of them are essence twins (see Glossary), which is why the death was so devastating to him. They also said that her death was a karmic repayment, something planned before the life began.

After the channeling was done, I asked him about the pastry story. Why had he said, "I don't understand"? To my great relief, the story was exactly true. But when he had asked her to tell about something they used to *share*, he meant something they used to *talk about*, or discuss. He was a well-educated man, but English was not his primary language, and he didn't realize that *share* could mean something broader. His wife, no doubt, was not expert in English either, but may have defined *share* with that broader meaning, or perhaps was interpreting his question as it came to her through my mind, through my understanding, since I was the channel. This illustrates that all communication has potential pitfalls, and apparent issues of accuracy may actually be issues of communication.

Incidentally, when people ask about a departed loved one, I don't usually channel them directly. Instead, Michael acts as a go-between, reporting what they say. This is easier, and doesn't disrupt Michael's energy work through me. Departed loved ones are usually in the room when I channel for someone, and I can often sense their presence and where they are, especially if the client asks about them.

A channeled entity doesn't necessarily know anything about a situation when first asked about it. When that is the case, everything needs to be "researched," and the entity will likely rely on the one asking to provide the relevant known facts as a springboard. The entity will then interpret the nonphysical information it finds in light of those facts. If the facts first given are incomplete or incorrect, the information may be mistranslated, even though the spirit of what is said may be accurate and even of great consequence and insight.

A woman once asked Michael about her son, showing me his picture. When Michael tuned in to him, they said that, in an odd way, his energy was not jelling with hers. She then revealed that her son had committed suicide, which, of course, explained what Michael was picking up. However, Michael could not have been expected to immediately know that her son had committed suicide—they were just beginning to get to know her and her situation, even if they already knew her essence well.

If someone withholds information from a channel, trying to test him, he is not appropriately participating in the process, and is inviting errors. Although it appears reasonable and logical that one should be able to test a channel in this way, it usually doesn't work. Withholding, or worse, falsifying information sets up a psychic block; it is like going to a doctor but not telling him the full truth, potentially setting up a self-fulfilling prophecy of failure. If there is actual hostility, conscious or unconscious, toward channels, channeled sources, or psychics, or a belief such as "I can never get accurate information," the psychic block is even stronger.

You may have experienced talking to someone who needed your help, and when a strong flow was established based on love and trust, wisdom popped out of your mouth that you didn't even know you had. The same principle is at work in channeling: when there is an organic need for information to be given as well as a wide-open-hearted receptivity, it is as if a vacuum is formed and information rushes from its source, through the channeled entity and the channel, to fill the vacuum in the person with the need. In other words, it is easy for the channeled entity to get the information, and he can even sometimes offer what might be seen as amazing knowledge. The reverse is also true: when there is not an organic need for information to be given or a wide-open-hearted receptivity, the information can be hard to get, or can even be blocked. That is partly why it can be difficult to answer test questions—there isn't an organic need for the information (the person already knows what he wanted the entity to tell him) so there is little flow established. Ironically, someone who is fully open and is asking for truly needed information might get precisely the kind of "proof" that a person trying to test a channel wants but cannot get because he is demanding it and not appropriately participating in the experience.

Channeled entities, being nonphysical, do not necessarily have easy access to outer, physical-plane details. The higher the plane, the more this is likely to be the case. Theoretically, any piece of information is available from the akashic records. In practice, it might require more energy than it is worth for a nonphysical entity to retrieve the information and transmit it through the channel, especially if the person asking already has it.

For example, an entity may not know offhand how many brothers and sisters you have, their ages, whether your parents are still alive, or your marital status. If, however, you describe a situation with a particular brother, they would likely be able to see your agreements and energetic connections with him, and provide you with information that supplements what you know and gives you added insight and understanding. If you are overly general or vague in the information you give them, they may give you a general or apparently incomplete answer. They may see energetic dynamics with various people who look like relatives, but not be able to be very concrete with you. They are not omniscient, and we can't expect them to expend an unreasonable amount of effort to look up details that are not materially relevant to our needs.

One client asked Michael what vitamins and minerals he needed. Michael named, for example, magnesium. Later I learned that the client was skeptical about the channeling, because he was already taking magnesium. It turned out that he had only been taking it for two weeks. All that Michael was saying was that he still needed magnesium; his need for it had not been satisfied in those two weeks. Actually, the fact that Michael said that he needed magnesium was a validation of the channeling, since a health practitioner, seeing the same need, had just prescribed it for him. Michael could not be expected to necessarily know what supplements the client was already taking, but they were able to see the need for the mineral in his body.

One form of psychic ability is telepathy—some psychics can pick specific thoughts and words, such as names, out of someone else's mind. I am occasionally slightly telepathic with close friends—I get words before they say them, for instance—but that really isn't my forte. If a channel is telepathic, the entity he channels may be able to use that facility to obtain details about a client, rather than through the means already discussed, such as retrieving them from the akashic records or from the client himself. There is not necessarily anything wrong with this, and some psychics and channels use telepathy frequently. However, in some cases, that might be an invasion of privacy, which, in my experience, Michael is scrupulous about avoiding. For example, if someone asks what someone else is thinking or feeling about a subject, they will go no further than making a conjecture based on how the other person's energy looks; they will not go "rummaging" around in someone's psyche, as they put it. And since I am not particularly telepathic, they don't have me to use as a "handy tool" anyway. Strictly speaking, they don't have to use a channel for telepathic information retrieval, but it is easier for them than directly reading a person without the use of a physical "instrument."

With or without telepathic skills, some psychics and channels have more skill than others at coming up with details, such as someone's name, that they did not previously know. (They might, for instance, have the skill of receiving and transmitting such information from people's spirit guides or other nonphysical friends who know them well.) Although such abilities can be impressive as well as entertaining, we presumably go to a channel to learn things we don't already know, or to reinforce and clarify what we have been sensing, rather than to be impressed or entertained. As one channel I know said, we already know what we had for breakfast—we do not necessarily get better insight or guidance from a channeled source who also knows that without our telling him.

Some channels and psychics want only a minimum of information from their clients—just brief, simple questions—so that they aren't influenced. However, I do not find that Michael is unduly influenced by the background that people give them. In fact, sometimes Michael's comments are surprising in light of the background they are given—situations might look quite different to Michael than they do to the people involved in them.

Channels and psychics may also want to challenge themselves to get as much information as possible on their own, without being told. If they are skillful at getting background details from sources other than their clients, they may not need much background from their clients. Again, that is impressive, but that is not how Michael works, at least through me.

Another value of giving background is that it focuses your questions. For instance, if you simply ask Michael to comment on your health, there are many levels on which they could approach that, and a huge amount of information that they could potentially give you. An energy block in your solar plexus may look to them like the most significant factor affecting your long-term health, and they might spend a lot of time exploring that. You might not yet even be aware of this block, but might be quite aware of a shoulder problem. Michael might not particularly notice that, especially if it's not very painful when you ask about it, and if it doesn't involve significant emotional or mental blocks. You might be disappointed that Michael didn't bring it up. Once you mention it, Michael would likely tune in to it, but they might view it as not going very deep—perhaps just some surface tension stemming from posture that could be corrected with bodywork. If you had wanted them to talk about your shoulder, it might have been best simply to ask them about it. (Michael generally requests "thumbnail sketches" outlining their symptoms anyway when people ask Michael through me about their health.) Channels and psychics who get background details telepathically or from guides may "get" without your asking that your shoulder is bothering you, but there is something to be said for asking for what you want in life, whether it is information or anything else.

It is important to validate that channeling is authentic, but there are ways to do that besides receiving details unknown to the channel. When one client asked Michael to tell him something about himself that "only a person from your plane of existence could know," Michael declined, giving this reply:

> The best way to self-validate channeling is to see if it rings true and aids your growth in specific ways. You can also validate our presence through your awareness of our energy that is pouring through the channel to you.
>
> We may sometimes provide information that seems amazing to you, but we provide information in the service of your highest good, not to impress you. We do not get information by rummaging through your subconscious—that would be a violation of your dignity. We rely on available sources such as the akashic records, your aura, and your guides.
>
> The retrieval of information is quite an involved process, and we do not expend more energy in seeking it than your needs warrant. If you asked us for obscure information that would not really benefit you, we would decline. It would be like asking someone to go to the New York Public Library and spend three hours hunting in the stacks for something trivial. Also, if we allowed people to require of us that we answer test types of questions, it would, in our view, demean the process of teaching, which is what we are about.
>
> It does not bother us that you have doubts about who we are and what is happening. In fact, we would prefer that you were a little doubtful. That way, you will take the material for what it is worth and not because it came from a causal entity.
>
> In any case, it is not important if we are a causal-plane entity, or anything else. What is important is your looking within and seeing if what we say is true for you. It is also important to

*you if you feel more balanced and centered as a result of being
in our energy.*

At the beginning of that session, the client reported feeling pressure
in his temples, which was due to resistance to the energy work. As
the session progressed, he relaxed. After the questions, Michael silently completed the energy work, as they usually do at the
conclusion of a session. Because this client had cleared out a lot and
had a large capacity to receive energy, Michael allowed the intensity
to gradually increase to a high level. (It's hard for Michael to do this
while discussion is occurring, because the focus is intellectual, not
energetic.) The client began to see and feel extraordinary light and
power, and blurted out, "If you had done this in the first place, I
wouldn't have made that request!" Michael explained that in the beginning, he was resisting a level of energy that was at about ten
percent of the present intensity. He had to be prepared for the increase.

Incidentally, the Yarbro books have a number of examples of Michael knowing extraordinary material details about people that the
channels could not have known. Since I was not a member of the
group profiled in these books, I do not know how commonplace that
was for them. However, the books do indicate that their content was
drawn from an enormous amount of material—the total output of
four channels over many years. (I do not have transcripts of most of
the private sessions I have conducted over the years.) Presumably,
Ms. Yarbro chose from that material the most impressive and interesting examples of their channeling. So perhaps, the "amazing"
aspect of the channels' work appears to have been more commonplace than it actually was. I also assume that these channels had
agreements with Michael to spread their teachings through mass-
market books, which might require a more dramatic kind of "proof" to
be accepted. Michael may have, at times, expended more energy in
order to get that kind of information.

One client, who, in Michael's terms, has an attitude of cynic,
later told me that after his first session, rather than accepting that I
was really channeling energy, he looked all over my apartment for a
machine misting LSD into the air, since he felt high, similar to his
LSD trips in the past! (I could get rich from selling such a machine, if
it were legal.) He had had a powerful experience of energy, but that
still wasn't validation enough for him. I had assumed that he was
dissatisfied with his session because Michael couldn't give him the
kinds of details he wanted. However, a mutual friend told me afterward that he couldn't wait to come back. Another cynic client
dismissed my channeling for her as "pop psychology." Then, months

later, she referred another client to me. Since a cynical or skeptical point of view is customary for cynics and skeptics, an unfavorable opinion from them may not be as serious as the same opinion from someone with an attitude of spiritualist or idealist.

Many people, especially those who consider themselves to be intellectuals, are automatically skeptical of anyone who purports to work with nonphysical phenomena, or anything else that can't be scientifically measured. Self-styled professional "debunkers" of psychics, channels, UFO's, and so forth, are an extreme example; although they cast themselves as being supremely rational, they have an emotional investment in denying the existence of what is beyond their conscious knowledge. I suspect that fear of the unknown plays a large part in this. I respect healthy skepticism—nothing should be taken purely on faith—but that, of course, is different from having one's mind made up in advance and then trying to prove one's rigid beliefs, dismissing out of hand what doesn't support them.

I do not have extensive experience with other channels, but my assumption, based on those I have met, is that most professional channels are sincere and authentic.[43] Perhaps people would not be so quick to judge a channel as being phony if they better understood how channeling works. As we have seen, making a genuine connection with a nonphysical entity does not necessarily imply accuracy and wisdom, and one cannot expect the same kind of assistance from every teacher and guide. Nevertheless, each one may have something useful to offer, and the presence of errors does not necessarily invalidate everything that is said.

We receive the most benefit from a channeling session (or psychic reading) if we not only listen literally, but try to catch the spirit of what is being said; the literal words may not always zero in precisely on our situation, but the general point being made may fit and be useful.

---

[43]I am not speaking here of storefront psychics who advertise channeling. There are many storefront psychics in New York City. My experience with them is limited, but my impression of them is that, at best, their work is generally superficial, and at worst, they are con artists. A common ploy is to offer an inexpensive reading, and then to tell their customers that some negative person or force is trying to control them; however, they, the psychics, can (for a large sum of money) light candles for them every day for a month and dispel the negativity (or some such thing). I would avoid any psychic or channel who emphasizes the negative rather than empowering their clients.

DELIBERATELY "WRONG" INFORMATION

Once in a while, information is withheld or given incorrectly because the person asking isn't ready to hear it. It might be too traumatic, or it would possibly interfere with completing a karma or lesson, or perhaps it is something best learned for himself. In cases like this, the greatest good may require sacrificing absolute accuracy per se.

Wrong information may also be used as a teaching technique designed to trigger further questions, especially when it is obviously contradictory, or to remind a questioner to trust his own perceptions, no matter what anyone else says.

Discounting lack of clarity in the channel, one usually hears what one needs to hear from a nonincarnate guide or teacher. However, deliberately wrong information is rare in channeling.

PREDICTIONS

Since the future, by definition, hasn't happened yet, it is impossible to make consistently accurate predictions. Some psychics and channeled sources are adept at picking up probabilities based on where things are heading, but since each individual has free will—probabilities are constantly shifting as we make choices—nobody knows for sure. Even when certain changes are more or less inevitable, the form they take and the way people react to them are not. Timing is especially difficult to predict, and even when different channels and psychics agree in their predictions about specific events, the dates often vary.

Sometimes people tell me that a psychic or a channeled entity told them that something terrible was going to happen, which upset them a great deal. That strikes me as inappropriate. I'm not suggesting that someone should lie if he sees a strong negative probability on the horizon, but it should be conveyed in such a way as to empower the person listening. Michael doesn't give "bad news." If they see someone creating a situation that he probably won't like, their approach might be to show him how he can create a more pleasing situation instead, if he's interested. Besides, since nothing is carved in stone before it happens, it is misleading to say that something is definitely, without a doubt, going to happen. Furthermore, because Michael's point of view is neutral, they may see what someone else might call "bad news" in a different light—for example, they might see a probable outcome as being simply another of the physical plane's growth-promoting challenges. Their approach may then be to show a client how he can make the best of that outcome if it arises.

It is wise to take predictions with a grain of salt. Rather than asking if and when an event will happen, it might be more useful to ask what percentage the probability is, and if there are agreements or karmas putting force behind its happening. For example, at a given moment, a person might have a sixty-two percent probability of getting a particular job, and the employer might have an essence-level agreement with him to hire him. That is a very high probability, since probabilities rarely rise to about eighty-five percent until something is actually in the process of happening; even a fifty percent probability is quite high. Nonetheless, people don't always keep their agreements, for a variety of reasons, and the person may not be hired. If, unexpectedly, someone comes along who seems better qualified or who is a friend of the company's owner, the probability might drop to thirty-seven percent, which is still fairly high, but, obviously, not overwhelming.

If we have an agreement to meet someone at a certain time, we may not be able to keep the "appointment," but if it's an important agreement, chances are that we will reschedule it and it will eventually work out. This is an organic, ever-changing world. Nothing is carved in stone. Every significant choice a person makes can change relevant probabilities.

We do not know for a certainty what the future will bring for ourselves or for you. That makes the game of life much more interesting and challenging. If everything could be predicted ahead of time, we would all have to be automatons, and if we are expressions of the Tao, then the Tao would likewise be an automaton. Fortunately, this is not the case. We cannot predict what others will do with assurance because others themselves do not know what they will do, and even if they think they know, they might change their minds. We can only give our best projections based on where things appear to be going, taking into account the relevant agreements and karmas. This is an art we are learning.

Imminent events are easier to predict. If an object is teetering precariously on the edge of a shelf, one could safely predict that it will fall. However, even in such a situation, someone might come along and move it.

It is a great fallacy that you need to predict the future to choose well now. Relying on predictions of the future weakens your capacity to make good choices. When you think that you have everything figured out, you may start to drift by on your pre-

conceived notions rather than playing the game in the present moment with all the skill and attention you can muster.[44]

Even if events do not go as our essence planned and predictions therefore prove wrong, sometimes things work out for the best anyway. A case in point was my apartment when I lived in Manhattan. Affordable apartments were next to impossible to find when I moved there, especially those larger than one-bedroom. However, my guides told me that I would find an inexpensive two-bedroom apartment to share. I got a photographic image of it, and a couple of my friends psychically saw similar images. Apparently, my guides were working on a few possible apartments that fit that description, but all of them fell through. I still found an affordable apartment, but it was a studio. It had been one of my guides' "back-up" choices, but they hadn't told me about it ahead of time. It was disappointing at first, but it turned out to suit my needs better in some respects than the envisioned apartment likely would have. I don't subscribe to the idea that *everything* works out for the best—the highest outworkings are sometimes thwarted because, again, people have free will—but I do believe that the universe is basically benevolent, and as a whole conspires to our highest good if we let it. Perhaps sometimes it does so in ways of which even our guides and essence are not aware.

WE ARE RESPONSIBLE

No one on any plane of existence is infallible or knows everything we need to know. In addition, we all have our own experience of reality and ways of describing it. There is no right and wrong in this regard, only infinite facets of truth. We do have much to learn from each other, and those on higher planes usually have more experience, greater resources of information, and a larger perspective than we do on the physical plane. However, their counsel is more accurately viewed as coming from loving friends than from a deity. No one is more "God" than anyone else.

We are each responsible for ourselves. We experience more growth if we don't do things merely because we think someone else, incarnate or not, told us to. It is well to examine what we hear others say with appreciation and respect, but we don't always hear what is actually meant, for one thing. More importantly, no one knows us better than we know ourselves, at least potentially. We must make

---

[44]Chapter Twenty-Three, "The Future," in my upcoming Summerjoy Michael book *Being in the World* also explores this topic.

our own decisions and mistakes, and form our own understanding, if we are to learn to guide the course of our lives wisely. Besides, true teachers don't tell people what to do. They give greater perspective and understanding so that their students can make well-informed choices. Beware of those who issue orders, or who are certain that they know what's best for someone else, even if they are being channeled from a higher plane. Just because material is channeled does not mean that it is appropriate or a fully realized expression of truth.

RECOGNIZING TRUTH

Channeled material, like everything else, must be interpreted through the understanding of the hearer. Sometimes we draw conclusions or make associations that are not valid, or we simply misunderstand. I am sometimes amazed at what clients say Michael said. The truth is precise; it is as important to hear what is not being said as what is.

The ability to recognize truth is crucial. Truth is always associated with love. It has a certain feel about it. It is not necessarily comfortable, but it is penetrating and ultimately liberating.

Often the truth or value of channeled material isn't fully apparent until later. It may seem at first to be deceptively simple or general. If we have that experience with something channeled for us, we have nothing to lose by living with it a while and seeing if it looks different later. One client told me that after her session, she wasn't particularly impressed, but two months later, she listened to her tapes and couldn't believe that Michael had said what they did; it was almost as if she hadn't heard it the first time. This is a common reaction.

In my brochure for new clients, Michael says:

You will get the most out of this session if you review the material in a week or two. It's hard for so much new input to soak in the first time. A defense against overload is to make it seem less than it is. This is normal, but often, our students find their channeling to be far more meaningful weeks or even months later. It is the mark of a good teacher (and we aspire to this) to give what the student is almost but not quite ready to hear. That way, we promote growth. Obviously, the material becomes more meaningful when the student is actually ready.

Our Western society's model of truth is based on polarity: something is either true or it isn't, and if it's true, something else must therefore be false. In my experience, two statements that seem contradictory can both be true, or at least, mostly true. I have sought to demonstrate that throughout this book.

Michael speaks of personal, world, and universal truths. That concept points out that something may be true for an individual or even many individuals, but not be true for everyone in the world, let alone in the universe. Gravity, for instance, is different everywhere on the planet, partly because of varying distances from the earth's core. If we didn't know that and saw two different measurements of earth's gravity reported, we would probably assume that one report was wrong. When we don't have enough information, when we lack "bridge information," we can tend to be judgmental and simplistic in our views. Truth is infinite, and is therefore vast enough to hold an infinite number of facets. Someone said that the measure of an idea's greatness is the degree to which its opposite is also true.

If there are poles of absolute truth and absolute falsehood, there is a long continuum in between, the infinite shades of gray between white and black. But more likely, absolute truth and absolute falsehood do not exist in the dimensional universe—only in the Tao is absolute truth. Pi, the ratio of the circumference of a circle to its diameter, refuses to be rounded off—it just keeps going into infinity: 3.14159265.... We do round off pi so that we can work with it—that is a convenience, but it is not the whole truth. With any spiritual teaching, we are working with rounded-off truth, because we cannot work directly with the whole truth—it's too big. I discussed models of reality in the Preface. We have no choice but to work with models. What else do we have?

However, a good model connects us to the infinite truth that it models, and although that cannot be fathomed, it can be felt. The more true we are to the truth of ourselves, the better we can recognize truth in models.

THE LARGER PERSPECTIVE

We are in the midst of a planetary transformation. There are many nonphysical beings who are assisting with it, whether we know it or not. Channeling is a means of consciously working with them. They are often as gratified to make the connection with us as we are with them. Used in a responsible way, channeling can be an important tool in our personal and collective growth.

Whether or not we call ourselves channels, it is becoming more and more essential that each of us develop our inner connections with the larger universe if we are to move creatively with the changes occurring.

Chapter 2

MICHAEL ON CHANNELING

COMING OUT OF ISOLATION

Everyone is capable of communicating with a broader spectrum of reality.

Those of us who are not in human form but whose vocation has a great deal to do with the human world find much satisfaction in being able to communicate directly with you through a channel. You will find that this phenomenon will become an increasingly valuable tool in the integration of the earth.

For a long time, people have lived largely in isolation, from other people and from themselves, as well as from those of us not in human form. Yet our participation is critical to the survival of the earth. You would not be able to function without our interaction. We are part of the ecology, you might say. On the other hand, your participation is critical to our existence as well. So you need us and we need you. Now you are awakening to the rich resource of the unseen assistance you have been receiving from both the physical and higher planes. Part of this awakening is the greater acceptance of the phenomenon called channeling.

Before the current dense human body became the status quo,[1] people could move easily between the physical and higher planes at will by changing their speed of vibration. Although they were focused on a particular plane, they could visit the others, including the physical, just as you may live in New York but visit other places to broaden your perspective. Now this is much more difficult. It is similar to what would happen if all forms of transportation and communication were taken away. Those in America might begin to think that Europeans were just a legend. Although you are still mostly without the means of transporting yourself to other planes, with channeling you do at least have the equivalent of shortwave radio—this is exciting. Hopefully, you will not stop there but will go on to reclaim the mobility symbolized by airplanes and other forms of transportation.

---

[1]Chapter Fourteen, "Previous Cycles," discusses this change.

It is big news on higher planes when the separation between the physical and higher planes is bridged at events such as channeled lectures! It happens so seldom, although it is happening increasingly. Those of us on higher planes see these events as opportunities to do some concentrated work with you. They are also fun for us.

You do not create in a vacuum. Your actions that are in alignment with truth, and hence for the higher good, are assisted and supported from a higher place, especially the astral plane, which has a particular connection with the physical plane. This does not belittle your own efforts, but if you were trying to create truly alone, you would have your work cut out for you.

THE PURPOSE OF CHANNELING

What is the purpose of channeling?

What is the purpose of telephones? They have no purpose, except to facilitate the purposes of those who use them for communication. Some people use channeling for selfish purposes. That is their choice. There is no law that states that channeling must only be used for the benefit of humanity. If you wish to channel Attila the Hun, and "Tillie" wants to be channeled, that is between the two of you. Channeling does not ensure that the source is holy.

Nonetheless, we would say that a superior use of channeling is to allow those who are not physical human beings, and who have worthy insight or information, to give it.

THE LARGENESS OF TRUTH

Why do different channels receive different pieces of the cosmic puzzle instead of the same truth?

The truth is very large. No one is big enough to contain all of it. It would be like a ninety-eight-pound woman giving birth to a three-thousand-pound baby. What comes through is generally what is most useful to the audience and most harmonious with the channel himself, in language that is most meaningful to those involved.

REAL OR IMAGINED?

Are the entities or energies that channels channel real or simply a figment of the channel's imagination, or both?

The best answer would be that we are real but that the way we manifest has much to do with the contents of the channel's subconscious. Most entities make liberal use of what is in the subconscious of the channel, because it is easier and teaches much to the channel. Furthermore, those listening also affect the material; we use what they bring as well. It is easier and it forges a connection with them. We have to use something, after all; we do not communicate in English or any other human language on the level where we are. Material foreign to the channel and listeners is harder to transmit. Also, speaking so that others can understand is a courtesy that you no doubt also extend.

We do not really care if our students believe that we are a causal entity. You may choose to think that the channel is just accessing some part of himself. You may even choose to believe that the channel is making it all up. It does not matter, because what we say is not true or false because we are the ones saying it. If it is true, it is true because it is true. If anything that is said resonates with you, you have the opportunity to verify for yourself that it is true, or at least useful for you as a way of looking at things. If it does not feel right to you, it does not matter who is speaking—even if it were God Himself, whoever that is for you. You still have to validate for yourself if something is true or not.

We suggest that you take this approach toward anything you hear or read: do not assume that anything is true or that it is false based on its source. Take the trouble, if you are interested, to find out if it is true based on your experience of it.

The Michael teachings are not the Truth, with a capital T. They are a model by means of which you can look at your life and gain some insight. The truth is present within you. The truth is the reality of your authentic being. As you become conscious of who you are, you can begin to validate for yourself anything you hear, if you so choose.

WHAT IS ACCESSED?

There are many levels of energy to which a channel can tune in, like the many bands on a radio. There are also many ways in the universe in which energies on the same level combine. Some energies are broader or more general in scope—they combine many energies—whereas some are narrower or more specific. We are a collective energy, that of a recombined entity or "spiritual family" of one thousand fifty souls, but we are relatively narrow in scope. Of course, wide is not better than narrow, just as blue is not better than yellow. There could be no wide without narrow, and vice versa.

The universe is incredibly vast. There are seven planes of creation, and infinite facets of reality. Theoretically, it is possible to channel any consciousness. You could actually channel the consciousness of a rock—it has consciousness. Like most universal consciousness, it does not use words, so there would need to be some translation, but it could be done. There are people who channel devas, which are of the physical plane even though most people do not see them. The most common consciousness channeled is that of astral-plane souls; this includes both those who are between human lifetimes and those who have completed the physical plane. Some of these sources are of a high caliber; some are not.

One can channel energies from the sun—the sun has consciousness. There are energies from other planets that can be channeled, including those of extraterrestrial beings. Sometimes these are inhabitants of the physical plane of other planets, although more often they are astral—on the astral plane, movement is much easier. [2]

The universe provides an infinite number of "radio stations" to which your "shortwave radio" can tune in. With a shortwave radio you can get broadcasts from all over the world. You do not hear those broadcasts if you have an ordinary AM/FM radio. You might say that more and more people are acquiring shortwave radios—in other words, fine-tuning their ability to receive other frequencies. So these consciousnesses are now being made available to humanity, some more

---

[2]Each planet, like everything in the universe, has seven planes, or seven aspects. There is one astral plane for the universe, just as there is one physical plane. The astral aspect of Earth, for instance, is connected to the astral aspect of, say, Venus, just as Earth's physical reality is connected by space with that of Venus.

accurately and fully than others. But nevertheless the trend is a positive one.

Is there a difference between channeling energies and specific entities or personalities?

Entities are energies—there is no distinction; both are consciousness. Every consciousness has a unique quality. When that unique quality is channeled through a person who also has a unique quality, it results in a particular flavor that might be identified as being a personality. Broader, more blended energies have a less specific quality or stamp than those more specific. For example, the consciousness of the sun as a whole is a broad blend and would probably not be interpreted as an entity so much as an energy, but it is fundamentally no different from us, except that we have a history of planetary sentience and can communicate more specifically with you.

Human personality, which is based on the body, overleaves, imprinting, and so forth, exists fully only on the physical plane. After death, only vestiges remain in what might be called the reincarnational self, which is, in effect, a subpersonality of the essence. If a reincarnational self is channeled, some sense of human personality can come through. Otherwise, there is no actual human personality in a channeled entity or energy. When entities such as ourselves who were once physically human are channeled from the causal plane or higher, there is no human personality in them because they have fully integrated their reincarnational selves, although human personality traits may be projected upon them by the channel or by those listening.

Even those who might be thought of as entities rather than energies can blend with one another, just as energies can blend. Most people would think of Seth,[3] for instance, as being wholly separate from Michael, which is not the case. Those on higher planes are not totally unified yet, but we do not experience nearly the degree of separation that is your experience on the physical plane. We have access, to some extent, to all the energies of the universe, although much of that access is more subliminal than conscious for us. You have that access as well, but not to as great an extent.

---

[3]Seth is the entity who was channeled by the late Jane Roberts. There are a number of Seth books available; I highly recommend them.

*Each consciousness is evolving individually, yet is con-
nected to the whole, which is also evolving. As participants in
the whole, we have access to all the parts. We are individual
and not individual at the same time in a way that is difficult to
describe in language; it must be experienced to be understood.
In general, we would say that the higher the plane of existence,
the more blended the energies. Therefore, it is harder to say
exactly who it is one is channeling, because of the number of
webs of connection that are generated as we evolve.*

TEACHING

*We grow by teaching. We benefit from the challenge of working
with you. After completing the physical and astral planes, each
person passes through this kind of teaching phase, although
not everyone has the privilege of being directly channeled.[4]
There are many ways in which nonincarnate souls impact the
physical plane, but being channeled is obviously a direct way.*

*We are not subject to time in the way you are. If you asked
an open-ended question in a year's time rather than now, our
answer would probably be more mature, not so much because
of our growth, but because of yours, and that of the channel.
You would be more open and available for deeper communion
with us, so you would probably attract to yourself a slightly
more advanced aspect of us. To put it another way: you would
be able to receive more of the capabilities we already have. It is
similar to a good school teacher with a good class being able to
do more than he can with a less receptive class, or a good actor
being able to give a better performance with a responsive audience than he can with one that is not. More of their resources
come forth when there is more room for those resources to be
received.*

*We give as much as can be given under what are always
limited circumstances—no one can receive an infinite amount—
but whatever can be given is sufficient. If we gave more than
could be received, it would be partly wasted, and perhaps even
harmful.[5]*

---

[4]Just as not every person is interested in being a channel, not every nonphysical soul is interested in being channeled. Channeling is done by
agreement between channeled entity and channel, usually made before the
channel incarnates.

[5]Michael teaches that no experience is ultimately wasted, since every mistake
becomes grist for the mill—we eventually learn something, at least on some

WHAT MICHAEL KNOWS

Much of the information we access requires interpretation. It is present in code, so to speak, and we must translate it into usable terms. Everyone has his own definitions and ways of translating thoughts into words. That is why the same information sounds different coming through different sources.

We generally know relatively few external facts about those who come to us for channeling. Theoretically, any available information can be obtained, but one has to weigh the value of the information versus the amount of effort it would take to retrieve it. From our causal plane perspective, we see the building blocks of life experiences. This, and not raw information, is our greatest value to those who come to us. People can validate us as a source not so much by whether we know something factual about them unknown to the channel, as by whether what we relay is in keeping with their experience and sheds light on it.

Practically speaking, not all information is available. To get information, there must be a source for it. If you ask us about something occurring on earth where those involved are not allowing a connection to higher planes, their guides may not be able to tell us much about it. And if there is considerable cloudiness or confusion around them or what they are doing, it may be difficult to tune in directly with clarity and accuracy.

SOMETHING TO WORK WITH

Channeled sources do not have a solution to every problem. For example, there is no medical cure for AIDS on the horizon at this moment, and even the wisest ones on the higher planes do not yet have many suggestions to make, as far as we know, on how to find one. The reason is that AIDS is a recent phenomenon, and research has not progressed very far. When there is enough of a body of research, those on higher planes may be able to see ramifications in that research that scientists do not see, and to correlate it with other sources of knowledge. Until

---

level, from everything we do. At the same time, growing through joy rather than pain by making the wisest choices we can is more efficient, not to mention pleasant. This topic is explored in my upcoming Summerjoy Michael book *Growing Through Joy*.

then, channeled sources cannot help that much. There has to be something to work with.

MULTIPLE PERSONALITIES

How does channeling differ from multiple personalities?

It is completely different. We are not a part of the personality structure of those through whom we channel. We are not of the physical or even astral planes. Our relationships with our channels are those of friends and colleagues. Multiple personalities is a disorder that usually stems from the absence of a strong sense of identity. The person starts confusing parts of past-life selves as being in the present. That could not accurately be said to be channeling.

CHANNELED ENTITIES' ACCENTS

Why do some channeled entities have thick accents, and some, none at all? Where do the accents come from?

The accent of a channeled entity may be a combination of the accents of several of its past-life selves, accessed for the purpose of translating thoughts into human language. Lives in which the personality was especially adept at language might have particular emphasis. It can also have to do with the past lives of the channel in which he either had a relationship with the channeled entity or was a channel—either of that entity or of another. In such cases, those aspects of self are brought in to assist. It also has to do with the manner of channeling. When the conscious self is more on hand to assist, the past-life selves are not as necessary.

RAISING THE VIBRATION

Since we do a lot of healing work through this channel, there is a need to raise his vibration to accommodate our vibration. Doing this too quickly would be like ripping something that was only intended to be stretched. As we begin to come in, we are "blowing up the balloon," filling the channel with increasing pressure. As this is done, little air-bubble-like pockets of impuri-

ties come to the surface, as in a water bed, and have to be re-leased. If they are not, they are amplified and could harm the channel, cloud the channeling, or both.

Those with whom we are speaking are included in an-other, larger balloon or energy field. We subtly work with clearing this container also. This is done by drawing the "bubbles" into the channel and gradually pricking holes in them, so to speak, squeezing out the air so that there is a feel-ing of evenness and smoothness in the person coming for healing and information. Many who come are so full of these bubbles of impurities that we can only do basic work, and as a consequence, cannot raise their vibration as high as we other-wise might. However, the work we do may set in motion a process that leads to more clearing, so that we could raise their vibration higher during a subsequent session.

DEPTH OF CHANNELING

We place no limitations on who can channel us. We are willing to be channeled by anyone who can accommodate us. How-ever, the further along you are in your movement as a soul, the more resources you have available.

Let's make an analogy. A twenty-four-year-old actor may be quite gifted. Perhaps he is given the opportunity to play a great Shakespearean role and does a credible job. But if he has the opportunity to play it again—let's say at the age of thirty-five—and if he has continued to grow as an actor, he will be able to bring more depth to it. This is not to say that the twenty-four-year-old and his performance are inadequate; they may be quite fine for what they are.

Similarly, an older soul who is channeling may be able to allow a greater depth to come through.

A SKILL TO DEVELOP

If you desire to learn to channel, it is certainly possible to do so. Keep in mind that, like any skill, it takes practice and dedica-tion. Should you choose to devote the time to learning this skill, you will necessarily be choosing not to develop others, so con-sider it carefully.

The qualifications for channeling are a deep desire to do it and a willingness to practice, cleanse your subconscious, and set aside your belief structures for the duration of the channeling.

Your conscious awareness is the main "road" on which your thoughts travel. It is used by many sources within you, including what is sometimes called the subconscious mind. Cleansing your subconscious so that clutter does not interfere and its usable raw material is available is a process that takes time and effort.

Ideally, a channel has all chakras open and available. In practice, the ability to open the seventh chakra is usually most important, especially if channeling verbally.

COMMUNICATING WITH THE INVISIBLE

Channeling can be defined as allowing another intelligence to speak through you. You can also communicate with an invisible source mentally, without it coming into your physical body and expressing through you. Here is a meditation that facilitates the latter:

To focus yourself, it is good to concentrate on something that is not distracting in order to keep your attention in one place. You can gaze through a candle flame, listen to some nonlinear music, such as chimes, or listen to your breathing. Once you feel deeply relaxed and present with yourself, state out loud what you wish to experience during that session. If you wish, for example, to receive visual images from your primary spirit guide, say that, and imagine a movie screen in your head. Then simply wait until the movie starts. Continue to focus on your breathing, the music, or the flame. Once you get images, describe them on a tape as they come, or write them down later if you feel confident that you will remember them. Afterward, work with the images as you would in interpreting a dream.

If you wish to receive words rather than images from your guide, prepare written, preferably open-ended questions ahead of time. You might imagine that you are sitting at a table with him, talking about what it is that you wish to know more about. As with the movie, wait until the conversation starts.

You can use this meditation for many different purposes, such as communicating with your "inner child" or your body consciousness. It is important to be clear about what you intend

61

to happen. You can also simply ask that whatever is for your highest good occur and then just remain in this state of openness. But if what you get is not what you were hoping for, next time you would want to specify what you would like to happen.

Whenever you work with the invisible in any way, you do so through your faculty of imagination. You have to be able to imagine yourself conversing with your guides, for instance, in order for that to occur. Letting your imagination run freely is essential to the success of guided meditations. If nothing comes, make something up. Soon, as the "pump" becomes "primed," reality will take over where imagination left off.

It is normal to wonder if you are making up everything you get. When you first start to access your guides or learn to channel, you may not yet have had much practice in translating from the invisible, so the translation may be rather rough. Your imagination may be filling in some of the gaps, or parts of yourself that you have ignored may take the opportunity to express themselves. With practice, you can quickly grow in your ability to translate specifically and accurately, and keep your unfinished business from interfering.

Whatever you get, avail yourself of what is offered with openness. Even if it comes primarily from your own psyche, it may be worthwhile. You are a wise and creative source yourself. Take it all in, not being too concerned at first about where it comes from or whether it is accurate. See if the information works for you. However, in time, you can sense the true happening when you are getting good material; it has a solidity to it. If you are in doubt, work with a channel or psychic you know to be competent, and get feedback. Usually, at least something besides pure imagination is happening. It may not be exactly what it purports to be, or it may have a mixture of sources. Nonetheless, your psyche has no reason to make up something "from scratch" when what you are asking for, such as information from a higher source, is available. When you ask for something, you usually get it. With work, you can clarify what is happening and improve your skills.

MINIMIZING STRESS

What can I do to minimize the stress of channeling on my body?

In preparing to channel, ask for the support of your inner resources and protect them with white light. Ask your soul to fill you with spiritual substance. Go through your body, cleansing your chakras. Notice areas that feel blocked and ask for release. Spend a moment in total stillness. A long meditation can be helpful, but it is not necessary.

After channeling, flush away any energetic debris that has accumulated. Release any draining cords of connection that have been attached to you by other people. Thank your inner resources and again surround them with white light. Ask your soul to replenish your supply of spiritual substance.

Channeling for people with little spiritual substance drains your own. It is a great service to them, but it can be quite a workout for both you and the entity being channeled.

WORKING WITH GROUP CONSCIOUSNESS

When we speak to a group, we first forge a spiritual connection with each person and sense what is occurring with him. Then we work to build a group consciousness. It is easier to address a unified group than a collection of isolated individuals. In group consciousness, individuality is still present, but the element of connectedness is added. Speaking with a unified group is not unlike speaking with an individual. The group consciousness has issues that can be sensed and addressed. They, of course, grow out of the issues of the individuals who comprise it, but group consciousness has its own "gestalt" that is unique to the moment.

Is there any special reason a specific group of people is drawn to you and this channel for any given lecture?

When a significant event is coming together, whoever has primary responsibility for it (such as us) broadcasts the equivalent of a radio signal "announcing" it to draw those both physical and nonphysical who might be interested in participating in the particular currents gathering. They can include your spirit guides and your discarnate loved ones who seek a greater sense of what is happening with you, as well as light workers and those who work with planetary energies as a whole. The signal strengthens in intensity as the event comes together.

People who, on an essence level, want to attend but choose not to on a personality level, for whatever reasons, could be said to be present in spirit but not in form. If there are many of them, there may be a feeling "in the air" of their absence. It is rather like having a committee meeting and some of the important members not showing up. You go on with your meeting, but there are some gaps.

We do not know exactly what is going to happen ahead of time. We listen as much as we speak. It is not our aim to give you the most entertaining and comfortable experience possible so that you have the same type of experience you might have at a good movie. You do not need us for that; you can go to a movie. Our goal is to serve your highest and greatest good. Often that involves specific energy work to clear blocks, which is not always comfortable, but which ultimately leads to a greater sense of well-being.

Everyone participating helps create what occurs in a group channeling session, not just those on higher planes. Those who are physical are generally present not just for their own benefit, but because they also wish to serve the greater good, even if that intention is not conscious. Astral "light workers" can help amplify and broadcast the generated energy to other people on the physical plane through the people's connections with those present.

Because of the subtle nature of this work, its effects are not immediately discernible by most. Someone who works with you in your office is not likely to come up to you after you participated in a group session and say, "Boy! You really zapped me with some energy last night, didn't you?" However, it has a cumulative effect. It is rather like introducing good food into your body. It contributes to the overall health of your body, but one glass of carrot juice is not likely to heal you. To the degree that you are open in group sessions, you receive and help transmit the highest possible quality and quantity of energy.

Is this *chi*, or healing energy?

Chi *is physical-plane energy. Ultimately, all energy springs from the Tao, and if there is a loving intent behind the expression of any energy, it is, generally speaking, healing energy. On the other hand, energy comes in infinite "flavors." In a group channeling session with us, you primarily experience our energy, which is of the causal plane. It vibrates more quickly than physical-plane energy, any physical-plane energy, including chi. The fact that it moves more quickly does not make it better, but it does make it concentrated and catalytic. Unless you are channeling, if you send someone energy, it is physical-plane energy, since you are physical. If it is a pure and loving offering, it is healing, since purity and love are always healing, no matter what the source of the energy is.*

HIGHER-PLANE ENERGY

This is my first time at one of your talks, and I've experienced a lot more spacing out than I normally would. Is that typical?

Causal-plane energy is more focused and concentrated than physical-plane energy. Because of its faster vibration, you experience it as a stimulant, lifting you to a higher place, and when it is expressed through a group, its power can be amplified. Although this can be a catalyst for healing and change, you are not used to the "altitude," so you get a little dizzy. In time, it becomes easier to stay alert in it.

In much the same way, we experience an upliftment by an infusion of energy from planes higher than where we dwell. One would not want to live all the time in an energy not of one's plane because it would be too intense, but higher-plane energy is valuable as an occasional boost.

Chapter 3

SESSIONS

The majority of Michael channels are in northern California. Throughout most of my career, I have been the only professional Michael channel in my area, with no established long-term community of Michael students. Because of that, I developed a somewhat different kind of channeling practice than those of most other Michael channels (and a different slant on the material, as well). The majority of my clients know little or nothing about the Michael teachings when they first come to me, so during their initial private session, I explain their Michael Reading chart before going into direct channeling with Michael. Sometimes I also explain the chart of a loved one, such as their mate, in conjunction with their own (and sometimes couples come together to a session).

I often channel charts ahead of time, several at once, on days when I am not seeing a client (or after a brief client session). I prepare much faster for sessions of chart channeling than for client sessions. My usual procedure is to quickly clear my chakras, ask within to put aside my conditioned consciousness, invite Michael in, and receive them into my crown, brow, and throat chakras, in that order. I then ask if we're ready; if we are, they nod my head yes, and we begin. Although it took much longer in the beginning, I can be ready to do charts in a couple of minutes, unless I'm tired and need to do a lot of clearing first. (If I'm channeling in the evening and didn't have much sleep the night before, I usually nap prior to channeling.) Even if I don't need to clear myself much before beginning, I may need to pause to do so periodically during a session, because Michael's energy, being cleansing, stirs up energetic "debris" in me. However, a session of channeling charts is still less physically tiring than a session with a client (although it is just as mentally tiring) because when channeling charts, there is no energy work to do with someone else.

When I first began channeling, I did most of it through conscious writing. Clients would give me a question. I would then go to the typewriter and get the answer, and give it to the client when I was done. After he read it, I would take his next question, and so forth. When I learned about channeling aloud from another Michael channel, that seemed more practical, and I practiced alone, with a tape recorder.

During the first couple of years, my channeling tended to be quite slow. Sometimes there were long pauses when Michael couldn't find a word they were looking for. Fortunately, that doesn't tend to happen anymore. This illustrates how the "instrument" (the channel) needs to be broken in by the "player" (the channeled entity). Channeling is a collaboration in which the channel needs to be able to move responsively with the entity being channeled.

With clients, I gradually bring Michael fully into my body, including all seven chakras. It generally takes about twenty minutes or more before Michael is ready to start talking. They also fill the space around me, including the client, with causal-plane energy, simultaneously raising the vibration and clearing away energetic debris, using my body as a sort of filter. After adequate clearing, they often quietly hold eye contact with clients while developing "alignment," continuing to clarify their aura and increase the light. They also usually do that for an extended period after the questions and answers are completed, and may spend a few moments between questions to clear any debris that may have accumulated. Sometimes, especially while the client and Michael, through me, are holding eye contact, the light becomes so intense that the client's face appears to me to blur, and clients have reported the same of my face. Also, there are sometimes moments when my face looks to the client like the negative of a photograph of it. As the energy work progresses, the client's aura sometimes becomes quite large, especially toward the end of the session, although Michael is careful to let it come back to a more normal size before the session concludes.

When my body is clearing energetic debris, whether mine or others', my body reacts in various ways, including yawning and something a little bit similar to hyperventilating or to the "breath of fire" in yoga, although I have not studied yoga and do not do it deliberately. (Most channels and healers do not exhibit such dramatic reactions to the clearing process. I understand that the Yarbro channel "Milly" simply sighs, for instance. It is also true that most channels do not do much energy work.) The rapid breathing happens less now; it has been replaced to some degree with a gentler quick inhalation. It was partly the result of incorrect posture creating a block in my neck, making the clearing process more jarring and draining. Craniosacral work[1] (which subtly adjusts the skull and the base of the spine) and lessons in the Alexander technique (which concerns how to sit, stand, and walk in balance) were helpful. The goal is to let my head "float" straight above my neck, so that energy can flow freely without "kinks in the hose."

---

[1]After some particularly effective craniosacral and other healing work, the rapid breathing disappeared for a few months, then gradually returned, but not as intensely.

Before clearing in whatever manner, I feel a mounting pressure and drowsiness, which climaxes of its own accord and releases through the breath. When it is complete for the moment, I feel lighter and clearer, and sometimes those for whom I am channeling report similar feelings. One client says that it feels like waves of energy coursing through his body. This clearing process is the most physically tiring part of channeling for me—it takes a lot of energy, especially when there is a lot of debris to clear in the client(s).

A psychic described the change he saw in my aura when Michael entered my body as an explosion of white light. He went on to say, "If I had been seeing it with physical eyes, I would have been blinded." Even people who have never seen auras before have seen my aura when I'm channeling; most often, it is described as being a golden or golden-white color.

Many clients have also reported that my face seems to change, looking much older or younger, or having a beard, or looking like a totally different person. Sometimes the images appear to be from past incarnations, and may be in historical garb. This usually occurs at the end of sessions, when the questions and answers are finished and Michael is working with clients purely energetically, raising their vibration while holding eye contact. This is a convenient time for nonphysical beings with close ties to the clients to "look in" on them through my physical eyes and make a direct contact, perhaps appearing as they did in a past life shared with the client. Michael's energy is still dominant, but I nonverbally "broadcast" energy from these beings, one at a time, which is superimposed upon Michael's. The purpose of such contact may be to help the clients process past-life issues.

> *The image might be of someone who was a teacher to the client in a past life, "coming back" to elucidate a truth to him. (That teacher may or may not be one of the person's current spirit guides.) The image might also be of one of the person's own past-life selves, now wiser, who is seeking in this lifetime to get a point across to the person.*[2]

> *We are not focused in personality, so we can allow the manifestation of whatever personality needs to be seen through us.*

---

[2]Our past-life selves continue to have a "life of their own" as kind of subpersonalities of our essence, and we can communicate with them. See the subchapter "Reincarnational Selves" in Chapter Twenty-five, "Reincarnation," or the Glossary.

Almost always, there are spirit guides and other astral-plane loved ones assisting with sessions. If an issue is being discussed that relates to lifetimes shared with them, they may participate more directly to help affect healing. They might also want to come through because of present-life issues they are helping with (or may just want to say hello, so to speak) but might appear in the garb of the last or most important lifetime they were with the clients. The garb resonates in the clients on some level even if they do not consciously recognize it.

One client told me that I momentarily looked like a gorilla! I asked her what gorillas represented to her, and she said that she had always slept with a gorilla doll—gorillas were comforting to her. So perhaps one of her guides, knowing this, appeared as a gorilla to let her know that everything was all right. Those who don't have physical bodies can appear to us in any form they wish, and are likely to choose a form that is meaningful to us. When my spirit guides first appeared to me visually (in my mind's eye), one of them, a playful, creative artisan soul, told me that he would appear to me in various symbols, such as a shaggy dog, a bird, or a ruddy-faced middle-aged man. Each symbol would represent a certain kind of message: the dog would represent a message about physical sexuality; the bird, about spirituality; and the man was a past-life self of the guide whom I had known—those messages would be "man-to-man talks."

When a client sees a face other than my own through me, he might also be seeing one of my past-life selves who knew him before, or even one of Michael's. Michael was once on the physical plane with many of those who are now their students.

If we were players in a past-life drama that is being touched, we may be seen in the garb of one of our past lifetimes, but this is rare.

The channeling of healing energy may be as important as the channeling of words. A chiropractor friend who referred a patient to me told me that the patient's body was noticeably changed after his session with Michael. Michael may appear to be just talking and listening, but they are also working intelligently and specifically on other levels. For example, if someone is asking about a relationship, Michael not only discusses it with him, but works with him energetically to help heal his issues regarding it. A by-product of all this energy work is that it imbued my small Manhattan apartment with a special atmosphere. Most people found it warm and nourishing. However, I had one guest who found that it made him feel buzzy and uncomfortable. (I wasn't channeling at the time.) After he left, I found that a fluorite crystal on my coffee table that I had had for years had broken apart into three pieces! Fluorite is an aura cleanser, among other things. I suspect that this guest was highly sensitive to higher energies, and they were activating needed cleansing in him.

I have a cat named Agape.[3] Whenever I begin to bring in Michael, Agape trots up and lies on the couch right next to my chair, soaking in the energy. When I am done, he gets up and goes somewhere else. *Michael's People*[4] has a passage about how much the channels' pets like Michael's energy.

If someone is sensitive to subtle energies, feeling Michael's energy may be the best way to validate that channeling is occurring. I once sat in the audience while three other people were channeling Michael, in a style very different from my own. For me, it was like being "inside out," because I am accustomed to feeling Michael's energy from within; instead, I was feeling it from without. When I became very relaxed, it put me in an altered state. Michael's energy through each channel felt different both in quantity and "shape"—one energy pattern was a wide "wall" of energy "coming at me" while another was a narrow, more gentle "beam," and the third manifested as a soft cloud around the channel—but all had the same basic causal-plane quality, which I experience as an intellectual, slightly "edgy" intensity.[5] Someone who once came to hear me channel for a group was skeptical at first—she was a client of the channel called "Milly" in the Yarbro books—but after she recognized the energy coming through me as having Michael's distinctive stamp, she could validate that I was indeed channeling Michael, despite the differences in my style and the kind of material coming through me.

The energy work is cumulative. In other words, if a client comes for a second session, we usually pick up where we left off at the end of the first session (after "getting up to speed"). This can be true even if a year has passed. A person's first session is generally one of laying a foundation, and may require a lot of "plowing" through and clearing dense blocks; subsequent sessions usually are easier and go to a higher place, although the work may not seem as dramatic—clearing

---

[3]I pronounce it in the modern Greek way, with the accent on the second syllable rather than the first: uh-*gah*-pee. Michael uses the older pronunciation—*ah*-guh-pay—when referring to unconditional love. I learned that *Agape* is fairly common as a woman's name in Greece today, using something close to the first pronunciation, and meaning "friendship."

[4]P. 248.

[5]In *Michael's Gemstone Dictionary*, by Judithann David and JP Van Hulle (Affinity Press, 1990), kyanite is recommended for connecting a person to the causal plane. To me, kyanite's energy feels much like Michael's. See Bibliography.

blocks is coarser work and may be more noticeable than the delicate work of raising one's vibration. If the client isn't sensitive to subtle energies, he may not realize how much is occurring.

Michael has lectured through me about how "heaven" or higher-plane energies need to be balanced with earth energies if we are to have a state of well-being. In other words, the more we work with higher energies, the more we need grounding. When I went to another channel once, the entity coming through him said that my body had a predominance of "celestial energy" and lacked sufficient "earth current." Obviously, I wasn't channeling at that moment, so there is a carry-over from the times I am channeling, as well as my tendency to not be fully "in my body" anyway. I am working to welcome more earth current into my body.

During channeling sessions, in addition to the standard question-and-answer format, Michael occasionally guides clients through inventive exercises. These might involve chakra balancing, visualization, or emotional release. Especially interesting is their work with couples, guiding them into a perception of the nature of the energy bonds between them and ways they might clarify and strengthen them. Michael also makes an excellent therapist.

Almost everyone who is drawn to come for a session or to study the Michael teachings is already one of Michael's students on an essence level. Part of Michael's work through me during a session is to forge an external bond with the client so that after the session, he has more access internally to Michael's support and energy. Feeling Michael's energy outside himself acts like a magnet drawing out their already existing essence connection. After several sessions, Michael might suggest that the client open directly to Michael within, channeling their energy if not their words during the session. The client then gets "stereo Michael," through me and internally.

My mode of transmission is usually deliberate and slow, although not as slow as it used to be. I endeavor to allow Michael to choose each word precisely so that it can be a vessel of spiritual impact, building energetic substance. The slowness can be especially pronounced in the beginning of a session, and seems to draw listeners into a more receptive state. Once there is alignment (and I am "warmed up"), the speed may pick up. When sessions channeled in this way are transcribed, the text is usually more articulate, "tight," and clear than if I am less alert and careful. However, when I am clearing a lot of energetic debris, it can be difficult for me to stay that precise, because the debris temporarily makes me a little drowsy.

I do observe that the best channeling, my own and others', occurs when the channeled entity is able to deeply and precisely engage with the person(s) listening. When each word is specifically appropriate for him, it can trigger greater realizations. I sometimes hear that, unbeknownst to me, Michael used a word or phrase that was key in the person's life. Occasionally I observe Michael using words that speak particularly well to a specific role. It makes sense that in general, words that stimulate understanding in a warrior, for instance, are not necessarily the same ones that do so in a priest.[6] Michael through me often doesn't answer questions immediately; instead, they take a moment or more to study the situation, delving beneath the surface to gather and process information, sometimes clearing energetic debris in the way.

Channeling has some similarities to a good aerobic workout. It consumes a lot of energy and leaves me feeling tired when I'm finished, although it is also stimulating; unless I'm totally "wiped out," I can't usually go to sleep for two or three hours afterward, and then I may want to "crash." Nonetheless, it is also beneficial for my body if I don't overdo it. Energy seems to move more freely in my body than it did before I began channeling.

In the beginning, I frequently got "channeling headaches," which felt something like being hit over the head with an iron frying pan. They sometimes came after channeling for as little as forty-five minutes. They resulted from my body not being used to the intense, causal-plane energy, and from the blocks in my body preventing it from moving freely. They seem to be largely gone now, but as with aerobics, too much channeling is still unwise.[7] I usually accept no more than one client a day, five times a week, and usually do no more than three days of channeling without a day off. I can go for as long as three and a half hours of questions and answers in a session now, but two hours or so is a more comfortable limit. Interestingly, five minutes of channeling doesn't feel that much less tiring than two hours, so I don't often bring Michael in to ask a quick question. (I do sometimes ask my essence to check with Michael about something, or communicate telepathically with Michael without bringing them into my body, but it's harder to get details that way.)

My sessions are unusual in that most of the time, they are open-ended. Since I don't normally schedule clients back-to-back, they are free to continue until they feel complete.

I asked Michael why they insisted on referring to people by their given first names in the Yarbro books, which can sound formal, but do not do this through me or the other channels I know. In other words, in Yarbro, a person known as Jim would have been called

---

[6]See Chapter Nine, "Roles."

[7]Channels have varying capacities for channeling, but JP Van Hulle has suggested that no one should channel Michael more than twelve hours a week.

"James," whereas he would be called "Jim" through me. Michael pointed out that although given names generally carry the true vibration of the personality, Michael's priority when I am channeling them is to put people at ease. The group Yarbro wrote about was closed, and involved the same people over a period of time who were used to Michael. Those of us who channel publicly constantly attract new people, and this tends to call for greater informality.

About half my clients come to me through word of mouth. I also run profile ads in two local new age magazines. They include my photograph so that people I have agreements with on an essence level can more easily recognize me.

Occasionally someone has a session because someone else gifted him with it, or maybe pushed him to come. These sessions are rarely as fruitful as when someone comes because he is drawn to come. I find that with the Michael teachings in general, they either immediately "ring bells" with someone, or they are not his "thing." There doesn't seem to be too much middle ground.

I started channeling public "Michael Speaks" group sessions in New York City in 1988, and have since done them in several cities. These evenings begin with a guided meditation that I channel from my essence to draw the group together.[8] The end of the meditation is silent, giving me a chance to bring in Michael. Michael usually speaks for about an hour, sometimes leading exercises and eliciting audience feedback. They then accept questions on the evening's topic. If there is time, they may also take questions on other subjects of general interest. (I request that people not ask strictly personal questions, since this tends to dilute the group experience.) Occasionally, some of us go out afterward to a nearby restaurant.

These are beautiful and powerful sharings, both inspirational and instructive. Michael usually doesn't discuss the technical aspects of their teachings, because there are almost always new people present. Even when we had regular monthly or twice-monthly gatherings in New York City, we never had a consistent group like the one depicted in the Yarbro books (although there were some people who were "regulars" for varying periods). The transcripts of these evenings account for about two-thirds of the material in the books in my Summerjoy Michael series, such as *Loving from Your Soul—Creating Powerful Relationships*. I usually don't announce a topic ahead of time, leaving Michael free to draw upon issues in the consciousness

---

[8]Forty-five of these are collected in my book, *Meditations for Self-Discovery— Guided Journeys for Communicating with Your Inner Self* (Summerjoy Press, 1995). See Bibliography.

of those present.[9] People often say later that they felt that Michael was speaking directly to them. With some people, major healing work occurs. Others report that points made by Michael become important themes for them during the following weeks. As with private sessions, some people relate having particularly vivid dreams afterward.

Over time, Michael has shifted their emphasis during these evenings from giving informational lectures to facilitating inner work, helping us explore and transform our relationship with ourselves and the world. Often Michael asks the group for feedback on the energy they are feeling, individually and in the group. As blocks are identified and discussed, they begin to clear. Those attending have the opportunity to practice discerning energy; hearing what Michael and others in the group are perceiving can help validate and clarify their own perceptions. Also, discovering that other people's experiences are often quite similar to our own during a group journey can be potent proof of our connectedness.

When I am traveling and don't have time to offer private sessions, I sometimes also work with small groups for which I channel answers to personal questions, rather than focusing on the group process. People often find that they learn as much from other people's answers as from their own, and sometimes common themes emerge. The energy work is as significant during these evenings as during the "Michael Speaks" and private sessions.

When I channel for myself, I do so in writing, usually at my computer. I bring Michael in to my upper three chakras, as I do when I'm channeling Michael Reading charts. Generally, I have collected and written out my questions over time, just as most of my clients do before a session with Michael. Also like my clients, I can ask further questions if an answer isn't clear to me. Normally, I do this in my mind, but sometimes I type those questions, too, so that I am going back and forth between myself and Michael. When channeling orally with a client, I might also occasionally interject a thought in my mind, such as "What about such-and-such?" but I usually don't speak aloud once Michael begins to speak through me, since I bring Michael in so deeply for the energy work and do not want to interrupt it, although if I must, the work usually "bounces back" quickly. Most other Michael channels do go back and forth between themselves and Michael during sessions with clients, at least occasionally. I understand that the channel known as Milly in the Yarbro books

---

[9]After one session, four people who had come together told me that they had been discussing a book about ascension, and had planned to ask Michael to talk about it. Before they had a chance to, Michael began their lecture by saying, "We'd like to speak about ascension."

sometimes required her private clients to transcribe Michael's answers for her while Michael was speaking, and had her clients read back the answers after each one. She then may have discussed Michael's answers with her clients before going on to the next question.

Many channels and psychics feel that they can't get good information for themselves because they tend to block themselves from hearing the truth or can't get it through their emotional charges intact. I've never hesitated to channel for myself, although I also don't hesitate to check with another channel or psychic as well, since no one can bring through more than a piece of the whole picture; seeing from another angle can be useful.

In channeling for oneself, it is especially important to put aside all opinions, beliefs, emotional charges, ego, and so forth. In fact, being willing to let go of all preconceptions in favor of a clearer view of truth is a prerequisite for excellence in all channeling, psychic work, counseling, writing, journalism, business, and art—for excellence in anything, really. There is at least some bias in all channeling, since channels are human. Most of our bias is invisible to us, and I can't know exactly how bias-free the channeling I do for myself is. I do know that I have a deep desire for the truth, and that, although Michael is always kind, they can be quite blunt with me when bluntness would cut through a defense against the truth. (Their level of bluntness with clients varies, based on a client's openness. Sometimes I observe them wording an answer very carefully to avoid coming up against a "wall." There's little point in giving an answer that won't be heard. In general, Michael is more blunt with me than with my clients, just as I am more blunt with myself than I am with other people.)

I don't channel for myself about personal matters very often anymore, partly because I don't have many questions I need to ask Michael. I more and more feel that I know what I need to do in my life, although sometimes I am stumped about something and am interested in what Michael would have to say about it. Another reason I don't channel for myself more often is that when I'm not channeling for clients or groups, I need to rest—I generally feel better if I don't channel too often. If I haven't channeled for a couple of weeks, I am more likely to "feel like" channeling.

When I do channel for myself, about either personal or general matters, I often find that what was previously unclear is crystal clear because I'm in Michael's energy, even if I still don't have enough intellectual understanding to articulate what I now see. It is as if Michael has lifted me to a summit to share their perspective. For example, as they were explaining a concept about body types that I hadn't understood, I got the whole picture almost at once, although

Michael had to explain further before I could articulate that knowing intellectually. Another example is when I ask Michael to address a disagreement, such as whether someone is a sage or a priest, [10] when there are good arguments supporting both sides. When Michael is explaining which one they see as being correct, and why, my doubts usually disappear—I see some of what Michael sees, and it feels right "in my bones." That's not to say that I trust everything I channel, but I usually find that if I keep asking the right questions until I get to the core of an issue, I not only get an intellectually satisfying answer but that feeling of seeing its rightness for myself.

In general when channeling, for both myself and others, what Michael says can seem simple and obvious, whereas it may not seem that way at all when we're not in Michael's energy—their energy illuminates the truth and makes it seem obvious. That can sometimes lead to the perception during or shortly after a session that Michael's answers are not very profound or substantial, whereas they may seem quite profound and meaningful later, when listening to the tape of the session or reading its transcript. On the other hand, their answers during a session often ring deeply true and seem both simple *and* profound at the same time. In either case, the session usually yields more understanding as the listener comes back "down to earth" with it and lives with it for a while.

Sometimes when I am channeling, I have a sense of what Michael is seeing or is going to say, and sometimes I don't. If they are reading a person's energy or a past life through me, I often catch a glimpse of what they are picking up and know where they are probably going to go with their answer, although my assumptions are not always correct. It seems to me that I'm only aware of the periphery of their perceptions—I'm not privy to their deeper research and thought processes.

Early in the evening during one "Michael Speaks," a woman complained about an unusual shoulder pain. As Michael studied it, I had no clue about what they were reading or were going to say about it, although I sometimes do under similar circumstances. Then they said that she wasn't carrying an emotional block, as others who had spoken earlier were. Instead, her shoulder pain was caused by a negative intellectual belief, not about the evening's topic, relationships, but about such things as channeling itself—she feared that maybe she would leave her body, for instance, and not be able to get back in. The woman was adamant that Michael was off-base. However, it usually no longer unnerves me when people don't validate what Michael says, because I know that although no source is com-

---

[10]See Chapter Nine, "Roles," or the Glossary.

pletely accurate, validation often comes later. Sure enough, about forty-five minutes after that, she walked out, which seemed to confirm what Michael had said, since the lecture itself probably would not have triggered that. Afterward, a psychic who was attending and sitting behind her said that he had read in her exactly what Michael had, which was good for me to hear, since I hadn't picked up anything myself (and it's always nice to receive validation).

I also frequently sense a particular word coming when I am channeling, but many times Michael surprises me by using a different word that is perhaps similar but is more precisely correct and has a feeling of penetrating rightness about it as it is being spoken. If later I am editing Michael's transcribed words for a book, those that felt right and even inevitable may now require editing to read as well as possible, partly because speech and writing are different media. I've also realized that one can't necessarily expect extemporaneously spoken words to seem perfectly polished, especially later in written form when there is time to scrutinize them; however, I do trust that those words that felt right in the moment were in fact right for that moment.

I have been doing an increasing number of sessions on the telephone. Clients who have had sessions both in person and on the telephone say that there is no difference in the energy work, although, obviously, the visual element is lacking on the telephone—no one, for instance, has reported seeing past-life images.

Again, every channel has different experiences; what I relate here should not be construed as being universal.

I often hear from clients that Michael's and my work with them has had a profound healing impact on their lives, through helping them identify and change limiting beliefs, transforming their energy patterns, or giving them more clarity about their challenges. This is very gratifying to me.

Working with Michael and other Michael students has been a great blessing in my life, too. Michael's energy has opened both my body and perceptions, and the Michael teachings have been a rich source of perspective and understanding for me. Their insights during sessions benefit me as well as the people to whom they are speaking—I learn something from just about every session. Through channeling, I am continually being exposed to beautiful truths. Nonetheless, integrating and applying them is a gradual process of growth, as it must be for everyone. Being human, I still don't always "grow through joy" (one of Michael's favorite expressions), but I am learning to. I am grateful for the constant reminders of truth, and for the excellent tools Michael has provided for our growth along our self-chosen paths.

Chapter 4

DIFFERENT MICHAEL FRAGMENTS

One of the reasons for the different styles and information coming through various Michael channels is that different Michael fragments (or essences) among the one thousand fifty warriors and kings are being channeled. Each fragment may identify itself as "we," like a spokesperson representing a company, but the entire entity doesn't have one voice.

We often think of oneness as being like drops of water blending in an ocean, losing all sense of individual identity. What actually happens as we ascend to higher planes is that we work together in our larger groupings much more cohesively. Individuality becomes less important, but it is not lost. Paradoxically, the more unified we become, the more our uniqueness is developed. This is illustrated by the way an organism evolves: each part becomes more specialized, yet the whole works together more effectively.

Michael is a name for a group of souls who are working together for specific purposes, one of which is called the Michael teachings. Each individual soul has its own slant on them. In *Michael's People,*[1] when asked about "a day in the life of Michael," Michael mentioned the various Michael fragments conferring with one another. If they were in total oneness, that obviously would not be necessary. Furthermore, in *Messages from Michael,*[2] they said, "We are integrated fragments of a larger entity," rather than saying that they are the whole entity.

Early on, Michael told me that I worked with a pool of around a dozen Michael fragments, mostly kings in cadence positions two, five, and six, which resonate with the roles of artisan, sage, and priest, respectively.[3] It makes sense that I would work with Michael fragments in these positions, since I am a creatively oriented sage with an inspirational life task. Later, they said that that pool had grown to over sixty, including those who speak, those who research, and those who do energy work. Over the years, I have opened "wider" to be able to handle more energy. When I am channeling for a large, receptive group, or for an individual who is especially open to energy and capable of receiving a large amount of it, that might call for a sizable number of Michael fragments to come forth. Also, the specific exper-

---

[1]P. 207.

[2]P. 54.

[3]See Chapter Eleven, "Cadences and Numbers," or the Glossary.

tise of particular fragments can affect which ones are "on duty" to handle the unique needs of an individual or group. In addition, fragments who have past-life or other connections with those for whom I am channeling might be drawn in. In a gestalt of group consensus and individual "volunteering," Michael tunes in to the situation when I am going to channel and senses which of its fragments are most appropriate.

However, I am not usually aware of any difference among the fragments I channel (or of how many are coming through), except an occasionally strong warrior presence. I seem more likely to channel warrior fragments for warrior clients. I imagine that a warrior channel is more likely to channel warrior fragments of Michael, and that a king is more likely to channel king fragments. Perhaps sages and priests, being cardinal or "exalted" roles, are also more likely to channel king fragments, since kings are cardinal as well.[4] Although there are no rules about this, it is true that "birds of a feather flock together." Another example of this principle is that a channel who is higher in male energy[5] is more likely to channel the male energy aspect of Michael, because that is what the channel is familiar with.

When I am channeling a large number of fragments at once, only one (or two) is the "mouthpiece," choosing words. This fragment(s) is drawn from a pool of about five or six "regulars" and four or five "part-timers" who work with me (out of about a hundred members of the 1050 in the Michael entity who routinely speak through all their various channels). A couple others might "research." The rest work with energy. I draw from a pool of about fifty fragments for the energy work, with as many as ten coming through at once. However, since there is a high level of unity among the various fragments, such divisions are not cut-and-dried; the various Michael fragments form an organic whole.

A few years ago, I channeled that the Yarbro group was also working mostly with kings, especially in positions one and two. The channels represented in the various non-Yarbro books each had their own agreements with Michael and drew from all cadence positions, but at the time I channeled the information, at least, there was a predominance of warriors in positions one and seven. These things might have changed or may change in the future.

---

[4]See Chapter Seven, "The Seven Fundamental Vibrations," or the Glossary.
[5]See Chapter Twelve, "Male/Female Energy Ratio."

Chapter 5

CHANNELING MICHAEL
INFORMATION MORE THAN ONCE

O ccasionally, when someone has received conflicting information from more than one channel, I am called upon to do Michael Reading chart "doctoring" to try to determine what information is correct. Before asking Michael to check the akashic records, we do extensive self-validation. I may ask the client exactly what Michael had said through the other channels, and in what context. For example, if Michael said, "You look like you're about sixth- or seventh-level mature" or "You look like a sage with a priest essence twin," Michael obviously wasn't committing to the information. They were probably reading his aura, perhaps in a group where it was hard to be certain, since auras can blend together in a group, or from a photograph during a telephone session, since reading photographs or a person's aura long-distance gives less information than reading the aura of a person who is physically present. On the other hand, if they said something with certainty in an in-person private session, it carries more weight. If the information had been given from the akashic records through a channel skilled at getting that kind of information, and if the information was the first given, it carries more weight still. I also go into further detail with the client about what the different roles, overleaves, etc., actually mean so that he can explore which are most true of his life, and I attempt to guess what is probably correct, based on my observations, as well. Only then do I ask Michael to give the information again; they usually confirm most of our conclusions, but they may not. If they don't, that could lead to more questions.

In my experience, the first information given is usually the most accurate if it comes through a channel who is clear and skilled in that kind of material, under favorable conditions. If the circumstances of a channeling are not ideal, such as in conditions of stress, fatigue, or distraction (in either the channel or client), mistakes are more likely to happen. Therefore, to self-validate, it can be valuable to consider what was going on each time information was given. If the information was incorrect the first time, the chances of it being correct the second time increase.

Even when channeled Michael teachings information is incorrect, it is still often plausible or has a logic to it. Consequently, it can be messy to sort out just what is correct, and self-validation can require delving more deeply. Even if a person is sure that certain information was incorrect, it can be worthwhile to examine it to see why it came up—it may convey something about what's happening in the client's life, even if it's not the correct Michael information. For example, once, not knowing that the information had already been given, I incorrectly channeled an artisan with a scholar essence twin as being a scholar. She said that friends had told her that she had been looking more scholarly lately. The incorrect information gave her a clue that she was drawing in more of her essence twin energy. (If our essence twin, or twin soul, has a different role, qualities of that role tend to "bleed through" our own, especially when the essence twin is discarnate.)

It is always possible to rationalize wrong information, to find reasons it is correct, just as it is possible to find reasons correct information is wrong. This is especially true when our understanding of what the information really means is not highly developed. For example, if I were new to the Michael teachings and someone told me that I am a king, I could "validate" that by noting that I am sometimes a perfectionist and am a good organizer, as many kings are. I could also "validate" priest because I tend to be compassionate, and artisan because I am somewhat creative. And so forth. But if I gained a deep working understanding of the roles, I would be able to see beyond the surface and eventually, at least, perceive what is actually true, which is that I am a sage, and that, in fact, I look and feel nothing like a king (and not much like a priest or an artisan, either).

There is no real harm in having incorrect Michael information—working to stay in the positive pole of priest, compassion, and out of the negative pole, zeal, is certainly a worthwhile endeavor for anyone. However, the correct information will ultimately be far more powerful and profound—recognizing my sagely oration and working for true expression[1] will have far more impact on my life. In the end, correct information rings more true and deep, and incorrect information doesn't quite fit. Still, correct information may not seem right if we don't fully understand what it means or what its limitations are. For example, if a person assumes that all servers like to take care of other people, and he doesn't, he may assume that he could not be a server. Or if someone has a goal of submission but is bossy at times (which could be explained by an occasional sliding to dominance, aggression or power mode, being a king or warrior, or any other number of factors), others might assume that submission couldn't be correct, not recognizing that the goal isn't about behaviors per se but about what motivates a person.

---

[1]These are the negative and positive poles, respectively, of sage.

I have discussed at length with Michael why Michael information is often inaccurate after the first time people ask for it. They explained that asking for specific information forms a sort of electrical circuit between the asker and the information, with the channel and channeled source as go-betweens. (They called this a "structural willingness to receive.") That circuit is strongest the first time the information is requested because there is an intrinsic need for the information—it hasn't been given before. The circuit is weaker subsequently if there is no organic need for the information to be given again.[2] Because of that, other influences can impinge more strongly than they otherwise would. That is not to say that the information will definitely be incorrect, but the chances grow.

One such possible impinging influence is the psychic projection of the person asking when he has a strong investment in certain information being correct. For example, if, from reading one of the Michael books, he is certain he is a sage, or very much hopes that he is, he may project that. The projection can appear to be the reality if it is strong enough, and can obscure the actual fact even for Michael when the circuit to receive the true information is weakened. Another influence that can obscure correct information is an aura that looks different than it usually does. For instance, a priest whose energy is scattered and who lacks a sense of higher purpose may resemble the other high-frequency role, artisan; artisans' auras are naturally diffuse. A third influence might come when a person has more than one essence sharing his body, or is working intimately with a nonincarnate essence; Michael might inadvertently read the information for an essence other than the primary "lease-holder."[3]

The problem of getting information more than once is not unique to the Michael teachings. It is often said that one's first intuition is the most accurate, even in mundane situations such as taking a multiple choice test. If you doubt your intuition and ask within again, what arises tends to be less certain and clear. When working with tarot cards about a particular problem, the first card drawn is usually the most apropos; if you keep drawing cards about the same

---

[2]This is true regardless of who the channel is each time or who asks for the information. If someone else had had my chart channeled without telling me, and then I have it channeled, the circuit is still weaker the second time. I may have a genuine need and desire for the information, but not a "structural" or organic need, since the information is, at least theoretically, available to me on the physical plane. It doesn't seem fair, but it does appear to work that way. Michael through me strongly encouraged a sharing of information in order to avoid such problems. This is part of being a good steward of what Michael gives us.

[3]See the subchapter "Combined Essence Energies" in Chapter Nine, "Roles."

problem, the waters become muddied, so to speak. Perhaps this reflects in part that the universe operates with an economy of effort: why ask for information twice when once will do?

A process of self-validation, like the one I outlined relative to Michael Reading chart "doctoring," can strengthen the circuit: after going through the process, there may now be an "organically" valid reason for the information to be given again, since what was first given was taken advantage of fully. An appropriate way to ask Michael again for the information would be something like this: "Such-and-such information was channeled for me. It doesn't seem right, for this reason. Could you please double-check it?"

Michael also told me that Michael students have made an agreement with Michael on an essence level to be good stewards of the information Michael gives, and not to ask unnecessarily for the same material to be looked up more than once.

The informational part of the teachings is a means to an end. We're really concerned with advancing growth, not with being a cosmic librarian.

Reconciling discrepancies teaches much about distinctions in the Michael system. For example, if a person is channeled as being second-level old on one occasion, and seventh-level mature on another, it can be quite educational to study the differences between those soul ages and try to determine which one is more true of him.[4] Discrepancies can also help keep channels and clients on their toes, so that no one assumes that a particular channel is infallible. Someone who needs lessons in self-validation, who perhaps has a desire to believe in the infallibility of a particular channel, or who tends to just accept whatever is given without engaging with it and considering it, is more likely to attract inaccurate information.

Some other channels I have spoken with confirm the difficulty in channeling Michael information more than once, and in *More Messages from Michael*,[5] the channels discussed how they "block" information if someone has already channeled it, even if they didn't know that. On the few occasions when I was unknowingly the second one to channel a person's Michael chart, or forgot that I had already channeled a chart and did it a second time, I did not "block"—the information flowed normally. Only once or twice did something seem "fishy." The charts were usually plausible, at least on the surface.

---

[4]See Chapter Fifteen, "Soul Age."
[5]P. 110.

However, I later discovered that most of the repeated material was wrong.

An acquaintance of mine went to four Michael channels when visiting northern California, and asked them all for his Michael information (which I had already given him). He didn't tell them he had already asked other channels, and didn't realize the problems involved in doing this. He thought that if the channels were "pure," he'd get identical information each time. That didn't happen, and he felt that indicated that the channels were "editing" the material. Actually, the results were fairly similar, since the information was being read from his aura in person, and some of it, such as his role and soul age, was pretty clear-cut. However, there were some differences in soul-age level and overleaves. Part of the problem, in addition to the weakened circuit, was that he didn't tell the channels that the information had already been channeled. Although his intent was not malicious, there was a lack of openness in that. I can understand his wish to try to validate a channel's accuracy, but when information is withheld, the session becomes more about "testing" the channel than about fully participating. Channeling is a delicate process that requires a complete investment by both the client and channel, including total good-faith cooperation and honesty, without any holding back. Telling Michael what was channeled previously can help them avoid inaccuracies. It alerts them that the circuit was probably weakened, and they can explore what was channeled previously to see if it has "roots" all the way back to the core of the person and shows up in his akashic records, or if it is merely somehow part of his appearance.

Channeling specific Michael information more than once is different from asking more than one channel or psychic what he picks up about, say, your health or a relationship, because with a general question, there are always more "pieces of the puzzle" that can be given, helping fill in the whole picture. Still, if a channeled entity or psychic told me something specific and I questioned its accuracy, I might check it with another source, but I would offer to tell him what had been said previously. As discussed earlier, some psychics, especially, may not want to know, but I would at least give him the option.

If someone requests a chart on a famous or historical person, I first consult *Celebrities—The Complete Michael Database*[6] by Emily Baumbach. It has a list of Michael information on about twelve hundred well-known figures, culled from the work of many channels. What I get may disagree, but the list provides a starting point. In fact,

---

[6]Causalworks, 1996. See Bibliography.

when Emily compiled the list, there were sometimes discrepancies among some of the contributing channels, and once in a while one channel got different information at different times. Emily, who also channels Michael, chose the information that felt most right to her at the time, and later changed her mind in some instances. Although it can be difficult to validate Michael information on people we do not personally know, we still have to decide for ourselves whether, for example, Shakespeare was a sage or a scholar, or whether Shirley MacLaine is an artisan or a sage.[7] Even when a channel is the first to ask for information on a particular celebrity, if Michael is reading it psychically, the lack of direct personal contact can interfere with the results. Not only is reading someone psychically without direct contact more difficult than in person, but a celebrity's media personality isn't necessarily genuine, and that can alter the way his energy looks.

Although Emily's book is an invaluable reference, Emily doesn't give us alternate channelings or who channeled information on someone first. Furthermore, there is no way to know if channels she didn't work with received information first on someone listed there, or if Michael information has already been channeled on those not listed. Michael has suggested to me that I check with other channels before channeling a chart on a celebrity or historical figure, but that isn't always practical, and I don't want to impose on other people's time.

There have been a few instances when a client has asked for someone's chart, and Michael has not been able to get the information because the essence of the prospective chart subject didn't want it to be given. In each case, the client told me afterward that the subject was intensely private or guarded. In general, a person's Michael information is a matter of public record—like a person's face—and asking for someone else's chart is usually not considered an invasion of his privacy. There is nothing on it that is either good or bad; it is all neutral, and there is nothing on it that could be used against a person. On the contrary, a chart can only help the cause of greater understanding. However, if an essence doesn't want it given out, it won't be, just as if a person doesn't want his face to be seen, he can keep it hidden.

---

[7]I channeled that Shakespeare was a scholar, confirming Yarbro, with scholar essence twin (to my surprise), and that Shirley MacLaine is a sage with a priest essence twin.

Part II

AN OVERVIEW OF THE MICHAEL TEACHINGS

Chapter 6

THE JOURNEY BEGINS

PERSONALITY, ESSENCE, AND SPARK

We are vast and multifaceted, and there are many ways of describing our various parts. However, the Michael teachings outline three basic levels of self: personality, essence (or soul),[1] and spark.

Our personality is our outermost level; it is who we are for this lifetime only. It is a composite of physical, mental, and emotional traits and is influenced by factors such as overleaves,[2] body type, heredity, imprinting, numerology, astrology, and many others. Our personality develops from what we learn in this lifetime.

Our essence animates our personality, providing our spiritual component. It is the part of us that continues from lifetime to lifetime on the physical plane, as well as through the six higher planes of creation in the universe. It is influenced by factors such as role, cadence position, entity, frequency, male/female energy ratio, and many others. Our essence develops from what we learn in all our earth lifetimes and our periods between lifetimes, the "astral interval." When our personality integrates lessons from our present lifetime, they become part of our essence's knowledge.

Our spark animates our essence. It is our core, the part of us that is a unit of consciousness of the Tao, which is also referred to as the "All That Is" or the "Ground of All Being." The Tao is what is beyond the universe, the source from which the universe springs. Thus far, the Michael teachings don't delineate traits on the spark's level as they do with the personality overleaves and essence roles. Our spark develops from what we learn in all our experiences in the universe.[3] When our essence integrates the experiences of our series of

---

[1]Michael generally uses the terms *essence* and *soul* interchangeably, although there are technical distinctions between them that are discussed in Chapter Twenty-Eight, "Levels of Self," along with other, more in-depth material on this general topic.

[2]*Overleaves* and other terms of the Michael teachings mentioned here, along with concepts such as reincarnation, will be defined and discussed in upcoming chapters. They are also defined in the Glossary.

[3]Our spark, which is our core, can only be reached through our essence, which connects our personality and our spark. For this reason, Michael often uses the word *essence* to include both essence and spark. However, technically, they are distinct.

earth lifetimes, as well as our higher-plane experiences, they become part of our spark's knowledge.

Our spark created our essence to enable us to express ourselves in the universe. Our essence, in turn, created our personality to enable us to express ourselves specifically on the physical plane. When a spark creates an essence, Michael refers to that as "casting" from the Tao.

CASTING FROM THE TAO

The Tao consists of an infinite number of sparks, or units of consciousness, that are at once wholly unified and individual, like the cells of our body. Some of these sparks are purely potential, and others have experienced varying degrees and kinds of realization in the universe and in the Tao itself. The Tao is the fundamental creator, and it created the universe to be its "workshop," a place where it could manifest and further know itself. The Tao pervades the universe with love, which is the animating force, the fundamental impulse, in all creation. Our spark, being part of the Tao, shares in the Tao's creativity. When we created our essence, we cast or extended ourselves from the Tao into the universe in order to expand the Tao. We explore, experience, and create in order to actualize more of the Tao's potential and bring back to it a wealth of new knowledge about itself. Since the Tao's nature is love, what we are really about, ultimately, is expanding love.[4]

This journey from the Tao into the universe and back to the Tao again has seven main "destinations." These are the universe's seven planes of creation.[5] Our first destination is the physical plane, which obviously is where we find ourselves now. When we complete the physical plane, we will next have a cycle of experience on the astral plane. When that is complete, we will move on to the causal plane, and so forth, until we have ascended through all the higher planes and are again fully focused in the Tao.

When we are cast from the Tao, we become a "fragment." During the middle of our time on the physical plane (the young soul cycle), we are at our most fragmented or individual. After that, our journey back to being fully focused in the Tao, which is the experience of total oneness, begins. (Humanity as a whole is on the verge of this—the average soul age on earth is sixth-level young; this will be a first-level

---

[4]See Chapter Four, "Expanding Love," in my Summerjoy Michael book *Loving from Your Soul—Creating Powerful Relationships.*
[5]See Chapter Twenty-Seven, "Planes of Creation."

mature planet probably within fifty years.) This journey involves in-
cremental steps of reunification. On the upper astral and lower
causal planes, our entity reunites; our entity is our spiritual family,
consisting of about a thousand souls. On the upper causal plane, our
cadre reunites; a cadre is a group of seven entities. At this point, we
experience enough unity that we are no longer considered fragments.
As we move through the three high planes, consecutively larger
groups of cadres reunite, until everything is reunited back into the
Tao.

I call the big "loop" to and from the Tao a "grand cycle," to differ-
entiate it from shorter cycles such as the old-soul cycle. It is like
taking a great journey around the world and returning home with a
much-expanded awareness. Someone on a journey around the world
may feel that his heart remains at home, no matter how wonderful
the journey is. On our journey through the universe, our heart could
be said to remain at home in the Tao. In casting from the Tao, we
never actually leave it; our spark is eternally a part of it.

Our essence is a sort of "vehicle" for the spark's journey. A spark
cannot live in the universe without a relatively dense form to anchor
it. Picture a spark cast from a fire—it is ephemeral, gone in a moment. So our essence gives our spark form in the universe. The
Michael teachings refer to the seven basic kinds of essences a spark
can create as the "roles" or "essence roles." They are *server, priest, artisan, sage, warrior, king,* and *scholar.* They are rather like the
various basic kinds of vehicles we can choose from if we wish to drive
on a trip: sedan, hatchback, truck, van, and so on. To continue the
analogy, the make and model of the vehicle, the kind of interior, the
color scheme, and the other choices we have when selecting a vehicle
roughly correspond to such elements of our essence as male/female
energy ratio, frequency, and the larger configurations in which we
participate, such as our entity—these modify the "basic vehicle."

When we are ready to incarnate on the physical plane, we have
several other choices to make that will further shape our experiences,
giving us a specific personality and set of circumstances so that we
can accomplish our life plan. These include our overleaves, body
type, agreements, and so on. We also choose our parents and physical body, and can, to a degree, influence our time of birth (which
affects our astrological influences). To continue the analogy of a trip,
the personality and circumstances we take on might be compared to
the motel and city where we spend a night.

Michael is fond of saying that all is choice. Obviously, the
choices of other people affect our lives, but we are the primary creators of our experience. Sometimes people complain, "I didn't choose
to be born." Although that's true on the level of personality, which is

the creation of our essence, on an inner level we *did* choose to be born. We are both creator and creation.

MICHAEL READING CHART

NAME

Date

ESSENCE (*N.I. – Not Incarnate*)

	INSPIRATION		EXPRESSION		ACTION		ASSIMILATION
	Ordinal	Cardinal	Ordinal	Cardinal	Ordinal	Cardinal	Neutral
ROLE	Server	Priest	Artisan	Sage	Warrior	King	Scholar

ESSENCE TWIN[1]

CADENCE[1]

CADRE/ENTITY

TASK COMPANION(S)

MALE/FEMALE ENERGY

---

[1]When I channel charts directly on paper rather than on computer, I circle the role, put a solid underline beneath the essence twin role, and a broken underline beneath the role that the cadence position (the first number in the string of three listed under "Cadence") resonates with, all on the "Role" line. This chart is my paper version.

FREQUENCY

SOUL AGE   1 2 3 4 5 6 7   Infant   Baby   Young   Mature   Old
MANIFESTING

PREVIOUS CYCLES

OVERLEAVES (Underlining indicates sliding goal, mode, or attitude; part of center; or secondary chief feature or body type.)

| | INSPIRATION | | EXPRESSION | | ACTION | | ASSIMILATION |
	Ordinal	Cardinal	Ordinal	Cardinal	Ordinal	Cardinal	Neutral
GOAL	Reevaluation	Growth	Discrimination	Acceptance	Submission	Dominance	Flow
MODE	Reserve	Passion	Caution	Power	Perseverance	Aggression	Observation
ATTITUDE	Stoic	Spiritualist	Skeptic	Idealist	Cynic	Realist	Pragmatist
CENTER	Emotional		Intellectual		Physical	Moving	Instinctive
CHIEF FEATURE	Self-Deprecation	Arrogance	Self-Destruction	Greed	Martyrdom	Impatience	Stubbornness
BODY TYPE	Lunar Plutonian	Saturnian	Jovial Neptunian	Mercurial	Venusian Uranian	Martial	Solar

Chapter 7

THE SEVEN FUNDAMENTAL VIBRATIONS

Mathematics has been described as the most spiritual of sciences. Through it, the universal order can be glimpsed. The whole of the Michael teachings could probably be described entirely through mathematics. The number *seven* is especially central to the teachings. In this chapter, we will look at the overall structure of the Michael teachings in terms of what might be called "the seven fundamental vibrations."

On the Michael Reading chart preceding this chapter, we can see that each role and overleaf is classified as being on one of four axes, or dominant universal qualities: inspiration, expression, action, and assimilation. The axes are fairly self-explanatory: a role or overleaf on the inspiration axis, for example, has an inspirational quality; in other words, it has to do with the inner world. (A definition of inspiration is "the act of drawing in.") The expression axis has to do with manifesting the inner world—for example, communication; it is the bridge between inspiration and action. The action axis relates to the outer world, or doing. The assimilation axis is objective and neutral.[1] It provides a resource for the other axes and helps integrate them.

Since the role is a person's primary way of being, we know that the primary way of being for servers and priests, the inspiration axis roles, is inspirational. In other words, servers and priests thrive on inspiration. They need to feel inspired and feel that they are inspiring others in order to feel that they are being themselves. They may also need to express themselves, act, and assimilate, but these impulses are not as important for them. Likewise, warriors and kings, the action axis roles, languish if they are not in a position to take tangible action. For scholars, having information to assimilate is as fundamental as having food to eat. And artisans and sages suffer if they do not have an opportunity to express themselves.

Each of the first three axes are divided into two parts, ordinal and cardinal.[2] Along with the assimilation axis, which is neutral (neither cardinal nor ordinal) and is not divided, that makes seven parts in all, making a position for each of the seven roles and overleaves.

---

[1]See the subchapter "Neutral Overleaves" in Chapter Eighteen, "Comments on Overleaves."

[2]The word *exalted* is a synonym for *cardinal*.

94

The ordinal side of an axis can be compared to a camera's zoom lens; it deals with the specific, concrete, and immediate. The cardinal side is like a wide-angle lens; it deals with the general, abstract, and far-reaching. The ordinal is contracted, oriented toward detail, whereas the cardinal is expanded, broad, and encompassing. Both sides are necessary, and contraction is not negative—it is not the same as restriction. In order to move, our muscles must both contract and expand.

This can be illustrated by looking at the expression axis roles, artisan (ordinal) and sage (cardinal). Artisans like to express themselves through the specific (e.g., through carving a piece of marble or styling someone's hair) whereas sages like to express themselves through the broad and encompassing (e.g., through communicating insights and ideas). Obviously, both characteristics are useful to the whole. Of course, artisans and any other role can also express themselves through communicating ideas, but that is a sage "specialty." Likewise, sages and any other role can express themselves through fine arts and trades, but that is an artisan "specialty."

Everything in the universe is energy at a particular frequency (speed of vibration). Sound is a band of frequencies that our ears are designed to receive. The musical note A above middle C is defined as 440 vibrations per second. If we multiply that by two, we get 880 vibrations per second, which is A one octave higher. If we keep multiplying what we get by two, we get higher and higher A's, until the human ear can't hear it. However, if we keep going, we move out of the realm of sound into other realms. At some point, we arrive at the realm of light, which is much faster than sound, and what had been the note A is now, say, the color red. There are people who actually perceive a particular color when hearing a particular musical pitch (although different people associate different colors with a particular pitch), and senses can overlap in other ways as well. This phenomenon is called "synesthesia." For someone who perceives color with music, the images can be complex, with particular colors associated with particular instruments and voices, and the colors of the notes themselves overlaid on them, sometimes blending.

Both music and color are external physical phenomena, but the same pattern exists for every level of being, including those described in the Michael teachings. In the realms of personality and essence, the overleaves and role are specific bands of frequency that correspond to each other. For the sake of analogy, let's say that the note A corresponds to the cardinal side of the inspiration axis. The octave would correspond to the specific realm in which this vibration manifested. High A might be like the role of priest, and A below middle C, the attitude of spiritualist. The words *priest* and *spiritualist* are attempts in the English language to represent how these vibrations manifest.

The seven planes of creation also sit on the axes. The messianic plane is the cardinal inspiration plane, and, as a plane, partakes of the same basic qualities as the role of priest and the attitude of spiritualist. Perhaps we could say that it corresponds to the A above high A.

Although there are an infinite number of points between one A and the next higher A, most Western music is built on the framework of the seven-note scale, and it seems natural to pick seven notes between those two A's as the primary elements of an A scale. Without such a frame of reference, music tends to sound like random notes. And though there are an infinite number of shades, there are seven colors in the rainbow, which help us distinguish what we see. In the same way, the seven roles give a concrete style, we might say, to the essence. The seven of each of the overleaves give focus to the personality: The seven goals give a specific direction or motivation to the personality. The seven modes give the personality a particular method. The seven attitudes give its perception an individual slant. And so on.

The roles and overleaves will be explored in detail in upcoming chapters, but much can be gleaned about them simply by looking at where they sit on the axes. Just from knowing that spiritualist, for example, is the cardinal inspiration attitude, we know that spiritualists have a broad, inspirational perspective. That can translate as an ability to see the myriad possibilities inherent in all things, or the working of higher forces. Because their view of life is so large, spiritualists can sometimes be "space cadets" when it comes to handling daily practicalities. However, it doesn't have to manifest that way—it depends on how the individual uses that overleaf. So the word *spiritualist* is "shorthand" for the cardinal inspiration attitude. It describes how the vibration we might call "A" in music manifests in the realm of human attitude. This analogy can be extended to all the other sets of seven elements described in the Michael teachings.

Chapter 8

COMMENTS ON
THE MICHAEL TEACHINGS

THE MICHAEL TEACHINGS ARE ABOUT ENERGIES

To continue the music analogy but in a different vein, let's look at the issue of theory versus experience. Understanding music theory can enhance our appreciation of music. However, music itself is sound, not words, and we can only truly understand it when we connect theory to direct experience through listening to music.[1]

Similarly, understanding "life theory" as taught by Michael can enhance our appreciation of life. However, as with music, it is difficult to truly understand the Michael teachings just through words. I find that people who know the Michael teachings only through books tend to develop misunderstandings. For instance, one client, a server, thought she was a warrior simply because she likes to be productive. To me, she looked and felt nothing like a warrior, but she had little way of knowing what a warrior looks and feels like just from reading books. We need to connect the theory with real life through direct observation and experience, particularly with other people whose Michael information has been validated, so we can know what the "music" "sounds" like.

The term *priest*, for instance, becomes more meaningful to us when we see the particular energy it represents in action within the lives of various people validated as being priests. Not only is it useful to observe priests in general, it is also helpful to compare and contrast young-soul priests and old-soul priests, priests with a goal of acceptance and priests with a goal of growth, priests and servers, priests and kings both in aggression mode, and so on. That way, the common threads stand out, and the effects of the other factors become clearer. Without such experience, we tend to oversimplify and jump to conclusions, to have theories rather than knowledge. Through experience, our understanding of the Michael teachings can keep growing indefinitely.

Learning the Michael teachings requires that we observe the energies behind behaviors rather than just behaviors themselves. Nothing in the Michael teachings is directly about behaviors.

---

[1]When Michael defines *theory* as the negative pole of the role of scholar, they are referring to concept divorced from experience.

Role, soul age, and so forth do not always lend themselves to recognition based on behavior alone. You must look deeper.[2]

Although certain energies tend to result in certain kinds of behavior, they don't necessarily, and we can't assume that a particular behavior automatically indicates that the person has a particular role, overleaf, male/female energy ratio, and so on. It is true, for example, that warriors tend to be highly productive, but people of other roles can be productive, too. The point is *why* a person is productive. Warriors are productive because of an instinctive drive to be active— warrior is the ordinal action role, so their productivity comes from the very fabric of their soul, from what they are. Others can be productive because of an overleaf such as aggression mode, which means that their method of operating is to be dynamic. Overleaves are personality traits that overlay the essence; therefore, overleaf energies do not come from as deep a place in a person as essence energies. A scholar in aggression mode may exhibit some behaviors that are superficially reminiscent of warriors, but he won't feel like a warrior (unless there is bleed-through from a warrior essence twin).

In writing about these teachings, it is necessary to describe behavioral tendencies, because describing energies themselves is difficult. It is like trying to describe the flavor of vanilla; only a taste makes what it is immediately clear. The language of wine critics is often parodied, but describing how a wine tastes is a great challenge. The same is true of describing the energetic quality of priests, for instance. Nevertheless, I have sought in this book to convey flavors alongside the more conceptual information.

POSITIVE AND NEGATIVE POLES

Energy itself is neutral, so nothing on a person's Michael Reading chart is intrinsically "good" or "bad." How energies manifest depends on whether they are based in love or fear—in the Michael teachings' terms, whether they are in their positive or negative poles. We can be in a negative pole chronically or just occasionally. We are more likely to be in a negative pole when we're under stress, and specific situations can trigger us to go into specific negative poles. Also, we can be in a negative pole strongly or mildly, and obviously or subtly.

If everything about two people was identical, including role, soul age, and overleaves, except that one of them was consistently in his

---

[2]A reminder: italicized, indented type such as this indicates a direct quotation from Michael that I channeled.

positive poles, and the other was consistently in his negative poles, these people would look very different. This could even be the case if one of them was heavily in just one negative pole. (A heavy chief feature can have a similar effect.[3])

I once channeled a Michael Reading chart for someone I was about to meet after just having spoken briefly with her on the phone. She was a fifth-level old king in acceptance and passion, and was emotionally centered, overleaves I usually like a lot. Her male/female energy ratio was complementary to mine, and she was in my essence twin's entity,[4] so I assumed that we would hit it off. When I met her, I found that she was strongly in the negative pole of king, tyranny. She was pushy, with a strong belief that she knew what others should be doing. True to her overleaves, she was passionate (mode) about being accepted (goal), but her tyranny drove others away and crowded out the warmth usually associated with acceptance. Old kings are usually more mellow, but even seventh-level old souls are not immune to *maya*, or illusion, which results from the negative pole of the role. In psychological terms, one might simply say that she was neurotic, but her chart paints a more specific picture. Although Michael Reading charts do not indicate the degree to which we are in our positive or negative poles, or the strength of our chief feature, they do provide a vocabulary for our pitfalls and how to avoid them—in other words, how we tend to manifest fear. They also illustrate our strengths, and how to build on them.

THE VALUE OF NAMING ENERGIES

The argument is sometimes made that if we know ourselves, we basically already know anything that might be conveyed on a Michael chart, or, for that matter, on an astrology chart, or on any other kind of reading. Why use an elaborate system to isolate the individual elements of essence and personality? Doesn't that just classify people?

Although many students of such systems use them simplistically to classify people, classifying energies is not the same as classifying people. After seeing the widely varying ways that particular energies defined by Michael manifest, it is clear that people cannot really be classified. We are each unique and unpredictable, although we have

---

[3]Our chief feature is our primary stumbling block. Chief features tend to trigger our negative poles. See Chapter Twenty-Three, "Chief Features."

[4]See Chapter Ten, "Cadres and Entities," and the subchapter "Essence Twins" in Chapter Seventeen, "Relationships," or the Glossary.

certain underlying forces in common. In naming the individual forces, we have tools for recognizing more specifically what's happening in our lives, and for making more specific choices concerning them. Otherwise, these forces might remain vague to us. Having the objectivity to describe a situation accurately is a powerful first step toward changing it. The Michael teachings offer a vocabulary for describing factors that may be difficult to "zero in" on otherwise.

For instance, a sage may grow up denying his impulse to express himself because others see it as an egotistical desire for attention, or as a superfluous interest. "That's very nice, but how are you going to make a living?" His denied essence energy is then more likely to come out destructively, through the negative pole, oration. Stuck in a job that gives him little opportunity to express himself, he may resort to loud, empty chatter or inappropriate humor. Learning that he is a sage and what that means can help him see his essential nature and what is required for his happiness. It is a validation that supports him in being true to himself when external validation is lacking. Identifying the negative pole gives him a tool for recognizing and avoiding inappropriate behavior.

Even if a sage is already manifesting his essential nature to a large extent, knowing about sage energy gives him much food for thought and opportunities to refine his experience of it. Knowing about the other roles can help him avoid judging himself and others for not having the same strengths and weaknesses.

Difficult overleaves (such as the attitude of cynic) and the chief features especially benefit from being named. A cynic in the negative pole, denigration, can easily become stuck in a morass of ugliness. Consciously knowing his attitude can help him avoid that without making himself wrong for naturally tending to have a more contradictory or "acidic" outlook. Someone in impatience may already know that he's impatient, but he may also feel powerless to do anything about it. Learning that his chief feature derives from a fear of missing out, and that it is an illusion that can be "photographed" (observed in action) and erased, can be most useful to him.

The Michael teachings can be fun—for example, it can be like a game to guess people's roles—but they are frivolous if they are not used as tools for growth.

VIEWING THE TEACHINGS AS A WHOLE

To truly understand the Michael teachings, everything in them needs to be viewed in light of everything else. For instance, I know a mature king in passion mode who doesn't look very passionate, except when he's angry, but he has no emotional centering, and was raised at a time when men were expected to hold their feelings in. In addition, kings are an action role, so they tend to demonstrate their passion through their actions, rather than expressing it or inspiring with it. Therefore, his enthusiasm may not be as evident as that of a sage or priest, for example. But we could say that for him, he's passionate—he's more passionate than he would be without that overleaf. I could validate passion mode for him by his statement that he wants to be fully enthusiastic about a task and be able to pour himself into it—that's typical of those in passion mode. They operate by opening the "faucet" all the way, and if they can't do that, they tend not to open it at all.

A warrior client with high male energy, a goal of dominance, a chief feature of impatience, and a mercurial body type, in the moving part of the physical center, but in caution mode, certainly doesn't look cautious in the classic sense. In fact, she looks impulsive to others because of the kind of risks she takes. But she did confirm that before acting, there is a quick moment of deliberation (the positive pole of caution mode)—she really does think before she acts.

I once channeled a partial chart for a woman who is a scholar with mostly neutral overleaves, which surprised her, since she felt herself to be anything but neutral. Only when she had me channel the rest of her chart did we discover that she has eighty-one percent male energy, which explained many of her issues.

So the various energies described by Michael are not separate compartments; each one affects the others, and must be seen in the context of the whole picture. The whole picture, of course, also includes many other factors besides those included on a Michael Reading chart. There is actually an infinite number of influences affecting each person. Astrology deals with the influences of the celestial bodies on our lives; usually, our astrological charts fit well with our Michael charts and complement them, but occasionally, the soul chooses a time of birth that brings in astrological influences different from or even contrary to those considered on the Michael chart. I, for example, am a Libra but have three planets and my ascendant in Scorpio, making me more intense and serious than an old sage in observation mode would normally be. Numerology tells us about the numerical influences of our dates of birth, as well as those of our names. Beyond numerology, I have long noticed that each individual name has a certain vibration, that each person named *Susan, Janet, Lester,* or *Bill* has a particular quality. The language and dialect we speak has an influence on our thinking and on our overall vibration, as well as where we're from. I'm originally from the Midwest, and that fact shows up not only in how I talk but in giving me a more "wholesome," less worldly quality. Age and overall life cir-cumstance are another influence: when I was in college, I noticed that, in general, freshmen had an innocence and brightness that seniors lacked—the freshmen were just beginning, while perhaps the seniors were tired from four years of college. Career also imparts a particular quality: medical doctors, for instance, share a demeanor and point of view that is quite different from the demeanor of, say, opera singers. All these factors contribute to who we are, and can be taken into account when studying a Michael Reading chart.

CHANGING TERMINOLOGY

When discussing the goals in Yarbro,[5] Michael said, "There is an in-termediate, neutral goal, which for the time being we can call 'stagnation.'" Evidently, they weren't satisfied that it was the best possible word. Other channels and students of the teachings have come up with alternatives such as *flow* (which I have adopted), *re-laxation*, and *equilibrium*. Perhaps there is no word in English that truly captures the quality of that vibration. A dictionary definition of *stagnation* is "an absence of movement, growth, or activity." Surely a soul would not incarnate with a goal of wasting its time, so this goal must contribute to growth in some way. The point of the assimila-tion-axis goal is to let go rather than trying to make things happen. Contrast this with the goal of growth, in which one deliberately goes after stimulation—it's a different approach, with different lessons. The positive pole of flow is suspension. To suspend is "to cause to be upheld by some invisible support." This suggests floating, like a leaf carried by a river. (The negative pole, inertia, suggests a rock at the bottom of a river, which is more like the connotation the word *stagna-tion* usually has.) Literally, flow is the opposite of stagnation—stagnant water is *not* flowing; but the approach of this goal could be described either as "going with the flow" or as stagnating, if we see stagnation as an absence of *self-induced* movement.[6]

The words *retardation* and *repression*, like *stagnation* and some other terms in the Yarbro books, have some negative connotations. If we remove the judgments around them and use them literally, they are probably more precise than their alternatives, *reevaluation* and *reserve*. For example, to retard simply means to make slow or slower, which is exactly what retardation does to the life of someone with this goal. (A *ritard* in a musical score is a direction to slow down.) One

---

[5]*Messages from Michael*, p. 106.
[6]See Chapter Nineteen, "Goals."

may use it to reevaluate, especially on unconscious levels, but the goal itself simply promotes, in the positive pole, atavism, or alternately, simplicity, a shedding of cultural imprinting to get "back to basics." Nonetheless, since it is not easy for people to accept the word *retardation* (people tend to think of mental retardation), I use *reevaluation*. I see it as a necessary compromise.

Likewise, the role many call "server" was referred to as "slave." Stripped of its societal implications, the word *slave* can be interpreted to simply mean someone wholly dedicated to service, and in some ways is accurately descriptive of this role. However, since people's feelings need to be taken into account, I think that *server* is a better term. Some people don't even like that, preferring *facilitator*, but to me, *facilitator* lacks specificity. In a way, all the roles facilitate something. Many spiritual teachings regard service as the highest path—Jesus was quoted as saying, "He that is greatest among you shall be your servant"[7]—so being called a server isn't demeaning, in my opinion.

There is much confusion over the terminology for the action-axis centers. Yarbro gives the terms *sexual* and *moving* for the ordinal and cardinal centers, respectively. In this context, Michael defines *sexual* broadly to mean any physical excitation, not just erotic. Because most people misunderstand this and have such charged feelings about the word *sexual*, I use the word *physical* for that center. Other channels have adopted the terms *moving* and *higher moving* for the ordinal and cardinal centers, respectively. So Yarbro's term for the cardinal center is other channels' term for the ordinal. Compounding the confusion is the fact that although *sex* can refer to mere copulation, in its most mature form it is a transcendent experience of higher energies, ultimately union with the cosmos. For this reason, Michael through me once said that a strong case could be made for calling the *cardinal* center "sexual," and the ordinal "moving." I later learned that in some of the Yarbro group's earliest channeling on this subject, Michael in fact did use the term *sexual* for the cardinal center, and *moving* for the ordinal. It mostly boils down to semantics. The point is to get a feel for the kinds of experiences being referred to when discussing these centers, whatever terms are used. (This subject is discussed in further detail in Chapter Twenty-Two, "Centers.")

In a Yarbro book, Michael referred to *one* of the words for a pole, implying that there are other words that could be used. There is certainly a wide range of qualities associated with any characteristic discussed in the Michael teachings.

---

[7]Matthew 23:11

Lastly, some people prefer the terms *focused* and *creative* energy to *male* and *female* energy. Since male energy specifically relates to the male body, and female energy relates to the female body, I have stuck with those terms. A man might be uncomfortable knowing that he has high female energy until he understands that it doesn't make him any less masculine in society's terms, although he may be more "laid back" than a man with high male energy. Likewise, although a woman with high male energy may be more career-oriented or other-wise outwardly directed than one with high female energy, it doesn't make her any less feminine in society's terms.

CHOICE

Michael is fond of saying that all is choice—we chose our overleaves, parents, even our essence role, speaking from the point of view of our spark. However, we tend to assume that on higher levels, we make choices in the same way we do on the physical plane, mentally mak-ing decisions. I can't imagine a spark of the Tao sitting around with its friends looking at travel brochures, and saying, "Earth looks real interesting—let's go there!" and then, "I think I'll do earth as a king. I haven't been a king in this universe yet. It'll be fun. Hey, Sid, do you want to be my essence twin?" Likewise, between lifetimes, I can't imagine my essence studying *The Higher Self Guide to Overleaves and Body Types.* I suspect that the choice process is organic in a way that is beyond our understanding. Relative to the rest of reality, our con-sciousness on the physical plane is rather crude. For one thing, as human beings, we necessarily view choice-making in terms of lan-guage; but like time, language as we know it is a construct of the physical plane. Nonetheless, on some level and in some way that may be incomprehensible to us now, we chose all the components of who we are—nothing is imposed upon us.

EVOLUTION OF THE MICHAEL TEACHINGS

The Michael teachings are not static, since both Michael and their channels are continually evolving and learning new things, as well as refining the way that they translate cosmic realities into human thought and the English language.

For instance, in the early days of the Yarbro group, Michael seemed to be urging their students to change their overleaves rather than simply be in the positive poles of whatever overleaves they had chosen for this lifetime. They seemed to feel that the goal of growth, power mode, and the attitude of spiritualist were the "best" ones for those on the spiritual path, and spoke at length about the negatives of most of the other overleaves, particularly the goal of rejection (referred to as "discrimination" in this book). I do not know whether this reflected a bias in the channel, "Jessica Lansing," or whether the Michael fragments being channeled were incomplete or unclear in their thinking. Perhaps the material itself was basically accurate but was missing additional material that would have balanced and clarified it. (In general, I find the Yarbro material to be both the most extraordinary and profound channeled material I have seen, and often cryptic and in need of clarification.) Whatever the case was, the material published in *Messages from Michael* a few years later had a markedly different presentation of the overleaves, with almost no encouragement to try to change them. Michael's approach was closer to the way I now understand overleaves: no overleaf is intrinsically "good" or "bad." Although some are more challenging to do well than others, and people are encouraged to slide (temporarily move) to an opposite overleaf under certain circumstances in order to find balance, every overleaf is seen as a potentially valuable tool for essence, probably chosen for good reason. This approach feels more right to me. However, it is possible that further clarification will come in the future.

No matter how excellent a channel is, it is important not to "deify" and "carve in stone" what comes through him, but instead let our understanding continue to evolve.

LIMITATIONS OF THE MICHAEL TEACHINGS

Like your physical body, the universe is complex. To make an analogy, the Michael teachings might be thought of as describing only the endocrine and lymphatic systems of the universe. There are many other systems at work.

Categories are convenient tools, but tend to lead to oversimplification. Reality is vast.

There are many parts of the Michael teachings that have not yet been received because the questions have not been asked. There is also some material that has not yet received wide dissemination.

Human language can only express a small part of our commu-nication. The rest must be perceived in essence through the higher centers.

There is no intrinsic value in simply knowing whether you are a sage or a priest, for example, according to our definitions. Like all information, it is only valuable if you use it. We present our teachings to aid you in your quest to understand, that you might journey into new territories of love.

Part III

ESSENCE

Chapter 9

ROLES

	ORDINAL	NEUTRAL	CARDINAL
INSPIRATION	*SERVER* + Service – Bondage		*PRIEST* + Compassion – Zeal
EXPRESSION	*ARTISAN* + Creation – Artifice		*SAGE* + Expression – Oration
ACTION	*WARRIOR* + Persuasion – Coercion		*KING* + Mastery – Tyranny
ASSIMILATION		*SCHOLAR* + Knowledge – Theory	

Our role is the type of soul we are, the spiritual archetype we embody.[1] Every soul has a particular role that determines his dominant way of being.[2] Although a soul can have only one role, there are secondary role influences from his essence twin and casting (mathematical position within the greater whole). We could say that our role is our primary style—it determines not so much *what* we do but *how* we tend to do whatever we choose to do. Anyone can do any activity, regardless of role, although each role tends to gravitate toward certain activities. For example, since sages are the cardinal expression role, they often like to disseminate information.

---

[1]"What's Your Role—An Introduction to the Michael Teachings," in the front matter just before Chapter One, gives some background on the roles. Also, each role is defined in the Glossary. Rather than explore each role in-depth separately, which is done in several other books, the roles are elucidated in relationship to each other and to other Michael traits, in this chapter and throughout this book. Most of the overleaves are handled similarly.

[2]The chart at the beginning of this chapter lists the seven roles, showing their axes (on the left), whether they are ordinal, cardinal, or neutral (on the top), and their positive and negative poles (beneath them). The charts at the beginning of the chapters on overleaves follow the same pattern.

However, a person should not assume that he is a sage just because he likes to do that—people of other roles may also have that characteristic. A role is not an exclusive, rigid set of behaviors.

For the same reason sages often like to disseminate information, they are also the quintessential actors and storytellers,[3] and there are probably more sages among actors than any other role. A sage actor can be colorful, expressive, and dramatic, with excellent timing. Jack Nicholson is a sage. A majority of comic actors, such as Whoopi Goldberg, Bill Murray, and Teri Garr, are sages. Nevertheless, there are a great many actors who are not sages, and they bring the qualities of their essence role to that profession.

An actor with the role of priest is likely to focus on how his performance can reveal some higher truth. A priest's style of acting can be intense, with much communicated through his eyes; Christopher Walken is a priest. An artisan's approach to acting emphasizes craftsmanship and technique—Meryl Streep is an artisan known for her extraordinary command of the craft of acting. A king's style of acting is commanding: Patrick Stewart, who played Captain Picard on *Star Trek—The Next Generation*, certainly acts in a kingly manner, and his Shakespearean training adds to the effect; Katharine Hepburn is another king[4] actor who commands enormous loyalty and respect. No actor can capture power and instinctive drive like one with the role of warrior—Marlon Brando is a perfect example. Servers, such as Doris Day, bring a nurturing warmth to their roles. (Ms. Day is now directing those qualities toward helping animals receive better treatment.) Scholars as actors study their parts as a means of learning about people, and can look a variety of ways as an actor; Vanessa Redgrave has been channeled as being a scholar, which illustrates that although scholar is the neutral role, scholars are not necessarily neutral people; many other factors can make for intensity in a person. Still, every scholar is dominantly assimilative—someone who studies, ruminates, digests, experiments, and so forth, as a primary way of being—as opposed to being dominantly inspirational, expressive, or active (referring to the four axes).

There are probably more artisans in the fine arts than the other roles, and the stereotypical artist looks more like the artisan role than the others; however, there are artists of all roles. Again, the role

---

[3]*Story* and *drama* are key words for sages. As a sage, I love musical theater because it uses various art forms, including music, dance, and costume and set design, to tell a story, heightening the drama.

[4]Since the essence has no gender, the term *king* applies to those in both male and female bodies; there is no role of *queen*. Likewise, there is no role of *priestess*.

has more to do with the way something is done than what is done. For example, painter Georgia O'Keefe demonstrated her warrior energy through both her subject matter and her style. She portrayed towering skyscrapers and cattle skeletons. Her style was focused and highly physical. Even her flowers were not "flowery" and had a sexual quality.

The quintessential chief executive is a king, but the United States has had presidents of all the roles; only John Kennedy was a recent U.S. president with a role of king. Jimmy Carter is a server, George Bush is a priest ("honorary scholar"), Gerald Ford is an artisan, Bill Clinton and Ronald Reagan are sages, Dwight Eisenhower was a warrior, and Richard Nixon was a scholar. It is easy to see how their styles as president reflected their roles. For example, Reagan was an actor and was called "the great communicator." Clinton is known for his social skills, his love of being in the public eye, and his saxophone playing. Both men are quintessential sages.

According to Yarbro, roughly twenty-five percent of the earth's population (and the sentient population of the entire cosmos) are servers, twenty-two percent are artisans, seventeen percent are warriors, fourteen percent are scholars, ten percent are sages, eight percent are priests, and four percent are kings. This follows the order of most ordinal to most cardinal, with the neutral role, scholar, comprising about one-seventh of the population. So about sixty-four percent of the population has an ordinal role, and twenty-two percent has a cardinal role, with, again, fourteen percent having the neutral role, scholar. On any planet, there may be historical periods during which these percentages vary. For example, there may be civilizations that attract many warriors but not many sages. In general, though, these percentages are fairly constant from planet to planet, according to my channeling, allowing for minor variations due to free will. Some planetary "experiments" call for slightly different mixes of roles. However, the Tao has found through past experience that these proportions work well: a planet lacking balance among the roles—one that is too ordinal or too cardinal, for instance—can invite added problems.

Those with cardinal roles—king, priest, and sage—tend to like to work with large numbers of people at a time, and focus on expansive ideas and projects. Those with ordinal roles—server, artisan, and warrior—tend to like to work one-on-one, and focus on the nitty-gritty. Scholars, the neutral role, are neither cardinal nor ordinal; they occupy the detached, objective position. However, they more often resemble the ordinal roles.

The cardinal roles have a more concentrated, penetrating, "wedge-like" quality; the ordinal roles have a less concentrated, more "rounded-off" interface with the world. For instance, inspirational energy from priests is usually perceived as being more intense than that from servers, who tend to have a more low-key, diffuse style. However, one can't jump to conclusions here either. I had one client whom I had channeled as being a server, but she seemed too intense to be a server. She had striking, powerful eyes more reminiscent of the role of priest (she was exotic looking in general). She had a no-nonsense, "don't-mess-with-me" style, and wasn't interested in serving others in the mundane, physical ways we often associate with servers. The only elements on her Michael Reading chart that may have accounted for these characteristics were her warrior (number three) casting and her occasional sliding to power mode (from caution). On the other hand, in a key way the role of priest didn't fit her, either: she wasn't drawn to working with large numbers of people or to inspiring people in an exalted way. In time, she validated that she was a server, realizing that she served people in nonmaterial ways, such as through often supporting her friends during emotional crises. (Perhaps she had "burned out" on the more mundane ways of serving in past lifetimes.)

ROLES AS ENERGIES

Often people identify with many of the roles. Our role is our dominant energy, but we have all the others in us as well, at least potentially.

Each role energy has a particular "flavor." Sometimes it's obvious in a person; sometimes it's not. Sages, for instance, have a certain tone that could be described as brassy, although its "volume" can be anywhere from quiet to loud. Other energies, such as essence twin role, casting,[5] overleaves, body type, life task, and imprinting, can either emphasize or de-emphasize the energy of the role.

For example, a warrior in caution mode or a server with the attitude of cynic can be like an actor cast against type, especially when in the negative poles. The usual warrior strength can be muted by caution, especially its negative pole, phobia. (In the positive pole, the warrior is simply deliberate.) Cynicism can put an edge on the normally nurturing server.

In addition, sometimes a person is afraid to manifest his true nature because of past experiences. A sage, for example, may be afraid of speaking up, even though the sage role is largely "about" communication, because doing so got him in trouble before; in such a case, the fear will tend to be a big issue, because a dominant part

---

[5]See Chapter Eleven, "Cadences and Numbers."

of his nature is blocked. Likewise, a king or warrior (or anyone else) might be afraid of using his power because of having misused it in the past.

When a person has had a lot of imprinting contrary to his role, sometimes his role isn't very evident simply because he's young and hasn't yet had time to assert who he is. Two teenage girls once came together to see me, and one of them was a king, which she found hard to believe, although her friend could validate it. I imagine that she looks more kingly now. If someone completes his midlife monad (usually in his mid-thirties), he generally throws off any remaining contrary imprinting that he no longer needs (if he ever needed it), fully revealing or "manifesting" his true essence. If someone doesn't complete it, he can remain stuck in his imprinting for the rest of his life (unfortunately, this is common).

In addition to past experiences and imprinting, we also all have a false ego that can obscure our true nature to some extent. Servers and priests, for instance, are the primary care-givers, and in their positive poles, they tend to be particularly warm and nurturing. However, in their negative poles, even they can occasionally be cold and self-centered, although their role will likely be evident in other ways. I once channeled a friend's mother as an old server; he had been certain that she was a young warrior (he had some negative judgments about both warriors and young souls). Michael explained that due to traumatic past-life experiences, she was a deeply wounded soul full of anger, and that that was masking her true essence.

It is also true that priests and servers sometimes need to be less involved with caring for others in order to balance their tendency to feel overly responsible for them; otherwise, they may not learn how to nurture themselves. In addition, because their vision of the higher good is so important to them, priests in their negative pole can tend to lay a lot of guilt and "should"s on themselves and others, leading to a quality of severity and heavy-handedness not unlike that of negative-pole warriors. Priests' positive pole, compassion, is the antidote to this.

I am a sage, and I also have a sage essence twin and a sage cadence position, yet sometimes people are surprised that I'm a sage, or at least assume that my essence twin influence must be something other than sage. In fact, when I visited part of the Michael community in northern California, various people guessed my role or essence twin role to be scholar, priest, server, and artisan, in addition to sage. Those who guessed scholar were probably seeing my serious, analytical side—I am intellectually centered, which makes me look a little like the scholar stereotype. (I am also in a number four, or scholar-position, cadence, which I discuss in Chapter Eleven, "Cadences and

Numbers.") I have a life task that is both expressive and inspirational, and my spiritual values are reflected in my writing, which may look somewhat priest-like. My goal of acceptance and my essence's altruistic bent give me a "nice guy" quality that may suggest to some the role of server. My songwriting and other creativity suggest both artisan and sage energy. Some people even think I'm a quiet person—not the sage stereotype—but I do talk a lot to people I'm close to, and have many people in my life who are important to me, which is typical for sages, the most social of roles. I also love to sing, act, lead groups, counsel, "network," write, and many other things that are common for sages. (When I was five, I wanted a typewriter for my Hanukah present, and was bitterly disappointed when I got a *toy* typewriter.) I have a sage's sense of humor,[6] although it does not always come out. (Humor can be a tonic for me, but I try to avoid the sage trap of being "on" all the time, "performing" my life rather than being genuine.) More importantly, expression, the name of both the sage's axis and positive pole, is what most deeply characterizes me. People who really know me and who are also familiar enough with the flavor of sages would probably know that I'm a sage.

There are many different kinds of intelligence, but one of the characteristics we frequently ascribe to intelligence is the ability to retain and manipulate large amounts of information. This is a scholar specialty; they tend to have "steel trap" minds, since it is in the nature of scholars to gather, organize, and store knowledge. They also tend to spend many lifetimes cultivating their intellect and often choose intellectual centering, so we generally think of them as being highly intelligent. However, I know a moving-centered scholar who is mentally retarded.[7] Obviously, he is not highly intelligent in this lifetime, even if he has been in many past lives. However, there is more subtle evidence of his scholar energy. For example, he has an encyclopedic memory for football statistics—he accumulates stacks of newspapers, refusing to throw them away until he has pored over the sports sections. He also remembers minutiae from the past. If the part of his brain responsible for such memory were also damaged, he would not even manifest these traits; you would have to look harder for evidence that he's a scholar, but if you're sensitive to what scholar energy feels like, you would probably still be able to validate him as a scholar. (Incidentally, it is often scholars and servers who incarnate into "differently abled" bodies; scholars, out of curiosity, and servers, to serve. However, most of us will have at least one lifetime in such a body.)

---

[6]See Appendix D, "Humor."
[7]See Chapter Twenty-Two, "Centers."

INFORMATION AND ROLES

Scholars are generally those most interested in the Michael teachings, followed by warriors. *Michael's People*[8] and all the Michael channels I know personally corroborate that. The first years of my practice were an extreme example of this, when perhaps a third to a half of my clients were scholars. Incidentally, patterns are continually changing in my practice (I will discuss this in greater depth later). Recently, I have been seeing and channeling charts for more priests than any other role, followed by sages, even though I saw few fellow sages early in my practice. My experience has no relationship to the percentages of roles on earth as a whole or even in the practices of other Michael channels, nor does it have any "cosmic" significance. It simply reflects the energies of my life at a particular time, which, for all of us, are complex and move somewhat unpredictably, like the tides. There is no concrete reason I have been seeing so many priests lately—it is just what is happening. An astrologer told me that she also experiences inexplicable patterns in her life, such as seeing three clients in a row who have Aquarius rising. Go figure!

In any case, it is easy to see why scholars and warriors are especially attracted to the Michael teachings. The Michael teachings are practical, structured, and informational. Warriors organize and structure the world. Scholars love information, and there are not many other metaphysical teachings that address the nuts and bolts of the larger picture. I have a few clients who have ordered ten or twenty Michael Reading charts at a time, profiling their family, friends, and coworkers. These clients are almost all scholars. It makes sense that Michael would create the kind of teachings they have, since the Michael entity is eighty percent warriors, and is in the number four or scholar position within its cadre.

When I explain and interpret Michael Reading charts for scholars, it often takes almost twice the time it takes for warriors. Most people sit quietly through their reading, so it's not because scholars ask a lot of questions. Somehow, they draw a lot of detail from me. Warriors, on the other hand, usually like speed and efficiency; this, too, is reflected in their readings.

In private channeling sessions, most questions concern personal issues, but many scholars seem to delight in getting their necessary personal questions out of the way so that they can seek general knowledge, asking the kinds of questions that those of other roles rarely do. They may explore the fine points of the Michael teachings, or of other metaphysical teachings, or discuss issues in the news, for

---

[8]P. 24.

instance. (Priests also tend to ask questions that other roles rarely ask, such as "How can I grow the most?" and "How can I best help others?")

Here are some comments from Michael about scholars and warriors:

Just as scholars tend to have a particular focus of energy in their minds, the action axis roles, especially warriors, tend to have a particular focus of energy in their hands, since the hands are often tools for action. They build the energetic facility of their hands from much doing. Wherever you have exercised your capabilities, you have more substance.

It is the nature of scholars to explore constantly for new knowledge. If existing knowledge sources have been exhausted, in the sense that everything the scholar wishes to study of resources currently available has been studied, the scholar is prone to creating new knowledge. He plays the game of "What would happen if...?"

Knowledge can be gained in many ways other than verbally. Theory, the negative pole of scholar, is more reliant on words. Becoming aware of more expansive avenues of communication can help scholars be in their positive pole.

Of course, it is not only scholars who are sometimes overly theoretical. People of any role who tend to use words as a substitute for direct experience can benefit from communicating more physically, emotionally, and spiritually.

The positive pole of scholar, knowledge, is not so much about *possessing* knowledge, although scholars usually have large storehouses of information, as it is about the *experience* of knowing: the positive-pole scholar *knows* rather than theorizes. More than the other roles, the scholar can know innately, without necessarily knowing how he knows. He can access the depths of what he has learned over many lifetimes.

One term cannot encompass the full range of a positive or negative pole. There is more to the negative pole of scholar, for instance, than theory. The terms *theory* and *oration*, the negative pole of sage, imply using words, which are a function of the intellectual center. In fact, *verbosity* has been used as an alternative term for the negative pole of sage. However, scholars and sages, like the other roles, can be in their negative poles without using words. The negative pole of scholar has to do with a separation from experience, projecting ideas *about* it rather than directly connecting with it. The negative pole of sage has to do with commanding attention without engaging in true communication. These negative poles can occur emotionally or physically—not all sages and scholars are highly verbal—although most often, they do occur intellectually, which is why the terms *theory* and *oration* are used.

People who are not intellectually centered or in the intellectual part of a center can still use their intellectual center, of course, but their access to it is not as direct. As mentioned, scholars tend to be associated with intellectual centering because they choose it so often. I've seen scholars who are emotionally centered for the first time in many lifetimes who are disoriented, especially if they are not in the intellectual part of the emotional center. It is like tying their strong hand behind their back to strengthen their weak one. Being both emotionally centered and in a female body for the first time in a while seems to be even more disorienting. The soul can't quite figure out "how this thing works."

If we are trying to guess someone's soul age, it can be valuable to know his role first. Mature souls are generally more intense and "attached" to the physical plane than old souls, but mature scholars, even if they are emotionally centered, can look less intense than old priests or warriors, since scholars are the neutral role.

Although the positive pole of scholar is knowledge, scholars, sages, and priests all tend to love knowledge. Scholars no doubt buy the most books by far, but sages and priests probably come in second and third. Scholars can be attracted to any interesting fact—pure knowledge, we might say. Sages emphasize insight—the "why" behind the facts—as well as pithy quotes and "news you can use." (Sages also tend to love magazines and newspapers, especially if they're entertaining.) Priests are attracted to "higher" or inspirational knowledge, and might mostly limit their reading to new age, religious, spiritual, or philosophical books. However, people of any role can love the particular kind of knowledge that is useful to its essence. For example, artisans and warriors might collect "how-to" books.

Also, although oration is the negative pole for sages, scholars, with their love of knowledge, and priests, with their need to inspire, can also be quite talkative. (Incidentally, simply talking a lot doesn't necessarily indicate negative-pole function.) When sages talk a lot, they tend to focus on their views or a "story," while scholars are more likely to give detailed "raw" information or theory, without sages' expressiveness and sense of drama. Priests often like to speak about what inspired them (or didn't). In their negative poles, sages talking too much are likely to irritate others, whereas scholars are likely to simply bore them, and priests might pressure or numb them. Sages tend to want people's attention on themselves in order to provide an audience for their self-expression, whereas scholars tend to want attention on the facts, and priests, on their vision of the higher good.

Our society tends to imprint males to talk less, and because kings and warriors emphasize action rather than expression, male warriors and kings are those most likely to be "the strong, silent type." Male artisans can also fit this stereotype, being quietly dreamy or moody. Nonetheless, people of any role can be either talkative or not, including sages, who may express themselves in other ways, or may simply be repressed.

Being intellectually centered may contribute to the tendency to be talkative, since it tends to make one more verbal. However, being verbal and talking a lot isn't the same thing—some people are quite verbal in writing and thinking, but don't talk much, and some people who are not particularly verbal are talkative—they may express their emotions or physical reactions through words, especially if they are in the intellectual part of another center, or they may simply be in the habit of saying whatever comes into their head, without thinking.

Nevertheless, it is probably safe to say that intellectually centered people in general are both more verbal and talk more than those with other centerings, and all other things being equal, sages, scholars, and, to a lesser extent, priests, tend to talk more than the other roles.

Sages who express themselves more through forms like art, dance, and bodywork than through words sometimes look like artisans, especially sages who are emotionally centered. Still, they usually emphasize communication more than technique. My mother was an emotionally centered sage, and her paintings contained a lot of symbolism and unspoken messages. This was more prominent than technical elements such as perspective and proportion, which artisans might emphasize.

Kings tend to have a healthy respect for knowledge, and although they don't generally seek it for its own sake, they often master whatever knowledge is relevant to their field of endeavor.

I've run into a few scholars who were certain they were sages, although they didn't have sage energy, as I recognize it. If a person is not familiar with how the energy of both roles feel, he could confuse them, since, as mentioned, they share a love of knowledge. Also, every role tends to have certain fears, and scholars often fear being boring. (Sages often fear not being heard.) Perhaps these scholars thought that being a sage is more "glamorous" or interesting to others. However, only the negative pole of scholar is boring—true knowledge is interesting—and there are some quite glamorous scholars around.

If in doubt whether someone is a scholar rather than a sage (or any other role, for that matter), use the "pack rat test." Most scholars I've observed (although not all, of course) have an extensive collection of some kind, most often books. Intellectually centered scholars may have a huge library of books, records, or computer disks. Emotionally centered scholars might save mementos such as letters and photographs, or clothes. Physically or moving-centered scholars might collect tools or recipes. (They also often love to travel, since it gives them an opportunity to study through their body.) Emotionally, physically, and moving-centered scholars still tend to have more books than the other roles, although not as many as intellectually centered scholars. (I once met one about my age with thirty thousand books!) Even if a scholar has disciplined himself to pare down his possessions, his inherent inclination is to save potentially useful things, since scholars provide resources for others, and want to have them on hand in case they're ever needed or just for their own "reference." Sages, on the other hand, might also like having a library, but they more often than scholars give away books they've already read, and in general try to find "good homes" for things they are not using. The difference between expression and assimilation is evident here.

Although a person of any role can have a good sense of humor, sages are especially noted for it, and, like comic actors, the majority of professional comedians are sages. When I see someone who finds most things funny or is continually laughing, my first guess is usually that he is a sage. A sage's laugh is frequently a cackle or a guffaw; titters come only when he tries to repress it, for example in a church or a funeral home. Sages seek to bring enlightenment. One way of doing this is through the lightness of humor and play. The humor of sages tends toward wit and cleverness. (Of course, not every sage is funny.) Warriors are also known for their humor, which is usually more earthy and hearty, as in the belly laugh. Puns and word play are a specialty of scholars, although, of course, punsters can be of any role.

While I was channeling for an old priest once, Michael guided him into simultaneously channeling them, although not verbally. I was fascinated later when he described the vivid, exalted visions he received while Michael's energy was in his body, very different from my experience. He also seemed to know empathically what Michael felt in being channeled, rather than just feeling his end of it. This seemed to be an apt reflection of his priest essence. Priests also seem to be the most vivid dreamers among the roles. (Artisans also tend to have extraordinary dreams, as well as daydreams.)

HOW ROLES APPEAR PHYSICALLY AND ENERGETICALLY

Occasionally, Michael students say that someone looks like a certain role. A person's physical traits result mainly from heredity and body type (which is partly hereditary). However, the role energy does exert subtle influences on how someone looks. It exerts a stronger influence on the qualities that come *through* physical traits, especially facial expressions. The following are some examples from my observation; they should not be taken as "rules" or as being universal, by any means.

Priests' eyes are one of the most clear-cut physical indications of role I've found: they are very warm and intense, either compassionate or severe, depending on whether the priest is in the positive or negative pole. Priests often receive comments from other people about their eyes. Warriors' eyes can also be intense, but in a cooler, earthier, sometimes metallic way. Servers' eyes are also warm but not as intense. In general, servers can look sweet, earnest, and comforting, or, in the negative pole, dull or downtrodden.

Kings can have narrow, wedge-shaped faces with long, regal noses and a contained, regal expression, sometimes as if to say, "We are not amused." Both warriors and kings have a "clean," no-frills, "let's get to the point or down to business" air about them. Warriors' faces can be flat and smooth. Warriors exude a quality of solidity and raw power. It is as if kings' faces are designed for focus, and warriors' faces for pushing through (like a blunt battering ram).

Scholars' neutrality can be harder to spot than the particular "colors" of the other roles, but it does manifest in the way they look. Their eyes, for instance, have a neutral, Van Gogh-ish quality—I can almost see swirling circles in front of them that perhaps allow scholars to observe without being seen too much. In general, scholars seem "washed" with an almost milky energy. Although scholars can be beautiful or handsome, like any other role, in my experience they are generally not striking, since they usually don't want to call too much attention to themselves. Sometimes I can guess someone to be a scholar only through a process of elimination—I figure that they can't be any of the other roles. On the other hand, scholars can look like any other role depending on what other influences are present. If, for instance, someone is a scholar with a priest essence twin, he may look like a priest because of the bleed-through against the neutral "backdrop." However, because the priest energy is being filtered through the translucent scholar energy, the priest energy isn't as strong or "pure" as it would be if he were a priest. (This will be discussed further in the next section.) In the negative pole, a scholar can sometimes seem colorless.

Artisans, servers, and scholars all tend to have a gentle, lower-key demeanor. Artisans frequently have a cloud-like air, and soft, rounded faces. "Pretty-boy" (as opposed to more rough-hewn) men and "adorable" or beautiful women in a Marilyn Monroe kind of way are many times artisans. They often like to express themselves through their clothes and adornments, hairstyles, and their body itself to create beauty and/or originality. This is also true of sages, although to a lesser extent. As you can imagine, many models are artisans and sages. Priests' smiles can be angelic, whereas sages' smiles often seem to have a little mischief in them. Sages' faces are highly expressive and are often good-looking or interesting, so as to capture the attention they need in order to fulfill their role.

In general, the solid roles —warriors, kings, and scholars—look more strong or "hard," and the fluid roles[9]—servers, priests, artisans, and sages—look more gentle or "soft," although I find that sages, particularly, can look either way. Depending on other influences, such as male/female energy ratio and essence twin role, I have sometimes mistaken a sage (especially in a male body) for a king, and vice versa, whereas I would be much less likely to mistake a server or an artisan for a king. So sage is the fluid role that can most easily look solid.

I asked some other Michael channels how the roles look to them. José Stevens pointed out the mirth in sages' eyes, and that sage males can have craggy, movie-star looks. Warriors' eyes tend to be narrow or close set, while kings' eyes tend to be far apart. Scholars can have a high forehead and a lot of facial wrinkles at a young age. They have a kind look as opposed to the compassion of priests. He also noted that artisans can look cute wearing anything, even a mop!

JP Van Hulle finds that priests tend to be the most striking and best-looking of the roles, with a strain who are tall and willowy. Kings and warriors are often short, and warriors can be thick, perhaps muscular or fat, with a thick neck. There is a strain of scholars who are stereotypically "nerdy": skinny and "weedy" with "ropey" muscles. (Of course, there are many scholars who do not fit this mold.) JP observes a "halo" of soft hair around servers' faces. Artisans can look dreamy-eyed or vague, with somewhat childlike faces; older artisans tend to have fewer wrinkles than other roles.

There are abundant exceptions to these generalizations, and discerning the role solely from the way someone looks is unreliable. Nevertheless, when combined with other perceptions, observing how

---

[9]Priests and artisans are the highest-frequency roles, and might, therefore, be called "gaseous" rather than "fluid," but generally they are included in the category "fluid roles" along with servers and sages.

a person looks can help us distinguish his role. As mentioned, when I have a photograph of a person for whom I am going to channel a Michael Reading chart, I usually try to guess his role. If what I guess turns out not to be his role, it is usually at least the role of his essence twin, or the role his cadence position resonates with.

A variation on this is psychically discerning the role (and overleaves, too) as it manifests in the aura. For example, artisans' auras tend to be soft and diffuse, whereas warriors' tend to be hard and compact. (Kings and scholars also tend to have auras that are dense and close to the body.) A king tends to send his energy down, while a priest tends to send his up. I do not see auras (although I can sense what is happening energetically with a person in a general sense). However, through some channels, Michael discerns the role and overleaves in that way rather than getting the information from the akashic records.

Incidentally, since artisans' auras tend to be the largest and most diffuse, artisans need to be especially aware of what I call "aural hygiene." In a crowd, there can be many other people in an artisan's aura, and he can pick up a lot of their energies, some of which can stay with him and weigh him down. It is a good idea for artisans to spend a few minutes each morning and evening clearing their aura. A simple way to do this is to imagine being washed by a rainstorm; the visualization itself isn't important—it is the intent to cleanse the aura and making time for it to happen that count. (This can benefit anyone, of course, but is particularly important for artisans, and, to a lesser extent, sages.)

It can work the other way around, too: if a crowd is in an artisan's aura, the crowd can take on the artisan's mood—the artisan *creates* the atmosphere.

What artisans pick up in their auras often bears little relationship to them—it is just debris, like the dust cloud around the Peanuts cartoon character Pigpen. That makes it easy to cleanse their auras. Priests, on the other hand, tend to pick up other people's negative energy as a result of their desire to offer healing. Their empathy allows them to feel what others feel, and they are natural healers. They can unconsciously draw off other people's blocked energies, but rather than dispersing them, they can store them in their own energy fields, which, of course, can become a burden to them. Sometimes it is not enough for priests to visualize cleansing their auras—they may also need to set boundaries and realize that it is not their responsibility to take on other people's "stuff." Whatever our role is, it is useful to learn to keep our energy field protected with a "teflon coating" of light. Just as healthy skin keeps intrusions out of our bodies, a healthy energy field has a strong energetic "skin."

SECONDARY ROLE INFLUENCES

Because of their neutrality, scholars are those most likely to look like another role, especially that of their essence twin. For instance, an emotionally centered scholar I know who has a discarnate artisan essence twin looks like a less-intense artisan. (Emotional centering sometimes makes scholars appear "unscholarly." However, one can assimilate emotionally as well as intellectually.) Another scholar with no essence twin looks somewhat like a sage due to the strong presence of two discarnate sage essences assisting her, yet at her core, she is assimilative rather than expressive. Imprinting, overleaves, or profession can also be influences. For example, one king who is studying expression in this lifetime chose a flamboyant sage mother to imprint her. She wants to be an actor, and, like many actors, she has taken on a persona somewhat resembling the sage archetype, since it is largely sages who have defined the style of actors. Likewise, any artist can take on something of an artisan persona.

When I can't figure out someone's role, I usually look at scholar first, and I might explore artisan as well. Since scholars study everything, they may in one life or another "impersonate" all the other roles. Artisans, being the most creative of the roles, also can "recreate" themselves in the image of the other roles, especially the role of scholar when they have a scholar essence twin and/or scholar cadence position.

Regardless of the role, sometimes the first impression given is that of the essence twin if its influence is strong. We tend to pick up the energy of our essence twin because the bond is so powerful. It is like people who are married resembling one another. This is especially true if the essence twin isn't incarnate, because it is then as if our essence twin is living inside us. I met a warrior with an artisan essence twin and casting (number two position in a number two cadence). Because of the double artisan influence, through the energy of the essence twin and through the "flavoring" of casting, she might be said to be an "honorary artisan." It shows up in her appearance: she wears striking, original clothes, and has a mass of soft blonde hair (perhaps correlating with the softness associated with artisan energy). However, closer examination reveals that her face and body are solid, compact, and strong, in spite of her petite frame. Her behavior is also warrior-like, more about action than expression.

Michael once told a warrior with a discarnate scholar essence twin (and a scholar spouse) that one reason he can so quickly know what action to take is his deep connection with scholar energy—he draws on the scholar resource of knowledge more internally than externally. He doesn't necessarily need to actually speak to a scholar to get the information he needs in order to make a sound decision.

INPUTS

One week I had two different clients who called frantically before their appointments, having lost my address. They reached my answering machine, but somehow figured out where I live and arrived early, thinking they were late. Amusingly, both were artisans. When an artisan friend of mine told me that he was marrying another artisan, I joked, "What? You'll never find your keys!"

Artisans have a reputation for the charming flakiness that sometimes accompanies high creativity. One reason is that artisans have five "inputs" or simultaneous "psychic (as in *psyche*) receivers." Artisans operate on five levels or "tracks" at the same time—they can receive and process five impressions from the outer world, either consciously or unconsciously—whereas warriors, for instance, operate on one. This facilitates the widest possible awareness of "what's out there," which aids creativity, because new creations are new combinations of already existing elements, and the artwork of artisans tends to have many levels. However, having five inputs can also be disorienting if artisans aren't well grounded, and can make concentration difficult. Artisans can seem not fully "there" when one is talking to them, whereas warriors are usually totally "there" or are not "there" at all. Sages have three inputs, with similar but lesser abilities and challenges in that regard. Sometimes artisans and sages compensate by being highly organized—with so many inputs, they have found that they need to be in order to keep track of everything "coming in" and all the projects they may be juggling at once. I am an example of this: I have a compulsion to write everything down and keep things in their place; otherwise, I don't feel that I have a handle on my life. (People sometimes think that I'm a Virgo, but there are not any Virgo influences in my astrology chart. Nonetheless, I have always been highly organized as well as detail-oriented. [10]) On the other hand, warriors, who have only one input and are the most focused of the roles, tend to be naturally organized, but they can also sometimes live in a mess and still feel that they can function effectively—being so focused, their sense of organization may be more internal. Also, warriors are normally "one thing at a time" people and artisans usu-

---

[10]One astrologer said that another factor in this is that I have Saturn conjunct my Mercury, bringing discipline to my mental processes.

ally have several projects going at once, but sometimes the opposite is true.

Some artisans like to do things "one at a time" because it is too disorienting for them otherwise. It helps them feel in control. On the other hand, there are warriors who, because they are only dealing with one input, can keep several balls in the air at once, so to speak, like jugglers.

Michael student Ed Hamerstrom suggested that the five inputs of artisans relate to 1) current reality, 2) the state of the work in progress, 3) the muse or vision of what he wants to create, 4) random unconscious stimulation that allows creativity, and 5) the application of that imagination, as in "What would happen if I try this here?" He suggested that the three inputs of sages relate to 1) current reality (the setting or basic situation), 2) what is being expressed, and 3) the audience. Michael said that that is a valid way of looking at their inputs.

The inputs are "slots" that can be filled in various ways or, at least, described in widely varying ways.

Scholars, kings, and warriors—the "solid" roles—have one input. Let's make an analogy here. Until recently, all television sets could display only one channel at a time. This is like having one input. Now there are televisions that can play a football game in the corner of the screen while the rest of the screen is taken up with Dallas reruns, or whatever. A person watching such a screen can receive two broadcasts at once. That is like having two inputs. The advantage of this is that two different sources can be integrated in some way. A person watching Dallas and a football game at the same time may see similarities and connections between the two that someone watching one show probably would not. He might, for instance, perceive Dallas characters and football players maneuvering toward their goals in similar ways. He may then try in some way to integrate the two shows, such as making a sculpture that illustrates the relationship between Dallas and a football game.

On the other hand, a person with a television set that plays only one image might be seen as a specialist in what was being viewed, either Dallas or the football game. If you are watching Dallas, you can explore everything about Dallas in full detail, noticing what all the characters are doing, wearing, and so on. This is of particular interest if, for instance, you are a scholar specializing in soap operas.

With a one-image set, you can change channels, either quickly or slowly, but you are not as well equipped to integrate the two programs in your consciousness as someone watching them simultaneously. You might also tune your set between two stations, but you would just get static.

The four roles with more than one input approach integration in different ways. Priests and servers each have two inputs. Priests are concerned with integrating their vision of what is higher or of greater ultimate importance into the immediate circumstance. Their "television screen," rather than having a second smaller image in the corner, has a horizontal line dividing it into higher and lower images. They view these two images simultaneously at all times. It is so natural to them that they take it for granted. The "screen" of servers is split with a vertical line, holding an image of the common good next to that of the immediate circumstance.

Sages have three inputs. Their screen is divided by two vertical lines into three side-by-side images that are more or less equal in size. Sages can use these three inputs to integrate the three other axes: inspiration, action, and assimilation. Sages are communicators and mediators. They interpret between warriors and priests, scholars and artisans, and so forth. They express what the other axes need to hear. Sages can also use these three inputs to integrate love, truth, and pure energy. By reconciling them, by sensing what is not only the most loving action, but simultaneously the most truthful and healing, you discover wisdom. Sages seek wisdom in the same way that warriors seek challenge and artisans seek originality.

Artisans have five inputs to help them in their quest. Their "screen" is divided into five sections similar to a pie divided into five pieces. These divisions, however, are not necessarily equal in size, and they can change. Images enter from the periphery of the screen toward the middle. What comes in through the piece of the pie labeled "A" might go back out in a different form through the piece "C." The images are constantly moving and changing. This allows artisans to arrange and rearrange realities, creating new ones as a result. [11]

---

[11] The number of inputs relates to the four axes. The "solid" roles, those on the action and assimilation axes, have one input—the focus that one input allows is suited for action and assimilation. The inspiration roles each have two inputs, again, appropriate for inspiration, which involves merging a

Suppose that at this moment, an artisan has Dallas *on input "A," football on input "B," "Tom and Jerry" cartoons on input "C," and so forth. He is likely to change some of or all the channels before the programs are finished. He senses when he has what he needs to create something new, and then moves on, seeking more raw material.*

There are inherent challenges in each way of inputting, and no way is better than another. The roles with one input have the advantage of greater stability. They can change channels but they still have just one image. Generally, those with one input wait for Dallas *to be over before tuning in to the news, or whatever. Also, being more focused, they tend to plan what they are going to "watch" ahead of time.*

The solid roles are basically dealing with what is. The inspirational roles want to add something higher or greater to what is. To do this, they have to simultaneously see what is as well as "that something more." The expression roles, with three or five inputs, want to change what is. In a sense, they have more "on their plates" than the other roles. Life may not seem so simple to them. However, they are designed to be this way, so seeing various realities simultaneously isn't foreign to them.

Although artisans, especially, and sages focus on creativity, all the roles can be creative in their own ways. The essential creativity of artisans and sages is to see new possibilities through combining diverse realities. The creativity of warriors, for example, is more straightforward. It is more likely to spring from an intimate knowledge of one reality than from drawing from more than one. If a warrior does draw from more than one, he does so deliberately rather than as an expression of his customary way of being, and he would tend to quickly refocus on one image.

You can learn to recognize inputs at work, but it isn't as simple as saying that sages and artisans are more "spacy" because they have more inputs, although that is sometimes the

---

higher or greater awareness with our immediate awareness. The roles of the expression axis have the highest number of inputs, three and five. Integrating diverse awareness is fundamental to creativity and expression.

It is interesting that none of the roles has four inputs. Ed Hamerstrom pointed out that the numbers *one, two, three,* and *five* are all prime, or indivisible, numbers. They are also Fibonacci numbers. Fibonacci numbers are a series starting zero, one, one, two, three, five, eight, thirteen, and so on, in which each number is the sum of the two numbers before it. Ed speculated that the number of inputs relates to these facts, that consciousness could only create more than one input by adding one to one, then two to one, and then three to two.

case. "Spaciness" is disorientation stemming from not being able to handle whatever is on the screen, whether it is one image or five. However, five images can be especially disorienting if they are not being integrated. [12]

Having multiple inputs brings diverse stimuli into one's thinking and feeling. This is not the same as having an excessively busy mind, which, by the way, is more common with those who are intellectually centered, because they tend to use their minds a great deal. Thinking tends to be more orderly and efficient when the mind is centered and serene. Nonetheless, when sages' minds, for instance, are centered, they are still receiving through their three inputs, and sages can shift their dominant attention among them. When scholars, who have one input, have busy minds, their content is likely to be on a single track or subject, rather than sages' three. Priests, when their minds are busy, tend to conduct a debate between "higher" and "lower" points of view. Incidentally, this can engender feelings of guilt if they judge themselves as not measuring up to their vision of higher function.

Thinking itself is output, not input, and output is on one track; in other words, you can only consciously think (or do) one thing at a time. If you seem to be thinking more than one thing at a time, you are actually rapidly switching your focus back and forth. If you have multiple inputs, you might be integrating the multiple "tracks" "playing" in the background into your thinking. This can occur whether or not you are consciously engaging with them; much integration occurs unconsciously. It is this integration that is the foundation of artisans' and sages' creativity.

RELATIONSHIPS AND ROLES

Every role has a unique friendship style. The ordinal roles—artisans, servers, and warriors—often prefer to focus on fewer but deeper friendships. Scholars, the neutral role, are also more likely to follow this path. They can also occasionally be more like the exalted roles—priests, kings, and sages—who are often drawn to having larger numbers of friends, or at least, acquaintances.

---

[12]One-input scholars can be spacy due to the "absent-minded-professor syndrome"—they're so absorbed in what they're studying that they disregard mundane aspects of life.

Artisans can often be contented being alone, working on their projects, although they can be warm and caring to those with whom they are friends. Servers have a natural ability to nurture, and sometimes know a great number of people from their service, yet may have difficulty making a true connection with them because of an inability to receive, to be served. Warriors typically have a few friends with whom they develop great loyalty and camaraderie.

Scholars tend to run into a lot of people, and can be stimulating friends, but are sometimes more drawn to study people than to befriend them. Sages, being the most social of all the roles, tend to devote the most energy to friendships, and have the highest number of them, but are sometimes less good at listening than talking. Priests also tend to have a lot of friends, and often want to take care of them. Although kings frequently have a lot of people around them, and tend to be quite steadfast in their friendships, they can sometimes find themselves in an ivory tower making statements such as "it's lonely at the top."

Of course, there are many exceptions to these generalizations.

The inspirational roles of server and priest, and the neutral role of scholar, tend to be the best listeners. Having higher female energy or simply being in a female body also generally facilitates listening. Kings and warriors are sometimes less adept at listening, because their focus is on action.

Roles on the same axis generally get along comfortably: servers and priests, warriors and kings, and artisans and sages. Other often-complementary combinations include scholars and warriors, and kings and servers. In fact, servers and scholars generally get along with all the roles. However, no matter what your role is, you will likely be in mate relationships with each of the roles throughout your many lifetimes in order to have a full experience of the physical plane.

The following lengthy quotation from Michael (which continues to the end of this subchapter) is from a private session with a mature scholar. He asked Michael to discuss how people of each role relate to those of the same role and each of the other six roles. This resulted in a total of twenty-eight pairs. Michael went in this order: scholar, server, priest, artisan, sage, warrior, and king. When each role was considered, there was one less pair than with the previous role because that pair had been covered already. So when they discussed kings, the only combination left was king-king, because kings' dynamics with the other roles had been covered already under each of the other roles.

Incidentally, the fact that this scholar would ask Michael for such extensive nonpersonal information in a private session is revealing of the scholar essence—as mentioned, in my experience it is virtually always scholars who do that. (The rest of the roles usually just stick with questions about their lives—life task, relationships, career, etc.)

Each of the roles correlates with a number between one and seven, in order from most ordinal to most cardinal, as follows: one—server; two—artisan; three—warrior; four—scholar; five—sage; six—priest; and seven—king. This will be discussed at length in the subchapter "Number Correlations" in Chapter Eleven, "Cadences and Numbers." If, in adding the numbers that correlate with two roles, the total is seven, there is optimal complementarity, in that the ordinal and cardinal perfectly balance one another, making a neutral combination. Those combinations are server and priest, artisan and sage, and warrior and scholar. The first two pairs are on the same axis. Although warriors and scholars are not, both are "solid" roles. And kings are already the seven-position role.

The combinations that add up to less than seven are ordinal and therefore more low-key; those that add up to more than seven are cardinal and therefore more intense. The degree of the relationship's ordinality or cardinality is the degree of the sum's distance from seven.

For instance, the server-artisan combination adds up to three, so it is a low-key relationship, combining the two most ordinal roles. A relationship consisting of two kings, the most cardinal role, adds up to fourteen. It is an intense, concentrated relationship, and can be tricky, with two "chiefs" and no "injun," although it will probably not be dull.

Although ordinal relationships can feel understimulated, and cardinal ones can feel overstimulated, this is not a ranking of the desirability of different combinations—any two roles can get along fine and have a rich, rewarding relationship. Also, the correlations of the numbers do not apply to the sums. For example, the server-artisan relationship, which, again, adds up to three, does not itself correlate with the role of warrior (the three-position role).

The ordinal roles, especially the most ordinal, servers, like interaction with cardinal roles because that is "exalting" for them. For example, in the server-sage combination, servers' behind-the-scenes support work is exalted through sages' large-scale expression. The servers are doing the ordinal work that is natural to them but find that it is magnified by association with the cardinal roles. The server-artisan, server-warrior, and server-scholar relationships are not particularly exalting for servers, although they might be quite warm and comfortable.

Michael's comments apply to all kinds of relationships, not just to mate relationships. However, Michael often used mate relationships as examples to illuminate the dynamics of particular role pairings. Being the most intimate and intense of relationships, they can best illustrate how role energies combine.

Keep in mind that there are many exceptions to the generalizations given below. A great number of other influences contribute to the gestalt of relationships, such as essence twin role, casting, overleaves, imprinting, and, most importantly, the unique chemistry between two unique individuals.

SCHOLAR-SCHOLAR: *Scholars see other scholars as particularly kindred, in ways that some of the roles cannot see others of their own role. Scholars can endlessly share notes, and therefore support each other in their endeavors; they share the alignment of colleagues. Unless the overleaves abrade or there is karma, it is unusual for two scholars not to get along.*

This relationship may lack spice. Being neutral to begin with, scholars are more attracted to what is not neutral, which makes for an interesting study; scholars are not so likely to want to study other scholars, although scholars may wish to study something with other scholars. Scholars would certainly not want to live in a world that was all scholars, but they would also not want to live in a world where there were no other scholars with whom to share notes.

SCHOLAR-KING: *Scholars and kings generally get along. Scholars tend to respect—not so much love—kings, but may not understand why kings can become impatient with them when they have trouble getting to the point, as they often do. Kings can master information quickly, which scholars like, and kings can match scholars' intellect. But kings tend to be generalists, whereas scholars might settle down to fifty years of studying one insect genus. Because scholars find this focused study to be so interesting, they may be hurt if kings do not share their fascination. They know that if kings do share their interest, kings can promulgate this interest near and far. But kings generally don't cooperate, and scholars can be impatient with this just as kings can be impatient with too much detail. Kings, though, are usually smart enough to recognize the necessity of scholars' contributions. So it tends to be a good solid relationship, if a little more distant than some others.*

SCHOLAR-WARRIOR: Warriors and scholars can be very good for each other. Warriors can bring out more of the "down and dirty" and the humor in scholars, so warriors tend to make better playmates for scholars than kings do. Warriors genuinely find scholars to be interesting. If warriors are in a hurry, they, too, can be impatient with scholars' penchant for detail, but if warriors have some time on their hands, they may be willing to entertain a lot of detail from scholars, asking questions, challenging, occasionally practicing some one-upmanship—and making a pretty good time out of it.

Since scholars are the number four position role and warriors are the number three—together they add up to seven—they sense that they can complement or add something to one another. One way in which they complement is that scholars, being the neutral role, can absorb warriors' focused, earthy energy.

SCHOLAR-SAGE: Sage and scholar is also a good combination. Both love knowledge and information. Scholars are sometimes envious of sages, because scholars tend to fear that they are not as "spicy," as interesting, as the other roles, and there is no role more potentially spicy than sages. (Sages feel that they have to be, in order to get everyone's attention.) The fact of the matter is that scholars are usually genuinely content not being in the limelight—being wallflowers, even—but your society rewards sages with acclaim much more often. If scholars feel a lack of self-esteem, they can be envious of sages.

I've noticed that scholars can easily find sages irritating because scholars want knowledge to be just caretaken: neutral and available. Sages, on the other hand, often want to elaborate on it or exaggerate it. Scholars distrust that, feeling that there's some distortion or ego in it.

A spice in your food can taste good in the right quantity, but can irritate if there's too much of it. Sages often feel the urge to exaggerate when they are fulfilling their role of storyteller. The story has to be made interesting, larger than life. Most people find movies, for example, that present stories faithfully—in life-size projections rather than larger-than-life—to be boring. They have to be magnified somehow. But sages can get carried away with this—just as any role can get carried away with whatever it is doing—and not respect boundaries. This can also be a factor in starting and expanding rumors.

There is a certain amount of heightening of reality that reality can tolerate without being distorted. In great art, reality may, in fact, be clarified by being heightened, by being put under a magnifying glass. That is really what sages are trying to do. However, if they lack skill or insight, they may distort it, which puts them in their negative pole, oration.

Scholars are more concerned about the purity of information, but they are not more dedicated to truth than sages. Scholars tend to see truth as fact; sages tend to see truth as what reveals the moral or insight of the story, since story is a big part of what sages are about.

Sages in the negative pole can be irritating to everyone, but we would not overemphasize the conflict between sages and scholars; generally, they are quite complementary. Scholars like how forthcoming sages are in providing information. Sages do not see it as an inconvenience, as a warrior, for example, might, if he's trying to get on to doing the next thing. Sages know that disseminating information is their job, their role. And sages see scholars as possible sources of "news they can use," although the way scholars operate is to take a big chunk of raw data and slowly distill it; if scholars give their knowledge before it has been well distilled, it can be more than is needed or can be used. Scholars are willing to provide data at any stage in the distillation process, because it is all interesting to them, but the other roles generally just want the end result: the fully distilled version, the conclusions, the bottom line.

That would also be why scholars like each other so much.

Right—there is mutual appreciation of the whole process. Sages, being an expression role, do not hesitate to express to scholars just what information they want or do not want. If they do this without tact, that can be offensive to scholars. Sages are usually pretty tactful, but sages who have a warrior essence twin or warrior casting,[13] for example, may be more blunt.

---

[13]See the subchapter "Number Correlations" in Chapter Eleven, "Cadences and Numbers."

Sages, warriors, and scholars all tend to have particularly well-developed senses of humor; so sages are another role that scholars can play with. However, scholars are prone to the kind of puns and word play sometimes called "groaners," and sages may tease scholars about this. Underneath, sages usually enjoy the word play or pun anyway. Sages do not really look down their noses at it (even though they may pretend to) because they appreciate all kinds of humor, even those that are not their own kind. If the humor is particularly complex or clever, sages may feel admiration and respect—even if it is not, in fact, all that funny. Wherever there is a demonstration of expressive ability, sages will acknowledge that on some level.

Scholars can be particularly humorous in their writing— often in a tongue-in-cheek way. Their humor is not as dramatic as that of sages, but it can be pleasant to read. Sages' humor tends to be more broad and accessible, and being expressive, it tends to work better in performance than scholars' humor. Scholars are not very often good at stand-up comedy, for example. They are just not expressive enough—unless they have a sage essence twin, or another expressive influence—to deliver their thoughts with enough spice. On paper it does not matter— the humor is all in the words themselves, and no role is more expert with words per se than scholars.

What about sages' ability with words?

Scholars are generally the most facile in vocabulary and the intrinsic use of words—what words go where—whereas sages are more clever in manipulating words and playing with their meanings, as with innuendo. The scholarly puns and word games are more about the structure of words themselves than about playing with their meaning, as sages are more prone to do. Sages, of course, can also be funny on paper with words, but scholars can be endless in their ability to mine the gold in words themselves.

SCHOLAR-ARTISAN: What these roles share in common is a large capability to do many types of things. With artisans, it is intrinsic, a natural affinity for fixing, designing, and making things.[14] For scholars, it more springs out of the knowledge that

---

[14]Once, an artisan friend of mine stopped by, and I happened to complain about the power button on my phonograph, which had not stayed down properly in years; he fixed it in about thirty seconds with a paper clip. That

has been gleaned through study. They also share in common a high ability for design and structure. However, we do not see this as the best combination for relationships, because both can be isolated or moody at times; there is not enough overlap between them—they are both just off doing their "thing," and their "things" often do not overlap, whereas with two scholars, their "things" more easily can. Of course, there are many exceptions to this, but, in general, this is not the strongest combination.

SCHOLAR-PRIEST: Scholars and priests work quite well together, because priests carry a great deal of concentrated higher energies, and scholars, being one of the three solid roles, and being neutral, are able to absorb a lot of that higher energy. So scholars feel grounding and also somewhat malleable to priests. Priests have the need to feel that others are receiving their inspiration, that they are acting on it. Sages have no such need; they just need to be heard, so they don't have to see the results, but priests do.

Also, scholars, perhaps more than the other roles, enjoy priests' inspiration and do not put up a lot of resistance to it, unless it has gotten them into deep trouble on a number of occasions. It would take quite a lot of negative experience with priests to make scholars wary. Warriors are much more prone to be wary of priests and resistant to them than scholars are.

Priests also appreciate knowledge, although when scholars and priests are together, the type of knowledge they share is usually higher knowledge, which to scholars is just one more category of interesting topics. Scholars, being neutral, are just as happy to discuss that as to discuss anything else, so it is not a problem. Priests would not be that interested in discussing a number of things of interest to scholars, but scholars can be perfectly happy with all areas of interest to priests.

Also, scholars can suffer from a dryness, a lack of emotion, and priests, being generally the deepest feeling of roles, can provide an antidote to this. So it can be quite warming for scholars to be around priests, unless scholars are, for example, trapped in the intellectual part of the intellectual center and do not want to be emotional or inspired, in which case they might have a wall to priests.

---

always seemed representative of artisans to me. Similarly, the stereotypical woman who fixes a broken-down car with her bobby pin is an artisan.

SCHOLAR-SERVER: Like scholars and artisans, scholars and servers tend to lack overlap. This combination can also get a little bland—there is not that much spice in servers either, although they often have a great deal of warmth. A scholar-server alliance might be chosen when both want to rest from a lot of stimulation or conflict, to have a safe harbor, to even be able to "zone out."

SERVER-SERVER: Unless, of course, the overleaves or other elements of personality abrade, servers are usually quite comfortable with other servers. There is nothing very exciting about that combination, but servers do not tend to seek excitement anyway.

SERVER-PRIEST: Servers and priests are a very good combination, because servers, like scholars, can absorb some of priests' higher intensity. They also share a quality of thriving on inspiration, so they can keep each other inspired, something that priests and scholars cannot—priests can inspire scholars, but scholars usually do not inspire priests very much, except perhaps if some symbolic information is given that reminds priests of a higher principle. Servers can inspire priests by their positive pole selflessness, goodness, and open heart. Romantically, this combination works especially well if priests are male and servers are female. If servers are male and they adhere to cultural sex-role imprinting, they may feel threatened by powerful female priests.

Priests and servers think along similar lines, but sometimes priests, being so preoccupied with higher concerns, are negligent of the mundane in ways that kings, for example, rarely would be. (Kings notice if the mundane is not done, although they may not do it themselves.) So in those pairings the servers, usually comfortably, handle the mundane, often to the relief of the priests.

SERVER-ARTISAN: Servers and artisans are a little better together than scholars and artisans, because when artisans are off doing their own thing, servers do not usually mind being temporarily ignored and supporting artisans behind the scenes. This can be useful if artisans are focused on some intense creativity. Also, artisans may be inspired to do better work in the creative process by the solid support of servers.

SERVER-SAGE: *Servers and sages can work quite well as long as the servers are not too much "by-the-book" kinds of people; some servers are, and sages do not tend to be—they like to play with the book, to stretch and expand it, rather than adhere strictly to any sort of pattern. (Sage is the five-position role, and the number five has a positive pole of expansion.) Servers who are bureaucratic, who see going by the book as what is best for the common good, tend to irritate sages to no end—and vice versa. However, if the servers are not doing their negative pole in that way, this is generally a good combination, because servers tend to be quite willing to let sages have the spotlight. Artisans, who also work well with sages, may or may not be willing to do that—they may just go off and do something else. They will not tend to try to stop sages from being in the spotlight, but servers are more likely to really listen and be supportive, fully receiving the expression of sages. Sages can be very grateful for that.*

Also, sages are often heart people. They may be quite intellectual and verbal, but they rarely become nearly as emotionally dry as scholars can be. Servers in their positive pole can epitomize the good heart, so servers and sages can love each other very deeply, in some ways more than servers and priests, because both servers and priests tend to stay busy taking care of other people. Servers might nurture priests, but priests might be out taking care of three hundred other people. Although sages might be entertaining three hundred other people, that is not as involving as the caretaking that priests engage in.

SERVER-WARRIOR: *Servers and warriors usually get along very well. Both tend to have much endurance, and it is easy for servers to view warriors' toil as benefiting the common good, even in the military, if that jibes with the servers' political beliefs. Warriors tend to like servers because they see servers as being down-to-earth and practical. Servers and warriors do not tend to fight as much as warriors can with most of the other roles.*

Servers and warriors are especially effective together as a team working together—for example, a server doctor and a warrior nurse would probably be very effective together in a high-stress situation. The higher the cardinality of the relationship—in other words, the higher the number of the combination's sum—the more stress there tends to be in the relationship. Sometimes that can be exciting and can make for a lot of energy, but it can sometimes be too much. In a high-stress situation such as a hospital emergency room or a battle front, the server-warrior combination, which adds up to only four, can be a calm center of productive work. The server-artisan combination would even be more calm, but not necessarily more productive.

SERVER-KING: This is probably the most comfortable pairing for kings. Kings like to be served; they feel that it frees them to serve the masses themselves. The seven and the one are two extremes, but in a sense they are right next to each other, too, if you make a circle out of the seven numbers. Kings serve in an exalted way—they serve the kingdom, looking at what is best for the overall picture. They do not feel that they have time for the mundane. That doesn't mean that they are lazy; it just means that they are occupied in other ways. So they like being served, and servers are generally thrilled to serve a king. However, in some of these pairings, servers get the short end of the stick. Kings can overwhelm and repress servers, which, of course, is not growthful for either role. Kings need to appreciate and respect the value of the service that servers render. Servers do not command respect, and usually do not demand it, either. Ideally, they inspire it. But they can be taken for granted, which is not to anyone's benefit.

It is hard for any role to feel that it can add something to kings; they seem complete—they are already the number seven role. But being in the number one position, servers are the role that comes closest to being able to add something to kings.

PRIEST-PRIEST: In general, members of the same role get along, but there can be some particular problems when two priests come together, depending on the soul age. Two young priests can be competitive. Two mature priests can overload one another, since there is so much of a particular kind of power here. However, a young and mature priest may do very well together, and old priests tend to get along fine with each other.

Marriages between two priests are rare, because both would tend to look for those who need their inspiration. Unless one of the priests is having a hard enough time that he needs to forgo seeking a "congregation" and is willing to sit still long enough to receive inspiration from the other priest, the two *would not find enough of a place in each other to put their intense energies.*

PRIEST-ARTISAN: This is a pretty good combination, as long as the artisans are not cynics or skeptics and do not repel the inspiration of the priests, and as long as priests are not in zeal, their negative pole, trying to shove something down the artisans' throats. Like scholars, artisans are pretty malleable. However, artisans are more changeable, chameleon-like, than scholars. Under duress, artisans may appear to go along with the priests' zeal, and then it may be proven out later that the artisans did not really go along. That can enrage priests; it may seem like a lack of being faithful to the cause, as with fundamentalist Christians with the role of priest, for example. Initially, artisans may cave in under duress, and then snap back to their more natural point of view. They may have been pretending to adopt the priests' views, or they may have actually swallowed them for the time being, but in either case, the priests would see the artisans' reversion as falsity.

Artisans can provide inspiration for priests, just as the opposite is true, because artisans can make much beauty for priests, who can be a little battered by being out there on the spiritual battlefronts, trying to help people in need. Priests can come home to an inspiring, comforting atmosphere of beauty provided by artisans, male or female.

PRIEST-SAGE: This combination can be problematic, or it can be quite good. The problem would be competition, trying to get the attention of the same congregation/audience. Since both are exalted (cardinal), and both often like to talk a great deal, it can be difficult for either role to feel that they are fully being received. And, in some ways, they tend to not understand each other very well.

On the other hand, they can get along quite well for a similar reason to the reason two scholars may get along—they may feel like colleagues; they may complement. Sages are an expression role but may feel a secondary impulse to inspire as well. So, for example, sage actors might want their performance not only to be technically good and to communicate what the author intended, but also to be inspiring, uplifting, and enlightening. Sages may see that as leaving the audience with more insight or understanding. Priests may see inspiration as more purely an emotional feeling of uplift and dedication. However, these two approaches are not at cross purposes, and sages and priests can work together as a team.

So if they are mature enough to give each other an opportunity to be fully received, the relationship can work quite well, but this combination can take more work than many of the others.

PRIEST-WARRIOR: Priests tend to be attracted to warriors, because warriors are, in some ways, opposite from them. Unbalanced priests can be cut off from the full and free ability to enjoy their body and the physical life itself, whereas warriors excel in enjoying the body and the physical life. Warriors are generally less attracted to priests than priests are to warriors because warriors may not be all that interested in being inspired, particularly in the younger soul cycles—they may not want to look up to the heavens if they are having a perfectly good time on the earth. They may also suspect that priests have the ulterior motive of trying to convert them. They may see priests as being rather like spies from the enemy camp. If warriors are converted—say, to a religion—then they may align with priests in converting others. More commonly, warriors would rather be free of what they would consider to be the limitations that priests seem to want to impose—especially if they are sexual. Warrior women may go along with their priest husbands' sexual limitations—against extramarital affairs, for example—as long as there is a good sex life in the marriage. Warriors have respect for boundaries, as long as those boundaries are not suffocating to their essence, and, more than the other roles, they need some kind of sexual outlet.

Warriors can be attracted to priests for priests' healing ability. Warriors can get pretty beat up in life, and when they are finally ready to receive help, no role is better than priests for ministering to them, both physically and spiritually. But if warriors are perfectly happy in their physical involvements, priests may not be all that attractive, except perhaps as an object of lust, as the "mysterious opposite."

PRIEST-KING: Surprisingly, priests and kings do not compete in the same way that priests and sages tend to. These two roles add up to thirteen, yet they are not competing for the same audience, because for kings, everything is in their domain, including priests, and kings see priests as fulfilling a valuable function in the whole. However, the partnership of priests and

139

kings is very concentrated. A priest with a king essence twin, or vice versa, has that partnership internally, and it is an intrinsically high-stress situation—such a soul feels a constant stretch, the sense that something exalted is required at all times. Priests and kings are "on duty" at virtually all times, making themselves available to their congregation and kingdom, respectively, and they can work well together. Priests, like servers, are also happy to minister to kings—not in particularly mundane ways, necessarily—it can be that, but someone else may be around to handle the mundane, since kings can have many people around them to help.

ARTISAN-ARTISAN: Artisans with other artisans can have a great variety of results—anywhere from very good to very bad. This combination is especially susceptible to the rest of the overleaves, but more often than not, it works pretty well. Artisans may not understand each other perfectly, but their lifestyles may meld quite comfortably because they tend to have a lot of flexibility. Artisans may have more excitement with warriors, but artisans can be frustrated by warriors' desire to structure. Artisans often like to live more by the seat of their pants, improvising as they go along, and generally this will not do for warriors, so there can be conflict there. Two artisans can be quite comfortable living in a certain amount of chaos with each other. We do not mean that artisans are necessarily messier than the other roles; we are just referring to the way their lives look. Artisans are less likely to have a "five-year plan," for example.

Artisans can fail to provide other artisans with what is needed in their relationships. There can be a feeling that one or both of the partners are neglecting the other because of being wrapped up in the project at hand. This combination usually works better if there is some overlap in the projects being worked on. For example, if the husband likes to work on their house, and the wife chooses colors and wallpaper, they can have much contentment together.

Many artisans like to feel anchored by the people around them. Generally, other artisans will not provide that, unless they have, say, a king or warrior essence twin, or perhaps very high male energy.

ARTISAN-SAGE: Sages can be anchoring for artisans, and they can have much joy together. Sages are often able to cultivate the humor in artisans, so that they are truly playmates. Sages can make it safe for artisans to be more childlike, whereas artisans may not feel that this is permitted with the other roles, even with other artisans—artisans may feel that they have to try to be more adult, because the relationship does not feel very well anchored. Sages, however, usually have a pretty good grasp on external realities, since they are the ones who interconnect and communicate with everyone. So with sages, artisans can feel anchored but at the same time have the ability to express themselves.

Sometimes sages push artisans to bring their creations before the public eye. That can be quite useful for artisans, but it may also bring up fear, since artisans are generally not as sturdy and do not feel that they hold up well in the public eye. So there can be a bit of a push-pull here. There is the need to put forth the artisans' works, but if sages push artisans too much, there may be too much fear coming out at once for artisans to deal with it constructively.

ARTISAN-WARRIOR: Artisans do not have to deal with that when teamed up with warriors, because warriors do not seek the public eye that much either, and warriors have more of a tendency to protect others. They would be protective toward artisans' sense of vulnerability. Warriors may also offer artisans some useful discipline, challenging them to complete a project they have been stalling on, for instance.

Warriors tend to be very appreciative of whatever artisans create. Warriors see what could be useful, how the world could work more efficiently, but unless it is a matter of simply jury-rigging something, they are generally not as good at actually coming up with the innovations that might achieve that. They can be in awe of the way that artisans can, often effortlessly, come up with new things.

On the negative side, warriors can lack understanding or even be intolerant of artisans' process. For warriors, life is a pretty simple business—you do what needs to be done. For artisans, life is a pretty complex business, and there are many variables to be played with. Warriors sometimes see artisans as having an "odd logic" that may actually be quite sound, but warriors do not see how it was arrived at, and therefore may tend to dismiss it.

So the artisan-warrior alliance, which is quite common, is fraught with mystery for both parties, yet there is an unmistakable attraction. Warriors like to have someone to protect and to receive their help, and artisans like to feel that strength, that simplicity.

Would you say that, more than the other roles, warriors equals male, and artisans equals female?

In a sense, yes. These two roles certainly correspond with the male and female archetypes in this culture. Servers also correspond with the feminine, but a different aspect of the feminine—more the family-oriented, reliable, down-to-earth feminine. Of course, king is another side of the masculine archetype. Kings bring the sense of "the buck stops here, everything's all right, I'm in control, leave it to me." In your culture, that has been viewed as perhaps the highest manifestation of manhood—that is a much admired and valued trait in men.

It is not surprising that people are becoming confused now that so many women are warriors and kings, and so many men are artisans and servers—and this will probably increase. The dynamics still hold true: warrior wives protect and shelter artisan husbands, even if the husbands are the main breadwinners and the wives are staying home—the wives still shelter and protect their husbands from the hurts of the world. The husbands still balance their wives, giving them a sense of creativity and unpredictability that is both fascinating and exasperating to warriors, since warriors tend to be fairly predictable people.

ARTISAN-KING: Artisan-king is an unusual combination in terms of mates; it is not so much a matter of opposites attracting, as with artisan-warrior. Do not take us too literally or make too much of this generalization, but it can be that because artisans and kings are so different—not merely opposite—they feel that the other is from a different planet. There is just not much overlap, whereas kings and servers can overlap much better because their thrusts are complementary.

Would you say that artisan-king is probably the most polar of any of the pairings, more than priest-warrior, in the sense of being nonoverlapping?

We would probably agree to that, although it is a close call. Priests and warriors run into a similar problem, but we would say there is more attraction between priests and warriors than between artisans and kings. Artisans and kings do not tend to magnetize each other; they do not tend to push each other's buttons that much, either—they just tend to occupy different realms. Warriors and priests do tend to push each other's buttons, as do warriors and artisans.

This dynamic is also true internally of kings with artisan essence twins, and vice versa. These energies combined in the same person can create a dichotomy, a sense of energies that do not have too much to do with each other. So let's say that a king has a nonincarnate artisan essence twin and has artisan casting, so he is an "honorary artisan" and has strong artisan influences; however, his artisan side is like a separate subpersonality. The exception to this is when seeking mastery in a craft or in any area of technique, such as making or fixing things. Also, most kings sometimes use artisans as a resource in order to gain desired mastery, since artisans tend to inherently know how to do many things. However, kings may be a little exasperated when trying to learn from artisans, because artisans cannot necessarily teach well, and kings tend to be impatient—they want to be given steps: one, two, three—"This is what you have to do to master this." Nonetheless, kings know that artisans do have the mastery they seek, and if they are smart, they just watch, observe, and pick up the desired skill from artisans more intuitively.

SAGE-SAGE: The only trouble spot between two sages is that both tend to be reluctant to yield the floor to the other. So if the sages involved have learned to be good listeners as well as good talkers—which is not very common—that problem is minimized. Sages can feel relieved to be in the presence of other sages who want to play, laugh, and joke, and who "get" and appreciate their jokes, especially if their sense of humor is a little off-the-wall. Sages' sense of humor that is meant for the mainstream, which includes all the roles, is more, you could say, commercial; sages tend to save their more eccentric or leading-edge humor for other sages and maybe artisans who will get it. Warriors and scholars also tend to appreciate sages' sense of humor, but do not always plug in to it in the same way.

Sages, then, can have much fun with each other. They can have long talks that may be in either their positive or negative pole, but often they have a sense of accomplishment through these conversations, and just the good feeling of being heard and received when each has enough time to share all he wishes to. On the other hand, these relationships can be shallow: if sages perform for each other instead of genuinely relating, there is not too much "glue" holding these relationships together or a sense of balance in them.

SAGE-WARRIOR: Sage-warrior is a good combination because there is the ability to laugh together, but whereas sages can procrastinate and play, warriors tend to exert pressure to get down to business as well. Warriors can play, but after the time for that has passed, warriors are ready to move on. So this is balancing.

Also, warriors are not generally very good at articulating, although there are exceptions to this—centering plays a part—and, of course, sages are expert at this, so sages can help warriors with their communication. Warriors sometimes feel that sages understand them well because warriors do not have to say everything—sages can intuit some of it, and warriors very much appreciate that. All the same, sages can put pressure on warriors to at least try to verbalize their feelings, because sages want to hear the words—the words are their validation—even if they already know, even if they are getting the communication nonverbally, which they often do.

SAGE-KING: Sages and kings can also get along very well. They do not tend to compete, as you might think they would. Sages can successfully convince kings to let down their hair and not be "on duty" all the time, although even then, even when recreating, kings do not tend to go off duty completely. Also, sages love to advise kings, to give information. However, if kings are in their negative pole, tyranny, it can quickly bring sages into their negative pole, oration, because in tyranny kings are not really listening to sages' advice. Then sages may start to bluster in order to try to make kings listen, to try to get through. Also, sages, like artisans, like to live a little bit by the seat of their pants; they do not like to toe the line. So if kings become bossy, there can be some big fights between kings and sages.

I think of the archetype of the court jester and king—it could be quite volatile and fraught with drama.

Right. Since sages are a cardinal role, they can generally hold their own with kings, unless they have a goal of submission or

*acceptance, which makes it harder for sages to fight. This com-
bination works best when kings' overleaves are relatively soft.
But sages generally do not mind fighting with kings, and kings
may secretly admire the sages' repartee. Kings may feel that
they can learn something from sages' retorts or insights.*

*WARRIOR-WARRIOR: Warriors almost always get along fine
with other warriors, and incidentally, since warrior is the number three position role, two warriors add up to six, one off from
seven. Warriors find in other warriors a common basis for living, and if there are complementary life tasks and they have
planned to be together in that lifetime, either as mates or in another close kind of relationship, they can, over time, fall in line
with each other. They may not overtly demonstrate or acknowledge that they are compromising with each other, but in time
they will gradually wear away each other's rough edges, and
fall into line with each other. They tend to have very good sex
together if they are otherwise compatible. Warriors generally do
not run into a problem with other warriors of wanting more sex
than their partners, which can come up with some of the other
roles and is very frustrating to warriors.*

*Warriors can easily find common values for raising chil-
dren and common political beliefs; when there is this alignment
between them, they can have a very orderly household. Problems can arise if they have artisan or priest children (or
rebellious sage children) who challenge them. On the surface it
looks like warriors want to maintain the order at all costs—they
want their children to go along with the program—but unconsciously, they often do not mind being challenged. In their
negative pole, they may be cruel, even, in repressing rebellious
actions, but in their positive pole, warriors have a strong sense
of fairness. If rebelliousness is proven to be for a good reason,
warriors will generally bend a certain amount with these children. For example, if the warriors are diehard business people,
Republican, right-wing churchgoer types, and they have an artisan child who wants to be an artist or actor, there may be
some problems for that artisan in having such parents. But the
parents will actually like being challenged, and if the child can
prove his talent and his will to follow through on a different
path than what his parents might have envisioned, they will
generally go along.*

145

WARRIOR-KING: Warrior-king is also generally an excellent combination. There tends to be mutual understanding and respect. Warriors see the leadership ability of kings, their ability to encompass the large picture of things—something warriors cannot necessarily do very well—so there is admiration, even awe, of this. But kings can greatly appreciate warriors' ability to dig in and do what needs to be done, in a way that kings may not do; kings may be waiting to delegate to someone else. (They may do the thing if no one shows up, sometimes reluctantly, and then may feel irritated about it.) So this is a quite complementary combination, usually generating a lot of loyalty.

There are no real major problems in this combination. There can be some huge fights, just as there can be between two warriors, but as long as the fights stay under control so that there is no demonstrated disloyalty or taking advantage of a known vulnerability in the other, these relationships are quite resilient in the face of a lot of fighting. (Deliberately bringing up a person's most vulnerable place in order to get the better of him is considered unfair play.)

Incidentally, artisans generally try to avoid fighting, and cannot handle it well in matings with warriors and kings. They can be confusing fighting partners for warriors and kings because they do not fight like warriors and kings do. They can be quite creative, subversive, and manipulative about it, often coming from left field. But artisans typically avoid conflict in the first place, and this can also be a problem in their relationships with warriors and kings, especially, who often like to bring their conflicts fully out into the open.

Sages and priests can better hold their own with warriors and kings than artisans or servers can when there is a disagreement. Servers typically react in fights with warriors and kings by trying to smooth things over. Like artisans, it is not in their nature to fight, but if they think that someone's basic needs are threatened, they will go to bat, and they can be quite persistent—persistence is their main fighting technique. For example if they see that child being abused, they can be like a little mouse at the toes of an elephant, staying with the problem until something is done. However, wherever they can, they placate.

KING-KING: When a king comes together with another king, it is like a summit conference. It is not so much a relationship as it is a joining of forces, a political alignment. Although these rela-

tionships do exist, they do not tend to be emotionally all that close. There might be a lot of respect, and if the female partner in a mated relationship has been raised to submit to the male, there may be a fairly high level of compatibility. However, if one of the partners feels that he or she has no kingdom, and if the other partner is not willing to be that kingdom, there can be a rather dysfunctional situation.

The role dynamics are generally more significant in relationships than the dynamics between any of the overleaves. However, certain overleaves are tricky, and when they are present they may be more important to look at than the role itself in terms of what may get in the way in a particular relationship. We mentioned two warriors getting along together well, but if one is a cynic and one is a spiritualist, or if one is in discrimination and the other is in acceptance, or if both have strong chief features, with one in arrogance and the other in martyrdom, for example, you could have some real problems, especially when you add that to warriors' volatility.

CORRELATING CHAKRAS AND ROLES

Chakras are points of energy in the body that focus certain issues for us, although there are varying ideas about which issues are handled by which chakras. Health problems in the area around each chakra are said to relate to that chakra's issues.

Most sources agree that the first chakra, at the base of the spine, has to do with grounding, survival, and security issues. The second chakra, just below the navel, relates to creativity. Both chakras have also been said to deal with sexuality. (The second chakra has been called both the sexual and the spleen chakra.) The third chakra, or the solar plexus, is just above the navel and is about power issues. Both the second and third chakras have also been correlated with human emotions. The fourth, or heart, chakra is about devotion and impersonal love. It has been placed both to the left of the spine, just under the physical heart, as well as along the spine, like the other chakras. It is the central chakra and is said to be where the soul connects with the physical body (particularly the location left of the spine).

The fifth chakra, at the base of the throat, is commonly acknowledged to be about communication and expression, in an obvious connection with the vocal cords. The sixth chakra, or the third eye, is the seat of both physical and higher vision, including intuition and psychic skills (such as clairvoyance). The seventh, or crown, chakra relates to purpose and union with the whole (which is why channels usually experience entities coming into their body through the crown).

I have seen many ideas about which chakras correlate with which roles, and cases can be made for each of them. One approach is to correlate chakras and roles based on which numbers the roles resonate with, as given in Yarbro.[15] For example, the role of server resonates with the number one, so server would be said to correlate with the first chakra. I like this approach best, but I still have reservations about it.

Like most of the approaches, it correlates the fifth, or communication chakra, with sage, the number five role. It also correlates the third, or power chakra, with warrior, the number three role, which is also common. For me, artisan, the number two role, works well with the second chakra, since it is about creativity. (King is also sometimes correlated with the second chakra.) It makes sense to me to correlate priest, the number six role, with the sixth chakra, or "third eye," the seat of perception and intuition; many spiritual teachers advocate meditating on the third eye. I also have no trouble with king, the number seven role, correlating with the crown chakra, which is where one connects with the larger universe, since kings organize the whole. (Kings wear crowns, too!)

Correlating server with the first chakra, which deals with survival and groundedness, and scholars with the fourth, or heart, chakra, works less well for me, at least at first glance. However, servers provide the essentials we all need for survival, and scholars provide the same consolidation and integration for others that the heart chakra provides internally.

A fairly common approach to correlating chakras and roles reverses the positions of servers and scholars, correlating scholar with the first chakra, since we store our foundational information there— for example, memories from past lifetimes—and servers with the heart chakra, since servers use it a lot—they tend to be nurturing. I have also seen warriors correlated with the first chakra, since they tend to have a lot of the instinctive drive associated with it. There are various other permutations as well, some that are radically different.

I think that, in the end, the chakras do not really correlate directly with the roles. Each role tends to emphasize certain chakras

---

[15]See the subchapter "Number Correlations" in Chapter Eleven, "Cadences and Numbers."

more than others, but no one chakra perfectly exemplifies a particular role. [16]

THE FOUR DIRECTIONS

Some Native American cultures see the direction south as representing innocence and trust; the north, wisdom and endurance; the east, illumination and new beginnings; and the west, death and introspection. A client asked about the correlation between the four directions and the four axes in the Michael teachings.

The four directions do not lend themselves to direct correlation with the four axes. Instead, specific roles emphasize specific combinations of directional energies. Although all the roles use all four energies, it is a matter of dominance.

Artisans: south and north.
Priests: north, west, and some south.
Servers: mostly west and some east.
Kings: east and west.
Warriors: west, south, and some east.
Scholars: north and south.
Sages: south and east.

TRANSCENDING POSITIVE AND NEGATIVE POLES

The game we play on the causal plane as kings and warriors is mostly not about positive and negative poles. We almost completely experience the essential nature of these roles and therefore transcend both negative and positive poles. As kings, for example, we are not concentrating on staying in mastery and avoiding tyranny. There is a vibration associated with us as kings that relates to mastery, but it is not our focus, because we have already played the game of dualities, and both mastery and tyranny are integrated into our consciousness.

The positive pole of scholar is knowledge, the negative pole, theory. When a scholar truly sees theory, knowledge becomes illuminated. He is then complete regarding that duality and is not limited by either theory or knowledge. He no longer

---

[16]See also the subchapter "Chakras and Centers" in Chapter Twenty-Two, "Centers."

merely has knowledge; he is the embodiment and process of knowledge, so he does not have to focus on it. He experiences the essential nature of the scholar vibration.

Expansion occurs through the positive poles—acting from love, in other words—but the experience of the negative poles, acting from fear, is not wasted. It contributes to your knowledge of love. You experience as much fear as you need to in order to clearly see it and fully awaken to the reality of love. As you do, you transcend both the negative and positive sides of things, and you develop the capacity to simply be.

Lessons about these dualities are usually not completed on the physical plane. They continue onto the astral plane until the entity recombines. Then a new game begins, which could not be played if the previous game had not been played.

NO HIERARCHY OF ROLES

It is not better to be one role than another. Some people think that it's better to be a king than a server. From the point of view of our spark, if we had wanted to be a king, we would be one. The roles describe various styles or ways of being; they are not measures of importance.

One client, since reading the Yarbro books, had been saying somewhat derogatorily of others who are heavy-handed in some way, "He's probably a warrior." She wasn't very happy to find out that she is one! I've run into that response in others, too. However, in the positive pole, warriors can have the comforting, earthy warmth of a blazing fire in a fireplace on a cold winter day. I often point out that Michael consists of eighty percent warriors.[17] A weakness, be it heavy-handedness or hypersensitivity, is often a distortion of a gift. A Mack truck may not be subtle, but it is strong, and strength is beautiful in its true expression. I think of warriors and kings as being like beams and girders supporting the rest of us: basic, unadorned, and strong.

That particular woman was sixth-level mature,[18] and had been going through a lot of difficulties, so some of the more typical warrior self-assertion was absent in her. Sixth levels are times of completion, karmic and otherwise, with other people. Those at sixth-level mature, especially, can look "shell-shocked" if they've been repaying a lot of

---

[17]Michael is an entity made up of eight hundred fifty warriors and two hundred kings.

[18]See Chapter Fifteen, "Soul Age."

karma (see Glossary). No doubt, her warrior confidence will return in a more refined form after her sixth-level lessons are complete.

COMBINED ESSENCE ENERGIES

Usually, channeling a Michael Reading chart is straightforward, but sometimes, Michael stops to tell me about something someone is doing that doesn't go "by the rules," which illustrates the vast range of possibilities available to us. An example is having more than one essence physically in one's body. Most of us draw on the energies of other essences, such as our spirit guides, but they generally remain astral. The more someone draws on other essences, especially when they are in his body, the more difficult it can be to psychically read his role and other essence information.

> In rare instances, more than one essence join energies and incarnate together. For convenience's sake, one has the silver cord connection to the body, [19] but the other essence(s) has just as much commitment to the life being lived and brings his own unique talents and insights into the life.
>
> This will not usually be undertaken if there is a great deal of karma to be repaid or a lot of personal agendas to be fulfilled, because that is a solo job. It is more common in situations where broad leadership and inspiration are needed.
>
> The man Jesus, before the entrance of the infinite soul, [20] was actually three essences in one body. The primary one was a seventh-level old king with a sage essence twin. The others were a priest with a scholar essence twin, and a king with a warrior essence twin, giving Jesus direct access to the five most cardinal role energies, emphasizing king energy. When an essence is incarnate only in a secondary position, he will often also incarnate separately in the same time frame and location, which was the case with these other two essences: they also incarnated in secondary positions as John the Baptist and the disciple John, respectively. [21]

---

[19]The *silver cord* refers to what connects the astral self to the physical body. Psychics often see it as being the color silver. It was originally a Biblical term, found in Ecclesiastes 12:6: "Or ever the silver cord be loosed,...Then shall the dust return to the earth as it was: and the spirit shall return unto God who gave it."

[20]See Chapter Twenty-Nine, "Infinite and Transcendental Souls."

[21]Through "Jessica Lansing," Michael said that the disciple John was an artisan. They also said that Paul and most of the disciples were priests.

These secondary essences can also come in after the life has begun. This is sometimes an alternative to a walk-in arrangement. A walk-in occurs when an essence takes over a body from another essence who chooses to leave it. When the body is shared, the primary essence still makes the choices, so usually no karma is incurred by the new essence(s). This arrangement can add life force and expand the person's energetic "palette." The new essence(s) benefits from having experiences he wouldn't otherwise be able to have. A fully incarnate secondary essence is a significant enough influence that Michael might dictate two sets of essence data for one person when I'm channeling his chart.

Here are some comments Michael made about situations involving combined essence energies (clients' names have been changed):

> *Charles is in a unique situation, in that his essence twin is not separately incarnate, but is blended into his earthly form.*

> *Jane's essence twin joined with her on a more or less permanent basis about two years ago. The role with Jane is a completely blended energy of server and king. The original 'occupant' is the server. Her attitude is less blended, the king side of her tending to use cynic, and the server using realist.*

One instance in which the essence energies aren't blended is an artisan who alternates about monthly with his king essence twin, going from gentleness to a sometimes dictatorial temper. This was bewildering to his employees. He was glad to hear that he's not schizophrenic! Michael said that the artisan is tired of the physical plane and needs to leave his body a great deal. This is his creative, if difficult, solution.

Another artisan (who has no essence twin) found a different, less noticeable solution to the same problem: he brought a similar artisan essence into his body to help out full-time.

The most extreme case I've seen of combining essences concerns a highly experimental scholar with an artisan essence twin who was bringing in one entity mate every several months, until there were seven total.

> *Since these fragments are already cycled off,[22] they bring him greater connection with the whole of his entity and its collective information.*

---

[22]*Cycled off* means being complete with the physical plane—the souls have completed their infant, baby, young, mature, and old soul cycles and are no

Michael described an adjustment period for them similar to that of walk-ins (discussed below), but easier.

One server was using this blending process as a prelude to walking out. A scholar had come in about three years prior to my channeling about it, and Michael said that in about ten more years, the scholar will have taken over entirely. The scholar already accounted for about sixty-five percent of the person's life force, but the imprinting and "ownership" was still the server's. Since the server was obviously in no hurry, this had the significant advantage of making the walk-in process uncharacteristically smooth and subtle.

Unless a person is familiar with a spiritual teaching about such things, he is not likely to be consciously aware that he is experiencing a blending of essence energies, or that a walk-in is occurring. However, if it happens in adulthood, he will probably notice that some kind of change has occurred. Those who are newly blending essence energies may find an expansion in their outlook or abilities. Walk-ins may notice a rather sudden shift in their preferences in such things as clothing or friends.

Walk-ins, incidentally, sometimes occur when a person is recovering from an illness or accident so that the new essence has a chance to adjust to the body and to the physical plane in general. Most of us get that opportunity during infancy and early childhood, when little is expected of us. It may be that the illness or accident was also the reason the previous essence negotiated the walk-in—he was tired of dealing with what was perhaps an unforeseen problem. A walk-in might be accompanied by a surge of energy or a new resolve to overcome limitations.

Walk-ins are not common. When they do occur, they do not necessarily indicate (contrary to popular belief) that an "older and wiser" soul has come into someone's body in order to bring enlightenment to the world. As with all such things, walk-ins are negotiated by those concerned; the incoming soul can be younger in soul age as well as older, and often has a more modest, personal reason for incarnating than transforming the world in general. Walking in to an adult body can appeal to a soul who sees no need to have another childhood experience at that time; perhaps he has only a few items on his "to do" list for that lifetime, and therefore does not need many years in the body. The soul walking out is usually concerned that the incoming soul will properly handle the responsibilities he is leaving behind (such as raising children).

---

longer physically incarnating. Their consciousness was fully focused on the astral plane. In becoming "roommates" with their entity mate, they were making an "encore" of sorts.

Chapter 10

CADRES AND ENTITIES

A cadre is a group of about seven thousand souls. It is divided into seven entities of about a thousand souls each. Each person is a member of an entity and its cadre. A cadre contains essences of all seven roles, but within an individual entity, two to four roles are usually represented.[1] Other members of our entity could be likened to our brothers and sisters, while members of other entities of our cadre could be compared to our first cousins, or our peers in the local community.[2]

AN ENTITY'S VIBRATION

Each entity carries a distinct vibration. Like a flavor or color, it can be hard to define in words what it is, but it can be recognized. Entities, which are sometimes called "spiritual families," are not unlike biological families, in which every member is unique, but carries the stamp of the family. Some people have learned to identify the vibration of many entities—they can meet someone and know that he is in a particular entity. Furthermore, there are "strains" within an entity, people who share even more particular qualities—they can even look alike. Again, it is similar to a family, where some members may share a common laugh, smile, walk, idiosyncrasy, or even look strikingly alike, although not everyone in the family does.

There is one entity whose members I often feel both attracted to and nervous around. Michael told me that in consecutive past lives, I experienced painful rejections from two members of that entity, and I now unconsciously equate members of that entity with rejection, which brings up in me a longing to be accepted by them, particularly

---

[1]There are unconventional cadres, such as my own, in which each entity contains all the roles.

[2]In Yarbro, Michael uses slightly different analogies: members of a primary cadence (discussed in the next chapter) are like family, members of an entity are like cousins, and members of other entities in the same cadre are like in-laws or step-relatives. I like comparing entities to families, partly because entities seem analogous to the general new age concept of "spiritual families."

Whatever analogy is chosen is a little arbitrary. I know many of my entity mates, for instance, and both analogies, siblings and cousins, work for me. Of course, people experience varying levels of closeness with both their siblings and cousins.

with my goal of acceptance. Being conscious of this pattern is helping me neutralize it.

One entity with which I am familiar has a number of strong women who are currently into wearing short, spiky "punk" haircuts. Members of my entity tend to be at least a little flamboyant (depending on the role and overleaves). I also know an entity that tends toward qualities such as kindness and gentleness.

Some members of another entity strike me as having a rough, bearish quality—they are warm in a gruff sort of way. Still another entity has a strain of members who seem particularly aggressive and/or abrasive to me. In fact, its whole cadre has something of that feeling to me, although there are members who do not. Of course, such perceptions are subjective; what I find abrasive may be someone else's definition of strength or even beauty.

The commonalities shared by cadre members are less specific than those shared by members of the same entity. I can usually tell if someone is in my cadre, although it would be hard to explain why— there's just a familiarity, perhaps even a sweetness, for me. Entity mates feel even more familiar. I may not realize when I first meet someone in my entity that he is an entity mate. However, after it is channeled, I can usually at least recognize the vibration and feel the connection. I usually like and feel comfortable with other members of my entity, although this relationship is not immune to problems that can arise between any two people, such as abrading (clashing) over-leaves, false personality (fear-based ego), or simple disappointment. Personality conflicts can always get in the way of essence connections, and even entity mate relationships can be karmic.

Just as each person has a life task and overall focus for his grand cycle, each entity has goals and interests, both short- and long-term. In fact, this is true of every grouping.

Entity mates share a common energy, and we are often attracted to people whose energy is more different from our own than that of our entity mates. Therefore, romantic relationships appear to be most common between members of directly neighboring entities in a cadre, whereas relationships within an entity are usually more brother-and-sisterly. Entity mates who are mated to one another sometimes describe their relationship as having something of that sibling quality. On the other hand, Yarbro[3] described mature and old soul members of the same primary cadence as often being "the best of friends or lovers." (A primary cadence is a group of seven souls who have the

---

[3]*More Messages from Michael*, p. 92.

same role; it is the "building block" of the entity.[4]) So being in the same entity does not prevent romantic involvement.

In order to begin incarnating on the physical plane, our entity must "fragment" into its individual essences. Members of our entity who have cycled off (completed) the physical plane begin to reunite on the middle astral plane while waiting for the rest of our entity to cycle off. They make themselves available to assist us. Like nonphysical essence twins, it is almost as if they live within us, providing us with an expanded "palette" of energies from which to draw. "Jessica Lansing" channeled Michael as saying that what Jung described as the collective unconscious was his perception of his reunited entity mates, with whom he was quite connected. It is possible to remember past lives of such entity mates almost as if they were our own.

THE NUMBERING OF CADRES

During my first year of channeling, I mostly saw members of my own cadre, which, in my channeling, Michael labeled Cadre Three. After that, I began to see significant numbers of members of the next three cadres, especially.

When I channel a Michael Reading chart, I include the person's cadre and entity numbers. Michael numbered the cadres through me in order of their average amount of planetary experience, so Cadre One is presently the most experienced cadre on earth; Michael assures me that planetary experience is measurable, although the difference in experience between two cadres with close numbers is negligible. Michael considers both the mean number of previous grand cycles, primarily, and also the mean soul age (which relates partly to when the cadre started incarnating) when they number cadres through me. I have channeled cadre numbers as high as twenty-three, out of what I presume are hundreds of thousands of cadres incarnating on earth. I suppose that this indicates that only members of the most experienced cadres are attracted to these teachings, and that the people they ask about are likewise in those cadres since "birds of a feather flock together." If I were to channel the chart of someone selected randomly from the middle of a distant country, someone having no connection with anything in my world of experience, it is likely that the cadre number would be quite high. Unlike the numbers one through seven associated with soul age level, entity, and cadence, the cadre numbers in this system have no energetic significance; they are simply a convenience for identification.

---

[4]See Chapter Eleven, "Cadences and Numbers."

Michael has numbered cadres differently through many of the northern California channels. What Michael calls Cadre Three through me is called Cadre One in the other system, and my Cadre Four is called Cadre Two. (I discuss the reasons for this in the next section.)

I come across members of what are labeled Cadres One and Two in my system only occasionally (they account for about three percent of the charts I have channeled). They mainly incarnate in the Orient. Those I do meet often have an interest in Eastern teachings, and/or have a drive to visit India, China, or other Asian destinations. These cadres are not themselves students of Michael; individual members may choose to study with Michael, and I have a couple of clients who are quite interested in the Michael teachings, but they don't often have the inclination because of the lack of an agreement to do so on a cadre level.

I have been keeping entity lists on my computer for those who wish to know about some of their entity mates, especially well-known members of their entity. Not surprisingly, I have by far the longest list for Cadre Three, with the most names for its second entity, which is my own. I have also recorded a high number of Cadre Three/Entity Four members, interesting in light of the fact that Michael through JP Van Hulle said that it is largely cycled off. Perhaps New York, my home from 1985 to 1995, is a hub for the "cleanup crew."

I see a disproportionate number of members of number two entities of other cadres, such as Cadre Four/Entity Two and Cadre Six/Entity Two. Perhaps because I am in a number two entity, there is a resonance.

Members of particular entities come to me as clients in waves.[5] It is as though one or two members of an entity come to see me, then

---

[5]There are other kinds of "waves" in my practice. For example, a woman who was the creative director for a major advertising agency came to see me. A few days later, another woman came who worked for the same firm, but she had not heard about me from the first woman, and she brought a friend who also worked in advertising.

This sort of thing happens frequently in my life, and it doesn't necessarily have great significance. During one period of about a year and a half, I met four different people who had some kind of personal connection with Shirley MacLaine. One of them gave her manuscripts of two of my books (without my asking him to) and another said that he would give her the Michael Reading chart I had channeled of her. I assumed that since these events were obviously not coincidental, they meant that I would be soon be working with Ms. MacLaine, which so far has not happened. That may have been one probability, or these events may have simply illustrated that related vibrations cluster together and come into one's life in "waves." I discuss a similar subject in the subchapter "patterns in channeling" in the next chap-

spread the word within their entity on an essence level. I begin to see its members more frequently in both private and group sessions, and they even turn up more often when I channel charts requested by people not in that entity. At group sessions, I have joked on occasion, "Welcome to the (such-and-such) entity reunion." At the next one, perhaps none of its members would be there. At a workshop I led at the NewLife Expo in New York, there were four members of Cadre Two, three in its third entity. At the next Expo, just one person from that entity was present at my workshop, but she had planned to attend the previous one and hadn't made it. (Most of the Cadre Two members I meet are at my Expo workshops.)

Sometimes I do a session with a particular entity's member, and then a friend of mine who is in that same entity drops by or calls during it or directly afterward. Or, I schedule two phone sessions back to back (which I rarely do), and the clients turn out to be not only in the same entity but of the same essence role. (That is a closer bond than being different roles in the same entity.) I don't know if all Michael channels have this experience. As a sage, I am constantly "networking," introducing people who need to meet; perhaps my experience as a channel in connecting entity mates is partly an outgrowth of that.

I can certainly validate the channeling in *Messages from Michael* that seventh-level old souls seek out their entity mates. That must be especially true for sages, being so social. I have had friendships or significant acquaintances with over fifty people channeled as being in my entity, and I have met several others. My mother was in my entity, and her paintings hang on the walls of my apartment. It is often entity mates who express admiration for her work or a sense of connection with her through it. (Members of neighboring entities, who might have known her in past lives, also sometimes comment on them.)

Being a nature lover, I had once sworn that I would never live in a big city, let alone one with a rather unpleasant climate. When I was somewhat spontaneously drawn to move to New York in 1985, I thought it was to pursue my passion for the theater. I never did work in the theater during my ten years there, although I was an avid theatergoer. I can now see that there was more to my compulsion to move there than that. In hindsight and with the benefit of the Michael information, it is clear that I had many agreements there, especially with other members of my cadre. I was constantly meeting people significant in my life who turned out to be in Cadre Three. I'm

---

ter, "Cadences and Numbers," and, especially, in the subchapter "Number of Past Lifetimes" in Chapter Twenty-Five, "Reincarnation."

sure that was more than chance, especially in light of how easy it was for me to move there: I had packed my things and was on the road from Colorado within ten days of having made the decision to make the move.

ENTITY LISTS

The following is a compilation of the entities of some well-known people. The Cadre Three lists were originally compiled by Michael channel Joya Pope and were based on the channeling and perceptions of various California-based channels. Over the years, I supplemented them from my own channeling. (Lists for all other cadres are exclusively from my channeling.) This kind of material can have a fairly high margin of error, and there were some discrepancies when Joya put the Cadre Three lists together, but perhaps they will give you a sense of the tenor of various entities. If you are in one of the entities or cadres listed, it can also alert you to some people with whom you might have an essence connection.

Being in the same entity or cadre can make for a strong connection. I was fascinated when I channeled Oskar Schindler as being in the same entity as Steven Spielberg, Cadre Three/Entity Five. (George Lucas is their entity mate as well.) You can also see on the lists that cadre mates include Hillary and Bill Clinton, Tipper and Al Gore, Madonna and Sean Penn, and Shirley MacLaine and Warren Beatty.

This compilation will be of most interest to those who are in what is called Cadre Three in my system, since the majority of people on this list are in it. That is because the channels who contributed to it and many of our clients are in Cadre Three. Since we are each most connected with other people in our own cadre, we would be most likely to ask about them. The fact that some entities have more names than others does not imply that there are more well-known people in them—this list is arbitrary, based only on who happened to be asked about.

The first number refers to the cadre and the second number is the position of the entity within that cadre, one through seven. For instance, 3/1 is Cadre Three/Entity One, or the first entity of Cadre Three. Cadre Four/Entity One is written as 4/1. Although both are number one entities, they are in different cadres.

3/1:   Winston Churchill, Sean Connery, Harrison Ford, Patti La-Belle, Kathy Najimy, Irving Penn, Mary Lou Retton, Oliver Stone, Tina Turner, Wendy Wasserstein, Virginia Woolf.

3/2: Randall Baer, Dave Barry, Candice Bergen, Betty Comden, Thomas Dolby, Duke Ellington, Werner Erhard, Paul Gauguin, Boy George, George Gershwin, Johann Goethe, Bob Goldthwait, Keith Jarrett, Jessica Lange, Madonna, Bob Marley, Bette Midler, Marilyn Monroe, David Niven, Conan O'Brien, Dolly Parton, Luciano Pavarotti, Rajneesh, Raphael, Dan Rather, Henri Rousseau, Haile Sellasie, William Shakespeare, William Shatner, Sting, Donald Sutherland, Elizabeth Taylor, Roger Woolger, Christopher Wren, Paramahansa Yogananda.

3/3: Bella Abzug, Johann Sebastian Bach, David Bowie, Barbara Brennan, David Byrne, Rodney Collin-Smith, Alan Cumming, Roger Ebert, Albert Einstein, Whoopi Goldberg, Tom Hanks, Pee Wee Herman, Gregory Hines, John Lennon, Muktananda, Maxfield Parrish, Kenny Rogers, Vincent Van Gogh, Mario Van Peebles, Debra Winger, Stevie Wonder, William Wordsworth.

3/4: John Bradshaw, Michael Feinstein, Martin Luther King, Wolfgang Amadeus Mozart, Anais Nin, Christopher Reeve, Wilhelm Reich, Diana Ross, Andreas Vollenweider, Patricia Zipprodt.

3/5: Julie Andrews, Ken Carey, John Cryer, Charles Dickens, Walt Disney, Tipper Gore, Jason Graae, Stanislov Grof, William Hurt, Michael Jackson, George Lucas, Rick Nelson, Peter O'Toole, River Phoenix, Peace Pilgrim, Chita Rivera, Anwar Sadat, Oskar Schindler, David Shire, Stephen Sondheim, Steven Spielberg, Roger Waters, Robin Williams.

3/6: Desi Arnaz, Jr., Matthew Fox, John Friedlander, Henry Kissinger, Krishna, Richard Maltby, Jr., Leonard Nimoy, Yoko Ono, Sean Penn, Gene Siskell.

3/7: Rosanna Arquette, Howard Ashman, Christopher Atkins, Ram Dass, Ellen Degeneres, Johnny Depp, Melissa Etheridge, Al Gore, Jr., R.P. Kaushik, kd lang, Julia Roberts, Stephen Schwartz, Martin Sheen, Gary Sinese, Oscar Wilde.

4/1: Otto von Bismarck, Hillary Clinton, Diane Keaton.

4/2: Bill Clinton, Garrison Keillor.

4/3: Gurumayi.

4/4: John Gotti.

4/5: Elijah.

5/1: Gertrude Stein.

5/2: Kevin Costner, Jack Kerouac.

6/1: Alexander Hamilton.

6/3: Harriet Tubman, Frederick von Mierers.

6/4: Shirley MacLaine.

6/5: Warren Beatty, Alan Menken.

6/7: The Dalai Lama.

7/5: Mikhail Gorbachev.

8/1: Lenny Bruce.

8/2: Lynn Andrews, Charles "Honi" Coles, James Earl Jones, Axl Rose.

8/6: Ross Perot.

8/7: David Pogue.

9/2: Nebuchadnezzar, Aidan Quinn.

9/5: Jiddu Krishnamurti.

10/3: Elwood Babbitt.

10/4: Moses.

12/3: Clarence Thomas.

12/7: Jane Roberts.

13/2: Aaron (Moses's brother).

14/3: Leonard Bernstein.

19/2: Michio Kushi.

23/2: Saddam Hussein.

CADRE GROUPS

According to my channeling, twelve cadres make up what Michael calls a cadre group, and seven cadre groups make up a greater cadre group.

A cadre group is reunited after cadres are reunited, generally on the messianic plane. On the buddhaic plane, cadre groups are united with one another, first in groups of seven (the greater cadre group).

Our entity (Michael) is a part of a cadre group that cycled off just before the current Cadre Group One cycled off, other than its two remaining cadres, which are well on their way to cycling off.

In other words, Cadres One and Two in my system are the last two cadres of an otherwise cycled-off cadre group, Cadre Group One, whereas ten of the twelve cadres of Cadre Group Two (my cadre group) are still incarnating. Someone in Cadre Two is in a different cadre group (One) than someone in Cadre Three (my cadre, which is the first cadre in Cadre Group Two), whereas someone in Cadre Four is in the same cadre group as someone in Cadre Three.

The following chart shows the twelve positions of my cadre group, Cadre Group Two. Next to them are the cadre numbers in my system.

CADRE GROUP TWO POSITIONS/
MY CADRE NUMBERS

First   position in Cadre Group Two / Cadre Three[6]

Second   position in Cadre Group Two / Cadre Four

Third   position in Cadre Group Two / Cadre Five

Fourth   position in Cadre Group Two / CYCLED OFF

Fifth   position in Cadre Group Two / Cadre Six

Sixth   position in Cadre Group Two / Cadre Seven

Seventh position in Cadre Group Two / CYCLED OFF

Eighth   position in Cadre Group Two / Cadre Eight

Ninth   position in Cadre Group Two / Cadre Nine

Tenth   position in Cadre Group Two / Cadre Ten

Eleventh position in Cadre Group Two / Cadre Eleven

Twelfth   position in Cadre Group Two / Cadre Thirteen[7]

The entire cadre group of which I am part has an agreement to study with Michael, so I am mainly attracting its members. The fact that my cadre is in the first position out of the twelve helps explain why it is called Cadre One through the other system—it is the first cadre among Michael's students. However, since I wish to identify the cadre of everyone whose chart I channel, I needed a numbering system that could encompass that, including Cadres One and Two in my system.

It might seem more consistent to number all cadres by their cadre group number and position, but the concept is relatively recent for me, and I know of no other channels who are working with it. Also, doing it that way would leave gaps, since some cadres have cycled off.

The concept of cadre groups helps explain the close bond we might feel with someone not in our cadre. [8] If someone in another en-

---

[6]In other words, what is called Cadre Three through me is in the first position of Cadre Group Two.

[7]Cadre Twelve belongs to Cadre Group Three, first position, but it is numbered before Cadre Thirteen because it is slightly "older" or more experienced, particularly because it began on the physical plane earlier. Such overlap is not uncommon. The first cadre of a cadre group does not have to wait for all the cadres of the previous cadre group to begin incarnating in order to begin incarnating itself.

[8]There is also the concept of "heart link" that explains a closeness with someone in another cadre that feels like a cadre connection. A heart link is a

tity of our cadre is like a first cousin, a member of another cadre in our cadre group could be likened to a second cousin.

How do the cadres within the cadre group interrelate?

Seventh entities, for one thing, tend to join with seventh entities of other cadres within a cadre group through essence twin connections. Those in your cadre group (Two) do this more than in most other cadre groups. We'd say about seventy-five percent of your seventh entity members choose essence twins in neighboring cadres within your cadre group. Your being in the first cadre of Cadre Group Two, your seventh entity members would tend to team up with members of the seventh cadre of your neighboring cadre, Cadre Four/Entity Seven, although people do skip around. Members of Cadre Thirteen (the twelfth member of your cadre group)/Entity Seven might team up with members of any other Cadre Group Two cadre in the seventh entity, or might have an essence twin connection with Cadre Group Three, especially Cadre Twelve/Entity Seven (the first cadre of Cadre Group Three).

So cadre groups themselves are linked.

Yes. Seven cadre groups make a greater cadre group.

Where does it end?

When cadres complete the buddhaic plane and are reabsorbed, so to speak, back into the Tao, they no longer exist as formations but are a part of the increasing fabric of the Tao. You might say that this reabsorption process drives the evolution of universes. As one cadre is reabsorbed into the Tao, it pulls along the other cadres in the cadre group who are still universal. When whole cadre groups are reabsorbed, they pull along their greater cadre group members who are still on a dimensional plane. This process has no end that we know of. Greater cadre groups are linked in groups of twelve again, we believe, and we are not certain what comes after them.

---

bond formed through life experience that does not end when the lifetime is completed. It can be forged regardless of cadre by any intense sharing, from being an exemplary parent or child, to saving someone's life. On average, my clients seem to have one heart link for every lifetime lived, although some people have many more or less. The number of heart links gives a good indication of how much of a "people person" someone is.

Are there essence twin connections outside of greater cadre groups?

Not that we know of.

I thought that essence twins were cast from the Tao simultaneously. How can members of different cadres, let alone cadre groups, be cast simultaneously?

You need to understand here what is meant by "simultaneously." Physical-plane time is not the measure of universes. It is an arbitrary division based on planetary circulations that relates mostly to itself and nothing else. Simultaneously means at the same universal frequency.

Essence twins are cast at a particular frequency; that is why they appear to be similar, or opposite sides of the same thing. There are also group frequencies shared, first by cadences, all the way up to the greater cadre groups and beyond. These common resonances are present in different aspects of the essence, each one providing a specific "overtone" in the unique "overtone series" of each essence.[9]

Let's say that your essence twin is in a different cadre group, and is cycled off. Would that put pressure on you to cycle off as well?

Yes, but you will probably stay pretty close in soul age to your essence twin as you move along anyway, so this is not a major issue.

Here is a summary of the organization of planetary sentient souls that Michael teaches (I will discuss cadences in the next chapter):

---

[9]See the subchapter "Number Correlations" in Chapter Eleven, "Cadences and Numbers," for an explanation of overtones and a related overtone analogy.

PLANETARY SENTIENT ORGANIZATION

SEVEN ESSENCES	=	ONE CADENCE
SEVEN CADENCES	=	ONE GREATER CADENCE (Forty-Nine Essences)
X GREATER CADENCES of X ROLES	=	ONE ENTITY (X=Varying Numbers) (About One Thousand Essences)
SEVEN ENTITIES	=	ONE CADRE (About Seven Thousand Essences)
TWELVE CADRES	=	ONE CADRE GROUP (About Eighty-Four Thousand Essences)
SEVEN CADRE GROUPS	=	ONE GREATER CADRE GROUP (Eighty-Four Cadres, about 588,000 Essences)
TWELVE GREATER CADRE GROUPS	=	ONE (Unnamed) (1008 Cadres, About Seven Million Essences)

Eventually, these linkages, directly or indirectly, include all sentient consciousness in the universe—they are part of the mechanics of oneness. The evolution of each part helps "pull" everything else along. By calling individual essences "fragments," Michael is communicating that we are each part of the larger whole—specifically, part of our entity. The entity is our larger identity, but since the entity is a part of the cadre, the cadre is a part of the cadre group, and so forth, ultimately, our identity is that of the Tao itself.

CADRES AND PREVIOUS CYCLES

We are often close to other essences with whom we were on other planets during previous grand cycles.[10] Many of them are in our cadre.

---

[10]See Chapter Fourteen, "Previous Cycles," or *grand cycle* in the Glossary.

Cadres are reformed each cycle, but as might be expected, many of the same sparks choose to band together more than once, so as to maintain continuity.

NONSENTIENT ORGANIZATIONAL PATTERNS

The pattern of organization outlined above applies only to sentient souls, who account for only about five percent of the Tao. Devas, for example, have another organizational pattern, and animal souls have still another. These are discussed in the following sections.

Incidentally, JP Van Hulle channeled that only about twenty-five percent of the Tao plays the universal game at all; the rest of it remains "uncast." If sentient souls account for about five percent of the Tao, that means that they account for about twenty percent of the consciousness operating in the dimensional universe. (Five divided by twenty-five equals twenty percent.)

Animals might occupy about another five percent of the Tao, devas perhaps four percent. Perhaps six percent is star consciousness, although that has many subdivisions. (An example is, of course, the sun, which actually permeates its whole solar system.) The other five percent is miscellaneous, such as free agent beings who help create new planets. The raw material of undeveloped planets and of the universe itself, although occupying much space, does not account for a large percentage of the Tao—maybe two percent. Planetary energies develop as sentient consciousness develops on them, in response to that developing sentience, in much the same way that male energy acts upon and shapes female energy. The more developed, mature planetary energies, such as earth or gaia energy, perhaps accounts for about one percent of the Tao. Although developed planets carry more of the Tao's consciousness than undeveloped ones, there are many more immature planets than mature ones.

ANIMAL HIVE SOULS

Animals have hive souls. The consciousness that incarnates in animal bodies has a much simpler organization than that of sentient consciousness. All consciousness that incarnates, for example, in cows derives fundamentally from one big group. There are simple subdivisions, but they are not nearly as com-

*plex as cadres and entities, for example. The hive soul's indi-
vidual fragments rotate among available experiences. It might
be a "sacred cow" in one lifetime, and live on a feed lot in another, to have a variety of experiences. Animals generally do
not have as many lifetimes as sentient souls, because there is
not as much available for them to learn.[11]*

Are animals in specific numerical positions within larger
groupings?

*No. There is a relatively simple, more chaotic structure within
hive souls. Several cat souls, for instance, may cluster together
around a consciousness that may not itself incarnate but brings
to focus a particular aspect of cat souldom.*

DEVIC "ENTITIES"

Devas are nature spirits who take care of the earth "behind the
scenes." They work with the mineral, plant, and animal kingdoms, as
well as with larger elements, such as the oceans, clouds, and mountains.[12] The more wild the area, the more devas there tend to be,
although there are also devas in urban areas, particularly where the
"vibes" are good. (Negative vibrations repel devas, which is partly why
plants tend to wither in them.) Germanic legends speak of
"elementals": the undines, or water spirits; the salamanders, or fire
spirits; the sylphs, or air spirits; and the gnomes, or earth spirits
(reputed to be rather nasty). A legend that became a popular nine-
teenth-century novel and a 1950's French play (done on Broadway
with Audrey Hepburn, called *Ondine*) was about a water "sprite" who
became an enchanting teenage girl and marries a knight. *The Little
Mermaid* derives from the same legend. Fairies, brownies, and
dwarves are other examples of devas. These beings vibrate slightly
slower than we do, and it is possible to see them when in a medita-
tive state. I understand that they can look much like they are
depicted in children's books. (I personally sense them more than see
them.)

Before we commit to a sentient cycle on a planet, we usually explore it first as a deva.[13] There are also "full-time" devas, who do not

---

[11]See also Chapter Eight, "Animals," of my upcoming Summerjoy Michael
book *Being in the World*.

[12]See also Chapter Twenty-Seven, "Planes of Creation."

[13]José Stevens discusses our devic stage in detail in *Tao to Earth*, and espe-

go on to a sentient cycle. We form into tentative sentient entities before our devic stage, and solidify those plans after it. However, when we are devas, we are not working out of a sentient entity—we join a devic grouping. The devic experience is less structured and formal than a sentient cycle, giving it more flexibility in that regard. Therefore, someone can join a devic grouping as a temporary "adjunct" rather than committing to a relatively long-term cycle.

> *A typical devic grouping or "entity" is made up of about one hundred fragments. Seven of these entities make up a devic "cadre." These entities and cadres may be highly specialized (ordinal), highly general (cardinal), or in between. One entity may consist of only oak tree devas, for example. If that is the case, its "cadre" may consist of seven oak deva entities, or may consist of a cross section of related tree species. A cadre may also be cross-special [related to the word species]. At the other end of the spectrum is a cadre that includes representation from all the physical systems on the planet. Such a cadre might help coordinate the activities of the more ordinal cadres, and can also be appropriate for pre-sentient souls who want to get an overview of the planet. "Career" devas are more likely to specialize.*
>
> *Since devic cadres are not as highly organized as sentient cadres (they don't need to be), they can be added to without major problems. It is complex to add a fragment to a sentient cadre, and it rarely happens.*

MICHAEL'S CADRE

Michael is the name of an entity that itself is a part of a cadre. The other entities of their cadre also teach on earth's physical and astral planes, but mostly nonverbally, through the body and emotions, rather than through the intellect. According to my channeling, Michael is in the fourth (or scholar) position in their cadre. The entity in the seventh position consists of three roles, artisans, sages, and priests. The other entities each have four or five roles in them.

Michael's cadre receives friendship and support from other causal cadres, mostly, and from cadres on higher planes. Although Michael experiences much more oneness with their larger groupings than we do on the physical plane, they are relatively self-reliant. Perhaps it relates to the nature of warriors and kings, who seek

cially, *Earth to Tao.*

challenge and mastery, respectively, and who tend to like to do things by themselves.

OTHER ASPECTS OF SENTIENT ORGANIZATION

To make an analogy, we can be members of various, sometimes overlapping organizations, in addition to being a member of our family, with its complex family tree. These organizations may be political, religious, or social. They may be on the community, national, or international level. They may be part-time or full-time, temporary or permanent. They may be small or large. If this is true of a human being during one lifetime, how much more true might it be of an eternal soul?

Seth, channeled by Jane Roberts, speaks of nine types of soul families, rather than seven. Ceanne DeRohan's *Right Use of Will* describes the organization of consciousness in an elaborate hierarchy. We are very complex, and there are many valid ways to describe the ways we relate to each other. Fundamentally, we tend to gather together wherever there are common interests.

Chapter 11

CADENCES AND NUMBERS

C adences are configurations of seven souls that, like entities and cadres, stay together for an entire grand cycle. They differ from temporary configurations (usually lasting several lifetimes) such as quadrates, sextants, triads, and so on that are formed, usually during the late baby and early young soul ages, for specific purposes relative to physical-plane tasks. A primary cadence is the smallest grouping of essences within an entity, and each member has the same role. There are many other kinds of cadences. We are part of more than one; occasionally, several.

Seven primary cadences join together into a greater cadence. So a greater cadence of servers, for example, consists of seven groups of seven servers, or forty-nine servers. Greater cadences also group together, although there can be any number of them—there doesn't have to be seven, and there may be just one. Series of greater cadences of various roles make up the entity.

Every essence has a particular numerical position within its entity based on its position within its cadence, its cadence's position within its greater cadence, and its greater cadence's position within its series of greater cadences. That is sometimes called its "casting." Along with our cadre, entity, and role, our casting precisely locates us within the universe, like our personal cellular phone number that travels with us. Theoretically, someone at the other end of the universe could locate a soul knowing that he's a server on earth in Cadre Twenty-Nine/Entity Four, with 3/2/6 casting. (Rarely, two souls with the same role in the same entity are channeled as having the same casting because there is more than one "pocket" of, say, servers within that entity, and the numbering starts over. Therefore, that theoretical caller from across the universe would need to know the "party's extension," or further locating information. This applies only to nonclassic entity structures, discussed shortly.)

Let's say that a scholar is in the third position of his cadence, and that that cadence is in the seventh position within its greater cadence. Let's also say that that greater cadence is in the fifth position out of however many greater cadences of scholars there are in that entity. In my system, that would be written as 3/7/5. That could be described as the essence's casting, or more commonly, it might be said that he has number three casting, because he is in the third position of his cadence. Cadence position, the first number of the three, is the most prominent casting influence. (The next section, "Number

Correlations," will explain how casting influences us.) The following diagram, "3/7/5 Casting," illustrates this casting, also assuming that this scholar is in an entity that is second within its cadre. Note that the seven pattern applies to the organization of the cadence, greater cadence, and cadre, but not directly to the entity; the entity contains varying numbers of greater cadences of generally two to four roles. (As mentioned, the entities of some cadres, including mine, each contain all seven roles, according to my channeling.) This hypothetical entity contains four roles, and a total of nine hundred thirty-one essences. The diagram's representation of the entity is a simplification of what can be a rather complex structure. The use of circles throughout the diagram is for convenience, and do not represent literal shapes. The numbering of the seven circles within a larger circle places the numbers resonating with particular roles on the same axis across from each other. For example, one and six are across from one another, and they resonate with the roles of server and priest, the inspiration axis roles. (Four, resonating with the neutral role, scholar, is in the middle.) As the diagram illustrates, each greater cadence consists of essences of only one role.

The second diagram, "Another View of Entity Two," illustrates the same position in a different way, using squares instead of circles, and placing the positions in numerical order. (It omits the cadre.) The larger squares each represent a greater cadence. The fifth greater cadence of scholars shows its forty-nine essences. The top row is cadence one; its positions one through seven go from left to right. The second row is cadence two, and so on.

I will use myself to give another example of casting. I am in the fifth position of my cadence, in a cadence that is in the fourth position of its greater cadence, in the third greater cadence of sages in my entity. I record that on my chart as 5/4/3. So my casting is 5/4/3, or more commonly, it would simply be said that I have number five casting.

Entities made up of essences who have had a lot of prior experience on other planets during previous grand cycles may develop a taste for the complex, and "classic" patterns may be altered. For example, classically, all the members of one role are grouped together within an entity. In an altered pattern, members of a role may be scattered throughout an entity in "pockets," even mixing with other roles within a cadence (although this is very rare).

3/7/5 CASTING
Of a Scholar in a Cadre's Second Entity

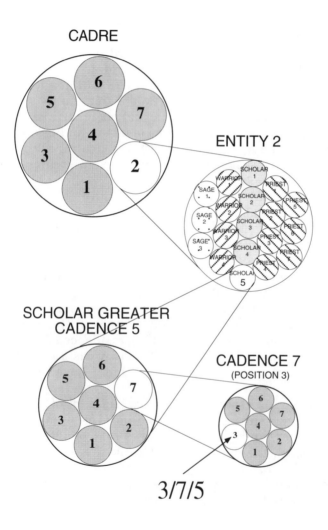

3/7/5

ANOTHER VIEW OF ENTITY TWO
And a Scholar with 3/7/5 Casting

(Each larger square is a greater cadence with 49 essences.)

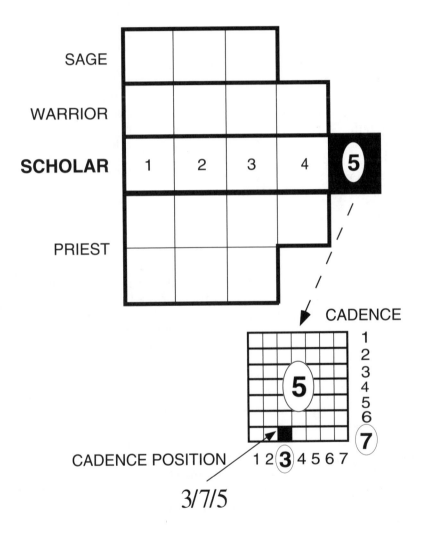

When greater cadences of one role are not all joined together, the third number in someone's casting (which refers to the position of the greater cadence), although valid, is not as strong. This also makes for a reduced solidarity of that role in the entity, but causes that role's quality to "break open" and have more impact on the entity as a whole. When an entity consists of more than one role that is not segregated into separate groupings of greater cadences, the entity as a whole is more homogenous, more of "one cloth."

If the number of essences in an entity is not divisible by seven, there are at least two possible reasons. The first is that some cadences may have gaps, most frequently at the end, to facilitate the entity structure desired by its members. In other words, all seven positions may not be filled. Since "all is choice," according to Michael, this is plausible, if unusual. (Greater cadences can also have gaps.) The second possible reason is what JP Van Hulle's channeling called "wild cards," essences who do not occupy a particular position, and are available to facilitate unusual entity tasks. There can be one to six wild cards in an entity. Wild cards are also unusual.

PATTERNS

One might think that the seven casting positions would come up with more or less equal frequency. However, that is not the case in my practice (which is not representative of the world as a whole). Most of my charts are now on a database, so it is easy for me to compute approximately how often each position has come up. Here are the seven positions, from greatest to least frequency of occurrence in my practice, with their percentages (if a position came up one-seventh of the time, that would be about fourteen percent): two—thirty-one percent; three—twenty-five percent; four—twelve percent; one—twelve percent; five—seven percent; six—seven percent; and seven—six percent. This was based on about twenty-seven hundred records.

As you can see, in my practice casting positions two and three have come up significantly more often than the others, at least so far—this could change. Early in my channeling career, the number three came up almost like a broken record. Then it subsided, while two took its place. For a while, four came up a lot, too, but then decreased in frequency, while one, which had been rare, began coming up more often.

174

Changing patterns such as these are commonplace with my Michael Readings, and in my life in general. As mentioned in the last chapter, things seem to come to me in clusters.[1]

> There are complicated vibrational factors, the sum of many different influences, that make certain waves come into one's life. These waves cannot necessarily be predicted or explained except in generalities.

One of the influences involved in my most often attracting numbers two, three, and four casting positions, in that order, is my own casting: 5/4/3. Two is the opposite of five (together they make seven) and three is the opposite of four.

NUMBER CORRELATIONS

Each number, one through seven, has particular qualities, with a positive and negative pole.[2] Each role and overleaf corresponds with one of these numbers, and shares its qualities. For instance, we can see on the following chart that the number six has a positive pole of harmony, and that the role of priest is the six-position role; therefore, priest is the harmonizing role. All the cardinal inspiration overleaves (under priest on the Michael chart) are in harmonizing positions; for instance, spiritualist is the harmonizing attitude, and growth is the harmonizing goal. It makes sense to think of the cardinal inspiration axis as harmonizing, just as it makes sense to think of the ordinal action axis (including the role of warrior) as enterprising.

Our casting determines how we tend to direct our role's energies. A scholar in the sixth position of his cadence would tend to use his scholarly knowledge as a harmonizing influence, and would have a somewhat priestly flavor. He might also study spiritual or religious subjects, since they are of special interest to priests. Having number six casting lets him work in the domain of priests without actually being one or looking and feeling that much like one.

Since five has a positive pole of expansion, a scholar in the fifth position of his cadence would tend to use his knowledge expansively,

---

[1] I further address these kinds of patterns in the subchapter "Number of Past Lifetimes" in Chapter Twenty-Five, "Reincarnation."

[2] This is not, by the way, numerology. Numerologists give readings based on one's birth date and name, using the numbers in different ways than Michael does, and using more of the numbers than one through seven. Michael's teachings about the numbers only apply to the seven roles, overleaves, levels, etc. within the Michael system.

and would have a somewhat sagely flavor. A magazine writer I know has a writing style and sense of humor that had struck me as sage-like, although he had also seemed to have sifted through and distilled a great deal of raw material, in a scholarly fashion, to come to his conclusions; he turned out to be a fifth-position scholar. He is a scholar who is an especially clear and colorful communicator.

The number three has a positive pole of enterprise and resonates with the role of warrior. A third-position scholar would emphasize knowledge that is productive and would also likely have a lot of initiative—for example, he might be better at starting and running a business than most scholars are. He won't have much of the feeling of instinctive drive that is the hallmark of warriors, but, like the typical warrior, he can, in his own way, be quite an effective achiever.

When first learning about the roles, it might have appeared that having only one role would be limiting. The influences coming from our casting and essence twin introduce much more complexity into the picture.

THE POLES OF NUMBERS
AND CORRELATIONS WITH ROLES

One	+ Purpose	- Simplicity	Server
Two	+ Stability	- Balance	Artisan
Three	+ Enterprise	- Versatility	Warrior
Four	+ Consolidation	- Achievement	Scholar
Five	+ Expansion	- Adventure	Sage
Six	+ Harmony	- Connection	Priest
Seven	+ Inculcation	- Eclecticism	King

CORRELATIONS OF NUMBERS
WITH GOALS, MODES, AND ATTITUDES

One	Reevaluation	Reserve	Stoic
Two	Discrimination	Caution	Skeptic
Three	Submission	Perseverance	Cynic
Four	Flow	Observation	Pragmatist
Five	Acceptance	Power	Idealist
Six	Growth	Passion	Spiritualist
Seven	Dominance	Aggression	Realist

One analogy for the influence of the numbers in one's casting is musical overtones. When a note sounds, a series of higher notes called "overtones" subtly resonates at the same time, "flavoring" it. A clarinet sounds different from a piano because the loudness of each of its overtones in relationship to the note played is different, due to its unique shape and materials. A "C" played on one instrument might have a higher "C" vibrating sympathetically relatively loudly, for example, while on another, "E"s and "G"s might stand out.

Likewise, each essence sounds a "tone" with a unique pattern of sympathetic vibrations. For instance, if the note "C" corresponds with the number one, I, as a sage (which resonates with five), am like a "G" with "G," "F," and "E" overtones from my 5/4/3 cadence position. It could be said that I am in the sage position of a scholar-position cadence in a warrior-position greater cadence, and this "flavors" my sage energy: I am like a G played on a saxophone, whereas another sage might be like a G played on a clarinet.

The first number in the three-number sequence is the strongest or most specific influence, but since I'm already a sage with a sage essence twin, it doesn't bring any really new qualities to my essence. It could be said that I'm an especially expansive sage. However, sages are already expansive by nature, or at least, adventurous, in the negative pole.[3] Although the second number would normally be a less-important influence, it is the first place in my chart that a new quality comes in, that of scholar, since I also have a sage essence twin. I can validate that I have a subtle flavor of the role of scholar. For example, I have an impulse to organize and conserve information. The third number is the least important or most diffuse influence, but I do have a bit of the warrior's efficiency and enterprising quality.

Suppose that someone is a warrior with a server essence twin, and his casting is 7/6/2. The numbers don't correlate with either the warrior or server energies, and each number is different, so there are five role influences out of a possible seven. In such a case, I wouldn't place much significance on the third number. If the numbers were 7/6/6, I would interpret the doubling of the six influence as adding a significant priest/harmonizing quality, perhaps equal to the seven king/inculcation quality. If the numbers were 7/7/7, the tripling of the king influence would be very significant—this would be a warrior who directs his power in a way that organizes, sums up, and brings

---

[3]Since numbers are abstract, their negative poles do not refer to destructive qualities (as other negative poles do) but simply to limited or narrow experiences of their vibration. It is not "bad" to be adventurous, for instance, but it is not as meaningful as being expansive. This will be discussed in more detail shortly.

to bear the lessons of whatever is done, probably with an eye to the service of others, since he has a server essence twin.

If the third number is a one—for example, 4/2/1—the second number takes on more importance. Every cadence in a first-position greater cadence (of a particular role in an entity) has a "pure" experience of its order within the greater cadence. Even though that number one still has its resonance with server and a positive pole of purpose, the fact that the greater cadence is first causes it to almost stand alone, without other greater cadences layered in front of it. So, in 4/2/1 casting, that essence and all his cadence mates have a pervasive, "pure" two-ness, or artisan resonance, since the cadence is second within its greater cadence, and the greater cadence itself is first among all the members of that role in that entity—no other greater cadence stands between it and the entity structure as a whole. That particular essence is in the scholar position within the cadence—it consolidates or brings together that two-ness, whereas its "neighbor," 5/2/1, expands it. The essence with 2/2/1 casting would have almost as strong a two-ness as someone with 2/2/2 casting, although the one influence would give it a slightly "sharper" or more directed (purposeful) quality. The one does have an influence, but its influence is mainly to impart a "stand-alone" quality that brings out the qualities of the number before it (the cadence's position within its greater cadence.) Servers do this as a role anyway—they stand alone in a certain self-sufficiency, bringing out the qualities of others—so, in a sense, this does not negate the server influence, but the number one brings more of its own flavor when it is the first or second casting number rather than the third (e.g., 1/7/6 or 3/1/2).

The first cadence in the first greater cadence of a role in an entity (positions 4/1/1 or 5/1/1, for example) would have even more of this stand-alone quality. A 6/1/1-position sage would have pure six casting, being the first sage in his entity to have number six casting. However, the number one also has some influence here, especially since it is doubled: this sage would be particularly purposeful in his harmonizing, and would likely work in fields that both priests and servers specialize in, such as the healing arts, using his communication abilities to bring harmony in that realm.

It's useful to see if these numbers underline other characteristics in a person. For example, let's look at a warrior with a server essence twin whose cadence numbers are 1/1/1. This person has a very strong server quality. He is another example of someone having an "honorary" role due to the influence of cadence position reinforcing that of essence twin role—this warrior could be said to be an honorary server. Since both warriors and servers tend to be tireless workers, he would likely have this quality. He would tend to be quite purposeful in using his powerful and protective warrior nature for the common good, which is a server emphasis. He might look like a cross between a warrior and a server—possessing both an instinctive drive and a nurturing quality—and at first glance, you might not be able to tell which role he is. An artisan with a server essence twin and 1/1/1 casting would have a very strong impulse to direct his creativity toward the service of others. Unless overleaves and imprinting influence him otherwise, he would probably be a gentle, sweet person. Nonetheless, since both this artisan and the above-mentioned warrior are the first-cast (most cardinal) essence of their role within their entity, they would also be extremely influential, having a kind of leading-edge thrust. Having three ones in a row brings the ultimate of that "stand alone" quality mentioned above, "potentizing" their role energy as well as flavoring it with a serverly thrust.

When there is a definite pattern in casting and essence twin role, there is usually a strong intention behind it. In the examples above, perhaps the sparks wanted to be as close to being a server as possible without actually being one (especially if they already were one during a previous cycle). Or perhaps the warrior's spark wanted to experience being a gentle warrior, since servers use the heart chakra a lot. By contrast, a spark might choose to be a warrior with all number five casting and a sage essence twin (honorary sage) to bring his productive energy into expressive endeavors.

The spark makes its choices with the whole grand cycle in mind, and matters of casting and so forth continue to have some relevance to the spark throughout the higher planes.

The number one, the lowest, most ordinal number, is in the most cardinal position of the seven numbers, since it is first. The physical plane is the number one plane; it is the most ordinal plane, yet is in the most cardinal position, in that it is first—it leads the way. This is also illustrated in the number one's correlation with the most ordinal role, server, and in the Biblical quote I used earlier in my discussion of terminology: "He that is greatest among you shall be your servant."[4] The role that some misconstrue as the most lowly is in the strongest position numerically, in the sense that the number one position tends to lead the way. And it may well be that servers are, in a sense, the most influential role, in their usually unassuming way. However, every position is strong in its own way; judgments of "strong" and "weak," and "low" and "high," do not have validity within the Michael teachings.

Servers' ordinality is reflected in the fact that, of all the roles, they can "do their thing" anywhere, without special circumstances,

---

[4]Matthew 23:11.

whereas kings, the most cardinal of roles, require some kind of "kingdom" in order to carry out their "mandate"—not easy to come by—in order to fully experience their kingliness.[5] Servers can serve under any circumstance; therefore, they manifest their essence the most easily and pass through the soul age levels the most quickly. The cardinality of their number one position is reflected by the strong quality of purpose (the positive pole of the number one) they can bring to their service. I also find that anyone in a number one cadence position is purposeful, and needs a purpose for anything he does. For instance, he is not likely to watch television unless he can see a purpose in it, such as learning something or gaining needed relaxation.

Kings are in the opposite situation from servers: they are the most cardinal role, and are in the most ordinal numerical position. Opposites have much in common, and, as mentioned, kings and servers have a special affinity for one another. In their own ways, both kings and servers are concerned with service, and also leadership. Kings tend to feel a responsibility to serve their "subjects." We could say that with kings, service is behind their leadership, and with servers, leadership is behind their service.

In the "Michael-Math" chapter of *More Messages from Michael*,[6] this was compared to the yin-yang symbol, in which the pattern "doubles back on itself." In other words, if we go far enough into yin, we come to yang, and yin has yang in its core—and vice versa. So when we take cardinality to its ultimate, we come to ordinality, and vice versa.

The number influences also apply to an entity's position within its cadre. When there is a dominance of one role in an entity, that role's energy tends to rub off on those of other roles in the entity. There are a lot of sages in my entity, so its members are known for having a sagely ebullience and expressiveness, even those who are not sages. However, it is in the second (artisan) position, so its sagely

---

[5]Artisans are the second most ordinal role and require only a structure to work with. Warriors, the third most ordinal role, require a challenge. Scholars are neutral, neither ordinal nor cardinal, and require a study. Sages are the third most cardinal role and require "wisdom" and someone(s) to whom to impart it. Priests, the second most cardinal role, require a higher ideal and a means to impart it. You'll notice that the more cardinal the role, the more difficult it can be to work out life circumstances so that the needs of essence can be met. A sage actor, for instance, may need to compete with many other actors for each opportunity to express himself on stage or in film, while servers face little competition for the opportunity to serve, and one can serve even under the most limited circumstances.

[6]P. 189.

boldness is flavored with an artisan-position aesthetic sensibility. George Gershwin and Madonna[7] are examples of famous people channeled as being in my entity who combine these qualities.

The fifth entity in my cadre, having a high artisan population, elegantly reflects the second entity; it is a similar but opposite situation. Artisans in this sage-position entity, such as Walt Disney and Steven Spielberg, are creative with sage-flavored (number five position) expansiveness. So the fifth entity has artisan energy with a sage-position "tilt," and the second entity has sage energy with an artisan-position tilt.

Number influences are also illustrated by the Michael entity itself. As mentioned, Michael is in the fourth (scholar) position within their cadre. Michael uses their warrior and king energy and efficiency to bring us a system of knowledge (positive pole of scholar).

Negative poles are constrictions that distort a vibration. It is easy to see why tyranny, the negative pole of king, for example, is negative. It is more difficult to understand why the negative poles of the numbers are negative. For instance, the negative pole of the number two is balance. Balance, obviously, is not "bad." Nonetheless, as it is used relative to the number two vibration in the Michael teachings, it signifies a limited experience of it.

Balance only concerns two elements, or two dimensions. Suppose, for example, that you have a twenty-pound weight in one hand. To balance it, you would put a twenty-pound weight in the other hand. Stability, on the other hand, concerns the whole, or three dimensions. Let's say that you are on a barge with a four-hundred-pound rock on it, and you don't want the barge to flip over. The best way to create stability may not be to put another four-hundred-pound rock in the opposite position. Instead, you might achieve stability (although not necessarily balance) by creating an intricate and beautiful asymmetrical pattern of rocks on the barge. So stability is a larger, more expansive experience of the number two than balance.

We are referring to the vibration that the number two resonates with, not necessarily to two objects or two things. Similarly, the number one resonates with a penetrating focus that can be simple in nature, in the negative pole, but also pur-

---

181

poseful and direct in the positive pole. It doesn't necessarily involve one thing.

Michael's comments above give some insight about how stability and balance relate to artisans. Artisans tend to have an aesthetic sensibility that looks for stability, or at least balance, in their creations. However, it is more than that—it relates to creating something that works.

Stability is not merely an aesthetic issue; it is germane to all creation. It implies that the whole works together—something stable is not expected to fall apart. Artisans, with their five inputs, bring together diverse elements. If these elements are not stabilized, there is no true creation, although there may be artifice, which has its own kind of balance. Stability is the foundation of creation. Artisans can easily become unstable, which undermines their ability to create.

ALTERNATE NUMBER CORRELATIONS

Here, again, are the correlations of the numbers one through seven with the roles, as well as with the planes of creation, as given in the Yarbro books.[8] Also included is the center that correlates with each plane but not necessarily with the role in the same position. For instance, the number two position role is artisan. The second plane of creation is the astral, which has an emotional quality and correlates with the emotional center. However, the role of artisan correlates with the intellectual center, since both are on the ordinal side of the expression axis.

Incidentally, I earlier mentioned that being in a sixth cadence position connects one with the astral plane, and the seventh position connects one with the causal plane, facilitating channeling. The astral plane is second, not sixth, but the upper astral is "home" to the sixth soul age, transcendental; the sixth position helps one "plug in" to guidance on this level, at the same time giving a messianic (sixth) plane feeling or resonance. It is similar with the seventh position. (Chapter Twenty-Nine covers "Infinite and Transcendental Souls.")

---

[8]See also Chapter Twenty-Seven, "Planes of Creation."

NUMBERS WITH ROLES, PLANES, AND CENTERS

	ROLE	PLANE	CENTER
One	Server	Physical	Physical[9]
Two	Artisan	Astral	Emotional
Three	Warrior	Causal	Intellectual
Four	Scholar	Akashic	Instinctive
Five	Sage	Mental	Higher Intellectual
Six	Priest	Messianic	Higher Emotional
Seven	King	Buddhaic	Moving[10]

In studying the chart above, it might seem more logical if the roles were rearranged to correlate with both the planes and the centers, as in the chart below. That would also make the ordinal and cardinal roles mirror each other. For instance, if the role of warrior were in the number one position rather than server, it would correlate with the physical plane. Then it would mirror the buddhaic plane and the number seven role of king, with which it shares the action axis. It would also correlate with the physical center, which is on the same axis. Following out this reasoning, the number two position would be server, mirroring the number six role of priest. It would line up with the emotional center, which is also on the same axis. The number three role would be artisan, mirroring the number five role of sage. It would line up with the intellectual center, which is likewise on the same axis. (With positions four through seven, the roles, planes, and centers already line up.)

ALTERNATE ROLE AND PLANE CORRELATIONS

	ROLE	PLANE	CENTER
One	Warrior	Physical	Physical
Two	Server	Astral	Emotional
Three	Artisan	Causal	Intellectual
Four	Scholar	Akashic	Instinctive
Five	Sage	Mental	Higher Intellectual

---

[9]Called the "sexual center" in the Yarbro books, and the "moving center" in some other Michael books. See Chapter Twenty-Two, "Centers."

[10]Called the "higher moving center" in some other Michael books. See Chapter Twenty-Two, "Centers."

| Six | Priest | Messianic | Higher Emotional |
| Seven | King | Buddhaic | Moving |

It would also be easy to make a case for the positive and negative poles of the numbers one to three, as channeled in Yarbro, applying equally well to these alternate assignations of role correlations. Servers tend to be purposeful in their dedication to service, but warriors can also be purposeful in their drive to get a job done—in fact, warriors are known as the most focused of the roles. They are also sometimes simple in their outlook. Artisans seek stability and balance in their aesthetic pursuits, but servers are known for promoting the stability of the family, and their presence has a balancing effect. Warriors are enterprising—they are often excellent in business, for example; they are usually not afraid to take the bull by the horns, and take risks. However, artisans are enterprising, too, in that they start a lot of projects. Enterprise fits with the artisan's mission to create new and original things. Artisans also tend to be versatile, in that they often know how to do many things.

All these points suggest the possibility that the number correlations in the Yarbro books were inaccurately channeled. Michael student Phil Wittmeyer proposed just that in an unpublished introduction to the Michael teachings; numbers are particularly prone to error in channeling, and he believes that the first three numbers were switched around.

However, as logical as the alternate correlations are, I see other evidence in support of the accuracy of what was initially channeled.

The entire "Michael-math" chapter in *More Messages from Michael* depends on Michael's original number assignments to the roles. If there was an error in channeling, it was more than just switching around three numbers. As originally channeled, the roles are numbered in order of most ordinal to most cardinal. That appears to be at least part of the rationale of those number/role correlations. Michael makes much of server being the most ordinal role.

Also, even though the same-axis roles don't mirror each other numerically, if we add them together on the inspiration and expression axes, they equal seven: one (server) plus six (priest) equals seven; two (artisan) plus five (sage) equals seven. On the action axis, kings already correlate with seven, but three (warrior) plus four (scholar) equals seven, and, as mentioned, warriors and scholars are known for having a special affinity.

I channeled about this issue, and found Michael's response to be most interesting. As usual when there appear to be discrepancies, there is validity in both points of view.

In one sense, there is symmetry in the reflection of higher and lower planes when correlated with centers and essence roles. In other words, warriors do correlate with the physical plane more than servers do, in the sense that warriors' energy is kinetic, and so is the physical plane's. The same is true for the astral plane and servers, and the causal plane and artisans. However, in another way of looking at it, in terms of cardinality and ordinality, the role of server correlates with the physical plane, in that both are the most ordinal of roles and planes.

You might wonder why the correlations are not the same in both the qualities of kinetic/emotional/intellectual, and ordinality to cardinality. The answer has to do with the structure of this universe. Servers need to be the most ordinal, so that the base of universal function be service and inspiration rather than action. The universe would be a different game if warriors were the most ordinal. The lack of symmetry in relationship to numbers and roles vis-à-vis the axes is deliberate. The fact that each axis occupies a different position in the higher and lower triads[11] ensures that one does not become predominant. If warriors were number one, and kings seven, the action axis would be predominant: first and last are the most powerful positions.

However, beginning the sentient progression with a kinetic plane, the physical, and ending with a kinetic plane, the buddhaic, before rejoining the Tao, makes sense because the first and last planes are closest to the Tao, and pure energy must precede its differentiation into love and truth. Therefore, there is symmetry with the planes.

We caution against looking only for symmetry. The universe must be both symmetrical and asymmetrical in order to grow.

There is symmetry when looking at the planes themselves, and asymmetry when looking at the soul's experience of the planes. The soul's experience of the physical plane, for instance, has a number one, serverly cast to it. To advance on the physical plane, the essence must toil with a steadfastness and even endure drudgery that the server essence is best equipped for. Physical-plane experience must have an inspirational resonance for there to be evolution. An action resonance on this action plane would be out of control.

---

[11]The upper triad is positions five through seven; the lower is positions one through three. Four is in the neutral position.

In addition, the number one resonates with the role of server (on all planes[12]) because in the soul's relationship with other essences, the foundation must be service.

OTHER KINDS OF CADENCES

Primary cadences consist of seven essences of the same role within an entity. Another type of cadence within an entity includes more than one role and preferably, each role represented in that entity. A third type spans the cadre, and other than that, it is like the second type; it contains a member of each entity, and preferably, someone of each role.

A fourth type is like a primary cadence in that it consists of only one role, but it spans the cadre, including one representative from each entity where possible. If it is a cadence of sages, for instance, and there are no sages in a particular entity, that entity will usually not be directly represented in the cadence. A sage with an essence twin in that entity might substitute. To illustrate: if the fourth entity of the cadre has no sages, a sage from the sixth entity with an essence twin in the fourth might substitute. In this case, no member of the fourth entity will be directly represented in this cross-cadre cadence, and it will have two members of the sixth entity.

JP Van Hulle has channeled about other types of cadences. One consists of everyone in a greater cadence who is in the same position within his primary cadence; for example, the seven essences in the number one position form a different kind of cadence. The members of such a cadence might have the following casting: 1/1/1, 1/2/1, 1/3/1, 1/4/1, 1/5/1, 1/6/1, and 1/7/1. She also channeled about cadences consisting of the essence in the first position of a greater cadence's first cadence, the essence in the second position of its second cadence, and so forth, "diagonally" across the greater cadence. The members of such a cadence might have the following casting: 1/1/1, 2/2/1, 3/3/1, 4/4/1, 5/5/1, 6/6/1, 7/7/1. Michael referred to the former as being like major chords in the "music" of the entity, and the latter as being like minor chords. In addition, they mentioned similar kinds of cadences spanning the cadre.

The purpose of the various "secondary" cadences is to bring together those who share certain mathematical commonalities, to

---

[12]The other number/role correlations also hold true on all planes.

take advantage of the unique configurations they provide. They are like a "branch" of consciousness within the entities and cadres that reflect on experience, like a corner of your mind of which you may not be fully conscious. Cadences do not necessarily convene meetings on the astral or higher planes to do something, although they can; even without such meetings, they still function as units of consciousness. The mathematical resonances are still there.

Throughout this book, I am referring to primary cadences when using the word *cadence* unless I state otherwise.

Chapter 12

MALE/FEMALE ENERGY RATIO

Each soul has a certain percentage of male energy and female energy, regardless of the gender of the physical body. For example, a man or a woman might have thirty-three percent male energy/sixty-seven percent female energy. The exact complement is a partner with a ratio of sixty-seven/thirty-three. All else being equal, you have more balancing sex with someone whose male/female energy ratio complements yours. Finding balance, of course, is very satisfying, but you might still be satisfied with a partner whose ratio does not balance yours.

Male energy is directed, focused, goal-oriented, productive, and outward-thrusting or positive-charged (as in a magnet). It corresponds with linear, left-brained thinking, and with doing. Its positive pole (as I channeled it) is exertion and penetration; its negative pole is intrusion. Female energy is creative, process-oriented, unstructured, and inward-drawing or negative-charged. It corresponds with circular, right-brained thinking, and with being. Its positive pole is expansion and generation; its negative pole is chaotic destruction. Female energy conditions the environment, whereas male energy structures it. The male body is designed to put male energy forward, and the female body is designed to put female energy forward, so there is a masculinity just from being in a male body, even when the soul is high in female energy, and vice versa. All else being equal, a man with seventy-five percent male energy is more focused and has more "drive" (not necessarily inappropriately) than a man with forty-five percent male energy, because there is more male energy there to put forward. Of course, the reverse is true regarding female energy and women.

Our male/female energy ratio remains constant from lifetime to lifetime. Although there are those who have a very high percentage of either male or female energy, most of my clients are fairly balanced in their male/female energy ratio, having no less than about thirty percent of each, making it easier to have a fairly complete experience of both sides of the creative process on earth. However, I've never run into anyone having precisely fifty percent of each. This suggests that our essence almost always likes to have at least a slight emphasis one way or another. Perhaps this is because a little imbalance promotes movement; a ratio of exactly fifty/fifty could create an internal stalemate.[1] However, the universe itself contains a balance of male and female energies.

I sense a subtle "shift" when crossing the line from forty-nine/fifty-one to fifty-one/forty-nine. In other words, it is significant which energy is dominant, even if that dominance is slight in terms of percentage. This doesn't imply, however, that if female energy is dominant, one is a female soul, or vice versa; the soul is without gender.

It is like weighing something on a balance scale. Adding one more small weight can tip the balance, and is significant, but its significance is still relative to the overall weight.

Since the feminine is receptive, it is perhaps not surprising that the majority of my clients are at least slightly higher in female energy.

In my observation, whether a person is male or female, it's a little more common for kings, warriors, and priests to be higher in male energy, and for artisans and servers to be higher in female energy, while scholars and sages seem pretty evenly split.

At least for the last few thousand years, the solid roles have generally favored the male body, and the fluid roles have generally favored the female, although there are many individual exceptions to this, as well as cultural variations. Souls choose a body that gives them the best of the particular opportunities for which they are looking. For example, in a culture in which women aren't allowed to read and many men do read, it's easy to see the attraction of the male body for scholars, especially those also choosing intellectual centering. Similarly, in a society in which women are sequestered, many warriors and kings would be enormously frustrated in the female body, although they might feel the need to occasionally incarnate in one anyway in order to maintain a balance. (Of course, they could choose to be female in a different society, but being female in the same society would give them a "taste of their own medicine," if they had participated in sequestering the females.) On the other hand, servers and artisans in that same society might find the female body better suited to their essences and the demands of the male body distracting. For example, if women do most of the handicrafts, that might outweigh the disadvantages of being female for an artisan, who might have less interest in the male activities of a particular culture, such as being a soldier or cowboy.

---

[1] I have heard Michael say through other channels that someone's ratio was fifty/fifty, but my impression was that they were estimating or rounding off numbers.

Our American masculine stereotype derives in large part from several generations in which many warriors incarnated into male bodies to fight the wars and do such things as "win the Wild West." Therefore, warriors, even with higher female energy in a female body, can seem masculine in this culture. The same is true of kings, and to a lesser extent, scholars.

Other factors, such as imprinting and overleaves, also influence the perception of masculinity and femininity. Strong overleaves such as dominance, power, and aggression—and, especially, imprinting from stereotypical role models—can also leave an impression of masculinity. None of this necessarily has anything to do with the male/female energy ratio. Nonetheless, all else being equal, someone with higher male energy is likelier to be thought of as being more masculine, and someone with higher female energy is likelier to be thought of as being more feminine.

Aidan Quinn, a high-male-energy artisan actor, is known for his blend of masculinity and vulnerability. (Sensitivity is an asset for creativity and is fairly common among artisans.) When Quinn played Stanley Kowalski in *A Streetcar Named Desire* on Broadway, a role made famous by high-male-energy warrior Marlon Brando, he was criticized not for his acting, but basically for not being a warrior with a large body. A warrior or king, even with higher female energy, can seem more "macho" to us than a high-male-energy server, artisan, or scholar, generally the most gentle of the roles. I met a scholar with seventy-one percent male energy but with a goal of acceptance, an overleaf that can also contribute to a gentle demeanor. His high male energy is not immediately obvious—he's sweet rather than macho. However, his high male energy is demonstrated by his large amount of accomplishment, and he can be aggressive in his own way. His doing is not the same as warrior or king action—much of it is writing, for instance—but he does direct a great deal of his energy into the outer world.

Male and female energies are not separate—they are "two ends of the same stick," opposite ways in which energy can move. A person's male/female energy ratio describes his tendencies of function rather than a static state. Even someone very high in male energy sometimes uses female energy; the "end of the stick" a person uses depends on the circumstance as well as his individual proclivity.

Male energy is sometimes referred to as "focused" energy, and female energy as "unfocused" or "creative" energy. *Focused* is a word often used by Michael students, and it can have slightly different meanings in different contexts. For example, warriors are the most focused of the roles, in the sense of having the most concentrated (earthy or dense) energies. This is reflected in their auras, which are usually compact and intense, as opposed to the auras of artisans, which are usually diffuse and soft. Warriors also have the strongest tendency to concentrate their attention; when a warrior is doing something, he tends not to be aware of other things, whereas an artisan, with five inputs, can hold five awarenesses simultaneously. Since male energy is also more concentrated than female energy, this is another reason we tend to associate warriors (and kings) with masculinity.

However, male energy is concentrated or focused in a different way: it is directional, whereas the focus of the warrior relates to density. Although all warriors (and kings) are action-oriented, the earthy power of a high-female-energy warrior, particularly in a female body, is less inclined to be directed at a particular goal than the power of a high-male-energy warrior, particularly in a male body. High-female-energy warrior women may also be drawn more to the inward or "mystical" "battle," rather than "charging" into the outer world. Even if the female energy isn't that high, the female body, in emphasizing the female energy that is there, can have a similar effect. However, the quest to overcome challenges (or, in the case of kings, to develop mastery) is still evident.

Male energy is similar to a laser beam: both move in one direction at a time, act on something else, and are designed for achievement; lasers, for instance, can be used to drill a hole in a diamond or perform eye surgery. Female energy is unfocused in the way that light from an incandescent bulb is—both move in all directions at once, providing an environment in which the creative process can occur; one can read and write, for instance, "within" a bulb's light. It could be said that male energy acts, and female energy receives action, or provides an atmosphere in which action can occur. Female energy also generates raw material for male energy to shape.

Here's another analogy: if water is energy, then water in a river is male energy, moving in a particular direction, and water in a lake is female energy, creating an environment for an abundance of plant and animal life.

Male and female energies cannot exist without each other. To make yet another analogy, if male energy is likened to an automobile engine, female energy is like the fuel the engine processes in order to propel the automobile forward. The fuel allows the engine to realize itself, but the reverse is also true: the engine allows the fuel to realize itself, to experience its value.

Male energy is more about shape, and female energy is more about content—that's why men tend to take care of a house's exterior, and women, its interior. Intellect is also more about shape, and emotions are more about content, which is why men tend to emphasize intellect, and women, emotions. Of course, cultural imprinting plays a part in this, and there are many individual exceptions to this, based on centering and role, in addition to male/female energy ratio, among other factors.

It would be valid to say that female energy creates within itself, and male energy creates outside itself. Both father and mother, for example, are obviously essential to create new life in the form of a baby. However, the mother provides the womb in which the creative process unfolds. This illustrates why female energy is also called "creative" energy—new things, whether ideas or babies, germinate and gestate within female energy. The father's role in pregnancy is more catalytic, although ideally, he also supports and protects mother and child (protection relates to shape), helps deliver the child into the world, and helps shape its development in it.

Another example of female and male energies working together is in the arts. Although the word *creative* here refers to any process of bringing forth something new, not merely to artistic creativity, artists generally emphasize female energy in their work. They can benefit greatly from the male energy function of a good agent, manager, dealer, or whatever, to help them shape their creations and put them out into the world. Male energy, being focused, helps manifest what is created and facilitates its impact in the world. Male energy is also responsible for the editing and shaping that is necessary in any artistic accomplishment.

The movement of life throughout the universe could be said to be based on the interplay of the feminine and masculine, or of being and doing. Male/female is a primary duality, and other true dualities are parallel to it: light/dark, order/chaos, yang/yin, hard/soft, rough/smooth, day/night, and so forth. Although light, order, and so on occupy the same position on their respective polarities as do dark, chaos, and so on, it should not be assumed that they are synonymous; they apply to different realms. Their correspondences can be educational, but each pair of dualities should be considered separately.

Today, many of us are trying to understand just what male and female energies are, since we are calling the old rigid stereotypes into question. There is a risk of replacing old rigid stereotypes with more politically correct rigid stereotypes. The destructive aspect of the masculine has been emphasized in recent years, but both the feminine and the masculine have destructive sides. (The evil witch in fairy tales is an example of the destructive feminine.) Love is the ultimate nature of everything, so it is not just the feminine that is loving. We tend to think of female energy as nurturing simply because it is undirected—it includes everything—but perhaps one could say that the feminine loves and nurtures in a being way, and the masculine does so in a doing way, and that we are each capable of loving in both ways.

As with everything else described in the Michael teachings, these energies can be talked about in terms of the ways they tend to behave, but they are not sets of behaviors. Energies are beyond behaviors, and can manifest in a variety of them. It can be difficult in this society to perceive and experience male and female energies directly, apart from our imprinting about them. Meditation can be a useful tool for this. When I have asked in meditation to put aside my conditioned beliefs and let my male energy come to the forefront of my consciousness, it has felt more dense, in the sense of being more weighty or thick, than female energy, parallel to the way that the male body is more dense than the female body. It makes sense that something more focused would feel denser. The two energies definitely feel different, but both are very beautiful in their pure state.

The unstructured quality of the feminine is not random in the sense of lacking order—it is experimental. Perhaps the term *creative chaos* is useful here to describe an aspect of the true feminine. Our society tends to fear and suppress all chaos, just as it has suppressed the feminine, but creative chaos is not destructive. In fact, it is a necessary part of the creative process. Like right-brained thinking, it leaves room for new things to develop. Rightly, the masculine and feminine serve one another, the masculine catalyzing and giving form to what the feminine creates through chaos. Each is necessary. Put another way, being makes space for doing, and doing expands being, when they are in right relationship to each other. If the masculine suppresses the feminine, the whole suffers, including the masculine's ability to do. We need balance between the masculine and feminine, both internally and externally.

There are many aspects of this balance. A soul that has several male or female lifetimes in a row, for example, can become unbalanced. The first lifetime returning to the other gender can be an uncomfortable adjustment. What it takes to maintain balance is different for each individual. One person may like to have seventy percent of his lifetimes be male, while another might feel balanced with fifteen percent. Those with substantially higher male energy usually prefer to have more male lifetimes than female, and vice versa. However, it is a matter of individual choice, and there are exceptions. In any case, virtually everyone has at least some male and some female lifetimes.

On average, those who have sixty percent female energy have about sixty percent female lifetimes, but there is variation among the roles and from individual to individual. The choice also depends on whether the male or female body is more appealing based on what is going on in the culture at the time. Right now, it is very interesting for scholars to be female in this culture, but that was not the case a hundred years ago.

Those with, say, seventy-five percent female energy are probably going to be at least a little uncomfortable at times in the male body, and might choose to have even less than twenty-five percent male lifetimes—they may have as few as ten percent if the male body feels foreign to them. But they may be completely comfortable during male lifetimes when they are not pressured to act outside of essence, pressured to be too focused or aggressive—for example, in a rather pacific culture—and when they have good, comfortable imprinting. So it is hard to generalize.

Although those who have very high female energy tend to avoid the male body, those who have very high male energy tend to avoid the female body even more. Those with high male energy need to put that energy out; there must be outlets for that that the female body might not provide in a repressive culture. So those with seventy-five percent male energy may have almost a hundred percent male lifetimes, especially among warriors and kings, who have a particular need to do. In the female body, they can suffer a great deal when their culture does not allow females to do anything of much outward significance.

However, there is also a problem if such souls avoid "taking their medicine" and having some female lifetimes. Although women will tend to be attracted to their intense male vibration, women will also tend to be frustrated by their almost total lack of understanding of them.

The most magnetic attraction for men having seventy-five percent male energy would be with women having seventy-five percent female energy. That can be even irresistible, but in terms of long-term marriage relationships, high-male-energy men might actually get along better with high-male-energy women. They are not so mystified by such women. Also, high-male-energy men and women can use their male energies cooperatively in doing things together, unless the men are intent on keeping the women subservient (which they often are if most of their lifetimes have been in patriarchal cultures).

Women who have more often been male in recent lifetimes are used to male prerogatives and are more likely to fight for equal rights as women. Women who have more often been female in recent lifetimes may be more conditioned to inequality and therefore may tend not to question it as much.

The type of body we are used to and our male/female energy ratio can affect our sexuality as well.

Souls high in male energy—let's say over seventy percent—are more likely to strongly emphasize heterosexuality in male lifetimes and be homosexual in female lifetimes. Souls high in female energy—say, over sixty-five percent—are more likely to emphasize heterosexuality in female lifetimes and be homosexual in male lifetimes, although less emphatically so, because the feminine is receptive; therefore, it can receive a soul of either gender who has high male energy.

This does not suggest that women with high male energy and men with high female energy are likely to be gay. Michael is simply stating that they are gay more often than women with high female energy and men with high male energy. Keep in mind that same-sex couples often have complementary male/female energy ratios.

Role is another factor in sexual orientation. Men and women of every role are gay and bisexual, but it is more common among sage and artisan males, and among scholar and priest females, because they tend to fit in least to our society's rigid gender stereotypes. For example, there are not a lot of male role models for sensitive, creative artisan boys, or for flamboyant, expressive sage boys; therefore, they may adopt female role models, or at least rebel against male stereotypes.[2] The majority of gay men do not fit the "flaming" stereotype, even the sages and artisans, but that stereotype owes more to the expression-axis roles than to the others: the love of fashion and decorating is in the artisan domain, and the love of high drama (opera, old movies, and larger-than-life stars) is sagely. (Those who seem to fit that stereotype are not necessarily sages or artisans— stereotypes, once established, take on a life of their own. Any boy who feels that he doesn't fit in as a male might adopt it as his identity.) Although the large majority of people of all roles, including the

---

[2]There are, of course, other reasons why someone may be gay or bisexual. For instance, Michael has said that older souls can be bisexual simply because they remember many lifetimes as both male and female and therefore are not strongly identified with their current body, since the soul has no gender. Also, they have said that virtually every soul will have at least one gay lifetime, since it is part of the "curriculum" of the physical plane. See also Chapter Twenty, "Sexuality," in my Summerjoy Michael book *Loving from Your Soul—Creating Powerful Relationships.*

expressive roles, identify as being heterosexual, the fact that artisans and sages dominate the arts also partly explains the high number of gay males in the arts. I also suspect that many stereotypical "fag hags" (women drawn to gay men) are sage and artisan females who sympathize—they may remember male lifetimes when they were in the same predicament, or may also dislike the "John Wayne" stereotype. (This is nothing against John Wayne, who was channeled as being a moving-centered young warrior in dominance and aggression; however, he was obviously not an appropriate role model for every male.)

The lesbian stereotype owes more to the scholar and priest roles than to the others. Although priests are inspirational and are, in a sense, a feminine role, priests also tend to be powerful and catalytic—like kings, they need to be received by the world; they want to have impact, if only spiritually—which has not, in general, been a trait much appreciated in women, although that is changing. Also, as mentioned, priests have a slight tendency toward having higher male energy. Scholars, as also mentioned, have tended to prefer the male body in recent millennia (like warriors and kings) and may not be completely comfortable in the female body. They also may not fit our society's female stereotype: scholars are often highly intelligent, and that can be threatening to patriarchal males. Also, like the other solid roles, they tend to express themselves in a straightforward, no-frills way, without the effulgence often associated with the female stereotype.

To a lesser extent, warriors and kings also provide some of the basis of the lesbian stereotype, which one might expect, since, as mentioned, these roles are also the basis of our masculine stereotype. Nevertheless, warrior and king women in general fit in to society's expectations a little better than priests and scholars do, since they can adapt to any structure fairly well—they can "get with the program" if it seems to be working. Also, warriors and kings tend to be highly sexual, and although warrior and king females may be attracted to other females if they have been male frequently, they may also want heterosexual experiences, which tend to be more sexually "explosive." (Even if they are exclusively heterosexual, they can still be at least somewhat the dominant partner.)

The business world, in emphasizing competition and bottom-line achievement, sometimes uses male energy in a distorted, extreme way, although much of business is naturally more male-energied. Since both men and women have both male and female energies, it isn't a problem for either sex to work in business. However, in my observation, higher-male-energy women seem to be more comfortable with it than higher-female-energy women. Sometimes a woman with higher female energy working in business feels brittle to me, as if she has to supplement her male energy with an artificial hardness to cope in the business world. She may have taken an executive position, for instance, because of lessons she wants to work on, such as being more assertive, but it may not feel very natural to her. A man with higher female energy may also not be all that attracted to the more aggressive aspects of business, but the male body makes coping with it easier, since, as mentioned, a person's male energy is forward in the male body. A woman with high male energy, especially if her role is warrior or king, might feel perfectly at home in an aggressive business environment, and might enjoy the additional challenge of opening the way for women in business.

The mean male/female energy ratio among the 1050 essences of the Michael entity is about fifty-four/forty-six, reflecting the fact the kings and warriors tend to slightly prefer having higher male energy. However, Michael's overall cadre, which includes all roles, has a mean ratio of about fifty/fifty.

On the level of the cadre, there is virtual equality of male-female energy ratio in most cases. On the level of the entity, there can be a slight tilt, and our entity has a little bit higher male energy, but that is not the main reason we come across as being more masculine. The fact that we are warriors and kings also adds to the perception within your culture that we are more masculine. However, the main reason is that those fragments who are interested in speaking through a channel rather than, say, researching or working energetically often have higher male energy.

Is that because in speaking, they're "protruding" into another reality?

Correct. The fragments who work through channels nonverbally to create atmosphere and "make for the event" tend to be higher in female energy.

So even on higher planes, there is reciprocity between those with higher male and higher female energies.

Chapter 13

FREQUENCY

Our frequency is the rate of vibration of our essence on a scale of one to a hundred. Slow frequencies feel steady, stable, or substantial. Fast frequencies feel effervescent, ethereal, or airy. Frequency ranges could be compared to solids, liquids, and gases such as ice, water, and steam. As with male/female energy ratio, the frequencies of my clients, more often than not, are midrange, from about forty to seventy, which suggests that it is more common to be "liquid" than to be "solid" or "gaseous."

Those with slower frequencies tend to move through their experiences more slowly and with a greater steadiness than those with faster frequencies. We don't mean that they are slow in their actions, but that they tend to move through the steps of their lives more slowly, with a definite, regular rhythm. On the other hand, those with rapid frequencies can tend to buzz, so to speak, with an edge and an uneven rhythm. They do not necessarily complete the physical plane more quickly, but they can have the same amount of experience in forty years that a slow-frequency person has in seventy—it is as if their engine runs faster. However, an experience at high frequency is not the same as one at low frequency. Frequency is another characteristic that allows for variety.

You usually feel most comfortable with people whose frequency is within about twenty points of yours. That puts you, in one sense, "on the same wavelength."

Priests and artisans tend to have higher frequencies. Kings, scholars, and especially warriors tend to have lower frequencies. Sages and servers can run the gamut. However, each spark is individual and may choose to vibrate at whatever frequency it wishes. Those who differ from the norm can contribute something valuable.

For example, high-frequency priests could be compared to steam that naturally leaves the pot when its lid is removed. They often like to "space out," dream, or meditate, leaving their bodies a lot. This allows them to connect with the higher elements of life. A relatively low-frequency priest may experience his priestliness in a more grounded and earthy way. Since priests tend to want to get beyond the physical plane, it is good to have some priests who have more natural resonance with it.

Frequencies are permanent for the whole grand cycle. However, you may not always manifest your frequency accurately. Someone who has a slower frequency may have been imprinted as a child to express himself at a higher one, or vice versa. If you are tired or overstimulated, that can affect the frequency you manifest as well.

Body type, role, and overleaves can affect the way frequency appears. For example, my frequency, sixty-four, is above average, but my body type, lunar, is the most passive, calm, and slow-moving of the seven types. [1] Also, neither my role, essence twin role, nor any of my overleaves are on the action axis except my chief feature, impatience. So I tend to move slowly unless I am deliberately doing otherwise (or am impatient). These factors do not modify my frequency itself—my fundamental vibration is still relatively quick and airy—but at first glance, someone might think that my frequency is lower, especially if my normally animated sagely expression is subdued. (The effervescence often associated with sages can be mistaken for high frequency, but sages can be effervescent on a lower musical pitch, so to speak.) On the other hand, if I had a mercurial body type, aggression mode, and so forth, someone might think that my frequency was higher than it is.

High frequency and low male energy (and vice versa) often accompany one another—they balance each other. A person who combines high male energy with the "buzziness" of high frequency can be intense, in the sense that his energy is moving both quickly and outward. I know a sage who has a frequency of eighty-one *and* seventy-two percent male energy, as well as a goal of dominance, passion mode, skeptic attitude, emotional centering, and a chief feature of impatience. I thought of stamping his chart "Warning—Danger!"

Likewise, people with low frequency and high female energy are often laid back and quiet; their energy, which is moving slowly to begin with, is drawn inward.

No configuration is "good" or "bad." In fact, there are pros and cons to every configuration of role, overleaves, frequency, and other factors of essence. Each is like a unique color scheme we chose for its unique creative possibilities.

The role itself has a frequency separate from the person's individual frequency. Artisans and priests are the high-frequency roles. An artisan with a frequency of thirty has a lower pitch, a slower and greater steadiness of vibration, than one with a frequency of seventy-

---

[1] See Chapter Twenty-Four, "Body Types."

five, but still feels airy compared to any warrior because of his role. However, his personal frequency would make him comfortable with a warrior whose frequency is around thirty, because they vibrate at about the same speed as individuals—they are both relatively "low-key"; the frequency of the role is separate. You might say that every trait described by Michael occupies a separate layer in a person. Referring again to the analogy of overtones, the vibration of one's role occupies a different octave or "band" in one's overtone series than the octave where one's individual frequency vibrates.

The mean frequency among the 1050 essences of the Michael entity is about forty-seven, reflecting the fact the kings and warriors tend to slightly prefer having a lower frequency. However, Michael's overall cadre, which includes all roles, has a mean frequency of about fifty.

Chapter 14

PREVIOUS CYCLES

As mentioned earlier, a grand cycle is the big "loop" beginning with the spark taking on an essence. It continues through having a series of lifetimes in a particular life form capable of sentience[1] on the physical plane of a particular planet (or group of planets that have space travel between them), and completing the higher planes of that planet. It concludes when the spark integrates its experiences back into the Tao.

Most people have completed cycles on other planets before beginning their current cycle on earth. Just as a series of lifetimes may have a theme, so may a series of cycles. Some of the people we are close to in this cycle may have been with us in previous cycles. For example, an essence mate is a person who was our essence twin[2] in a previous cycle. When I included essence mates on Michael Reading charts, about half of those I channeled listed at least one essence mate. Essence mate relationships tend to be close and deep, but without the intensity of the present essence twin relationship; they are like relationships with former lovers who are now good friends. Some of us also have close relationships with people who were our task companion[3] in a previous cycle. There is no term for this relationship, but we generally work well with such people; the relationship is task companion-like, but not as compelling.

As a tree grows, it generates concentric internal rings that can be seen when it is cut. Similarly, each lifetime puts a "ring" of experience "around" our essence, and each grand cycle puts one around our spark. When this cycle is complete, it will be fully integrated into our spark, just as when this lifetime is complete, it will be fully integrated into our essence. The core of our spark is unchanging. It is the ultimate "I" who experiences.

---

[1]Sentient souls are those who have self-awareness and can function intellectually. (See Chapter Twenty-Six, "Sentience.")

[2]Our essence twin is the soul closest to us, and most similar to us on an essence level. See also the subchapter "Essence Twins" in Chapter Seventeen, "Relationships," or the Glossary.

[3]A task companion helps us with our life task, and vice versa. See also the subchapter "Task Companions" in Chapter Seventeen, "Relationships," or the Glossary.

Four is the average number of previous cycles for human beings in general, and the average for Americans is five and a half.[4] The highest number for anyone on earth is nineteen. The man Jesus, for example, before the entrance of the infinite soul,[5] had nineteen previous cycles; he was relatively very experienced at the planetary "game." Buddha, on the other hand, had fourteen, and Krishna had thirteen, more commonly found numbers. The average member of the Michael entity has had about eight and seven-eighths previous cycles, with eighteen being the highest number of any fragment in their entity.

The number of previous grand cycles of my clients has ranged from eight to eighteen, and eleven or twelve is most typical. I have run into a couple of people who were said by Michael to have had eleven and a half or fourteen and a half previous cycles. Somewhere along the way, they cut short a cycle and went "back to the Tao" early. That is something like suicide, but on the essence level.

The Tao is always generating new sparks for sentient cycles. There are people on earth with no previous cycles, although they likely have had other universal experiences.[6] However, it would be more typical for such a spark to join an entity on a less complex planet. Also, essences with a relatively high number of previous cycles more typically incarnate on more advanced planets where the average number of previous cycles is higher. Such planets are all over, but in general closer to the center of the universe than earth. They are often quite intellectually and/or technologically oriented, even in their early stages. Their infant soul cycles produce societies that are more complex than an earth infant soul society, although they are still characterized by relative simplicity. By the mature soul cycle, such societies tend to be more advanced in their abilities to work together cohesively and even telepathically, like one large or-

---

[4]These figures apply only to human beings. According to my channeling, dolphins and whales, earth's other sentient species, have an average of about six and two-fifths previous cycles, making the average for both of earth's sentient species (humanity along with dolphins and whales) about four and three-fifths.

[5]An infinite soul is not an individual "fragment" of an unrecombined entity, as we all are; it is a representative of a reunited cadre bringing the Tao to bear directly on the physical plane through one of the three high planes. A seventh-level old soul who is complete with the physical plane "walks out" of his body, and the infinite soul "walks in." The four historical manifestations of an infinite soul were through Jesus, Buddha, Krishna, and Lao-tzu. See also Chapter Twenty-Nine, "Infinite and Transcendental Souls."

[6]Other universal experiences include being a deva, being part of the consciousness of a star, or helping design new planets. There are countless other "jobs" available.

ganism. This could look to us like individuality is sacrificed (extraterrestrials visiting earth are often described as lacking individuality and emotion), but it's just a different game. Entities and cadres are more unified on the physical plane in such cases.

Those on such planets might find the lack of complexity here a little boring. Earth is considered "suburban"—not quite the "sticks," but not "cosmopolitan" either. However, every planet has unique challenges, and earth is a particularly important experiment, primarily about balancing opposites. Also, everything is by choice, so everyone who is here has chosen, on some level, to be here.

The more sentient cycles a spark has had, the higher its level of sentience, because it gains experience. It becomes more complex, with increased capacity for subtlety and nuance. It is like a later model of a machine being more sophisticated, with more parts, than earlier models, because of what was learned through the earlier models. Nevertheless, no doubt the earlier models worked fine, and future models will make those that are now state-of-the-art look simple— everything like this is relative. We exist on an infinite continuum. Someone with nineteen previous cycles looks quite complex on earth, but might look simple on a more cosmopolitan planet. Likewise, someone with two previous cycles might look complex somewhere else. Even someone with no previous cycles is sophisticated compared to nonsentient consciousness. It is also true that everything in the universe is perfect as it is.

One Michael student wrote me that he had been channeled by another Michael channel as having had three previous cycles. After reading an article I wrote that discussed the subject, he felt inferior. It is possible that the channeling he received was referring to something else—terms can be defined differently through different channels, or there might be different ways of measuring such things as previous cycles.[7] Even if the channeling was referring to the same thing, increased complexity does not make one superior. I know two people with eighteen previous cycles: one is a loving and "enlightened" person; the other looks like a mess. The point is not to be complex but to expand the Tao through the expression of love through our uniqueness. An infant soul with no previous cycles who has agape, or unconditional love, at his level is "winning the game."[8]

---

[7]In general, I seem to get higher previous cycle numbers and lower soul ages (see Chapter Fifteen, "Soul Age") than some of the other Michael channels whose channeling I hear about. I do not know if that is because of differing clienteles, semantics, or inaccuracies.

[8]The final state of agape is one of total unconditional love for everything. Michael considers this to be the ultimate goal of all sentient evolution.

In general, those with more previous cycles can better afford the luxury, so to speak, of studying something "nonessential" like the Michael teachings, since they have had more practice with the basics of physical plane life. Although each planet has new lessons, there are certain skills common to all physical-plane experiences, so the repetitions are helpful. It is like proficiency at one sport making it easier to learn another.

Michael told me that the previous cycle concept was not given to the group responsible for the Yarbro books (although it was hinted at) partly because they didn't feel that the books' audience was ready for it. The more fundamental material is difficult enough to grasp. Another reason may be that the group didn't ask about it.

On another occasion, when I asked about the history of earth, they said that at one time, there were two separate strains of sentients on land, those with a relatively high average number of previous cycles, and those with relatively few. The so-called higher sentients inhabited ethereal bodies (physical bodies at a faster rate of vibration than our present bodies), while the "lower" tried out various experimental bipedal mammalian forms that the higher sentients regarded as animals. At that time, the whole earth, including all its life forms, was of a lighter density. The "fall of man"[9] and of the earth itself into a heavier density had to do with the higher sentients mating with the lower, and with true animals, which created sometimes-pathetic half-breeds or "things" of various kinds. An earlier version of our present body was brought in from planets in the "Dog Star" system as a solution to the problems that resulted, "standardizing" the sentient body for humanity. It was similar to the lower sentient bodies already here, and therefore was easily adapted to this planet.[10] However, it was more sophisticated in its mental capabilities. It allowed for a broad range of sentience levels to incarnate, although our present version of it is now less flexible and more dense than it was originally, because of the heavier density of earth itself. Although our present body is still fairly flexible, it may be too complex for some and too limited for others; some souls feel like they're "in over their heads" and others feel hamstrung because the "human animal" just won't seem to do what they want it to. Despite these limitations, most of us are able to at least "make do" and put our human sojourn to good use. Dolphin and whale essences occupy a narrower range of

---

[9]Michael told me that they dislike that term because it is judgmental.

[10]In experiments in which people are not exposed to sunlight or clocks, they begin to go on twenty-five-hour-day schedules, sleeping and waking an hour later each day. According to JP Van Hulle's channeling, the planet our bodies were "imported" from had twenty-five hour days rather than twenty-four.

sentience, somewhere between the human extremes in terms of number of previous cycles, although their average number of previous cycles (six and two-fifths) is higher than that of humanity (four).

Many members of Cadre Three began their present cycle as infant souls in these bodies on planets in the Sirius system, and continued it on earth after they were transported here. Since that was so long ago, it doesn't affect them much now. There are very few other cadres still incarnating that came to earth mid-cycle. One (that I am not familiar with) is just now beginning to incarnate here; it is from a recently exploded planet relatively close to earth, according to my channeling.

Also, some of us completed a cycle on earth in the ethereal life form, rejoined the Tao, and then began another cycle in these human bodies, since every life form allows for a unique set of experiences. It is very rare for a spark to have two cycles in the same life form on the same planet; that would be like getting the same degree at the same college twice.[11]

Not only was our present body useful in solving a problem here on earth, it needed a new home anyway. Its previous home was five interrelated planets where another sentient species dominated. As our species began to host sentient souls in their infant soul cycle, it was in danger of enslavement as if it were an intelligent animal. Also, two of the five planets, where it might have become dominant, became uninhabitable—one exploded, and one became poisoned by gas leaking from its core. Eventually, working under essence-level agreements, more enlightened members of the dominant species, who wanted to protect our species, "seeded" earth with it. According to JP Van Hulle's channeling, "Bigfoot" sightings are of members of that

---

[11]Before channeling information on the "fall of man," I had been exposed to other channeled material on this subject by Ceanne DeRohan in *Right Use of Will* and Ruth Montgomery in *The World Before.* (Contact me if you're interested in reading excerpts from what I have channeled about *The Right Use of Will*—I may write a paper on the subject.) I had also been exposed to information about Sirius and other historical material that came through Michael channel JP Van Hulle. In my channeling, Michael drew on and integrated some of this material, adding new insights and information (such as on the sentience levels).

I would be in a better position to channel on this subject with depth and breadth if there was more raw material in my subconscious. If some ambitious scholar waded through all the sometimes-contradictory metaphysical literature about earth's history and wrote a concise summary of the various views, I could probably channel a reasonably complete and accurate overview, tying most of it together. In the meantime, I present the information here as incomplete, but perhaps of interest anyway.

dominant species who are continuing to observe the progress of their "experiment."

In the following, Michael explores the relationship between soul age (one's age on a particular planet) and previous cycles.

Since I completed all the soul ages on several planets before this one, does my soul age on this planet matter?

You have never experienced second-level mature on this planet. You were once on a planet, for example, in which your life form was plant-like; it did not move very quickly. The processes of photosynthesis were your predominant experiences. Your day-to-day life was very different from your life here. In addition, that cycle was not as a king, but as a scholar, so that also changes your experience. Although the fundamental lessons of second-level mature on that planet are relevant to you now, the facts of them are not. Therefore, you have the opportunity to strengthen and expand those lessons, to experience them in different ways. That is why you came to this planet. It offers new horizons, new combinations of factors.

Some spiritual teachers say that time is an illusion. That statement is valid, although it is also true that time is real within its scope of influence and cannot be ignored. For instance, the fact that time is an illusion is not a valid excuse for being late for an appointment made beneath the convenient umbrella of physical-plane time. [12] However, even on the physical plane, time is not all-encompassing or totally rigid, and in the large picture, everything is simultaneous—the inter-relationships of the various levels of our inner reality are not governed by time. "Now" is a higher reality than time; everything exists now, not now in this moment in time, but in the now that is beyond time. These interrelating levels of reality include our previous (and potential future) cycles. Although our spark *experiences* them progressively, they also exist simultaneously: our previous cycles are all present in our spark like integrated subpersonalities.

When you are focused in the Tao, you might never think about your past planetary experiences, although the fruits of them are manifest in your spark. Only when contemplating another cycle might past cycles be recalled and reviewed. That is when they are most relevant.

---

[12] See the chapters "Time" and "Beyond Time" in my upcoming Summerjoy Michael book *Being in the World.*

Chapter 15

SOUL AGE

SOUL AGE	FOCUS	PERCEPTION[1]
INFANT + innocent openness – terrified aversion[2]	Survival	Me, not me
BABY + formation and structuring – rigidity	Structure	Me, other me's
YOUNG + worthwhile accomplishment – self-centeredness	Success	Me, you
MATURE + resonant perception – subjective perception	Relationships	You as you perceive yourself
OLD + inclusiveness – undirectedness	Context	You as part of something greater
TRANSCEN- *DENTAL*	Social revolution	Synthesis
INFINITE	Spiritual revolution	Tao

---

[1]To expand on these summaries, here are quotes from *Messages from Michael*, pp. 70-79, "The infant soul perceives itself and the world around it as simply 'me' and 'not me.'...The baby soul perceives itself and the world around it as 'me' and 'many other me's.'...The young soul perceives itself as 'me' and it perceives you as 'you.'...The mature soul perceives others as they perceive themselves....The old soul perceives others as a part of something greater that includes itself....The transcendental soul perceives the synthesis....And the infinite soul perceives the Tao."

[2]I channeled these positive and negative poles for the five soul ages usually experienced on the physical plane. I do not consider them to be the "ultimate" terms, but perhaps they fill a gap, at least for now.

WHAT IS SOUL AGE?

O ur physical age is obviously the age of our body, which advances during this present lifetime only. Our soul age advances over our many lifetimes on this planet. The age of our spark, which roughly correlates with our number of previous cycles, advances over our many planetary experiences. So someone can be young in body, old in soul, and be a "middle-aged" spark—or any other combination. Each kind of age affects our perceptions in specific ways.

Physical age is measured by the number of years we have lived. However, it could also be described by the stage of development we are in, with its unique lessons and vantage point from which we view the world. Infants, by necessity, see things in terms of their survival. Babies look for structure, something they can hold onto while they're learning to walk, figuratively as well as literally. Youngsters begin to learn to master the outer world. Adolescents begin to cultivate their inner world and one-on-one relationships. College-age post-adolescents develop an overview, gaining a greater sense of the context of their lives. And so forth.

Physical aging occurs at a similar pace for everyone, since it is largely dictated by biology. However, we cannot measure soul age using the number of years or lifetimes logged, since the soul develops through experience, not just through "putting in time." Therefore, we categorize it in terms of changing perspective, parallel to the stages of an individual lifetime: infant (infancy), baby (toddler), young (childhood), mature (adolescence), and old (post-adolescence). Completing the old soul cycle, and hence, the physical plane, is like college graduation for the soul.[3]

Being called a baby or an adolescent, for instance, is usually considered derogatory when describing an adult. However, the terms and analogies used to convey what the soul ages are about are not derogatory in any way—they are only illustrations designed to show the parallels between the processes of human development within an individual lifetime and the development of the soul over many lifetimes. Soul ages simply tell us the types of lessons that are dominant

---

[3]Analogies have their limitations, and should not be taken too literally. In *Messages from Michael* (p. 90), Michael compared soul ages to the stages of education, using a slightly different analogy: infant soul—kindergarten; baby soul—elementary school; young soul—high school; mature soul—college; and old soul—out in the world. However, elsewhere (p. 55) they say, "The mature soul has all of the conflicts of the celestial adolescent or young adult," suggesting that mature souls could be compared to either the high school or college ages. No doubt, other analogies could also be used.

at particular stages. Our soul age is where we are on a "loop" that actually has no beginning or end. Being a younger soul does not prevent us from being on the spiritual path or from doing anything we wish to do, although each soul age tends to be interested in certain activities more than others due to the specific emphases of the age.

> *Soul age perspective relates less to the way you think about things when you deliberately think about them—your philosophy, for instance—and more to how you habitually see things when you are washing dishes or driving a car. It is your view from the mundane, so to speak.*

The chart at the beginning of the chapter summarizes how those of each soul age perceive other people. Infant souls do not yet have a basis for making sense of what is "out there"—they only know that it is "not me." Baby souls, focused as they are on bringing people together under the umbrella of civilization, see others, sometimes simplistically, as being "just like me." They can become confused and upset when those "other me's" act differently than expected. Young souls, learning to impact the world, see others as "you"s they can impact. Mature souls, delving into their inner world and exploring relatedness, can keenly feel other people's "stuff," and perceive it in the same way they perceive their own. This can make for much intensity and, often, subjectivity. Old souls tend to be more detached, and try to see themselves and others within a larger context.

Transcendental and infinite souls will be covered in Chapter Twenty-Nine. These souls normally dwell on higher planes and very rarely come directly to the physical plane; when they do, it is to assist in social or spiritual transformation. A transcendental soul is a representative of a reunited entity, and an infinite soul is a representative of a reunited cadre. Transcendental souls perceive others as self and directly experience what others feel. Infinite souls exist in oneness with everything, almost to the same extent as the Tao itself, since the infinite soul is the Tao's "messenger."

Soul age describes our primary perspective and lessons with regard to the physical plane. When we are astral, we are not focusing on learning about physical-plane survival, structure, success, relationships, or context, so soul age is largely irrelevant (although our overall level of development is not). Our perspective from the astral plane regarding the physical plane is relatively neutral, because it comes from outside the physical-plane game. It's similar to when you finish playing in an athletic event—the game looks different from the locker room than it did on the field. Another analogy is being on vacation from school: practically speaking, it matters little whether you're a freshman or senior when you aren't "cracking the books." Our existence on the astral plane has its own lessons, but they are relatively unstructured and might be viewed as "extra-curricular" when compared to the physical-plane curriculum.

The majority of my clients are mature souls, with old souls accounting for most of the rest. Once in a while, I channel for young souls. So far, I have never channeled privately for a baby or infant soul. This is probably typical of most Michael channels, except that there are many old souls in northern California, so channels there may see more old souls than mature.

The average soul age on earth today is sixth-level young, but within fifty years or so, it should be first-level mature; this is called the "mature-soul shift." It is a momentous time for humanity because we are not only moving into a new average soul age, but we are changing directions. The infant, baby, and young soul cycles all move in the same direction—toward greater focus on the outer world. Once that is reasonably well mastered, the soul changes direction; upon beginning the mature soul cycle, it starts moving toward greater focus on the inner world. The old soul cycle moves in the same direction as the mature, taking the mature soul lessons to a higher level.

I don't notice much difference in general between my mature and old soul clients in terms of their degree of interest in and dedication to the spiritual path. The main difference I perceive is that mature souls feel more intense and dramatic, whereas old souls feel more casual, light, and airy (unless they are carrying substantial unresolved traumas, but that is still relatively on the surface). Also, mature souls tend to concentrate on the more immediate, two-dimensional aspects of their relationships (their specific, direct connection with another person), whereas old souls tend to see their relationships within a more complex web of three-dimensional interrelatedness.

According to *Messages from Michael*,[4] "The baby souls and infant souls together equal the number of old souls now." However, in the Winter 1987 issue of a short-lived publication of new material from the Yarbro group, *The Michael Messenger*, the following breakdown was given: ten percent infant, twenty-three percent baby, thirty-two percent young, twenty-four percent mature, and eleven percent old. (This was said to be valid for cetaceans—dolphins and whales—as well as for humans.) This breakdown seems reasonable to me. Perhaps the wording of that quote should have been: The infant souls (approximately) equal the number of old souls now.

---

[4]Pp. 79-80.

Through me, Michael gave the following breakdown of soul ages in the U.S.: three percent infant, fifteen percent baby, thirty-eight percent young, thirty-two percent mature, and twelve percent old.

Yarbro gave mottos for each of the soul ages:

INFANT:	Let's not do it.
BABY:	Do it right or don't do it at all.
YOUNG:	Do it my way.
MATURE:	Do it anyplace but here.
OLD:	You do what you want and I will do what I want.

A client asked Michael through me for more positive restatements of them. This is what they came up with:

INFANT:	Let's try it.
BABY:	Let's do it well.
YOUNG:	Let me apply myself to this situation.
MATURE:	Respect my boundaries.
OLD:	Let's respect different points of view.

SEVEN SOUL AGES

Although we only experience five soul ages on the physical plane, we will each experience being a member of our entity and cadre when they are reunited on higher planes. In other words, we will experience the sixth and seventh soul ages, transcendental and infinite, but probably not on the physical plane.

Laeh Maggie Garfield, in her book *How the Universe Works*, suggests a scheme of seven soul ages that are experienced by everyone on the physical plane: *infant, toddler, teenage, adult, mature, old,* and *volunteer*.[5] Her explanations differ from Michael's in various ways, but in general, her approach is similar. She seems to arrive at seven physical-plane soul ages by dividing Michael's *mature soul cycle* into *adult* and *mature*. Her designation *volunteer soul* would be described by Michael as a "seventh-level old soul transcendental," who has no remaining karma and could cycle off, but reincarnates mainly to be helpful to others. Her terms *toddler* and *teenage* are fundamentally equivalent to Michael's terms *baby* and *young*. She describes each soul age, and the seven levels of each soul age, as correlating with the chakra in the same numerical position.

---

[5]Garfield does not mention the source of her ideas.

SOUL AGE LEVELS

There are seven levels to each soul age. In our first physical-plane lifetime, we are a first-level infant soul. We may have one lifetime at that level, or ten, depending on how quickly we complete that stage. Some souls (especially priests) like to complete each level as quickly as possible, while others (particularly scholars and warriors) like to take their time and have a more thorough experience, not missing anything that looks interesting; it is an individual choice, and it is not "better" to go more quickly or slowly. Your choice is what is right for you, and it benefits the Tao for there to be a variety of "speeds" in this regard. After completing first-level infant, we move to second-level infant, and so forth. Normally, when we complete a level, it is at the end of one lifetime, and we begin our next lifetime at the next level, but it is also possible to move from one level to the next in the middle of a lifetime, particularly if we didn't have much left to finish from the earlier level. When we complete seventh-level infant, we move into first-level baby and repeat the seven levels higher in the spiral, so to speak. When we complete seventh-level old, we "cycle off"—that is, we no longer incarnate on the physical plane. We start a new "game" on the astral plane.

Each soul age level is a particular stage in the realization of that soul age's perspective. I like the analogy that JP Van Hulle channeled, comparing the levels to going to the beach: At first level, we stick our toe in the water. At second level, we are in the water up to our waist (half in and half out). At third level, we dive in and are completely submerged. At fourth level, we reemerge, fully "wet" with that soul age's perspective. At fifth level, we splash around and play. At sixth level, others splash us. And at seventh level, we return to the shore.

At first-level mature, for instance, a person is just beginning to see the world in terms of relatedness; much of his perspective is still focused on the outer world, as it was when he was a young soul, although he has a feeling of needing more than worldly success. At second level, a person is drawn more deeply into mature soul perspective, and can compare it to young soul perspective. Then there is a need to reconcile those two views, which can lead to inner conflict: "Which is more important, career or relationships?" for instance. The third-level mature soul is fully enmeshed in mature soul perspective, but doesn't yet have the ability to confidently operate in it out in the world. He may feel the need to be less public while he discerns and evaluates. (Since the young soul cycle is about success, the third-level young soul may be more active in the world than before, but still without full confidence.)

Fourth level is in the middle—three levels have gone before, and three more are to come. It could be seen as the balance point, the place where the soul feels, "I've got it!" He is fully functioning at that soul age's fundamental perspective—his foundation is in place—and can authoritatively carry it into the world. The fourth-level mature soul feels confident of his abilities in relationships. His relationships tend to be intense and central in his life, which may look at times like a soap opera, as can that of any mature soul, but the drama can be fun, too.

Naturally, once the foundation is in place, the soul wants to expand in new directions, which he does at fifth level, accessing and integrating more peripheral strands of experience. The fifth-level mature soul may have unusual or even eccentric ways of being and relating to others. At sixth level, the soul "looks at his watch" and says, in effect, "I'm almost done with this soul age, and I need to tie up loose ends, particularly with other people." This is a busy time for the soul, and can require many lifetimes to complete, particularly if the soul has a lot of karma to repay. Since the mature soul cycle is the most intense soul age to begin with, a person who is sixth-level mature can have a difficult time. After a few lifetimes of repaying difficult karmas, he can look shell-shocked, a little like one of those cartoon characters who keeps getting hit over the head with a frying pan, so that tweety birds are flying around the bumps. It is especially important for those who are at the sixth level to stay up to date with their internal processing of their experiences so that they develop conscious awareness; otherwise, they can quickly develop a large "backlog." It can also be helpful for anyone who has had a difficult life of paying back much karma to realize that that is just a phase of development—every soul has lifetimes like that—and doesn't indicate that he is a "bad person."

Seventh level reminds me of an old McDonald's commercial, "You deserve a break today...." Especially after the rigors of sixth-level mature, the soul feels ready for less intensity, and although there is still plenty of work to do, there can be a tendency toward complacency or even laziness. At seventh-level, the emphasis is on completing unfinished business with oneself rather than with others. Since seventh level is the culmination of the soul age, the soul wants to review what he has learned during all seven levels before moving on. A good way to do that is to teach it to at least one other person (the cardinal roles may teach it to many).

In Chapter Eleven, "Cadences and Numbers," we discussed the positive and negative poles of the numbers one through seven. The list is reprinted below, since these poles also apply to the seven soul age levels. At the first level, we enter into the purpose of the soul age, perhaps oversimplifying it. At the second, we stabilize our new perceptions, in the least balancing them with those of the previous soul age. At the third, we work to fully use our new perceptions profitably in the enterprise of our life, or at least with some versatility. That leads right into the fourth level, at which we consolidate (which means "to unite into one system or whole, to make strong, secure, firm, or coherent") that soul age's perception, or can at least comfortably achieve from it. At the fifth level, we expand the perceptions of that soul age, or at least have adventures with it. At the sixth, we harmonize or at least forge connections among the soul age's various lessons and loose ends, especially with other people. And at the seventh level, we inculcate (instill) the lessons all the way through ourselves and at least one other person; we sum up the soul age, or at least eclectically contain the individual elements of it.

POSITIVE AND NEGATIVE POLES OF NUMBERS

One	+ Purpose	- Simplicity
Two	+ Stability	- Balance
Three	+ Enterprise	- Versatility
Four	+ Consolidation	- Achievement
Five	+ Expansion	- Adventure
Six	+ Harmony	- Connection
Seven	+ Inculcation	- Eclecticism

MANIFESTED SOUL AGE

On my Michael Reading charts, I channel both a person's true soul age and the soul age he is manifesting at the time I channel the chart. Our manifested soul age is the average level of our personality's perspective at a given time; it can change relatively rapidly if it is lower than our true soul age. I've had clients who rose from manifesting second-level mature, for example, to fourth-level mature in a matter of months. Our true soul age is our level of potential function, the perspective of our inner self. It is more significant and impactive than our manifested age, which is more on the surface.

In every lifetime, we manifest first-level infant at birth, since our body is not capable of sustaining a higher perspective; our true soul age may be evident, but it is not engaged, because on the level of personality, we have to focus on infant soul lessons such as survival. As we get older, our manifested soul age can increase up to our highest level of previous attainment in past lifetimes. However, we might become stuck at a certain level, at least in some area of our life. For example, a mature soul may manifest young because he doesn't want to face some difficult relationship issues; he's more comfortable focusing on success. Or an old soul may manifest mature, because he is not willing to give up some attachments. It is similar to an adult being emotionally younger than his true age in some way because of a trauma that occurred in the past—he is staying at that place until he is willing or able to deal with it.

We also might deliberately manifest at a particular level longer than would otherwise be necessary to review some lessons. For example, an old soul may need a "brushup" on young-soul lessons regarding success and money, and may spend the first half of his life focused on business endeavors. I am not implying that everyone working in the business world is manifesting young—it is more subtle than that. Our manifested soul age is the dominant focus of our lives, no matter what we are doing externally. Someone manifesting as a mature soul in business, for instance, is likely to be most interested in the relationship aspects of business, even if he is required to spend a lot of time dealing with other aspects of it.

Soul age manifestation is sometimes a mixed bag. A fifth-level old soul may be manifesting young in the area of money, for example, mature in the area of relationships, and old in most other areas. The energies that these perspectives generate might combine to form a composite manifested age of seventh-level mature. Since it can be an average, manifested soul age may not always seem to completely fit. Again, true soul age is more important anyway, since it describes the real person rather than what is happening at the moment on the surface.

Surprisingly, soul age can sometimes advance even if it is not fully manifested.

If someone is manifesting a younger soul age, he may still be gleaning valuable experience. He may, for example, be on his last lifetime as a first-level mature soul, and his review of some baby and young lessons may be all he needs in order to move on to second-level mature.

A third-level old soul may not have developed fully in certain types of relationships when he was a mature soul. For instance, he may have developed a strong mature-soul perspective in sexual, male-female relationships, but not have had much experience with mature soul male bonding. Maybe he did not have much opportunity.

In any case, when a problem arises in this area, he may not have many resources to fall back on. He may simply not know how to share emotional intimacy with another man, how to trust without being competitive. He is where he would have been as a mature soul when he would have normally first handled this issue. Doing so now might help him advance to fourth-level old. Once he integrates the mature soul lessons in this area, he is likely to move on to old soul lessons in it, since that is his true perspective. Old soul bonding, by the way, is deeper, yet less personal.

He does not have to manifest third-level old in all aspects of his life to advance to fourth level, as long as he fills in the gaps he needs to fill.

A person may also need to review some lessons that he already learned because they have not been reinforced for several lifetimes. As the saying goes, "Use it or lose it."

Once, Michael commented on a chart:

Steve is manifesting slightly higher than his own soul level due to imprinting.

He was sixth-level mature manifesting at seventh. I would have thought that impossible, but the client confirmed that it was true. I suppose that means that he is living from a perspective that he has not yet "earned." Perhaps it is like the disciples of spiritual masters who are given experiences they couldn't have had on their own, and who then must grow into them. Since Michael has only made this comment through me once, I assume that this sort of thing is rare.[6]

In the following passage, Michael discusses how a person can benefit from being imprinted by an older soul without actually manifesting older than his true soul age.

A mature soul, for instance, virtually never manifests old. However, if he is imprinted by someone who is old, he can learn helpful skills.

Suppose that a busy forty-five-year-old has a seventy-two-year-old semi-retired friend. The semi-retired friend sees the workaday world from a perspective that is farther away. He has come through its drama and knows what is on the other

---

[6]Psychic John Friedlander suggested that a person could also manifest older than his true soul age when combining energies with other essences who are older. See "Combined Essence Energies" in Chapter Nine, "Roles."

side. Therefore, he does not take it as seriously as the forty-five-year-old does. The forty-five-year-old can adopt some of his friend's philosophy of life, learning to be more detached, but he is still in the midst of the workaday world—he has not yet come through the other side of it, so he does not yet know for himself what his friend knows.

Likewise, the mature soul is still in the midst of the drama of life. He cannot stop being in it while he is still in it. It would not be beneficial to skip over that whole portion of development. He would always be hobbled by the lack of that experiential movement. But he can learn from old souls, who naturally find it easier to have a detached viewpoint (although they do not always have it either).

Mature soul lessons are just as significant and valid as old soul or any other lessons.

Many older souls who have manifested younger than their true soul age for a number of lifetimes are beginning to manifest more accurately because of the media. The media provides a way for any group to know about and communicate with other members. For older souls, who see the world in a larger way than the average or mainstream person, there are now many books and other media that help reinforce that way of seeing.

Manifesting our true soul age is not the same as manifesting our essence, which occurs after we dispose of whatever childhood imprinting we carry that taught us to appear different than we really are—we begin to look like our actual role and overleaves across the board. We can manifest our essence without yet manifesting our true soul age, and without necessarily being in the positive poles of our role and overleaves (which is the experience of true personality). After we are manifesting our essence, we will occasionally be in our negative poles, like all human beings, but at least they will be *our* negative poles, not a simulation of our parents' or someone else's negative poles.

Sometimes people are distressed to learn that they are not manifesting their true soul age—they see it as a sign that they are behind in their spiritual growth. That is not necessarily the case. This idea stems in part from the belief that "older is better" when it comes to soul age. We may feel more integrated when we manifest our true soul age, since our inner and outer perspectives are more aligned, but perhaps a more accurate indication of where we are spiritually is how much we are in our positive poles.

217

CAN SOUL AGE REGRESS?

Once we have been through a developmental experience, it cannot be lost. We may forget its lessons, but the experience is always there to draw upon. Therefore, soul age does not regress, and it is rare for manifested soul age to backtrack as well. When someone seems to regress in life, it is usually due to an increase in false personality—in other words, he is going into his negative poles more frequently; his false ego is more in control, and his essence, less. But this doesn't necessarily mean that he is manifesting a younger soul age. Any soul age can be experienced from either positive or negative poles. Soul age simply indicates the nature of our lessons, not whether we are succeeding in them.

Once, Michael indicated that a person who had "sold out" may have dropped back a level or two in manifested soul age, but that it wasn't a significant change; the minor backtracking wasn't the "selling out." If, for example, he had been manifesting third-level mature, which is a quiet time of internalizing mature soul perspective, and later he began to again manifest second-level mature, which is a time of balancing young soul (outer world) and mature soul (inner world) lessons, that was not the cause of the increased dominance of his false ego.

Someone who seems to be regressing may actually be moving forward but be meeting new, more difficult challenges that have temporarily "thrown him for a loop."

OLDER IS NOT BETTER

It is not better to be an old soul than to be mature or young, just as it isn't better to be forty-five years old than it is to be thirty-two or fourteen. A young person may be wise, and an old person foolish. A baby soul may be loving, and an old soul spiteful. People of every soul age are capable of manifesting their true personality—that is, of acting out of their positive poles, which are motivated by love. Younger souls are simply less experienced than older souls, not having completed as many monads.[7] They are less fully tested, one could say.

Having compassion for others through knowledge of oneself is possible at any soul age.

---

[7] See the subchapter "Monads" in Chapter Seventeen, "Relationships."

An infant soul can be appropriate and responsible, but is not ready to handle larger responsibilities. He is generally not attracted to situations beyond his abilities. It is similar to a child, who can be appropriate and responsible, but for a smaller sphere than an adult can be. You would not expect a five-year-old to hold down a nine-to-five job, for example.

Advancement is not as important as experience. You do advance, because you are in motion, but you are here to experience life in every facet. Some facets of life are easier than others, but each step of development is necessary. If you were to skip over one, you would be left with a gap.

The more conscious you are in your growth process, the more quickly you grow. However, this does not necessarily translate into moving more quickly from second-level mature to third-level mature, for instance. It is not necessarily desirable for you to move from second to third mature as quickly as possible. Your soul age simply indicates your point of perspective. It is not inferior to be second-level mature rather than third-level mature; all points of perspective are valid. However, if you are ready to move from second mature to third, and you bring more awareness to the process, it may happen more quickly because you will be in a better position to avoid becoming stuck.

On the other hand, it may be appropriate for you to have an extensive experience of being at second-level mature. If that's the case, you will do so more expansively if you are growing consciously, but you will not necessarily finish it more quickly. The object of the game is not to move through the soul ages as quickly as possible. It is to move through them in the way you choose to move through them. Choice is the "name of the game." Some people are more attracted to the mature soul perspective and spend more time in it; others are more attracted to the young or old-soul perspectives. It is individual.

Soul age is similar in some respects to physical age. When you are sixty, no matter how intelligent, mature, appropriate, or healthy you are or are not, you go through certain experiences; the sixty-year-old body brings with it a certain perspective—you cannot escape that. Likewise with the eleven-year-old body: an eleven-year-old girl may mimic a seventeen-year-old, wearing makeup and dating, but she probably does not yet have the physical capacity to support a sexual relationship, for instance. Two eleven-year-olds can be quite different, yet both *share the eleven-year-old experience. In the same way, two people of the same soul age share a common perspective, even though the specifics of their lives may be quite different.*

Old souls tend to be tolerant and inclusive, and at least try to be open to other ways of looking at things. However, they may become upset by people whose points of view are rigid and exclusive. So if they are trying to respect different points of view, they may not respect people whose points of view do not respect other points of view.

So they can't be tolerant of intolerance?

They can be, but because they're still learning this tolerance, still learning to see the larger picture, this can be a touchy issue. They may become indignant when others are overtly intolerant—they project their issue. They are at a more advanced level in this lesson than younger souls, so they can be a little arrogant about the fact that they would never be so overtly intolerant. Nonetheless, they know that they are not really completely tolerant either, so it can be a struggle.

Overt intolerance would probably not evoke the same level of reaction from, say, mature souls, who are more likely to just shake their heads in dismay and want the "offenders" to get as far away from themselves as possible—they do not want others to project feelings into their space that are going to be difficult for them to process—but they will not necessarily think about it further.

Mature souls need to have their emotional boundaries respected. Baby souls are generally more concerned with behavioral boundaries than emotional ones, so they do not tend to become "bent out of shape" if others are, say, emotionally ugly in their space, although they might be appalled if the behavior seems inappropriate. Mature souls, however, would tend to take in that ugliness, and therefore need to keep others out of their space when they cannot process it. Although they may know their own boundaries, they do not automatically know what other people's boundaries are, since they tend to be rather subjective, so others may need to tell them.

It is hard to understand a soul age older than your own. However, every soul age is arrogant about other soul ages in certain ways. As mentioned, old souls can be arrogant about those who are intolerant. Mature souls can be arrogant about those who are not taking life as seriously as they are, who do

*not care as deeply and fervently about their values or who do
not take values seriously at all. Young souls can be arrogant
about those who are not able to cut it in the world, those who
seem to be misfits. Baby souls can be intolerant of those who
are not "following the program," who are not being a "good boy"
or girl, falling into line. And infant souls can be arrogant toward
those whom they think are making life too complicated or who
are too disconnected from the practical aspects of survival.*

*Everyone looks at things from his own point of view, and
that is why the Michael teachings are offered—so that people
will understand that there are good reasons for others seeing
things differently.*

It is ironic that in our society, most people want to be physically
young, but those who learn of the Michael teachings often want to be
old souls. Part of the reason for this is confusion over the term *old
soul*. In common new age parlance, saying that someone is an old
soul is a compliment; it implies depth and innate knowledge. However, in the Michael teachings, it simply refers to a particular stage in
our developmental process.

Being an old soul is not all that different from being physically
old. Whether speaking of our body or our essence, being old means
that we have gone through particular stages of experience, which
may or may not result in increased wisdom. Wisdom relates to having
a conscious awareness of the meaning of one's experience, and is
available at any stage. Naturally, a larger perspective can come with
greater experience, but that is not, of itself, wisdom.

Anyone manifesting his true personality—that is, anyone in his
positive poles—is having a degree of essence contact within, no matter what his soul age is or how many previous cycles he has had.[8]
This is a function of orienting in love. Essence contact, with our own
essence or with that of another person, brings growth and wisdom.

Soul age identifies how old we are on this planet, as opposed to
how many other planetary cycles we have experienced. The impression of being an old soul, as it is meant in common new age parlance,
can derive from many factors, but the number of previous cycles
probably contributes more to that than soul age as Michael defines it.

---

[8]Essence contact occurs when the personality makes a direct connection
with either his own essence or the essence of another person. It is necessary
in order for spiritual growth to occur. It can be a powerful and life-changing
experience, or relatively mild. Even though your essence is, ultimately, who
you are, your personality can be cut off from it by being identified with a false
ego and acting too strongly from the illusion of separateness.

Having had many previous cycles does impart the look of having been "around the block a few times."

Just as a person who is twelve years old in this lifetime can seem wise because he's had many past lives, a person can be young on this planet but seem deep because of having many other planetary experiences "under his belt." A young soul with fourteen previous cycles may in certain ways appear older than an old soul with five, although the young soul is primarily outwardly focused, whereas the old soul emphasizes the larger context and tends to be more casual about life on the physical plane. The young soul remembers, on some level, having been a mature and old soul fourteen times before. The circumstances each time were unique, but the fundamentals were the same.

If we think of the old soul cycle as being equivalent to being in college, an old soul with three previous cycles might be compared to a person attending a community college, whereas someone with ten might be compared to a person attending a state university, and someone with seventeen might be compared to a person attending a rigorous private college—each is at the same point in his process, but with different levels of complexity.

However, soul age, number of previous cycles, and also physical age are merely quantitative measures of potential levels of sophistication or complexity. The depth and quality of the specific lessons that an individual has gained are at least as important. Extensive spiritual study and practice, for example, or simply maintaining high levels of integrity, in this lifetime or in past lives, can contribute to the impression of being older. A young soul (as defined in the Michael teachings) who has lived many lifetimes with a relatively high consciousness tends to seem older than an old soul who has not. Imprinting by older souls can also give an impression of being older.

We must be careful in these and all other teachings not to classify people. We are each incredibly vast and complex, and the measures and descriptions provided by the Michael teachings are not intended to pigeonhole people. We are not limited by the elements described in these teachings; rather, they focus us, making us more specific. Anyone can choose to study and pursue the spiritual path, no matter what quantity of experience he has had in terms of soul age or previous cycles. However, those with more experience are more likely to gravitate toward it; those with less experience may feel that they have their hands full dealing with the basics of physical-plane life.

Although the Yarbro books stated that each soul age has its merits and that no soul age is better or worse than another,[9] the descriptions of the soul ages may sound most complimentary to the old soul. As mentioned, they stated that the old soul motto is "You do what you want, and I will do what I want" whereas the young soul motto is "Do it my way." Although there is certainly truth to this, it is important to catch the spirit of Michael's words, rather than adhere to the letter of them, especially when they are obviously generalities. In another example of generalities in *Messages from Michael*, Michael said that young souls almost always seek higher education, usually graduate degrees.[10] If the average person on earth is a young soul, that would imply that the average person seeks graduate degrees. Obviously, that is not the case—the average person on earth cannot afford higher education of any kind, although he might desire it. However, the spirit of what Michael said here is clear: young souls are motivated toward the greatest possible outer accomplishment, in whatever sphere. This manifests more obviously in people with higher male energy, which moves outward and is naturally more achievement-oriented than female energy. It is also more obvious with warriors and kings, who are motivated to seek challenge and mastery, respectively. (Incidentally, discerning distinctions between similar-sounding characteristics, such as male energy's focus, and young souls' motivation toward success, is very helpful in learning the Michael teachings well.) Still, anyone will tend to seek success more at the young soul age than at the others—a young soul priest in the clergy, for instance, might have the ambition to become the head of his church, whereas an old priest would not likely seek that position for its own sake; he would probably have to feel that holding it would bring much good to all concerned. Otherwise, he most likely wouldn't bother.

The reason young souls may give evidence of the motto "Do it my way" more often than those of other soul ages is that their lessons are about impacting the outer world. Some do that more appropriately than others. I know young souls who have learned to respect other people's points of view, and older souls who have not.

Young souls do not yet have the ability to see a lot of perspectives at once. They can be tolerant, certainly, but the very nature of the young soul cycle does not lend itself to an overarching view of reality. There is much emphasis on individuality and success, so it is easy to see why the young

---

[9]*More Messages from Michael*, p. 28.

[10]*Messages from Michael*, p. 72.

soul would often want you to do things his way. Although this is not the highest possible point of view, it does not necessarily indicate negative pole function. There are young soul philanthropists, for example, who are genuinely motivated by a desire to use their success for the benefit of others. In fact, they may measure their success by how much they are able to do for others, which is a very enlightened approach. They may think that others should do what they are doing, or at least that more people ought to do it, and there would be much truth in that opinion.

Each soul age has a higher or larger native perspective than the one preceding it. The old soul perspective is to leave other people alone, to let them do what they need to do in life. Although you might be able to teach a young soul this in principle, it is not so easy for him to see why he should do this and to apply this principle, particularly when it gets close to home— for example, with other family members. Of course, it depends on his role, too—a young king or warrior will almost have to imprint others with his way of doing things, whereas an artisan in submission may still want you to do things his way, but not as intensely.

Young souls need to apply themselves to their environment, not so much to make others "do it my way," but just to have the experience of having maximum impact. They actually are not necessarily all that attached to a particular way; if you can show them a more effective or workable way, they will generally quickly adapt to that, as long as they can internalize that way and then apply it to the environment themselves. That can manifest as the type of person who always has to think that your idea was actually his.

The young soul need to impact the outer world is not the same as warrior persuasion (positive pole) and coercion (negative pole), which come from who they are rather than from their soul age perspective. Warriors carry an organic, instinctive drive to structure the world, to act in it with power. The young soul perspective is focused on the outer world, but it can manifest through the expression, inspiration, or assimilation axes as well as through the action axis. That young priest in the previous example would be motivated to rise to a high position within his church as part of the development of his ability to deal with the world's structures. A young priest who is a doctor might have a goal of becoming the Surgeon General, the head of the AMA, or the chief administrator of a local hospital. That doesn't mean that he will be chosen for the desired position, but he has a built-in motivation for seeking it. Since we are in the world for many lifetimes, we certainly don't want to come and go without ever having learned how to make full use of the institutions here. The young soul cycle is the time when obtaining those skills is emphasized. People of other soul ages may also seek a high position, but their main reason is likely to be different. A mature soul who wants to be the Surgeon General might see it primarily as an opportunity to find more meaning in his life, or even to do something great in the world. (Mature souls are responsible for the majority of artistic masterpieces, for instance, because the mature soul cycle concerns exploring our depth, seeking the profound.) The young priest might also care about his life having meaning or about achieving greatness, but that is not likely to be his dominant reason for seeking a high position. Young souls emphasize spreading their wings, so to speak.

Young souls test their self-sufficiency and independence to see how much they can do on their own before beginning the mature-soul process of developing interdependence. I know a young soul with wealthy parents who is a single mother. She works as a bartender and accepts little money from them except for her daughter's education—she strongly values making it on her own. I, on the other hand, as an old soul, would probably be perfectly content to live on the dole of wealthy parents!—that is, if there were no major strings attached. I have felt ready to "retire" since childhood. I have little need to accomplish in the world, except as that gives me opportunities for expression (which sages require) and, specifically, to complete my life tasks. Like most of us, I do have to work for a living, which has the advantage of helping keep me productive and careful about how I use my time. Without direction, old souls can easily succumb to laziness, since achieving success or even greatness is not a strong motivation. Old souls tend to take the attitude, "Well, it won't matter a hundred years from now" (I know an old scholar in his eighties fond of saying that) whereas mature souls tend to take the physical plane more seriously than the other soul ages—everything tends to matter a lot to them. *Messages from Michael*[11] referred to old kings who are "vagabonds and hoboes" and to old artisans' "unfinished masterpieces." Old souls often do have high standards of excellence, but must have strong reasons to follow through: either the requirements of survival, or preferably, a sense of mission. It is ironic that issues about survival, prevalent during the infant soul cycle, can reemerge as the old soul prepares to cycle off. There are many old soul "New Agers" who barely make it financially. Unlike young souls, old souls are little able to suffer hardship in order to "make it to the top." If

---

[11]Pp. 100-101.

they don't like what they're doing, they have a hard time making themselves do it. They can seem undisciplined, but they can be quite disciplined relative to tasks they care about. Old souls tend to take the longest time of any soul age to come into their own, to "find themselves." Part of the reason is that the older the soul, the more levels he has to review before manifesting his true soul age.[12] Most old souls do not manifest their true soul age before their mid-thirties, if they do at all. (Roughly two-thirds of all people never fully manifest their true soul age, whatever it is.)

Of course, any soul age can have problems related to survival. Obviously, even young souls can lose their jobs, for instance, and have trouble keeping food on the table. Mature souls can be so absorbed in their inner process that they have little energy left over for making a living. In the U.S., those of all soul ages and roles who are trying to support themselves in the arts often have a difficult time making a living unless they've made it to the top of their field, since there is so little support for the arts and so much competition. Furthermore, even many young souls would be glad not to have to work for a living, particularly if they didn't like their work (and were still able to "keep up with the Joneses"), although they might seek success in other ways. A young server I know would prefer to stay home and raise her children full-time, although she is quite successful in her career. She might define success in terms of how well she is able to take care of her children, or she might feel that she has already demonstrated her ability to be successful in her career, so that she no longer feels the need to continue to pursue that. This brings us back to the fact that the Michael teachings are about energies rather than specific behaviors. Each soul age has a particular energetic quality and perspective that can be discerned, even if, for example, a young soul does not appear to be highly oriented toward outward success, as it is usually defined, during this lifetime.

A few people have asked me, with a little awe, what it is like to be seventh-level old. A couple of people have even been suspicious that I "awarded" myself that designation. Being seventh-level old is not an award or worthy of awe, despite beliefs to the contrary. We live in a society that tends to see things in terms of becoming the "top dog," and being seventh-level old might be interpreted as being the top dog,

---

[12]The scientific principle "ontogeny recapitulates phylogeny" explains why, in the development of a human fetus, it temporarily has "gills," for instance: it is reviewing the stages of its prior evolution, and apparently, gills were once part of our physical ancestors' equipment. In the same way, in a single lifetime, a seventh-level old soul must review each level of the infant, baby, young, mature, and old stages before manifesting seventh-level old. That's why a young soul can come into his own earlier than an old soul can.

in terms of soul age. Since the U.S. is a sixth-level young country (in a sixth-level young world), there are so many people seeking the top positions that it is not surprising that our society is based on a hierarchical view that fosters competition. However, this paradigm is changing, and, in any case, we need to put aside this hierarchical view of life if we are to understand the Michael teachings, or any true spiritual teaching. Again, old is just old.

Like every soul age and level, seventh-level old has its own peculiar traits. Understandably, those who are seventh-level old (or late sixth-level old) are often meticulous about not owing anything to anyone, even in seemingly trivial ways, or otherwise leaving any loose ends in their lives, because of their thrust toward completing not just the old soul cycle, but the entire physical-plane cycle of incarnation. Seventh-level old souls may also have a particularly strong drive to complete a mission of some sort, but they can be especially late bloomers as well, since there are so many prior soul age levels to "review" before manifesting their true soul age. One repays karmas with others during sixth levels, whereas seventh-level lessons are more self-karmic (internal), so seventh-level old souls can have a quality of seeming less a part of the world. Seventh-level old souls can carry the general old soul impression of "marching to a different drummer" to its ultimate. They often have a hard time fitting into schedules or other people's expectations—they can take "what really matters," however they define that, quite seriously, but they are often casual about the form of things. Not every seventh-level old soul is intelligent, wise, or even a "nice" person, let alone "enlightened"—it depends on the individual. But, again, certain kinds of lessons are emphasized at seventh-level old, as with all the soul ages and levels.

Although each soul age brings a larger perspective, no stage necessarily sees things inaccurately. In climbing a mountain, we first see aspects of the valley in great detail, but we don't see the whole thing. When we get higher, we see the panorama, but the details aren't as vivid. Our memory of the details can help us when we reach the higher levels. We need each step—they are all "right." The pleasure is as much in the experience of climbing as in reaching the top. With the soul, every "top" is the bottom of a new level anyway, so there is no end to the journey.

Within an individual lifetime, the goal is hardly to get old and die, but to experience something valuable along the way. Loving parents enjoy watching every step of their children's progress. Likewise, we can see each stage of our own development as being beautiful. Some spiritual people want to finish their development and regain union with the Tao as quickly as possible. If that had been our spark's attitude in the beginning, we never would have chosen to be cast from the Tao.

Granted, the physical plane is not a picnic at this time. We might occasionally wonder what could have possibly motivated us to come here. However, there have been easier, more pleasant times, and there probably will be again. In any case, we will ultimately see everything we pass through as having been valuable.

Some New Age students have been told by other channels or psychics that they are on their last lifetime here, and are confused if they are told by Michael that they are not seventh-level old. A theory has arisen among some Michael students that the soul age pattern will be transcended in the coming "shift."[13] Perhaps movement through the levels will speed up, since there will presumably be less resistance to growth. However, I doubt that they could be dispensed with altogether—soul ages are merely natural developmental stages—and "instant enlightenment" would not be all that valuable anyway. Growth that is not fully experienced and integrated is flimsy. It is like a plant that grows too fast, without developing adequate roots—it can be easily blown over.

Some channels have gotten information that the earth's population will be vastly decreased in the coming times, making far fewer bodies available for incarnation. This could explain the "last lifetime" idea. Perhaps many of us are tying up enough karmic and other loose ends so that we can take extended "vacations." The world we would return to later to continue our cycle would be very different, probably much more pleasant.

We choose whether or not to cycle off. Permission does not have to be granted by somebody else. However, if we try to do it before we are ready, it will become obvious that we weren't ready, and we will feel the need for a "return engagement." If we have not completed seventh-level old, we will not feel ready. It is a little like sex: we may pause in the middle of it, but it usually doesn't feel complete until after orgasm. Being complete with the physical plane can also be compared to an individual lifetime: sometimes people die young, but a life isn't normally viewed as complete unless a person lives to old age.

I asked Michael about Ramtha, a soul on the astral plane who claimed, through channel J.Z. Knight, to have lived only one lifetime, thirty-five thousand years ago in Atlantis. He says he then reached "enlightenment" and therefore no longer needed to incarnate.

---

[13]See the next subchapter, "Planetary Shift."

Ramtha is a warrior who was on his last lifetime, and cycled off. From Ramtha's point of view as a personality, it was his only lifetime—the personality only lives once. From his essence's point of view, it was not.

Most people see enlightenment as a state of all-knowing perfection, which I do not believe is possible. I do not see either Michael or Ramtha as being in that state. To me, enlightenment means being awake to our essence and able to live genuinely in the present moment, in accordance with love and truth.[14] Theoretically, a first-level infant soul could be enlightened, according to that definition, but he would still have an enormous amount to learn, as, in fact, we all do, no matter where we are on the "loop."

Some people assume that they are old souls because of their strong interest in spiritual teachings. However, that is not necessarily the case, and many old souls are not consciously interested in spiritual teachings. Such interest can also be stimulated by imprinting, past-life experiences, overleaves (the attitude of spiritualist, for instance, can contribute), or role (priest, especially), or may simply be an object of study, just as some people are interested in studying animals or the design of bridges.

In addition, being interested in the New Age or in spiritual teachings is not the same as being on the spiritual path, which implies a deep commitment to spiritual values and a willingness to undergo rigorous self-examination. Of course, often they coexist, but there are many people on the spiritual path who are not conversant in spiritual teachings. Likewise, there are people associated with the New Age who are not on the spiritual path, although it is a matter of degree, and no one can judge for certain whether someone else is on the path. Love is what the spiritual path is ultimately about. Love, of itself, has little to do with soul age, although presumably, our experience of love matures as we go along.

Being an old soul does not guarantee being on the spiritual path either—or, as mentioned, even being a pleasant person. There are tendencies in those directions—we might say that an old soul has room in his life for spiritual things because of the lessons already completed. But, as Michael is so fond of reminding us, all is by choice. An old soul may not choose to become involved with spirituality in a given lifetime. He may have other interests that are higher priorities for him. On the other hand, I know many mature and even

---

[14]In *Messages from Michael*, p. 114, Michael defines "enlightenment" as extinguishing the chief feature, which I think amounts to the same thing, since the chief feature prevents essence contact.

young souls who are interested in spiritual teachings and who are on the spiritual path. Nonetheless, the predominant lessons and perspectives of their soul age are evident in their lives.

PLANETARY SHIFT

Messages from Michael gave the average soul age on earth as fifth-level young (it is now sixth-level). Through JP Van Hulle, Michael said that the Harmonic Convergence[15] marked the beginning of the shift into mature soul perception. This may not be a contradiction. In my channeling, Michael differentiated between average soul age and average consciousness. Although the average soul age may still be late young, mature soul consciousness is beginning to have proportionately more influence. This can be observed in the popularization of interests such as ecology, myth, and emotion-based psychologies. These relate to our inner world and to our connection with others, which are of greater interest to mature souls than to young souls. So a person can be a young soul, dealing primarily with young soul lessons, and still have values or a heightened consciousness about issues usually of stronger interest to mature souls.

> *Earth is a young soul planet, but mature soul consciousness is beginning to hold sway. Part of the reason is that young soul separateness, played out to its ultimate negative-pole conclusion, resulted in World War II's awesome destruction. People are disillusioned and open to more connectedness, especially with the specter of nuclear destruction hanging over their heads.*

Although the "coming event" of a mature soul planet is casting its shadow, so to speak, profound change will not likely manifest until the average soul age is actually mature, which will probably occur in about fifty years. Nonetheless, it is undeniable that we are in an important transition. Major planetary change during this era has been predicted for a long time (for example, in ancient Hopi prophecies). There are many ways to look at this.

---

[15]The Harmonic Convergence was a coming together of astrological influences on August 16, 1987 that was said to mark the beginning of the New Age.

The soul age shift is related to the New Age,[16] the astrological shift from Pisces to Aquarius,[17] and the possible polar shift.[18] They all fit together; their timing is not by accident. We choose to emphasize the soul age shift.

The shift from young to mature is the most radical shift that can occur in any people's history. The shift from baby to young, for example, is significant, of course, but it is a movement in the same direction as before, toward more effective and powerful outward function. The shift from young to mature is a change in direction, toward inner and higher values. Of course, this could not occur if there had not first been the young soul cycle. The shift from mature to old again is not a shift in direction, just in focus.

Currently yours is a young soul society in a young soul world. Because of the pervasive mass media, those of other soul ages are conditioned by young soul values. Even infant souls living in tribes now sometimes have televisions and want the material possessions promulgated by young soul media; their surface thinking is along the lines of young soul thinking. As the world shifts to a mature soul consciousness, new values will become more generally accepted, and the media will also likely help promote them, accelerating their spread.

Mature soul consciousness will create societies in which there is more emphasis on caring for those who are less fortunate. There will also be more of a balance between the masculine and the feminine. This should lead to a lessening of aggressive tendencies. There is a possibility that within a few hundred years, war will be completely eliminated. Humanity's ability to destroy the earth can actually accelerate the shift, because it encourages people to realize that it is in their best interests to find peaceful solutions to conflicts.

Young souls are great at building civilizations. The young soul cycle has contributed a great deal—we are not critical of it.

---

[16]The New Age is a long-predicted time of higher human consciousness leading to world peace and harmony. Some people call it the "Now Age," since they believe that we are now in the beginning stages of that time.

[17]According to astrology, the earth moves through approximately two thousand year cycles governed by a particular astrological sign. We are currently in a transition between the Piscean Age and the Aquarian Age.

[18]Many psychics and channels have predicted that a shift of the earth's axis, changing the location of the North and South Poles, will occur around the year 2000. See Chapter Twenty-Two, "The Earth Shift," in my upcoming Summerjoy Michael book *Being in the World.*

But particularly in this civilization, young soul consciousness has manifested in an extreme way. Young souls always tend to be more independent, but the sense of isolation and separateness of young souls in this civilization has been excessive. So this step in your growth will be most welcome, provided you do not destroy the surface of the planet first. That is a very real danger.

Although New Age thinking contains ideas and phenomena that are not embraced by many mature and old souls (such as reincarnation, channeling, crystals, and UFO's), in some ways, the coming of the mature soul cycle is the coming of the New Age—the mature soul cycle is a major part of what is new. However, the coming New Age is also more than that; it is, hopefully, a time of cleansing and transformation, so that the world's vibration is raised.

When did we shift from baby to young?

It was about two thousand years ago.

So obviously, we don't have to have a polar shift, with massive earth changes, to have a soul age shift, correct?

Right. The last pole shift was about twelve thousand years ago.

Were we infant souls then? If so, was Atlantis an infant soul civilization?

Atlantis was at sixth-level young at the time of its demise. The average soul age of a planet is one thing; individual nations have their own average age that may be different. During the time of Atlantis, there were other nations that were at infant or baby soul stages. Atlantis itself began as a nation at late-level baby and went through a wave of maturation all the way through late-level old. Then a new wave of souls came in at predominantly young and again moved through old. Then once more it drew a number of young souls who had spent their infant and baby soul cycles in other civilizations and were attracted to Atlantis because of the particular opportunities that were there at that time.

When Atlantis was primarily young-souled, there were still many mature and old souls around, and infant and baby souls as well. Many infant souls incarnated as servants. (We are not speaking of the essence role, server.) They saw this as a fast track to growth.

This is not the first time on earth that the average human soul age has been late young shifting to early mature. In the course of the progression of sentient life on a planet, there can be many waves of souls progressing from infant soul to old.

We anticipate that the next shift, from mature to old, will occur in about one thousand years.

Why can this be achieved in half the time that it took from baby to young?

People are able to learn from what has gone before; they have the tools to advance more quickly.

Chapter 16

LIFE PLAN

Before incarnating, we usually plan each lifetime in detail. The overall blueprint is called our "life plan." Its centerpiece, the most important thing we want to accomplish, is our "life task." We usually begin working directly on our life task (or tasks—we can have more than one) after completing our "midlife monad"[1] in our middle to late thirties. Although we all have intuitive access to our plan, asking a channeled source about it can validate and shed new light on our sensings.

Rarely (at least in my experience) is a life task specifically to do a certain earthly job, such as to fix television sets. Television might have been just a probability when the life task was chosen.

Here are some examples of life tasks I have channeled: using the entertainment media to inspire in others a love of love and truth; working for world peace on a grass roots level; helping people learn how to survive gracefully and prosper under harsh circumstances; and integrating the lessons of many past lives. All are specific, yet broad enough to have many possible ways of fulfilling them. Of course, these are summaries. One person's life task could fill several pages and have many parts to it. What a channeled source relates is usually what is most relevant at the time. Also, the way that it is stated can vary greatly, since everything in the akashic records must be translated.

Every life task is a focused way of allowing our essence to manifest in our life, and any time we are aligned with our essence, whatever we are doing contributes to our completing our life task, if only indirectly.

Not everything in our lives is planned out ahead of time. Plans are usually made, but they are flexible frameworks within which we create our lives. There are usually several alternatives, and sometimes plans have to be changed.

It's like modifying the blueprint after we start building our house. Perhaps we discover that the land is too wet for a basement, or that brick has become too expensive, so we go with an alternate plan we made earlier. If none of our alternate plans work out either,

---

[1]Our midlife monad is a life passage in which our genuine role, overleaves, and life path emerge wherever they were obscured by what we were conditioned to be. Those who do not successfully complete the midlife monad tend to remain stuck in their restrictive imprinting. See also the subchapter "Monads" in Chapter Seventeen, "Relationships," or the Glossary.

we may improvise a new one that we hadn't thought of earlier but that works fine. Furthermore, the blueprint only specifies the basic design of the house. Once the house is built, it can be made to look many different ways through decorating and landscaping choices, for instance. Our life plan provides us with a framework, but we must continually build upon it.

A major part of our life plan is our agreements. An agreement is a decision made by two souls, usually before incarnating, to work together on the physical plane in a particular way. There are many kinds of agreements, including to help one another in a variety of ways or to have a particular kind of relationship, such as that of mate or parent/child. Agreements ensure that we'll have some help available, but they are not "sacred." What is chosen can be unchosen. For example, people make an average of about nine mate agreements before incarnating, according to my channeling. Obviously, most of us don't intend to be in that many long-term relationships, but the agreements provide us with a number of other people whom we've already "okayed" as being compatible partners in terms of our life plan. Sometimes those with whom we made mate agreements are unavailable or feel unsuitable once we meet on the physical plane—for one thing, personality does not always reveal essence, and an essence we're close to may have a distorted or neurotic personality in this lifetime. Our lives may have turned out differently than expected and a union may no longer seem appropriate, but checking out our mate agreements is preferable to "starting from scratch."[2]

Some people are disappointed when they learn that they don't have a mate agreement with someone to whom they are attracted. We might say that if we choose to mate with someone, we are making a mate agreement on the spot; everybody has free will. Not having a mate agreement doesn't invalidate a relationship. Agreements can put us a step ahead, but there are many other factors that contribute to successful relationships. We can have excellent relationships with people with whom we have no agreements, or whom we have never even known in past lives.

When planning an upcoming lifetime, we may make a child agreement with another soul who is open to being our parent when we're ready to be born. We may make this agreement even before that prospective parent has incarnated, or we may make it on an essence level once the parent is physical. If the agreement is made before the

---

[2]See also Chapter Eighteen, "Finding Your Mate and Developing Intimacy," in my Summerjoy Michael book *Loving from Your Soul—Creating Powerful Relationships.*

parent is mated, as is usually the case, the agreement is made with an individual rather than with a couple, since it is not known for certain with whom the parent will mate. However, there's a high probability that we will also have at least a somewhat close connection with the soul who becomes our other parent; it is unlikely that someone with whom we'd make a child agreement would mate with someone who is a stranger to us.[3]

As with mate agreements, we prioritize our child agreements if we make more than one at a time, and our prospective parents prioritize theirs as well. If our first-choice parent decides not to have children after all, or if we never make it to the top of his or her "list," or if the only body available through him is male, and we want a female body (or vice versa), we go on to the next prospective parent on our list or make another child agreement. Women who become pregnant despite having carefully used birth control may have a child agreement with a soul very eager to be born through them. On an essence level, these women might be thinking how much fun it would be to parent that soul, or what a good idea it would be to complete an outstanding karma with him. Nonetheless, a mother always has the right to choose not to have a child, for whatever reason. Our personality has a different point of view than our essence; on a personality level, we may be thinking that we can't afford a child, or that the timing isn't good in terms of our career. Our personality is on the "front lines" of our life, and may have a better grasp of practicalities, although if our personality goes along with our essence and ends up in a corner because of it, our essence usually at least finds a way to solve the problems that arise. Our essence sees the larger picture of our life better than our personality does, and may be in a better position to know what will work out best for us in the end. However, our essence is not infallible, and does not impose its will.

If a couple has five children, for example, the first, third, and fifth child may have had agreements with the father, and the second and fourth, with the mother. In other words, the couple usually alternates between their individual child agreements, although that is a matter of essence-level negotiation. If the first fetus is especially appropriate for one of the essences with whom the mother has a child agreement, that essence might be born as their first child, even if the

---

[3]When they are planning to reincarnate, most souls know what kind of situation and body into which they wish to be born. However, younger souls may leave it to their more-experienced guides to come up with some appropriate possibilities for them. They then choose the one that looks best to them. Likewise, younger souls expecting a child may leave it to their guides to find a suitable soul to incarnate in that child. Older souls tend to take more responsibility for the process.

child "takes after" its father. The second child would then probably be one of the essences with whom the father has a child agreement. So even if a child looks and acts more like one parent, that is not necessarily the parent with whom he made the child agreement.

If it is decided on an essence level before conception that a particular soul will be born to a couple, that soul may be present at conception "supervising" the "construction" of its body from the very beginning. Some couples have experienced knowing during intercourse that they have conceived and that the soul of the child was present with them. The soul might have even been able to influence the event to the extent of guiding a particular sperm to the egg.

Parenthetically, I have a theory, based on anecdotal evidence, that the first boy mainly takes after the father, the second, after the mother, and that the first girl mainly takes after the mother, the second, after the father. By "take after," I mean that the child has dominant physical and personality traits of that parent. So there seems to be even a biological "taking turns."

Not everything that happens to us is part of our life plan. Sometimes people say that there's no such thing as an accident, or fatalistically view everything that happens as "meant to be." Actually, sometimes mishaps are accidental, in the sense of not being intended on any level. There is always a cause, but occasionally it's just carelessness or chance. Similarly, sicknesses do sometimes occur merely because resistance is low and "something is going around." There are not grand, metaphysical reasons for everything. Each situation must be looked at with fresh eyes to see what it really is. If everything in the universe was "fated" to occur, not only would that negate free will, but the game would be boring. That which is unplanned and unexpected is the wild card that makes life challenging and interesting. Even though most of us incarnated with some kind of life plan, each of us is also constantly making choices that interact with those of other people and change the "landscape," making the execution of that plan a matter of much alertness, intelligence, and skill.

Chapter 17

RELATIONSHIPS

There are many reasons we might resonate with another person. We may have shared important past lives or even previous grand cycles. We may have been friends between lives on the astral plane, perhaps working together on a project for the benefit of those on the physical plane. We may have been one another's spirit guides. We may both be members of the same configuration such as a quadrate or sextant.[1] We may be members of the same cadence, entity, or cadre. Or we may have a permanent soul relationship such as essence twin, essence mate, or task companion.

It is also possible that we have never met before, but have the same or complementary role or overleaves. We might be close in soul age, or simply share common qualities or interests.

ESSENCE TWINS

An essence twin is a soul we team up with for an entire grand cycle to reflect ourselves back to us; it is the most intense relationship we can have. It is synonymous with the terms *twin flame* and *twin soul*, but not necessarily with *soul mate*.

I once attended a workshop at which we were instructed at one point to choose a partner for some exercises. We shared some intense processes with that partner, and then came back to the whole group and continued on. This was repeated throughout the workshop with the same partner. Although the majority of the workshop was not spent working with the partner, the time that was spent in process with him was crucial, and usually, a strong bond developed between the partners. An essence twin relationship is rather like that.

Lessons you learn tend to be communicated to your essence twin, and vice versa.

You could see your essence twin as being like your work partner, in terms of your inner work as opposed to your life tasks. Your growth helps your essence twin indirectly, because of the energy you share.

---

[1]Quadrates and sextants are long-term groupings of four and six souls, respectively. See also Glossary.

> *The task companion relationship emphasizes how you handle things. The essence twin relationship emphasizes how you feel about things.*

Essence twins classically have opposite male/female energy ratios, and the same casting (positions within their cadence and greater cadence). However, this is not always the case. Choice rather than mathematics makes two souls twins, although mathematical correlations can support the relationship. As mentioned earlier, cadres made up of essences with a relatively high number of previous cycles tend to be more experimental, and don't necessarily stick to "classic Michael" in their design. Essence twins who plan to meet each other often choose opposite body types,[2] although there is no "rule" requiring this.

I know my essence twin, although not very well—we have never lived in the same city. We have some major things in common, and she has said things that helped validate for me my channeling that she is my essence twin (I also double-checked with another channel). On a personality level, our connection is friendly but not particularly close or compelling, although the essence twin relationship often is. (This illustrates that close soul connections do not always translate into close personality connections, and the people most important in our lives are not necessarily that close to us on an essence level.) My essence twin has been said to look like she could be my sister. Her body type is neither similar nor opposite to mine, so the resemblance is not due to body type. Our casting is not the same, either, and our male/female energy ratios are not quite opposite. However, a psychic who saw her picture said that the higher frequencies of our auras are very similar in color and shape. (I do not know any of my task companions in the flesh, but Yarbro said that, even more than essence twins, task companions are often thought to look or talk alike.)

Our essence twin is typically in a different entity than our own but in the same cadre. We may find that entity's vibration to be particularly complementary to our own because our essence twin is in it, or we might have chosen to have an essence twin in that entity because we found it complementary in the first place. Our essence twin is usually someone we have known in previous grand cycles.

In *More Messages from Michael*,[3] Michael said that essence twins are "never in the same entity." However, in *Messages from Michael*,[4] the wording was "are not often part of the same entity, but are part of

---

[2] See Chapter Twenty-Four, "Body Types," or the Glossary.
[3] P. 42.
[4] P. 193.

different entities that were cast at the same time." This illustrates how through even the same channel or group of channels, at least slightly differing information can come through. There is no unequivocal way of proving whether the "never" is correct. I channeled that one couple, both kings, are essence twins in the same entity, but that could have been an error. However, the words *never* and *always* send up red flags for me. The universe does have order and design, and it is possible that some *never*s are correct—I don't wish to say that a *never* can never be correct! But I'm more comfortable with the wording in *Messages from Michael, not often*, in light of Michael's teaching that "all is choice." The universe's order and design relate to its male energy, which gives structure and shape; female energy relates to "creative chaos," the fact that there are unlimited possibilities.

I presume that "different entities that were cast at the same time" refers to entities in the same cadre, since cadres were defined that way elsewhere in Yarbro. In Chapter Ten, "Cadres and Entities," I discuss essence twin connections outside the cadre with other cadres in the cadre group. I suppose that they could also be seen as having been "cast at the same time."

More than any other relationship, the essence twin relationship is the "glue" that holds the whole together. The reuniting of a cadre's seven entities on higher planes is, in part, the reunification of the essence twins within that cadre. The later reunification of a cadre group's twelve cadres is also, in part, the reunification of those essence twins who are in different cadres.

On my Michael Reading charts, I channel the essence twin and task companion(s) as being either nonincarnate or incarnate (male or female). If the soul is incarnate and the chart's subject knows him, he could be a friend, acquaintance, or relative. If he doesn't know him, there could either be plans to meet in a certain number of years, or no plans to meet in this lifetime.

When Michael says through me that the essence twin (or task companion) is a friend, they mean that they are picking up a substantial amount of connection personality-to-personality, as opposed to essence connection. They do not necessarily mean that the essence twin is currently in the person's life; he could have been a childhood friend. When Michael says that someone is an acquaintance, they mean that there is less personality connection, but at least, it appears to Michael that the chart's subject has met him in the flesh. A friend or acquaintance who is also a relative will be channeled as being a relative.

When the subject has met his essence twin, Michael says whether the essence twin is younger or older than the chart's subject, or is about the same age, but sometimes they add a question mark. Michael doesn't get this particular information from the akashic records; they read it psychically. They aren't always certain if the essence twin is actually younger, for instance, or just looks that way. Michael is trying to help the "chartee" identify his essence twin (and channeling names unknown to the channel is very difficult). However, looking in the akashic records for the essence twin's day of birth, in terms of our calendar, or for other highly temporal information, would be like looking for a needle in a haystack, and not worth the energy it would require. On the other hand, most Michael Reading chart information, such as the goal, is easier to get from the records: it is a core and ongoing factor in life. Also, Michael does look up in the records whether the essence twin is incarnate, and, if so, the gender, as well as whether they have agreed to meet.

When the essence twin is a friend, acquaintance, or relative, sometimes it can be difficult to figure out just who it is. I have my clients send me photographs of people who seem to fit the description, and check them with Michael. Eventually, we usually (but not always) find out who it is. It is especially hard when the person is merely an acquaintance, who might be consciously forgotten, although it is subliminally comforting to have met in the flesh those souls closest to us, even if they are not overtly involved in our lives.

When we are deeply involved with our essence twin on the physical plane, that relationship can be so compelling as to distract us from our life task or other things we wish to accomplish. That is why we don't necessarily get together often with our essence twin on the physical plane. On the other hand, the very intensity of it can bring up important issues.

Your essence twin reflects you back to yourself—your short-comings as well as your strengths—like a finely polished mirror. Working with your essence twin is a good way to process your blocks.

We mirror our essence twin not only because of our mathematical correlations, if any, but because of having had so many experiences together, both on and off the physical plane. It is like a couple who have been together for fifty years. They tend to pick up one another's mannerisms and idiosyncrasies, and communicate almost telepathically. They may start to look like their partner's other half, but they are still individuals.

When our essence twin is not incarnate, it is almost as if that soul is living within us—in our vest pocket, so to speak. The bleed-through is noticeably stronger than when our essence twin is incarnate. For example, an artisan with a king essence twin looks much more kingly when his essence twin is not incarnate. If your essence twin dies while you are alive, the bleed-through immediately increases.

As with most entities, the members of the Michael entity have essence twins of all roles, but besides twinning with fellow warriors and kings, Michael has a particularly high number of sage and artisan essence twins. On the higher planes, the essence twin bleed-through is even more pronounced than it is on the physical plane, since much more unity is experienced. The sage energy bleeding through helps Michael communicate more articulately, and the artisan energy aids their creativity in choosing words and their ability to work with the complex structures inherent in their teachings.

In Chapter Twenty-Five, "Reincarnation," I will discuss how an essence can have more than one incarnation in the same time frame. Our essence twin may be channeled as being not incarnate even though its essence has one or more incarnations in this time frame—our essence twin has a reincarnational self but we are not bonded to it. The way it works is that every time we incarnate, we bond with our essence twin in a particular way. We either bond directly with his essence, or with a reincarnational personality that is going to be in the same time frame. We either agree to know that personality or not. The influence of our essence twin is weakest when we are bonded to a reincarnational personality we have no plans to meet. It is strongest when we are bonded directly to his nonincarnate essence.

In *Messages from Michael*, it was stated that six times out of seven, our essence twin is of the same role. In the experience of several other channels, including me, the reverse seems to be true. My channeling indicates that neither view is actually wrong. Those with fewer previous grand cycles usually like to have a relatively "pure" experience of an essence role. Being a scholar with a scholar essence twin gives us concentrated scholar energy to work with. Since the average human being has had about four previous cycles, it is probably true on the whole that six out of seven times, a person's essence twin has the same role as he does. However, once we have done a planetary cycle as a scholar with a scholar essence twin, we might like to try being a scholar with a king essence twin, to vary the energy. The channels who find that roughly six out of seven people seem to have essence twins of different roles may be working with those from cadres consisting of essences with a higher average number of previous cycles. These cadres are not necessarily constructed in typical patterns.

About five percent of us have no essence twin. A lesson of a cycle without an essence twin may be self-sufficiency, finding balance and completeness within, experiencing our reflection within ourselves rather than externally. We might choose a fairly balanced male/female energy ratio to facilitate this. People with no essence twin sometimes tell me, when they learn of it, that they aren't surprised; they always had a sense of doing this planet "solo." They may need to be especially deliberate about drawing in support from others. Sometimes they team up with someone who functions like an essence twin for a lifetime or a series of lifetimes. I refer to them as "surrogate essence twins."

Those who have an essence twin also occasionally adopt a surrogate when the original is not incarnate or is busy elsewhere. He usually has the same role as the original, and otherwise resembles him in various ways.

Incidentally, we can be attracted to someone who reminds us of our essence twin, even if we do not have an agreement to work together in an essence-twin-like way.

TASK COMPANIONS

A task companion is another soul we team up with at the beginning of a grand cycle. We work together with our task companion, supporting one another in our life tasks, which are complementary. Sometimes, people have more than one task companion. One is chosen at the beginning of the grand cycle, and up to three others are added along the way, usually during the infant soul cycle. On less than one percent of the charts I have channeled, Michael said that the person had no task companion.

We often work with our task companion and essence twin in the dream state, especially if we don't know them "in the flesh." A nonincarnate task companion is often one of our spirit guides, specializing in working with us on our life task. If we "tune in" to our guides visually, they may appear to us in the form of one of their reincarnational personalities whom we knew in prior lifetimes that are significant for us now. If we know the role of our task companion and get visual images from our guides, it might be interesting to see if we can pick out our task companion. For example, if we have an artisan task companion, we might explore whether one of our guides seems especially inventive and chameleon-like. If so, that might be our task companion. (We could also ask this guide if he is our task companion, but we shouldn't assume that our astral friends understand the Michael terminology.)

The Yarbro books implied that we have only one task companion. Perhaps the task companions added after the grand cycle begins, which I and other Michael channels have been told about, would be considered "synthetic" in the Yarbro perspective, although Michael tells me that they function in the same way as the originally chosen task companion. Yarbro also emphasized that one's task companion is never of the same role. However, I have channeled charts for more than a few people on which the task companion had the same role. It is possible that my channeling was in error, or that what I channeled was a "synthetic" task companion—my charts do not specify when a task companion was chosen. If I do channel a task companion of the same role and ask Michael, "Are you sure?" so far they have always replied in the affirmative.

I once channeled a client's chart that listed two task companions. Later, someone else was also said to be the client's task companion. Michael explained that they wished to encourage the client to first question who that person was to her before they told her that he was her task companion.

NONPHYSICAL SUPPORT

Often clients are disgruntled to find that both their essence twin and task companion(s) are not incarnate. Michael said that many of us like to "take turns" with them being on the physical plane so that we have plenty of support astrally. This can make our lifetime more intense and productive. When they are incarnate at the same time we are, they may be too busy with their own lives to be there for us as much as we might like them to be. Of course, there are lifetimes in which one or more of them are incarnate and very much involved in our lives.

Sometimes a person's essence twin or task companion is incarnate, but they don't plan to meet. Everything is by choice, and two souls do not necessarily choose to be in the same place at the same time, no matter how close they are. For instance, if you live in the U.S. and your essence twin is a ninety-year-old woman living in Mongolia, meeting is probably not practical, so it is easy to understand why you didn't plan to meet. However, you likely work together out-of-body in the dream state.

Occasionally, someone meets his essence twin or task companion but never becomes close; he may not even remember him. However, such contact may facilitate their astral communication. Since, as mentioned, the essence twin relationship, especially, can be so absorbing, they may not have wanted to become more than acquaintances in this lifetime, in order to keep from being distracted from other matters on which they wanted to concentrate.

SOUL MATES?

The concept of soul mate, if defined as your one-and-only per-fect mate, is not valid for most essences, who desire a variety of experiences. However, some essences are extremely at-tached to one another, and do not rest until the other is found if they have an agreement to mate, especially if they are essence twins.[5]

When our essence twin is incarnate and we have our primary mate agreement with him (which doesn't happen often), a psychic or chan-nel might discern that person as being our soul mate, since there is such an intense bond.

However, if incarnate, our essence twin (or task companion) is not necessarily our dream lover or "soul mate." In fact, sometimes we don't get along with him. This soul can also be our mother or father, best friend, business partner, or even nemesis. It is helpful to be in a variety of circumstances with this soul.

One metaphysical concept states that if we are male, there may be another person who is the embodiment of our female energy, and vice versa. This person is considered to be our other half. This con-cept has no direct correlation in the Michael teachings, but perhaps it stems from the fact that essence twins often have opposite male/female energy ratios. Nevertheless, our essence twin is a sepa-rate soul. Only our reincarnational selves could be said to share our essence. It is true that essence twins are a unit, just as our cadence and entity are units. Together, essence twins are something more than two individuals—they form a joint consciousness. This is true of every unit of two or more essences—for example, our entity has a collective consciousness. In fact, humanity as a whole has a collective consciousness.

MONADS

Monads are essential experiences. You might say that they are the "courses" of the "University of Life" on earth. To get your "degree," you have to complete a minimum number of them. Al-though the curriculum is not the same for everyone, there are some "basic" courses that most people take.

---

[5]See also my Summerjoy Michael book *Loving from Your Soul—Creating Pow-erful Relationships.*

You set up any monads you intend to do when you are making your life plan before incarnating. Most of them are reciprocal. You usually do one side in one lifetime, the other side in another, with the same essence. That gives you more specific information about the monad. It is like a scientific experiment in which you use controls, keeping every factor the same except what you are testing for so that you can see where the variations are. You generally feel pulled more intensely into a monadal relationship than you do into a nonmonadal relationship. You are not likely to do two major monads in one lifetime, although you might.

The most common monad is teacher/student. In it, you agree before a lifetime begins to be either a teacher or student with another person. On the teacher side, you are not necessarily a school teacher, but may be a mentor or a friend, usually an older person to the one being taught. You learn about the teacher/student relationship. Exploring the act of teaching itself is as important as what is specifically being taught. To learn about teaching, you must have a student. If you are on the student side, you are learning about being a student, about receiving knowledge. Such a monad normally lasts many years.

Sometimes teacher/student monads are done with therapists or spiritual teachers, but the teacher/student monad can be done within the context of a sibling, mate, or any other kind of relationship.

Do we sometimes have lifetimes in which we do not work on any monads?

Yes. Everything is by choice, and it is important not to take on too much in one lifetime. If you have a lifetime that is devoted to repaying a lot of karma, you may choose not to also involve yourself in monads. However, the monadal relationship is a foundational one and is intimately connected with the evolution of the soul on the physical plane.

Messages from Michael stated that monads are only done once. According to my channeling, it is true that most people do them only once.

However, those with many previous cycles, with their boundless energy for advanced experimenting, often choose to do the monads several times, each time in different ways.

Completing monads more than once makes possible "love monads." Love monads are formed when two essences have completed all the major monads together. If, for example, a person has love monads with five other essences, he obviously has completed each of the major monads at least five times. That suggests that he has been quite busy on the physical plane, and probably has had many past lives. Love monads are only possible in the old soul cycle, since some of the monads are not done until then.

There is no set number of monads that we must do to complete our cycle on the physical plane, but Michael channel Aaron Christeaan compiled a list of over thirty, and there are variations possible on those as well.[6] The monads we actually do are a matter of choice.

One monad involves mature souls honorably serving a corrupt master. We might wonder why the soul might wish to undertake such a negative experience. I think of it as being like an inoculation: in this case, once we've completed and validated the monad, our naiveté regarding leaders is likely to be gone forever—in the future, we will use more discernment about whom and what we serve.

Incidentally, in *More Messages from Michael*,[7] Michael said that many people around Hitler were doing this monad, which suggests that Hitler was doing the same monad with several people.

A tandem monad is one in which two people align with each other so that they are going through the same or similar experiences at about the same time, in order to support each other through them. I have an old friend with whom I am doing a tandem monad, and it's a running joke between us about how parallel our lives are in certain respects. I have another friend with whom I am also doing this monad, but it wasn't planned before this lifetime began; after I moved to New York and we became close, we decided on an essence level to initiate it and began to notice that we were synchronized. (This illustrates how parts of our life plan are improvised as we go along.) For instance, in one conversation we discovered that we had both just begun taking voice lessons again (from different teachers) and had found that, after two lessons, a lot of things had come together for us that hadn't during lessons taken in previous years; we were both excited about that, but neither of us had been consistent in practicing. We also find that our inner process is somewhat synchronized, so that we often have similar realizations or breakthroughs simultaneously.

---

[6]See *Michael—The Basic Teachings* by Aaron Christeaan, JP Van Hulle, and M.C. Clark (Michael Educational Foundation, 1988), pp. 189-196, for a list of monads.

[7]P. 185.

In addition to monadal relationships, there are seven internal monads,[8] which concern our relationship with ourselves rather than with others. These have also been called "milestones." The first is birth. The second is the emergence of an awareness of self as a separate individual, usually by the age of two. The third occurs around the age of eighteen, when a person leaves the "nest." The fourth happens at the time of the midlife crisis. The fifth or "senior citizen's" internal monad usually occurs between the ages of sixty-five and seventy-five when a person reflects on his life, on what he has accomplished versus what he set out to do. The sixth is the beginning of the dying process, and the seventh is death itself. Here are some comments Michael made about the midlife monad, which is particularly difficult:

> *During the first half of your life, your emphasis is usually on completing the majority of your karmas, if any, and on preparing for your life task. During the second half, you have the opportunity to apply the lessons you learned during the first half and to begin working directly on your life task. The fourth internal (midlife) monad is the transition between these two periods. During it, you internalize the lessons of your life thus far and choose a course for the future that will allow you to fulfill your life task. You also shed elements of your imprinting that no longer serve you. The theme of the fourth internal monad might be said to be "To thine own self be true." You must know yourself to be able to be true to yourself. Therefore, during this monad you will probably need to get to know yourself better.*
>
> *If you begin this monad having already shed a great deal of unneeded or contrary imprinting, and if you know yourself fairly well and are pretty clear on your life task, this transition is relatively painless. It only becomes a midlife crisis when all this work has to be compressed into a short period of time.*
>
> *This monad usually occurs from about age thirty-five to thirty-seven. However, it can occur as much as ten years earlier or later.*

---

[8]See also *Messages from Michael*, pp. 215-217, *More Messages from Michael*, p. 32, and *Michael's People*, pp. 38-39 and p. 106.

KARMA [9]

In the Yarbro books, karma was specifically defined to mean a significant abridgment of another person's right of free choice without prior agreement, such as murder. Michael through me sometimes refers to this as a "major karma." Murder creates a significant energy imbalance because it robs someone of his physical body and all the effort he invested into setting up that lifetime. The murderer owes his victim that energy. A person who forms a karmic bond by murdering someone will, in a future lifetime, either be murdered by him, which cancels the debt with an opposite action, or will save his life, which is a more enlightened, joyful way of repaying such a debt. In rare instances, the energy imbalance is neutralized through "grace," in which the murderer fully realizes his infringement, and both parties are able and willing to forgive the karma without acting it out physically.

Another example of a major karma is a thief robbing a large amount of money that someone worked to save, causing significant hardships that the victim cannot recover from, thereby reducing the choices available to the victim. The money doesn't belong to the thief; it is "magnetically" linked to the person who generated it, and "tries" to return to its rightful owner, like a wave impelled to the shore, where it can return to equilibrium.

Through some other channels, Michael defines karma more broadly, as being any intense experience. This is more in keeping with the general new age use of the word. This would include lesser energy imbalances that do not significantly abridge another's right of free choice or alter the course of his lifetime. Michael through me calls these "intermediate" and "minor" karmas. (In *Michael's People*, [10] Michael refers to the repayment of intermediate karmas as "acts of restitution.") An example of an intermediate karma might be a business owner firing an employee unfairly; the owner has the right to do it, and although the employee might suffer some temporary hardship, it doesn't generally cause major long-term harm. However, "what goes around comes around." If the owner lacks fairness with his employees, he is likely to attract that sort of treatment in the future for himself. It may or may not come from those whom he treated unfairly. This differs from major karma, in which the "books" must be "balanced" with the same party.

---

[9] See also Chapter Twelve, "Karma," in my upcoming Summerjoy Michael book *Being in the World*.

[10] P. 34.

If, in a future lifetime, the former owner were to meet the former employee, the former owner might feel guilty or rejecting, depending on whether he was repentant. If he felt guilty, he might feel an impulse to help his former employee in a way roughly commensurate with the harm he had caused. If he follows his impulse, he may engage in an act of restitution, probably not knowing why he wants to be so "generous."

If the former owner was not repentant, and the former employee had not resolved his feelings about what had happened, the former employee might inexplicably feel nervous, angry, or even the desire to "get even." If the former employee now happened to be in a position to unfairly fire the former owner, he might do that, or he might choose to put aside his "irrational" feelings and act with integrity. This is obviously a milder experience of karma than if the former owner had murdered him; in that case, the former employee would likely feel powerful waves of energy seeking to be rebalanced. Although there is always free choice, he might feel overwhelmingly compelled to reciprocate what was done to him, or to allow the other person to make it up to him, especially if that was in their life plans. Minor and intermediate karmas are not centrally compelling in a lifetime in the way that major karma is. Only major karmas must be repaid before a soul cycles off. However, most of a soul's intermediate and minor karmas will also be repaid in the passage of many lifetimes.

Of course, getting even, which can be an element of any kind of negative karmic repayment, tends to perpetuate patterns of injustice. The history of civilization could be couched in terms of vicious circles of getting even. There is always a choice about how a karmic debt is repaid. If an essence plans to repay a karmic debt in an upcoming lifetime, the means of repayment is likely to be discussed with the essence to whom the debt is owed. An essence may even agree to incarnate and be murdered at a particular time in order to repay a debt. Even if a person did not agree to repay a particular karma in this lifetime, if he gets involved with someone to whom he owes a debt and the "ball starts rolling," he may repay it anyway. Once he is drawn into the whirlwind of a major karma, it can be difficult to extract himself from it until the karmic "ribbon" is "burned," since its energies are so powerful.

Let's say, for example, that in a past life a person murdered someone with whom he has a close soul-level connection. Let's also say that they did not plan to settle that debt in this lifetime—they felt that it would be better to work on some other lessons together beforehand. So they meet and become involved with one another. There may be an underlying discomfort due to the outstanding karma—the one who had been murdered may at times feel an inexplicable nervousness or wariness in the other person's presence, and the one who had murdered may still carry the unresolved emotions that led to the murder in the first place. However, their basically close soul-level connection draws them together and they seek to work things out with each other. If they get to a point in their relationship similar to the point at which the karma was incurred the "last time around," they may find that they have grown enough to deal with the challenges that arise in a more mature way. They may also find themselves again engulfed by the emotions that come up. In the heat of the moment, the one who killed may kill again, incurring more karma, or the one who had been murdered may this time be the murderer—the energy imbalance of the original karma may surface in full primal force, like a tidal wave, and seek to right itself any way it can.

After a karmic debt is repaid, those involved can carry "karmic residues," leftover ill feelings that will usually, in time, fade away. If we meet someone who at first triggers negative feelings in us, but whom we come to like or feel neutral about, this could indicate that we were dispersing karmic residues.

Sometimes people assume that every difficult relationship is karmic—that is not the case. Some people are just hard to get along with, or push a lot of our buttons. Also, people can develop patterns of behavior with each other after several lifetimes together that may not be fully productive, but are not karmic. With deliberate work, these patterns can be changed. An example might be two people who basically love each other but habitually compete rather than support one another. There is no energy imbalance here, just an encrusted way of relating.

There is also what Michael calls "self-karma," which could be defined as an energy imbalance within oneself caused by false, limiting beliefs acquired in past experiences, either in past lives or earlier in this lifetime. This can result in a disease, for instance, that requires a righting of the internal imbalance in order to heal. Seventh-level lifetimes, whether young or old, are often taken up with attempting to deal with self-karmas.

If, for example, a person harbors bigotry without overtly acting it out and tangibly harming someone, he has not incurred a karmic debt, but he may generate self-karma and feel compelled into situations that bring him face to face with his bigotry. Someone who hates members of a particular religious group or race may, in a later lifetime, choose to be born into it so as to deal with that bigotry, just as he might had he incurred a karmic debt with a member of that group or race. However, specific prejudices are fixations of the personality and are not, per se, carried from lifetime to lifetime, although the tendency to have prejudice is. Prejudice is a projection of some rejected part of self. The exact object of a person's prejudice depends on the culture into which he is born: he will tend to hate whatever group is "popular" to hate in that culture. For instance, in one lifetime his prejudice may be fixated on Roman Catholics; in another, on blacks. However, there can also be patterns from lifetime to lifetime: for example, people may be misogynistic and/or homophobic in many of their male lifetimes if their male energy tends to reject their female energy. Coming to terms with prejudice is a way of learning to love and accept all parts of oneself. Whether a person does this through repaying a karmic debt owed another person, or internally, by dealing with self-karma, the fundamental lessons are the same, since our relationships with others reflect our relationship with ourselves. When a prejudice arises in us, it can be useful to ask ourselves what part of ourselves that particular group represents to us.

CORDING

A cord is a psychic connection with another person that transmits energy. Cording is designed primarily for parents to be connected with their children as if through an invisible umbilical cord. Cords allow parents to provide supplemental life support for their children until they can become energetically independent (during adolescence). They also allow parents to be aware of what is happening with their children. Adults can "run" a couple of small children off their "battery," since theirs are so much larger, but not other adults. Adults are too big— they consume too much energy—to run off other people's batteries. The size of cords can vary; one that is large can seriously drain someone's energy.

Although cords are not designed for adults to be energetically dependent on other adults, cording among adults is common. Most people both cord others and are corded by others. There may be a net loss of energy, a net gain, or it may come out equal. However, it is preferable for adults not to allow anyone to cord them other than those who are literally dependent on them for survival, such as children or an invalid. Most adults are capable of living from their own internal source of energy.

Cording is not the same as a shared bond, which does not take energy from another but provides connection. A shared bond looks similar to a cord, but it does not transmit a substantial amount of energy. It is more like a telephone line that is available when needed for communication than like the power cord of an appliance that is constantly drawing energy.

To eliminate cords, close your eyes and visualize them. Notice their location, color, and size, and follow them out to see to whom they connect. Then ask your inner self to let them go and dissolve them in the light. You will probably need to do this regularly for a while, since cording and being corded tend to be habitual. If you do this a couple of times a day for a few weeks, those who attempt to reestablish a cord with you will probably become tired of it and stop.

If a particular cord is not dissolving, you might explore what your "payoff" is in letting that person cord you. Is it assuaging some guilt or misplaced sense of responsibility you have regarding him?

When you release a major cord, you may find that it leaves a "stub," or at least some rawness, if not an "open wound." Spend some time continuing to release and heal it until the area is totally smooth. If the wound is open, it is easier for others to re-cord you. Visualize a specific color you find healing for this wound and keep it there. It should be different in color from the cord. For example, if the cord looks red, you might fill the wound with a blue-green "salve."

If you feel the need to cord others, you can work on developing a stronger knowledge of your inner source.

Are essence twins corded?

Essence twins are not necessarily corded in the way we are speaking of here. They share a permanent connection on an essence level. Cording is on the physical level.

Part IV

OVERLEAVES

Chapter 18

COMMENTS ON OVERLEAVES

Overleaves are personality traits that "overlay" the essence. We choose them before a lifetime begins[1] to facilitate the purposes of that lifetime, and usually select a new combination of them for each lifetime. The overleaves include the goal, mode, attitude, center, and chief feature. The goal influences what we do; the mode, how we do it; the attitude, why we do it; the center, the part of self from which we do it; and the chief feature, what tends to block or distort our doing.

CHOOSING OVERLEAVES

When planning your upcoming lifetime, you think about what you want to achieve, what your "bottom line" is, and then choose the tools, including overleaves, that will facilitate that.

Do overleaves follow a pattern from one lifetime to another?

If you have a series of lifetimes in which the general theme is acceptance, for instance, you might choose that goal each time. Or, you might like to alternate acceptance, growth, and flow, going among these three goals from lifetime to lifetime. The patterns followed are individual.

Choosing overleaves is an art. As with anything else, you learn more about it as you go along. You might learn, for example, that it is not a very good idea to combine an attitude of cynic with a goal of acceptance. Nonetheless, some people can pull it off.

Overleaves, of course, are chosen. Therefore, it is natural for individuals to have more affinity for certain ones. However, there are combinations of overleaves that are best suited to the accomplishment of certain purposes. When essences contemplate incarnating, it is to their benefit to choose the appropriate tools. Sometimes this is done hastily, like a carpenter who

---

[1]Exceptions are the center, chosen at the second internal monad (age two), and chief feature, chosen at the third (around age twenty), although we make tentative choices before birth and stay with them about 90% of the time.

rushes to work without bringing the right tools, but after a while, one learns that doing that makes life harder.

There are spirit guides who do nothing but help others plan their overleaves.

In your true personality, which springs from the positive poles of your overleaves, your overleaves are not as noticeable as when the "harsh edges" of the negative poles are in play. Overleaves are always a factor, but in their positive poles, they are not limiting.

The more you are aligned with your essence, the more flexibly you use your overleaves. They are like a musical instrument. If you are a master of the violin, you find ways to get the best sound out of it. Rather than railing against its restrictions (it is not, after all, a trombone), you get it to do all the things you want it to do, something someone less skilled may not be able to do.

Suppose that you have a goal of dominance. As you are aligned with your essence, not only do you work to stay in the positive pole, leadership, but you redefine and expand it. One way to do this is to make more use of the sliding mechanism,[2] in this case, from dominance to submission.

At one time or another, you have probably done all the overleaves; at some level, you remember what they are like. If occasions arise that call for the use of other goals, for example, such as acceptance, you can summon that energy. However, it will be more effort than using dominance or submission, if dominance is your goal. Your own overleaves are most natural for you.

Overleaves are not cut-and-dried. When you are fully conscious, you choose behavior consistent with your goals and needs at the time. Having free will, you are, in a sense, always free to choose your overleaves, not just at the initiation of a new life. However, if you have chosen appropriately in the beginning, and barring a vast change in direction, those overleaves will serve you well most of the time. They give you a structure, so you can focus on other choices.

---

[2]As mentioned, *sliding* means temporarily moving to another overleaf. See the next subchapter, "Neutral Overleaves," or the Glossary.

My goal is acceptance, but for a while, I was also using the energy of growth. Through another channel, Michael picked it up in my energy. Our "native" overleaves are, by definition, most natural for us, so acceptance is more comfortable for me. However, I needed some growth energy temporarily; it helped me do some intensive healing and learn a lot in a short period of time.

In *Messages from Michael*,[3] Michael said, "Balance implies obsolescence of the overleaves." I don't think that they were implying that when one is balanced, one no longer has overleaves, but that in balance, they are not limiting factors. Overleaves are simply a framework. Taking any overleaf to an extreme pushes us into its negative pole. Sliding to the positive pole of its opposite overleaf can bring us to balance. For instance, someone being overly accepting becomes ingratiating (ingratiation is acceptance's negative pole). By temporarily sliding to sophistication, the positive pole of the opposite goal, discrimination—in other words, by deliberately being discriminating about what we accept or the way in which we accept what comes to us, and by limiting how far we'll go in order to be accepted by others—we can return to the positive pole of acceptance, agape. In Yarbro,[4] this was called the "hands-across" technique (or the "hands-through" technique for the assimilation axis overleaves, which can slide to any of the other axes).

Each essence has individual characteristics apart from overleaves. In addition to the factors already discussed, such as casting, male/female energy ratio, and so forth, each essence has had its own unique history and experiences that have shaped it. Beyond that, the spark behind each essence brings its experiences from other planets in previous cycles, and from other universal experiences. Therefore, every essence has evolved unique characteristics. These characteristics are not as specific as overleaves, but sometimes resemble them. For example, an essence can tend to be rather pragmatic in a general sense. As a result, he may choose pragmatist as an attitude more often than average.

Everyone, at one time or another, chooses each overleaf. If we are in an overleaf that emphasizes our natural tendency, it will be especially strong. A mild manifestation of an overleaf probably indicates that the essence's proclivities are in another direction.

There is a certain amount of chance in the way each essence evolves over its lifetimes. Before each lifetime, we choose overleaves and life circumstances to give us the experiences we seek, but often things go differently than we expect them to, since everyone has free

---

[3]P. 238.

[4]*Messages from Michael*, pp. 211-214.

will and there is always the possibility of someone forming karma with us, interrupting our plans. Because none of us have yet mastered the game of life, we don't always handle these interruptions with equanimity; we are sometimes traumatized and form faulty conclusions about what got us into trouble and how to avoid that in the future (just as the personality does within one lifetime). This may cause us to develop more heavily in one direction than another. There's nothing actually wrong with this, since all experience can ultimately lead to growth, and the imbalances we form lead to our being "experts" in certain areas of human function. Nevertheless, those of us on a spiritual path may feel the need to deliberately place ourselves in situations that challenge our preconceptions and force us to become more balanced.

To illustrate, Michael told one client, a scholar, that his essence has some prejudice against passion mode, feeling that its abandon gets him into trouble. Therefore, he doesn't do that mode often and hasn't developed very fully his ability to be passionate. He prefers reserve mode, which is his mode in this lifetime, and *has* developed the ability to be restrained—he's more comfortable feeling that he is in control of himself. Since he could tend to be almost hermit-like, he chose a goal of dominance so that he would put himself out in front of other people more, although dominance looks more subtle in him than it would in most people, just as passion mode does during lifetimes when he takes on that overleaf. He may feel that he doesn't know how to be passionate, even though it might not actually be that difficult for him when he is able to circumvent his aversion, perhaps using a crutch such as alcohol, which might prime the pump, so to speak. (People with uncomfortable overleaves often turn to alcohol, drugs, or other addictions.) Overleaves overlay and bring out certain qualities of essence; the overlay of passion mode isn't going to make this person "wild and crazy," since that quality isn't well developed in his essence to begin with, and scholars do not tend to be all that intense anyway (although there are exceptions). However, Michael pointed out that the highest good is sometimes served by "jumping in with both feet," just as it is also sometimes served by being restrained. Therefore, this scholar will eventually probably want to become more comfortable with passion.

A true idealist overlooks the practical to institute the utopian, and is sometimes able to do the seemingly impossible thing, thereby changing the world. A person with an attitude of idealist but whose essence feels uncomfortable taking eccentric paths if they seem logistically impractical may be pulled forward by his attitude, but with his feet dragging, so to speak.

I have a client with an attitude of cynic who has validated it—she does tend to notice first what won't work—but she manifests it gently; one wouldn't guess her to be a cynic unless one knew her well. With most people who have it, this attitude stands out strongly. I would assume that her essence tends to view life in an open, encompassing way, and that, therefore, she doesn't choose the attitude of cynic often. (It is generally not chosen often anyway, but some people choose it more frequently than other people.)

Many souls do not have strong opinions about overleaves, particularly younger souls, who have not yet had time to develop a lot of prejudices about them. They may have quite different overleaves from lifetime to lifetime, but as they become older, they can become a little more settled in their ways. However, if they are smart, they will pick the overleaves that are actually most useful for the lifetime rather than going with the ones they are most comfortable with.

Sometimes it becomes evident to a soul that it chose the wrong overleaves for the "job." During the first seven years of life, when the personality is still quite unformed, the soul can change the overleaves relatively easily. However, later in life, once the personality is more set, the essence may have no way to produce the needed changes, because the die has been cast. If someone then comes into a teaching such as this one and sees that things are not working very well, he can consciously cooperate with his essence in a remolding of his personality, but that is not generally an easy thing.

If it is just a matter of sliding across an axis more often, that is not a big problem, and usually, that is what people end up doing: the cynic becomes an almost full-time realist. He still maintains the basic lens through which the cynic views the world, but his more overt expression of attitude is realistic. It would be much more difficult for a person to change his primary centering, for example. Suppose that he has chosen the intellectual center but simply does not have the capability of good intellectual function, due to a lack of acculturation for that—a lack of good intellectual food growing up—or perhaps because of damage to the brain that occurred unexpectedly. Such a person might be better off with one of the other centers, particularly the physical center. However, a frustrating, unsuccessful attempt to change the center can create a lot of discomfort. Again, a conscious teaching such as this can help a person affect such a change more easily.

Abrading overleaves are those that tend to clash, especially in their negative poles, either internally or with other people. For instance, someone with a goal of discrimination can feel prickly to someone with a goal of acceptance, who may be particularly sensitive to the possibility that the person in discrimination (which was originally called "rejection") will reject him—it is especially important to someone in acceptance to be accepted. An example of internally abrading overleaves is a person having both a goal of acceptance and an attitude of cynic, whose negative poles are ingratiation and denigration. It's hard to get someone to accept us if we're denigrating him. Internally abrading overleaves may be chosen as a challenge, to see if the individual can balance apparently opposing qualities. They may also be chosen simply out of ignorance. However, no combination of overleaves is inherently "bad" or is necessarily troublesome to a particular individual. The key to handling any overleaf or combination of overleaves well is staying in the positive pole(s) as fully as possible. Positive-pole behavior, which is love-based, is harmonious and pleasing, no matter what the overleaves (or role) are.

NEUTRAL OVERLEAVES

Neutral overleaves are those on the assimilation axis. Unlike the other three axes, which are divided into cardinal and ordinal sides, the assimilation axis is undivided and is neither ordinal nor cardinal; it is instead neutral.

Neutral overleaves lack a push or pull toward a particular pattern of expression. They are impartial in that sense. They "like" all the patterns and are committed to none. They have no color of their own, rather like white light, which is often described as being above all the colors, but might be better described as being in the center of them. Like white light bent through a prism, the neutral axis lends itself to differentiation without being that differentiation itself. White can be seen as having no color, or as all colors, all possibilities, rolled into one.

The neutral overleaves go with whatever seems best in the moment. In the case of pragmatist, for instance, what seems best is what appears to be the most practical. Of course, the neutral position, like all positions, is essential to the whole.

Stubbornness, the neutral chief feature, is uncommitted fear. Rather than fearing something specific, such as being judged by others (arrogance), or missing out (impatience), stubbornness just fears whatever it does not yet know. This translates into a fear of change or movement. In stubbornness, one does not move at all, rather than moving in a specific direction, such as away from judgment or toward certain experiences.

Sometimes a neutral overleaf is chosen not so much for itself as for the flexibility it gives, since neutral overleaves can slide to all others. Overleaves on the three other axes can slide only to their "partners" on the axis. For example, caution mode can slide to power, and vice versa. Most people with a neutral overleaf have one or two others to which they occasionally slide, but some people spend little time in the neutral overleaf itself, just using it as a convenient means of getting to others. In fact, some people slide around constantly, and there are even those who slide to everything.

COMBINED OVERLEAF ENERGIES

Earlier, we discussed people with more than one essence in their body. Occasionally, people also combine overleaf energies. Some do more than one overleaf simultaneously, rather than sliding to one at a time. One client of mine blends the energies of two attitudes, using seventy percent realist and thirty percent cynic. Another combines two goals, dominance (seventy-five percent) and reevaluation (twenty-five percent), which is not "supposed" to happen, since they are not on the same axis. This is more challenging and uncommon. It could probably be said that dominance is his "official" goal, but that he is permanently "pulling in" some energy of reevaluation to blend with it for a specific purpose, similarly to the way that I have a goal of acceptance but temporarily took on growth energy as well.

Here is a more extreme example of this:

Gene's goal is a blend of five equally, a very unusual arrangement, excluding dominance and discrimination.

In this case, his "official" goal is probably flow, which is neutral, with him using the sliding mechanism to reach the others but holding the energies simultaneously instead.

The next example is even more unusual.

Sally's attitude is unspecified. She blends all seven energies.

Again, she is probably using the neutral attitude, pragmatist, to reach the others, but reaches them simultaneously rather than consecutively.

> *Jim has an equal emotional and moving center, with very little in the intellectual center.*[5]

Perhaps in this case, one center, say, the emotional, is the "official" one, and he accesses his moving center through the moving part of the emotional center, but he uses them, again, simultaneously.

Some of us simultaneously hold as many as three chief features. They can be blended, as with a stubborn martyr, or separate, as with someone who is both self-destructive and arrogant. This is different than sliding between chief features, focusing on one at a time.

Some people have unusual sliding patterns. For example:

> *Fred slides between flow and submission, constantly alternating between them, and experiencing each almost equally.*

One warrior permanently alternates between growth and dominance, which, again, isn't "supposed" to happen.

If we view each overleaf as representing a particular realm of energies rather than a rigid structure, it is easier to understand how overleaf energies can be combined. One physical realm of energies is light: there are seven colors in the rainbow, but they can also be combined to produce various hues.

Combining overleaf energies is rare, but as it is said, exceptions prove the rules. They also show that the universe is flexible, and, as in Alice's Restaurant, "You can get anything you want."

PERSONALITY VERSUS ESSENCE

One dictionary definition of essence is "the real or ultimate nature of a thing...as opposed to its existence." Our essence is our individual source, our higher self, the primary influence in our life, but it is a spiritual influence. Our overleaves and other personality traits provide the details that specifically identify us as the person we are in this lifetime.

---

[5]The primary center is the aspect of self from which a person normally responds—either the emotional, intellectual, physical, or moving center. The part of center is where a person's secondary responses originate. See also Chapter Twenty-Two, "Centers," or the Glossary.

If the essence in your body "walked out," and a new one "walked in," you would not immediately become a totally different person. In the beginning, your overleaves, as well as your body, memories, imprinting, and other elements of your personality, as well as your life circumstances, would remain the same, although you might find yourself feeling and looking at things differently. Over time, your new essence would gradually adapt those elements, even your body, to "his" purposes. "He" (which is now you) might choose a new set of overleaves, but it can take up to seven years for him to "install" them. This illustrates the fundamental yet general influence of the essence.

Those who have experienced past-life regression know how different our personalities can be from lifetime to lifetime, even though there are common threads. This also illustrates the difference between essence and personality.

A person can have a highly expressive essence, for instance— let's say he's an artisan with a sage essence twin and is in a number two (artisan) cadence position. However, in this particular lifetime, that person might have a highly inspirational personality—let's say his goal is growth, his mode is reserve, his attitude is spiritualist, and he is in the emotional center. These are all inspiration-axis overleaves. In observing such a person, you could probably perceive an inspirational quality, perhaps an added warmth, "superimposed" over his basic nature, which is expressive.

Chapter 19

GOALS

	ORDINAL	NEUTRAL	CARDINAL
INSPIRATION	*REEVALUATION* + Atavism – Withdrawal		*GROWTH* + Comprehension – Confusion
EXPRESSION	*DISCRIMINATION* + Sophistication – Prejudice		*ACCEPTANCE* + Agape – Ingratiation
ACTION	*SUBMISSION* + Devotion – Subservience		*DOMINANCE* + Leadership – Dictatorship
ASSIMILATION		*FLOW* + Suspension – Inertia	

Our goal is our primary motivation, what drives us, the general bottom line we want to accomplish in any situation we're in. As with the other overleaves, our goal normally stays the same throughout our life. Having a goal, however, doesn't mean that we achieve it.

For example, people with a goal of acceptance do not necessarily find it easy to accept difficult situations. In fact, they often find themselves in situations that are difficult to accept. Nonetheless, they usually bring to the challenge tools that can assist them, such as open-heartedness and agreeableness. (The positive pole of acceptance is agape, but one doesn't have to achieve total unconditional love in order to be in the positive pole. A certain magnanimity or even tolerance is adequate.) Also, other overleaves, such as the attitude of cynic, may abrade, making the challenge greater, and the chief feature is always an obstacle to meeting the goal. However, when acceptance is our goal, it is a major issue whether or not we achieve it. Similarly, those with a goal of flow may not actually be relaxed people who let things come to them gracefully and easily, but that is what they most aspire to be, and if they are blocking that experience, this, too, will be a major life issue.

This applies to the other overleaves. Having an overleaf does not ensure that we are good at it. For instance, an emotionally centered person is not necessarily in touch with his true feelings, although he does tend to react emotionally. An intellectually centered person is not necessarily intelligent. And only in the positive pole is a pragmatist truly practical.

Our goal is more about our relationship with our life situations than about our relationship with ourselves. For example, people in the positive pole of flow seem to have an easier time making a living and otherwise getting along in the world than those with other goals. I sometimes joke that flow is the goal that the rest of us wish we had chosen. I know one scholar in flow, for example, who receives disability income for a relatively minor injury, and has flowed from one house-sitting or other rent-free situation to another for a few years. This has given her more opportunity to study and do deep inner work. However, I don't think that her inner process has been easier than anyone else's. We all have parts of ourselves that need healing.

Although flow is sometimes chosen for a rest from outer stress and striving, it can be chosen for other reasons as well. For example, a person may choose flow, which is the neutral goal, simply to slide to other goals, giving him a lot of flexibility as to which goal energy he will use at any given time.

Growth, at forty percent of the population, and acceptance, at thirty percent, are the two most popular goals. Growth is a state of movement, of seeking new experiences, new stimuli to which to respond. To move, we must be unbalanced. When we walk, most of the time, we are "falling" forward. Acceptance is a state of stillness and balance, being peaceful about what happens. People in growth tend to be in motion, and those in acceptance tend to "plunk down." I would imagine, for example, that adult education classes are filled with people in growth, who tend to be busy and continually trying to learn something. I am in acceptance, and I don't have much motivation to go out and do those types of things. I think that I feel overstimulated more easily than those in growth. Still, those in growth can become overstimulated and, as a result, go into the negative pole, confusion.

Acceptance is a "natural overleaf" for sages, since both are on the cardinal side of the expression axis. When sages have a goal of acceptance, it can be "overkill," since sages tend to naturally seek acceptance anyway in order to have an "audience" for their self-expression. In the negative pole, a sage in acceptance can go to extremes in "bending over backward" to win favor, and have a tendency to obsess about those who don't seem to accept them rather than focusing on those who do.

Bill Clinton, an obvious sage, has been criticized for being ingratiating. I channeled that he is a young sage with a goal of growth, but others have channeled that he is a mature sage in acceptance. (Incidentally, Ronald Reagan has also been channeled as being a mature sage in acceptance, although he was said to be a young sage in Yarbro.) Clinton's public behavior is certainly reminiscent of acceptance, but it is unclear whether acceptance is actually his goal. His behavior may just be a result of his political survival instinct, perhaps stemming from an overwhelming young-soul need to succeed. He had been more willing to hold to unpopular stands before his 1980 defeat for reelection as Arkansas's governor. Also, in his private life, he has been known to have a quick temper and may be less accommodating than he appears to be publicly. In addition, part of what is seen as ingratiation may be his sagely diplomacy, attempting to integrate opposing points of view, and a common sage trait of collecting insights from others.

A friend who is a mild-mannered old scholar with a distaste for authority figures is also in dominance, which troubled him when he learned of it. Nonetheless, he had to admit that in every situation in which he finds himself, people spontaneously come to him expecting him to lead. I suggested that he regard the positive pole as leadership by example and by finding win-win solutions.

The positive pole of submission, devotion, is reminiscent of servers, whose positive pole is service. However, submission, like dominance, is on the action axis, so it involves doing: someone in submission devotes himself through action. Servers obviously also act, but for them, service is more a state of being; action is a means to inspire more than an end in and of itself. Mother Teresa, who was channeled as being a server in submission, combined these traits. Since, in this society, we have expected men to be dominant and women to be submissive, a woman in dominance may seem more masculine, even with higher female energy, and a man in submission, even with higher male energy, may seem more feminine. However, submission is also a natural overleaf of warriors, and manifests in their devotion to their principles (and, often, their leaders).

A friend of mine with a goal of submission is a woman artisan with higher male energy (and a feminist); however, she would probably strike most people as being higher in female energy if they didn't really understand what male and female energy refer to. Her artisan softness and love of fashion and beauty, her imprinting, and her goal all conspire to emphasize what is considered feminine. In the negative pole of submission, subservience, she feels subservient to her circumstances—helpless and stuck—even though she would not likely allow herself to be overtly subservient to another person. Her devotion to spiritual truths, particularly as represented in the books she reads (she is intellectually centered), is a manifestation of submission's positive pole.

Discrimination and reevaluation are the rarest goals. Discrimination motivates someone to discern and be selective—people in discrimination sometimes have a squinty look in their eyes, as if they're trying to discern visually—but the negative pole, prejudice, causes people to indiscriminately reject others from their lives. A mature sage I know who has this goal was described by his ex-wife as driving everyone away from himself—an especially painful thing for a sage (sages being the most social of the roles). Even in the positive pole and even for sages, people in discrimination tend to be "picky" about who their friends are, as well as about everything else important to them. It is a good idea for those in discrimination to deliberately slide to acceptance once they decide to open to friendship so that they can accept their friends as they are.[1]

Clients in reevaluation tell me things such as "My dream is to have a cabin in the mountains (or a cottage by the shore) where I can be alone." However, wanting to escape from the "big, bad world" is not the same as being motivated to reevaluate. Those with a goal of growth are prone to overstimulation, and often slide to reevaluation in order to "catch up" on processing all the input they have received. People who are autistic or who are institutionalized much of their lives sometimes have this goal; it appears that nothing is happening with them, but they may actually be unconsciously processing a lot of unresolved experiences from past lives. Of course, when processing is conscious, it can be accomplished more quickly and efficiently, but not everyone is capable of conscious processing.

In the following, Michael answered a question about how those with various goals approach service.

There are no hard-and-fast rules about this, but in general, those with a goal of submission are more interested in service than those with a goal of reevaluation or discrimination. Those with a goal of growth are likely to be more concerned with their own process, but may be interested in serving others if that supports their growth. Those with a goal of acceptance may serve others, especially in terms of helping others accept themselves, perhaps by simply being a loving presence for them, but will not tend to do as much in service as someone whose goal is

---

[1]See Chapter Twenty-One, "Attitudes," for a further discussion of discrimination, particularly as it compares with the attitude of cynic.

on the action axis, submission or dominance. Someone in acceptance is more likely to offer kind words, for example, in service, since acceptance is an expression axis goal. Since growth and reevaluation are inspirational goals, people with these goals tend to serve others, if they have a service thrust, through inspirational means, wanting to help others with their own growth or reevaluation, for instance.

Spiritual growth is not the same as the goal of growth. Spiritual growth results from being in the positive pole of any overleaf, which allows for essence contact. The goal indicates the type of growth experiences a person tends to look for. With a goal of growth, you set up challenges and attempt to meet or overcome them. In acceptance, your emphasis is accepting what you cannot overcome or change. To truly overcome, accept, flow, discriminate, lead, devote, or reevaluate can contribute equally to spiritual growth.

Chapter 20

MODES

	ORDINAL	NEUTRAL	CARDINAL
INSPIRATION	*RESERVE* + Restraint – Inhibition		*PASSION* + Self-Actualization – Identification
EXPRESSION	*CAUTION* + Deliberation – Phobia		*POWER* + Authority – Oppression
ACTION	*PERSEVERANCE* + Persistence – Immutability		*AGGRESSION* + Dynamism – Belligerence
ASSIMILATION		*OBSERVATION* + Clarity – Surveillance	

Our mode is our primary way of carrying out our goal, and our general way of operating in the world. It is usually our most visible overleaf. By contrast, our goal, for example, is what motivates us, which is not necessarily obvious. We might have to observe someone's pattern of choices over time to discern that he has a goal of growth, but passion mode, on the same side of the same axis, is likely to be apparent quickly in the way he does whatever he does.

Observation, on the assimilation axis, is by far the most common mode—in fact, half the population is in observation. However, since it is neutral, one can slide from it to any of the other modes, which is partly why it is chosen so often. For example, I am in observation sliding to passion and perseverance. I didn't want to be in passion full-time, and didn't want to be in reserve (passion's "partner" on the inspiration axis); observation allows me to use the energy of passion mode when it is appropriate for me. The positive pole of observation mode is clarity; in the negative pole, surveillance, we observe things that are none of our business, that don't add to our clarity. People in observation are more prone to stare, often without being aware of doing it, than those with other modes.

I think of passion mode as boundlessly letting one's inner energy flow "down" and "out," pulling out all the stops, bringing enthusiasm and high spirits. It reminds me of Howard Huge, the very large dog in the comics. Passion's partner on the inspiration axis, reserve mode, is the opposite; it draws one's inner energy "up" and "in," as a ballet dancer does, promoting containment and grace. It is about boundaries, whereas passion is about releasing boundaries. Passion amplifies, whereas reserve shuns exaggeration.

Power mode, being expressive, exudes energy with fullness in all directions. (All of the cardinal, or exalted, overleaves have this wide-open, expanded quality.) People in power mode often look "macho," whether male or female—they seem to have a lot of self-confidence and appear to know what they're talking about. If we know that people in power mode naturally come on strong, we can take that into account and not be intimidated or doubt our own perceptions. Caution, its opposite, controls its expression deliberately. In the positive pole, people in caution mode look both ways before crossing the street, so to speak; in the negative pole, they don't cross the street at all—they say things such as "I want to, but I'd better not." Caution mode may be chosen if a person has tended in recent past lives to be impulsive.

Aggression mode pulls out all the stops in terms of action, since it is the cardinal action mode. It does a number of things at the same time, with high energy. I have a scholar friend in aggression mode who could talk to me on the phone while grading papers (she was a school teacher) and washing dishes. Its opposite, perseverance, concentrates on one particular action, staying with it until it is complete. In the negative pole, perseverance reminds me of the cartoon bulldog that does not let go of the mailman's leg—in perseverance, one can stay with something that would be better let go. Perseverance works well in life situations in which it would be otherwise easy to give up. José Stevens observes that those in aggression mode often have a jutting jaw, and those in perseverance can have pursed lips.

Since, as mentioned, about half the population is in observation mode, and about another thirty percent is in caution mode, the remaining twenty percent of the population accounts for the other five modes. If you observe people, say, sitting in a bus station, you might notice that about half of them are observing, looking fairly neutral, and about another thirty percent look cautious. Among the rest, you may be able to see evidence of the other modes: some people appearing dynamic (aggression mode) or restrained (reserve), for instance.

In the subchapter "Number Correlations" in Chapter Eleven, "Cadences and Numbers," we discussed how each of the roles and overleaves have a numerical position in the progression from most ordinal to most cardinal. The role of server, for instance, and all the overleaves on the ordinal side of the inspiration axis are in the number one position—they are the most ordinal, or contracted. The role of king and all the overleaves on the cardinal side of the action axis are in the number seven position—they are the most cardinal, or expanded. Michael student Kent Babcock pointed out how the modes illustrate this progression:

One/reserve holds back.

Two/caution is reluctant.

Three/perseverance commits to action within a narrow range.

Four/observation is neutral.

Five/power thrusts outward, bold yet diffuse.

Six/passion releases inhibitions and increases intensity.

Seven/aggression is the most conspicuously strong since it is focused on tangible actions.

Kent noted the inward, private nature of the first three, and the expansive, affecting nature of the last three. He also pointed out that "this progression can be understood as a natural flow from the most yin (reserve) to the most yang (aggression)." These observations could also be applied to the other overleaves.

Chapter 21

ATTITUDES

	ORDINAL	NEUTRAL	CARDINAL
INSPIRATION	*STOIC* + Tranquility – Resignation		*SPIRITUALIST* + Verification – Faith
EXPRESSION	*SKEPTIC* + Investigation – Suspicion		*IDEALIST* + Coalescence – Abstraction
ACTION	*CYNIC* + Contradiction – Denigration		*REALIST* + Perception – Supposition
ASSIMILATION		*PRAGMATIST* + Practicality – Dogmatism	

Our attitude is our primary "slant" on life. Of all the overleaves, attitudes are the most flexible. Although our originally chosen attitude is our most natural way of seeing the world, we usually use other attitudes fairly often. We can all be realistic, for example. However, unless we have the attitude of realist, or are using the sliding mechanism to reach it from cynic or pragmatist, we are not experiencing that energy purely; we are superimposing the realist attitude over our own. For example, my realism as an idealist is not the same as the realism of someone who actually has the attitude of realist.

I know a cynic, normally "the devil's advocate," who uses the negative pole of spiritualist, faith, when he doesn't want to see something "negative." He is not truly using the spiritualist attitude, with its panorama of possibilities. He isn't purely using cynic either; he is mixing the two energies.

A friend who is a pragmatist sliding to spiritualist is one of the best examples of spiritualist I have met. He uses pragmatist at his job, but most often, he slides to spiritualist and stays there. His conversation is a never-ending stream of possible things he or others could do. I suppose that his being an artisan, with so much creativity and five inputs, also contributes to this.

I find spiritualist to be one of the most softening overleaves. Someone with an otherwise strong chart, such as a warrior in dominance and power, is a significantly more gentle person as a spiritualist. If he were a skeptic or cynic, two difficult attitudes, he could tend to be prickly or harsh in his negative poles. As a spiritualist, his negative poles tend to come on less strong.

Stoic is the other inspirational attitude. Whereas spiritualist, being cardinal, is expansive ("anything is possible" might be its motto), stoic, being ordinal, is contracted. Stoics stay within, feeling that whatever is going on out there isn't that important (their motto regarding outer possibilities might be "whatever—it doesn't matter that much"). In the negative pole, serenity gives way to resignation, not attempting to impact the world because "what's the use?"

Both realists and pragmatists have a "sensible," relatively unweighted view of things, but they are different and look different. Realist is on the action axis, so realists tend to focus on external, objective realities: "that's the way things are." Realists are realistic in the ordinary sense of the word. In the negative pole, realists suppose what reality is rather than truly perceiving it; they can also see the wide range of factual elements of a situation without recognizing which are most significant, and can have trouble making up their minds. Pragmatist is on the assimilation axis, which is neutral. In the absence of a point of view weighted in one direction or another—such as that things could be improved (idealist) or that it doesn't really matter (stoic)—pragmatists see things, almost by default, in terms of what works best. They like to be efficient and practical. However, what looks practical to one person may not look that way to someone else. In the negative pole, pragmatists dogmatically stick to a rule book—what was established as being the most "appropriate" in the past—and therefore lack spontaneity; they also don't "take time to smell the roses," since that isn't "practical."

Both realists and cynics tend to see things in black-and-white terms: it either is, or it isn't. Realists emphasize what is, and cynics, what isn't. I'm not suggesting that they can't appreciate the shades of gray in an argument; instead, I'm referring to a matter-of-fact quality in their view of life that is, in general, typical of the action axis.

The cynic attitude exerts an influence on its environment not unlike that of an acid; it cuts through. In the positive pole, it cuts through the tarnish to get to the metal. In the negative pole, it cuts through the metal, too—it destroys.

Cynics have the advantage of not being very easy to disappoint, because they tend not to have a lot of positive expectations. In the negative pole, particularly, they tend to have negative expectations, but in the positive pole, they tend not to have many expectations at all. The cynic simply does not see the world as a place where dreams can come true, as the idealist might, but that doesn't mean that the positive-pole cynic is unhappy about that: he can have pleasure in reality as it is, not unlike the realist.

More than realists, positive-pole cynics play the role of protectors (like warriors), making certain that the false does not destroy or prevail—that the tarnish does not destroy the metal—but without necessarily providing polish for the metal, the wherewithal to make it shine beautifully. In other words, cynics can cut away the tarnish, but without bringing forth an inspirational vision of the possibility of something more or higher; that is for the spiritualist or idealist to do.

In the negative pole, cynics tend to believe that the tarnish will prevail anyway, and what difference does it make if their acid therefore eats away at some of the metal itself? It is an exceedingly harsh view.

In the positive pole, the cynic attitude can provide a sharp-edged tool for the use of a person's curiosity. Cynic can also be useful when someone wants to feel that he has full permission to explore the hidden side of life, what other people do not acknowledge or talk about. Many comedians are cynics because humor can unearth hidden areas and bring them to light; it can release tension through showing what people want to acknowledge but don't feel that they can.

Cynic is not a particularly easy overleaf to use, but the soul does not always like to do what is easiest.

In fact, cynic is the most difficult attitude to do well, and is perhaps the most difficult of all overleaves. In the negative pole, denigration, it can make a person "prickly." I have sometimes found cynics (and, to a lesser degree, skeptics) difficult to channel for, since the channeling process requires a certain level of trust and willingness to participate, which may not come easily for them. Some cynics and skeptics, on the other hand, use their attitude to help them validate the information they receive without letting it get in the way of their receiving it in the first place. The positive pole, contradiction, might express itself as making sure something is really worthy by challenging its performance—for example, kicking the tires when checking out a used car, or pulling on a chain to find its weak link. Cynic is known as the warrior attitude, since both are on the ordinal side of the action axis, and *challenge* is a key word for both.

Although most cynics have an acidic quality, in the positive pole, contradiction, it can be appealing (as with all positive poles). Someone might choose to be a cynic for that acidic quality, since it facilitates cutting through b.s. The cynic's world view emphasizes what isn't working or what won't work, which can be useful in business, for example.

One client I channeled to be a cynic seemed to be handling it appropriately. He didn't have a particularly negative attitude (to which cynics are especially prone). At a workshop, he said that he was certain I had gotten it wrong, that he is a realist, that he objectively focuses on how things are. As I discussed it with him, he contradicted everything I said, again, doing so pretty appropriately. Others in the group agreed that they were getting a good demonstration of the positive pole of cynic. It is true that cynics can slide to realist, although Michael didn't pick up any significant sliding with him when I checked with them.

Cynic and the goal of discrimination have some commonalities. However, discriminators tend to focus more on what isn't of high quality aesthetically (being on the expression axis), whereas cynics, as mentioned, tend to focus more on what doesn't work well (being on the action axis). These are the two overleaves most prone to becoming bogged down in negativity (cynics perhaps slightly more than discriminators, although it depends on the degree they are in their negative poles), and are not chosen often. Although cynic can be a little more harsh than discrimination, negative-pole discriminators are more prone to be self-critical and hard on themselves, expressing their discrimination both inwardly and outwardly (the expression axis bridges the inspiration and action axes), whereas negative-pole cynics, being on the action axis, tend more to act harshly on just the outside world.

The negative pole of discrimination is usually a little easier to handle than the negative pole of cynic. Yet, in some cases, discrimination's negative pole can leave him feeling even more miserable than cynic's, because in discrimination, there still are, or can be, high expectations. There is the ambition to find the sublime, the perfect, the exactly right, the highest—yet everything around (and within, too) may seem to disappoint. Therefore, the discriminator can give up on ever finding that beauty, that sublime thing. There may be the prejudice—the pre-decided idea—that something is trash anyway, so why not just classify it as trash, and save the trouble of actually discriminating? The hope for the beauty is still there, but a certain laziness kicks in.

Also, the discriminator can be overly confident in his ability to make those judgments that separate the wheat from the chaff. Often, particularly in younger souls, there is less capability to truly do this than the person thinks. This goal works better when there is at least some humility. The older soul discriminator who is fairly honest with himself acknowledges his limitations, knowing that he is not always able to discriminate because he has not had the requisite experiences. He sees himself as a student for a while when he is learning to discriminate in a new area.

The cynic does not need training in the same way because the testing is done then and there, on the spot, although past experience may cause the cynic to be especially susceptible to the negative pole. Again, there can be laziness, not going through the testing and just saying that such and such is always a particular way. However, in prejudice, the negative pole of discrimination, habitual criticism is directed toward something specific, whereas denigration, the negative pole of cynic, is broader, as with the curmudgeon who denigrates everything. If there is something the cynic has previously tested and found wanting, he can be quite opinionated—not unlike the discriminator—but there is not a strong sense with the negative-pole cynic that he is attacking that one particular thing as much as he is using his negative opinion of it to "prove" how terrible everything is—his opinion is part of his overall outlook at that moment. His tendency, then, is to have ill will toward all, whereas the negative pole discriminator may, on the one hand, be very negative about one thing, and be quite opinionated that something else is the absolute best, because discriminators have a need to find the best, and they need to express whatever they have found to be the best as being the best, since discrimination is an expression-axis goal.

The attitude of skeptic has some similarities to that of cynic. The perceptions of both cynics and skeptics tend to be negative, not necessarily in the sense of destructive, but in the sense that they emphasize what isn't or what might not be. However, skeptics don't have the same acidic quality that cynics do—their skepticism feels more intellectual (skeptic is on the ordinal expression axis, as is the intellectual center). Skeptics often enjoy debating, and make excellent interviewers and scientists. They seem to want to be convinced, and *are* convinced if the opposing arguments satisfy them. If you win over a skeptic, he can be the greatest champion of your ideas. It's more difficult to convince cynics—they tend to just keep on contradicting. Comedians tend to be either cynics or skeptics (and, as mentioned, sages). They can use their negative perceptions for a positive (constructive) purpose, helping us see and laugh at things we might otherwise ignore.

Since I am an idealist, I can best discuss the influence of attitude and how it interacts with our other overleaves and role by exploring idealism.

IDEALISM

When I first learned about the Michael teachings from a friend, she told me about the seven attitudes. We both knew without question that I am an idealist. It is natural for me to see things in terms of how they can be improved or "should be." For instance, one of my ideals is aesthetic beauty. Unless I deliberately use another attitude, such as stoic or realist, I can't help but notice how much better something would look if it were cleaned, painted, repaired, and so on. I can feel uncomfortable if I am not in a position to do something about it.

Here's another example of that: I feel that people "should" return phone calls. (Being a sage factors into this: communication is very important to me.) The fact is that many people do not return calls, for whatever reasons, and that is their choice. Although that is sometimes surprising and disappointing, I am learning to be realistic and work sensibly with things as they are, rather than railing against what I cannot change. This also relates to my goal of acceptance.

Also, I write songs, and think that lyrics should rhyme accurately and consistently. I notice it when they don't. However, I remind myself that others may not feel that that's important, and that they are not "wrong" for having a different ideal, or none at all, regarding the craft of lyric writing.

In the positive pole, coalescence, the idealist energetically and optimistically takes whatever action he can to make a difference in the world. Idealism is on the expression axis, and especially since I am a sage, I tend to express my views as a way of bringing change. For example, there is a lot of criticism about the power of the *New York Times* theater critic. I wrote the *Times* a letter with several potential solutions. (It wasn't printed.) Also, I make suggestions to businesses when I encounter what appear to be unnecessary problems in their operation. However, it is important for an idealist to choose carefully what projects he takes on, because there are so many worthwhile possibilities—almost everything looks like it could be improved.

In the negative pole, abstraction or naiveté, I sometimes assume that because things "should" be a certain way, they are, and I don't recognize how they actually are. Other ways that I've done the negative pole include unrealistically getting my hopes up, counting my chickens before they're hatched, idealizing people, not seeing the writing on the wall, being oblivious to what's really going on, and so on. I do the negative pole less and less as I get older.

Simplicity is an ideal of mine. For example, I have given much thought to how tax laws could be made simple and more fair. However, that is abstraction, since I have no influence over the tax laws, and my ideas would not be politically popular anyway. If this issue were a high priority to me, I could devote a lot of energy to campaigning for my ideas, and maybe create some momentum around them, but I have many other such ideas as well. If I don't have time to pursue them, it is a waste of time to think endlessly about them. Coalescence is grounded in what I have the power to change. A negative-pole idealist can spend a lot of time tilting at windmills. Perhaps there is a place for tilting at windmills—it may inspire people or plant a seed for the future—but the best of ideas "on paper" are worth little if they aren't practical. Sliding to the positive pole of skeptic, investigation, can help expose the limitations of situations or of those involved, resulting in more workable ideas and less naiveté.[1]

I am intellectually centered, and I often slide to skeptic (as well as discrimination) in intellectual pursuits. I examine ideas closely for inconsistencies, discrepancies, and so on. I can be a persistent questioner and a relentless investigator. I am skeptical of my own channeling at times. Such skepticism is not for its own sake, but in service to ideals such as truth, accuracy, and clarity (the positive pole of my mode, observation).

My goal, acceptance, motivates me to attempt to love things exactly as they are. Since idealism sees how things can be improved, this can create conflict, but it doesn't have to. Substituting the word *and* for *or* is useful in this situation: "I fully accept this situation *and* I see how it can be improved. I do whatever I can to change things *and* I don't worry about what I can't." Acceptance can balance idealism and keep it from robbing joy from life, since the world seldom lives up to high ideals.

---

[1]This is another example of the "hands-across" technique, which involves using the positive pole across the axis from your role or one of your overleaves to get back into your own positive pole. It involves crossing two sets of opposites: from ordinal to cardinal (or vice versa) and from negative pole to positive.

Idealism, sage, and acceptance are all on the cardinal side of the expression axis, and share certain attributes. Sages are already attracted to insights and ideas. Idealism focuses those ideas on how things could be improved and finding creative solutions to problems. This is particularly useful in counseling and brainstorming. Acceptance is warm and inclusive of others, which helps them feel comfortable receiving an idealistic sage's suggestions.

Idealists tend to be harder on themselves than those with other attitudes, because they can see how they "should" be; their idealistic quest to improve things can include themselves. When I was younger, I tended to focus on my flaws and be self-conscious about them. This fed my self-deprecation and arrogance, my chief features at the time.[2] Now, although I am still never fully satisfied with my life skills, I am more accepting of myself and more neutral about my imperfections. I see them as things I'm working on but not as measures of my worth. At the same time, idealism has assisted my growth. For example, I often ask myself how I could have handled a situation better, especially if it was uncomfortable. I constantly learn from this.

My current chief feature is impatience. I am continually working to improve my use of time, planning better so that I don't feel that I have to rush. This helps me reduce my belief that there isn't enough of it.

I chose idealism so I could help bring change. Learning to stay in the positive pole allows me to do that more effectively.

---

[2]We do not settle on a chief feature until about the age of twenty, and even after then, the chief feature can change or be eliminated altogether if the person works on it enough. The other overleaves normally remain the same for the entire lifetime.

Chapter 22

CENTERS

	ORDINAL	NEUTRAL	CARDINAL
INSPIRATION	*EMOTIONAL*[1] + Sensibility – Sentimentality		*HIGHER EMOTIONAL* + Empathy – Intuition
EXPRESSION	*INTELLECTUAL* + Thought – Reason		*HIGHER INTELLECTUAL* + Integration – Telepathy
ACTION	*PHYSICAL* + Amoral – Erotic		*MOVING* + Enduring – Energetic
ASSIMILATION		*INSTINCTIVE* + Atomic – Anatomic	

O ur centers are the seven aspects of self that experience our lives. Four of them are routinely accessible: the intellectual, emotional, physical (on the ordinal action axis), and moving (cardinal action) centers.[2] One of the four is primary for us, depending on whether we process incoming stimuli and respond to it mainly

---

[1]*Messages from Michael* and *The Michael Handbook* place the intellectual center, which is verbal, on the expression axis, and the emotional center, which is mute, on the inspiration axis. However, *Michael—The Basic Teachings* reverses these positions. I use the first arrangement. I see both emotions and the inspiration axis as relating to the inner realms, and words as being means of expression.

[2]I chose the term *physical center* for the ordinal action center. The Yarbro books use the term *sexual center*. Some other channels use the term *moving center*, which they define as including both physical excitation and larger-scale movement.

For the cardinal action center, Yarbro uses the term *moving center*, which I have also adopted. Some other channels use the term *higher moving center*, which they use to describe transcendent experiences of pure energy. Both approaches have validity.

from our intellect, emotions, or body (either by physical excitation or by larger-scale movement).[3]

A person can be quite intellectual without being in the intellectual center; for example, most scholars and many sages have well-developed intellects regardless of centering. Decisions are most effectively made from the intellectual center, using reason (while taking emotions and "gut" or physical feelings into account). A person who is emotionally centered may react emotionally but still make decisions (which are not necessarily reactions) logically and rationally. Learning to use our centers appropriately is like learning to use the right tools for specific jobs.

Similarly, a person can be quite emotional yet not be emotionally centered; all the fluid roles tend to be at least somewhat emotional. And someone can be quite physical—being athletic or a dancer, for instance—without being in one of the body centers. Warriors and kings, for example, tend to be physically oriented. However, a person in one of the body centers tends to be more physical than he otherwise would be, just as someone in the emotional center tends to be more emotional and a person in the intellectual center, more intellectual.

We might view our center as our control station or center of gravity. For example, if we are intellectually centered, our intellect is where we coordinate our internal activities. When we receive stimuli, we process them intellectually. Then we funnel them into one of the other centers for further processing, most often through our "part" of center. For instance, if we are in the emotional part of the intellectual center, our intellect would most often funnel a stimulus to our emotional center through the emotional part of our intellectual center.

Each center has seven parts. Six of them are like doorways connecting it to every other center. For example, the intellectual center has the intellectual, emotional, physical, instinctive, higher intellectual, higher emotional, and moving parts. The intellectual part of the intellectual center is the place of "pure" intellect.[4] Again, four of the parts of any center are routinely accessible: the intellectual, emotional, physical, and moving.

The part of our center indicates how we tend to express or articulate our response, or from where our next response tends to

---

[3]Some other channels say that three centers rather than four are commonly available as primary centers: the intellectual, emotional, and moving (ordinal action) centers. However, in Yarbro, Michael makes it a point to say that the moving (cardinal action) center is the only routinely accessible higher center.

[4]A soul must be able to use the intellectual part of the intellectual center to be considered sentient. See also Chapter Twenty-Six, "Sentience."

come. Although one part of our center usually predominates, we can use all the parts of our primary center to reach all the other centers. So being in the emotional part of the moving center, for instance, doesn't prevent someone from also frequently reacting from the intellectual part of his moving center as well. In fact, the more balanced a person is, the more all his parts of center are available to him. However, since our centering springs from either the intellect, emotions, or body, and our part of center usually uses another of these three aspects of self, we are generally left with one of the three that we don't use as much. That can be the "weak link" in our chain, and we need to be especially conscious about using it in order to be better balanced.

For example, if we are in the emotional part of the intellectual center, our weak link may be our physical and/or moving centers—i.e. taking action, since these are the action-axis centers. With this centering, we tend to feel things about our thoughts. From there, we can go into our emotional center itself (probably through its intellectual part) and have direct emotional experience. After feeling and processing our emotions fully, the right action should be clear. If we are "trapped" in the emotional part of our intellectual center, we go around in circles; the appropriate response is "short-circuited." We do not actually get into our emotional center, and we do not think effectively either. Instead, incomplete feelings about our thoughts stimulate additional incomplete thoughts, without leading to productive resolution and action. This can manifest as patterns such as worry, depression, and even obsession. Focusing on our weak link—i.e., deciding what action to take—can help us get out of the trap. To do this, we first need to allow our thinking to be clear, objective, and complete. It may be useful to quiet the emotional part of our intellectual center with something such as gentle music, or spending time in nature. We will probably also want to explore our emotions to see and fully experience what we are really feeling, since the patterns of the trap are often ways of avoiding our true feelings.

To stay out of whatever our particular trap is, we need to make certain that our emotional, intellectual, and action centers are each adequately developed and available.[5]

All the centers are present in all people, but usually not fully available and operative. All the centers are "appropriate," but certain ones are more appropriate for certain circumstances.

---

[5]*Earth to Tao* by José Stevens has a chapter, "Balancing the Centers," that sheds more light on the traps.

Someone intellectually centered is likely to get to his moving center through the moving part of his intellectual center, whether or not that is his main part of center. He would think through what he wants to do, and then act on it. However, pretty soon, the moving center itself would take over. To give an example, suppose that you decided to exercise. You would think through what you wanted to do, set it up, and start exercising. Your mind might be active at first, continuing to guide your movements, but after a while, your body itself would take over, hopefully, and its own wisdom of how to exercise itself would come forth. You would then be in the moving center.

There is no real limitation in having a specific primary center, whether it is the intellectual, emotional, physical, or moving center, because through it, you can access all the other centers. As you mature, you learn to use all the parts of your center as means of accessing the other centers.

Ideally, all of a person's centers would be well developed, and some people use centers other than their primary one quite a bit. A scholar who is not intellectually centered, for instance, is still likely to have a strong intellect and use it a lot, due to having spent many lifetimes working with it. He just doesn't react to stimuli intellectually; in other words, his intellect does not become immediately excited and engaged in response to stimuli, although he may generally be quite analytical. Likewise, sages and priests who are not emotionally centered are still likely to have a lot of emotional activity. However, a person's center is usually the most prominent part of him, at least to other people, since it is our reactions that other people most often see. A person with no emotional centering (who is not in the emotional center, and not in the emotional part of another center) may look unemotional to others, even if he feels his emotions keenly. A person with no intellectual centering may appear impulsive—he doesn't tend to react analytically or articulate his reactions intellectually. A person with no physical or moving centering may appear inert—his body may be quite vital or sensual, but that might not be obvious to others.

There has been some disagreement as to whether people can be in the emotional part of the emotional center, the intellectual part of the intellectual center, and so forth. I have channeled that some people have such centerings. One person whom I channeled as being in the moving part of the moving center was described by his wife as never sitting still. Obviously, he thinks and feels, like everyone, but his responses are almost all with his body. In *Messages from Mi-*

chael,[6] Michael spoke of *most* people combining two different centers by being in a part of a center, implying, of course, that not all people do that.

Often, emotionally centered people have a watery or soft quality in their eyes. Intellectually centered people tend to have sharper eyes, and the slowest reactions—we might even be able to observe the "gears clicking" as they take time to analyze. Physically centered people might seem particularly sexual or physical, and those in the moving center might be known as people of action. However, the action-axis centers can seem more transparent than the others—it's harder to see a body reacting in excitation, or to tell if a person's movement is his first reaction or is "bouncing off" a thought or emotion—so a person who looks like he might be intellectually (or emotionally) centered might actually be in the intellectual (or emotional) part of the physical or moving center. If I'm uncertain when trying to perceive what someone's centering is (and I am not channeling), I generally figure that it's one of the action-axis centers. Someone in the intellectual part of the moving center, for example, who has been strongly intellectually acculturated, may look similar to someone who is intellectually centered. On closer examination, however, the intellect feels one step removed, since its reactions first come through the body. It is rather like a scholar with strong artisan essence twin influence: he may look like a "watered-down" artisan, because the artisan energy is filtered through his neutral scholar energy.

ACTION-AXIS CENTERS

I attended a concert of African music with a friend who is in the emotional part of the physical center. The concert included a lot of drumming and dancing. My friend found that it made her high, whereas I, who am in the emotional part of the intellectual center, just mildly enjoyed it. I could sense that her body was surging with an energy that felt like electricity—it was as if every cell in her body was excited. My body, on the other hand, was fairly calm. I kept wishing that I could understand what the words to the songs meant, and how the dances and music were used in the lives of the people.

That seems characteristic of our respective centers. For me, it was understand first, feel second, and maybe vibrate later. For her, it was vibrate first, feel second, and maybe understand later.

---

[6]P. 114.

I did, incidentally, start to vibrate after a while, partly with her help. She has a saturnian body type,[7] which is positive and active. Mine is lunar, which is negative and passive. These are polar opposites, and therefore magnetically attract, so it was easy for our bodies to exchange energies. I put my arm around her, and the electricity in her body started moving into mine a bit. I felt that my body was grounding hers. However, my body never vibrated to the extent that hers did.

We tend to gravitate toward entertainment that most stimulates our primary center. I go to far more theater than to concerts or opera. Theater is often a dominantly intellectually centered experience, being so verbal. My friend also enjoys theater, and opera as well, which is dominantly an emotionally centered experience. Nonetheless, physically centered experiences like that African music concert are her favorite. I imagine that those who most enjoy watching sporting events tend to be in one of the action centers, although people can become both emotionally and intellectually stimulated by them as well.

Another friend in the physical center told me that when she's upset, she may feel nauseous before she realizes intellectually or emotionally that she's upset. Also, others can tell what she's feeling by looking at her facial expressions before she has registered intellectually or emotionally that she feels that way—people see her automatic physical reaction.

Although you use your moving center whenever you move, if you do not primarily live from your moving center and respond by movement, you cannot be said to be moving centered. If you are moving centered, you are likely to move more often than if you are not moving centered. Those who move only if they have to are usually not moving or physically centered.

Other action-axis overleaves, such as aggression or impatience, can encourage greater use of the body (action-axis) centers.

As mentioned, the Yarbro books referred to the ordinal action center as the "sexual center." In my practice, I use the term *physical* for it because people can easily misunderstand the term *sexual* in this context. Michael used it to mean any form of physical excitation, which is also experienced in most athletics and can even be experienced when doing an activity such as cooking.

In Yarbro, the positive and negative poles of the sexual center are amoral and erotic. The dictionary defines amoral as "outside the

---

[7]See Chapter Twenty-Four, "Body Types."

sphere to which moral judgments apply" and gives the example, "infants are amoral." That suggests innocence or purity. Negative poles limit the scope of a particular vibration. Although, of course, eroticism is not "bad," it is a more limited or narrow expression of this energy. If we are in the negative pole while hiking, skiing, or cooking, for example, it doesn't necessarily mean that we are sexually aroused. It may mean that we are stuck in a limited aspect of the energy: we are perhaps using the excitation merely to stimulate ourselves rather than to participate expansively in what we are doing. It is like being concerned only about our own pleasure during sex, rather than enjoying participating in the full experience with our partner.

In Yarbro, the positive and negative poles of the moving center are enduring and energetic.[8] Again, there is nothing wrong with being energetic, but it is a more limited experience than tapping into endurance. In endurance, a rhythm is established, bringing ease and a "high" (this being a cardinal, or higher, center). Moving-center highs are sometimes experienced by people such as dancers, orchestral conductors, accomplished meditators, and athletes, and by anyone during sex. In such highs, the body can seem to be moving almost by itself; the body's higher knowledge takes over. It can even seem as if one is in slow motion, or as if time is standing still.

> *The excitation of the body sexually is, of itself, of the ordinal center, but when it opens the body to higher energies, toward the greater fulfillment of the sexual act, there is a shift to the cardinal center.*

When sex is more than physical excitation, it can also be a gateway into the higher emotional and higher intellectual centers.

A sense of timelessness and effortless intensity can also be experienced in the other higher centers. This might have to do with the fact that the higher centers resonate with the higher planes of creation, in which physical time doesn't apply. In Yarbro,[9] Michael spoke of the appearance of time slowing down relating to the "enhanced concentration of the higher intellectual center." Elsewhere,[10] Michael said that "some actors, particularly those actors who are sages, expe-

---

[8]Other northern California Michael channels and students who have adopted the terms *moving* and *higher moving* for the action-axis centers use the terms *productive/frenetic* and *beauty/desire* for their poles. (Like the Yarbro channels, I use the term *frenetic* as the negative pole of the mercurial body type.)
[9]*Michael's People*, p. 70.
[10]*Messages from Michael*, p. 278.

rience the higher intellectual center when acting, in that the role seems to do itself." The higher intellectual center and the role of sage are both on the cardinal expression axis.

The moving center is the only higher center that is relatively easy to access. That is partly because false personality is more threatened by higher emotional and intellectual accomplishment than by one that is purely energetic, and therefore, in a sense, less specific or defined—it is "just a sensation." The transcendent experiences associated with the higher centers, such as a moving-center high, occur when we are in them intensely and in the positive poles. One may experience a mild moving-center high in an aerobics class, for instance, and an intense, blissful high during a dance performance.

Higher centers expand or "exalt," as Michael puts it, what occurs in the ordinal centers. All the ordinal centers involve some sort of excitation: intellectual, emotional, or physical. Excitation is response on a small scale. The excitation in sex is a good illustration of the physical center. When one slides to the moving center in sex, there is a larger response; it can take the form of moving the body as a whole, which is a larger response than the excitation or vibration of its parts. In addition, it can take the form of bringing the body into a transcendent experience of energy, which can also occur in meditation and other experiences. Like rhythmic movement during sex, this is an expansion of scope in the body's energy. The moving center isn't "better" than the physical center; in fact, we couldn't have one without the other, and there is much reciprocity between them. Experiencing the positive pole of any center is pleasurable. The amount of pleasure, again, depends on the intensity. The difference between the cardinal and ordinal centers is similar to the difference between any other cardinal and ordinal overleaf—the cardinal is simply expanded. However, with the higher emotional and intellectual centers, we would not generally want to be that expanded in everyday life.

Some of those who use the moving center more than the physical center are channeled through me as being in the moving part of the physical center because they get to the moving center through the moving part of the physical center. Their first reaction is physical excitation, which warms up their body, so to speak, quickly leading to larger, more encompassing movement.

An essence may not choose a centering if he thinks that it won't be reinforced and developed in a particular culture. In *More Messages from Michael*, Michael said that sexual centering is rare because our society does not acculturate for it.[11] Perhaps many of the people who

---

[11]Pp. 277-278.

quickly go into the moving center from the physical do so because it isn't considered okay, by and large, to be in bodily excitation, whereas reacting by taking action is considered more acceptable. In the database of charts I've channeled (which, again, isn't necessarily representative), about 41% are intellectually centered, 21% are emotionally centered, and 38% are bodily centered. I didn't start asking Michael to specify ordinal or cardinal for the body centers until 1992; since then, about a third have been physically centered (a rate of about 13% of all charts) and two-thirds moving centered (25%).

ENGAGING WITH EMOTIONS

When you experience pure emotion, you are in the emotional part of your emotional center. If you are intellectually centered, you would normally get there through the emotional part of your intellectual center. You might, for instance, observe the form and understand the beauty of something, have feelings about that understanding, and then go into the emotional center itself, feeling inspired by that beauty.

Someone in the intellectual part of the emotional center, on the other hand, would tend to feel inspired by the beauty first. He might feel communion with it, or it might evoke memories. He might then verbally articulate his feelings.

Everyone has emotions, just as everyone has thoughts and everyone has physical reactions and movements. However, when we are not emotionally centered, we don't respond from our emotions; our emotions are not directly excited by stimuli because they are not "forward." When we are in the emotional part of a center, we at least have easier access to them. Those who are neither emotionally centered nor in the emotional part of another center can seem cool and unemotional. The emotions are the "weak link in the chain," as I put it earlier. This seems especially true of those who are in the physical or moving center, and for the solid roles (kings, warriors, and scholars). Priests, for instance, access certain emotions through their positive pole, compassion. Nonetheless, they still seem less emotional when they are not in the emotional center or the emotional part of another center.

We all react to stimuli to some degree, mainly from our center. Some people react more strongly than others, depending on imprinting, body type,[12] overleaves, and so forth. Of course, it also depends

---

[12]For example, the martial body type is more volatile than the lunar type.

on the situation, including how much charge, positive or negative, a person has about it, and his general level of stress. Someone who easily loses his temper, for instance, may be volatile because he carries a lot of negative charge and doesn't have a lot of inhibitions about expressing it. He is not necessarily emotionally centered. He might, for instance, be physically centered: a bodily sensation of being threatened may stimulate the emotion of anger through the emotional part of his physical center. If he is trapped there, he cannot reach the emotional center itself and therefore deal constructively with his anger. Instead, he directs his anger back into his body, becoming more and more agitated. Similarly, in someone intellectually centered, the belief that he is threatened could stimulate anger through the emotional part of that center. If he is trapped there, he would direct his anger back into his mind, becoming obsessive.

Someone who tends to react irrationally or unreasonably is not necessarily emotionally centered either; a person can be intellectually centered but be irrational—just because the reaction comes from the mind doesn't mean that the thinking is objective or clear, and an emotional reaction can also be reasonable. Also, people who cry a lot may just be under a lot of stress and are not necessarily emotionally centered, although they often are (especially men, who are generally imprinted not to cry; their centering may make it difficult for them to fully succumb to that imprinting). However, emotionally centered people live and react predominantly from their emotions—they feel first; their emotions, whether large or subdued, are continually "out front" in their interface with the world.

Sensations of pleasure or sexual arousal derive, of course, from the body, although they are sometimes interpreted as being the emotion of love. If someone gives us pleasure, that can foster the growth of loving feelings, but those feelings are distinct from the pleasurable sensations. Similarly, when we're physically tired, we're more susceptible to feeling emotionally "cranky," but again, these are distinct experiences—we don't always feel cranky when we're tired. Also, emotions and intellect can manifest in the body, as when our body feels light or tingly when we feel happy, or when our stomach churns when we think about a problem over and over. The latter is especially common with those trapped in the physical part of the intellectual center.

When someone in the physical center is angry, upset, or elated, he is likely to experience it first in his body as some kind of excitation. He may feel burning in his gut, or light-headedness. If he is in the intellectual part of the physical center, he may verbalize his reaction, shouting an epithet or talking about why he's so happy. Only then might he actually feel his anger or joy in the emotional center, and only if he is not in his trap. The trap, again, is a "broken record" experience. With this centering, it could lead to endless thinking or talking about his reaction, stimulating more reaction, rather than experiencing the emotional quality of it.

> *Someone in the intellectual part of the physical center might consider himself to be quite emotional, but especially if he is in his trap, most people probably won't know about it very often, because his responses to stimulation do not emanate from his emotional center.*
>
> *However, he can become well-balanced by developing free access to his emotions through the emotional part of his physical center. In other words, he can learn to express his emotions in a way appropriate for him. If he does, the designation "intellectual part of the physical center," although still accurate, may become a little limiting. That still may be his most customary centering, but it could also be said that he is secondarily in the emotional part.*

It is especially easy for someone in the physical center to go into the moving part of the physical center, even if that isn't his customary part of center, since the physical and moving centers are on the same axis and are so closely related, For example, a person who becomes physically excited may then hit, or jump for joy. The reverse is also true: a moving centered person can go especially easily into the physical part of the moving center, becoming excited by movement.

CORRELATING CHAKRAS AND CENTERS

As with the roles and chakras, there are differing ideas about how the centers and chakras correlate, and again, one can make a case for each, depending upon the basis used for correlating them. However, I have come to the conclusion that correlations such as these are like analogies that eventually break down. Although a center may have a particularly strong influence on a chakra, the centers are not really located in one particular part of the physical or energy body. For example, we associate the intellect with the brain, and both the sixth and seventh chakras are seated in the region of the brain; however, emotion and movement are also directed from the brain. Since we communicate verbally through the throat, the throat chakra could be said to be the seat of the intellectual center, but we can just as easily express emotional sounds through it, and the intellectual center may also need to use the heart chakra at times.

It might be more correct to view each chakra as a "modular slot" or "window" capable of accommodating input from any of the centers, in addition to its own native "work station" function in the body. More than one center can work through a chakra, and a center can work with more than one chakra. Which center is dominant in a chakra varies from person to person, depending on his life task, gender, male/female energy ratio, and so forth. It can also change during a person's life, depending on his needs.

For example, Michael told me that my higher emotional center correlates especially with my throat chakra, helping make singing an emotional, inspirational experience for me. One way in which energy flows in the body is up and down through the chakras, so having neighboring chakras correlate with certain centers can be useful in particular circumstances. My higher intellectual center has a particular correlation with my third eye, which is useful in channeling, since Michael's energy first comes into my body through the adjacent crown chakra, which in me especially correlates with my moving (cardinal action-axis) center.

Perhaps when the various chakra-center correlations were channeled, they were each based on the "calibrations" of a particular individual present at the time, or of the most common pattern in that specific group—Michael read what they saw and maybe assumed it to be universal. If that particular Michael fragment had never been asked about it before and had not given it any thought or discussed it with other members of the Michael entity, that would have been an easy mistake for them to make.

Incidentally, the third eye, which relates to the pituitary gland, is commonly numbered as the sixth chakra, and the crown chakra, which relates to the pineal gland, is commonly numbered as the seventh. However, Michael through me once numbered the crown chakra as the sixth. The crown, of course, is on the top of the head, and the crown chakra is accessed from there. However, the crown chakra's emanations are centered near the pineal, and they explained that the pineal itself is actually a bit lower than the pituitary. I later discovered that some chakra charts also number the crown chakra as the sixth and the third eye as the seventh, and Michael through "Jessica Lansing" once did the same thing. Nevertheless, I now stick with the more common numbering.

HIGHER EMOTIONAL AND INTELLECTUAL CENTERS

Intensely accessing the higher emotional and higher intellectual centers brings those revelatory, life-changing experiences that usually only occur when we are under a great deal of stress—our backs are against the wall, so to speak, and life circumstances force us either to open to something higher or to be engulfed by the stresses. However, opening widely a higher center when it has been closed is like exercising intensely when we're out of shape and without warming up first—it's a shock to the system. It is preferable to open and access our higher centers deliberately, a little bit at a time.

> *Opening your higher centers is a major goal of the spiritual path, and a key to happiness. You open them by opening to love, truth, and higher energies. This allows you to contribute to humanity in the most significant way possible.*
>
> *Generally, people do not often reach the positive poles of the higher intellectual and emotional centers (integration and empathy) in any profound way. Understanding some aspects of truth, for instance, is not the same as integration, which ultimately brings an all-encompassing, profound awareness of truth. That requires a foundation of stability. Otherwise, the experience can be startling, at best, and shattering, at worst.*[13]

We gain the stability of which Michael speaks through ongoing spiritual growth, particularly through balancing our other centers. That means having all of them open and available, and reacting from the center that is most appropriate for the situation: reacting intellectually when a reasoned response is required, responding emotionally when that is called for, and taking action when that would be the most beneficial course. (Again, we can reach all our centers through the various parts of our primary center, whatever it is.) Reacting from an inappropriate center is like using a screwdriver when a hammer is needed—it wastes energy and creates problems. An example is responding to someone's pain by intellectualizing, when expressing a loving emotion might help heal the pain; an intellectual response is probably inappropriate, even for those who are intellectually centered. Balance gives us a foundation for higher center experiences, so that when intense love, truth, or pure energy starts pouring through us, we don't lose our bearings.

---

[13]Michael discusses opening the higher centers in more detail in my Summerjoy Michael books *Loving from Your Soul—Creating Powerful Relationships* and the upcoming *Opening to Healing Energy*.

Chapter 23

CHIEF FEATURES

	ORDINAL	NEUTRAL	CARDINAL
INSPIRATION	*SELF-DEPRECATION* + Humility – Abasement		*ARROGANCE* + Pride – Vanity
Fear of	*Inadequacy*		*Vulnerability*
EXPRESSION	*SELF-DESTRUCTION* + Sacrifice – Immolation		*GREED* + Egotism – Voracity
Fear of	*Loss of Control*		*Want or Loss*
ACTION	*MARTYRDOM* + Selflessness – Mortification		*IMPATIENCE* + Audacity – Intolerance
Fear of	*Worthlessness*		*Missing Out*
ASSIMILATION		*STUBBORNNESS* + Determination – Obstinacy	
Fear of		*Dealing with New Situations*	

O ur chief feature (or chief obstacle, as I now refer to it in my practice) is our Achilles' heel or primary stumbling block—it is the focus of our fears and illusions. Since it is our dominant blind spot, it can be hard to recognize it, and even if we acknowledge it in theory, it can be difficult to recognize in action (although, no doubt, we can see other people's chief features plain as day!). The chief feature can be blatant, or it can be relatively subtle, especially after we've been working for a while on extinguishing it. The chief feature can also be relatively mild; it may not be a major focus during a particular lifetime, so its influence may be relatively minor.

As with the other overleaves, we can slide across the axis, or to any of the other chief features from the neutral position, which is stubbornness. We can also hold a secondary chief feature, which is simultaneous rather than alternating. According to *Michael's People*,[1]

---

[1] Pp. 51-52.

the secondary chief feature distorts the attitude, whereas the (primary) chief feature distorts the goal. Usually, the secondary chief feature is more at work in personal relationships. Although I recall *Michael's People* saying that everyone has a secondary chief feature, I do not consistently get secondaries on the charts I channel. (Rarely, I get two secondaries.)

The chief feature and the negative poles of the role and other overleaves are activated by fear.[2] Ironically, they make matters worse because they generate inappropriate responses, and then it seems that more fear is warranted when these responses don't work. For example, stubbornness is a fear of change, but when we resist change, we make things worse for ourselves by creating conflict, making it appear that even more fear is warranted, which can lead to still more stubbornness. The inappropriate responses build on themselves, increasing the hold of the false personality and maya. False personality is made up of the chief feature and the negative poles of the overleaves; maya means illusion, and relates to the essence, particularly the negative pole of the role.

Fear's purpose in the scheme of things is to alert us when there is a genuine threat to our physical safety so that we will take the necessary steps to ensure our protection. Fear springs largely from the body's survival urge, and the body's ultimate fear is the fear of death. Our chief feature stems from what we falsely and habitually perceive as the greatest threat to our survival. In arrogance, one believes, "If others criticize me, I will die." In self-deprecation, one believes, "If I cannot improve myself and become adequate somehow, I will die." In impatience, one believes, "If I don't beat the race against time, if I miss out, I will die." In martyrdom, one believes, "If I don't become worthy and prove my worth, I will die." In self-destruction, one believes, "If I lose control, I will die." In greed, one believes, "If I don't get enough, I will die." And in stubbornness, one believes, "If things change, I will die."

These fear-based beliefs, although illusions, can be self-fulfilling prophecies. With self-destruction, a person can be so afraid of dying through losing control that he directs his anger toward himself and implodes, becoming seriously ill or dulling his discomfort through substance abuse. In another scenario, the pressure builds up to the point at which he explodes uncontrollably, creating exactly what he had been dreading. In greed, a person can die, or at least suffer, from having too much; too much food can lead to obesity; too much money can become a heavy responsibility; and so on. The arrogance that is

---

[2]Both the positive and negative poles of the chief features are fear-based; the positive poles are merely the lesser of the two evils.

supposed to protect a person from the barbs of others can make him a target for them; acting superior to others can cause them to want to put him in his place; criticizing others can make them want to criticize him. Self-deprecation's fear of inadequacy can lead to actual inadequacy and failure, from a person trying too hard and getting in his own way, or from not making an effort at all. The impatient person may actually miss out by trying to pack in too much and then being late. The martyr becomes a victim of his self-inflicted pain. And a stubborn person's resistance to change can cause changes to be negative that would not have been otherwise.

Our essence settles on a chief feature at the beginning of adulthood, usually around the age of twenty in this culture. Before that, we might "play with" various chief features, or even all of them, especially during adolescence.

The chief feature isn't manufactured out of nothing. It is made up of previously latent fears, from past lives or earlier in the present lifetime. Concentrating them into a chief feature makes it easier for us to recognize and work on them. Overcoming these particular fears becomes the focus of our growth. People with no chief feature may be focusing on growth in other ways.

Each pair of chief features, like the other overleaves, are opposites. The inspiration axis chief features are arrogance, which perceives self in an inflated way, and self-deprecation, which perceives self in a deflated way. The expression axis chief features are greed, which attempts to add to the self, and self-destruction, which attempts to subtract from it. The action axis chief features are impatience, which audaciously tries to make things happen in the environment, and martyrdom, which experiences the environment as acting on itself. The assimilation axis chief feature is stubbornness; it is neutral and not a member of a pair.

The chief features are defensive. The cardinal chief features artificially expand the self in defense, while the ordinal ones artificially contract it.

Our psychological shadow, or dark side, includes our chief feature and the negative poles of our role and overleaves. However, everyone's shadow goes beyond them and is unique.

Michael's main tool for reducing our chief feature is simply to "photograph" it, noticing it when it is influencing us. If we can do that, we can begin to anticipate when it is likely to be activated, and can take steps to avoid it.

Regression into past lives or early childhood can be another useful tool for working with the chief feature. For example, someone in arrogance might unconsciously be reacting to a past life in which the judgments of others were literally fatal to him. Regressing to that lifetime can help him realize on a gut level that he is not at risk in his present situation.

Affirmations are also useful. The following affirmation can help someone in arrogance: "It is all right if others judge and criticize me. I love and accept myself." Welcoming what was feared reduces its power over us. Along these lines, it can also be helpful to recognize the valuable lessons offered by what is feared. Again, with arrogance, we can realize that many people are judgmental, and it is impossible to avoid the judgments of others all the time. However, although we do not need to take them personally, we can learn from them; we can explore what is valid in the criticism we receive and use it to grow into, ultimately, a happier person.

Let's look at the chief features individually. Since we've been using arrogance as an example, we'll begin there.

ARROGANCE

I knew a person who was quite intelligent and seemed to think that that made him better than most people. I was surprised when Michael said that he had no chief feature—I was sure that he was in arrogance. Michael said that he used the style of arrogance consciously to achieve his goals. Because it did not spring from fear and was not unconscious, it is not a chief feature. A person can have a big ego and be self-important and still not have the chief feature of arrogance.

Arrogance is a fear of vulnerability, of being judged and found wanting. This may manifest in the form of overt arrogance, as a "first-strike" defense: the arrogant person hopes that by criticizing those who appear to be threats before they have a chance to criticize him, he will be safe.[3] He may also criticize himself before others have a chance to do so, hoping that "if I'm perfect, no one will judge me," which can look like self-deprecation, although it is not a fear of inadequacy motivating him. (However, those in arrogance frequently slide to self-deprecation, and vice versa.) Those in both of these chief features can be painfully self-conscious, and everyone in arrogance has, by definition, a shell around himself to some degree. However, not everyone with a shell around himself, or who is critical (or self-critical), is in arrogance. Again, it is a matter of what the motivation

---

[3]Although chief features can always cause problems in relationships, two people manifesting arrogance in this way can have a particularly hard time together, for obvious reasons. Two people in heavy stubbornness can also have an especially difficult relationship.

is. A shell, or being critical, is indicative of this chief feature only when it is motivated by a desire to avoid being judged and found wanting. Cynics and discriminators, for example, can also be critical.

STUBBORNNESS

Stubbornness is the chief feature that my clients most often think that they don't have when they do. Its position on the assimilation axis gives it neutrality and contributes to its invisibility—it's harder to see something neutral. It manifests not so much by doing something as by not doing something, by digging in one's heels and not moving. Someone who is classically stubborn is inflexible and difficult to deal with—he insists on his own way. However, stubbornness is not always so blatant. One of its subtler manifestations can be when someone sticks with an approach or a way of thinking that is not working.[4] It can also masquerade as perseverance or integrity. People who tend to say no first may be in stubbornness, or may have an attitude of skeptic or cynic. Although it's hard for us to see our stubbornness, others feel it when they run up against it—it's like hitting an invisible wall.

A useful affirmation for stubbornness is: I am fluid and flexible, and welcome change. The changes in my life bring blessings and growth.

IMPATIENCE

Impatience, on the other hand, is the chief feature that my clients most often think they have when they don't. Like most terms in the Michael teachings, impatience has a more narrow definition than it does in common usage. It specifically refers to a habitual, irrational fear of missing out. Its negative pole, intolerance, isn't ordinary prejudice; it springs from this fear, and often manifests as testiness when someone seems to be delaying us. Drivers who are always trying to go faster than traffic conditions gracefully allow often have this chief feature. Impatience is characterized by a restless malaise and a lack of grace. In impatience, we "push the river" or "strip our gears" trying to get to the next thing.

---

[4]There are common threads among the overleaves and role on the same column on the Michael Reading chart. Stubbornness, on the assimilation axis, is reminiscent of the negative poles of the other assimilation axis overleaves and the role of scholar: *dogmatism* (pragmatist); *inertia*, which relates to becoming stuck (flow); and *theory* (scholar), for example.

I once assumed that a king I know who claimed to have no patience and who tends to be irritable, critical, and short-tempered is in impatience. However, Michael said that he is in arrogance (as well as tyranny, the negative pole of king). I was able to validate that by observing that he is not the type to constantly look at his watch, curse when forced to wait, or drive overly aggressively—all telltale signs of impatience. However, the testiness of impatience can look similar to the criticalness of arrogance.

Time is usually a big issue for people in impatience. One type of person in impatience chronically arrives late after trying to cram one more thing into his schedule before leaving—he doesn't want to miss out on other, last-minute things. He takes a phone call he doesn't have time for, tries to "kill two birds with one stone" by fitting in an errand, and so forth. (I speak from experience!) Another type usually arrives excessively early because he doesn't want to miss out on the event at hand. He then impatiently waits for it to start, hurrying it along if he can.

However, impatience is more than issues about time. I know someone who chronically tries to fit in too many activities, and then runs late and hurries, but is not in impatience, even as a secondary chief feature; she is in self-deprecation and growth. She is motivated to rush not so much because she fears missing out, but because she fears being inadequate, and is trying to "catch up," to gain the skills and experiences that would make her "adequate." The goal of growth motivates her to seek stimulation and be busy; our chief feature distorts our goal, so self-deprecation's fear of inadequacy causes her to seek growth with an edge of desperation, which sometimes interferes with or blocks her ability to grow, whereas my impatience can do the same with my ability to accept myself and my situations.

Most of us are impatient, in the generic sense of the word, when we don't understand why other people are different from us, why they don't care about something we do or aren't as good at something as we are. For example, a sage may be irritated with someone of another role who doesn't communicate well; a king may be critical of someone who doesn't strive for excellence; and a server may be intolerant of someone who doesn't care deeply about the common good. This is not the same as the chief feature of impatience, because it is not sourced in a fear of missing out; it is simply a lack of understanding or acceptance of the differences between people. A major purpose of the Michael teachings is to illuminate the reasons for those differences so that we can learn to be loving rather than judgmental.

In impatience, it can be helpful to affirm: I have all the time I need in order to do each thing I need to do and to experience everything I wish to experience; everything is in order.

MARTYRDOM

Martyrdom brings up images of loudly proclaimed suffering or silent manipulation. However, like all chief features, martyrdom can be subtle. I have sometimes seen it manifest as chronic back pain in people who don't complain or otherwise act like martyrs. They unconsciously put into their body their belief in their unworthiness and need to suffer. Although it's true for all of us that there are negative influences in our lives beyond our control, if we are not in martyrdom, we tend to take them in stride; someone in martyrdom might instead see them, at least unconsciously, as confirmation that he is a victim of outside forces that are conspiring against him. He may rail against them, yet feel that he must somehow deserve his treatment.

I have heard a couple of people say, upon learning that martyrdom is their chief feature, "Oh, no! My mother was a martyr, and I always swore I would never be that way!" Maybe these people chose mothers in martyrdom to see their own similar beliefs. Rebellion certainly indicates a charge around the issue, but usually does not bring deep changes, even if it involves swinging to opposite behaviors. Of course, this applies to all the chief features.

All chief features are problematic, and the problems they cause are in proportion to their severity. Nonetheless, martyrdom and self-destruction generally seem to create the biggest problems in terms of life events. I've seen people who were unconsciously controlled by these chief features suffer painful deaths or prison terms because of them. Although the ultimate goal is to eliminate one's chief feature altogether, it can be useful for someone with these chief features to temporarily slide to impatience or greed.

Those in martyrdom can benefit from affirming: I deserve the blessings of life; I am worthy of them just for being who I am.

SELF-DEPRECATION

Sometimes people confuse self-deprecation with martyrdom. It is useful to consider the axes. Martyrdom is on the action axis, which relates to the external world. In martyrdom, people *do* things to prove their worth. They feel that they don't deserve external rewards. Self-deprecation is on the inspiration axis, which relates to the internal world. We might say that in self-deprecation, someone has trouble feeling inspired about himself. He feels that he doesn't have what it takes within to "measure up." He tries to make himself seem smaller than he is, just as someone in arrogance tries to make himself seem larger than he is.

More than the other chief features, a little self-deprecation can sometimes be comfortable for other people; someone in self-deprecation generally isn't a threatening authority figure. However, after a while, self-deprecation can get on other people's nerves, just like all the other chief features.

A useful affirmation for self-deprecation is: I am fully capable of doing everything I wish to do.

GREED AND SELF-DESTRUCTION

I come across greed and self-destruction less often than the other chief features. They are more often chosen by younger souls, and I don't see that many younger souls in my practice. By the same token, arrogance and self-deprecation are more often chosen by older souls (because of the self-worth issues that naturally come up during the later cycles). Stubbornness, impatience, and martyrdom seem universally "popular" among all soul ages.

In *More Messages from Michael*,[5] Michael defined self-destruction as a fear of loss of control. Elsewhere,[6] they said that in self-destruction, one can be authoritarian and can be thought of as difficult. In *Michael's People*,[7] they related it to a childhood of neglect and rigidity, resulting in a feeling of having no control over one's life, often leading to extreme self-discipline as a compensation. Despite *Celebrities—The Complete Michael Database* listing Nancy Reagan's chief feature as arrogance, I think of her as exemplifying self-destruction—she seemed to feel the need to use authoritarian means to control the Reagan White House. Along with reserve mode (negative pole, inhibition), this chief feature might have contributed to her being "uptight." Hillary Clinton may have the same chief feature, to a lesser extent, although JP Van Hulle channeled her as being in stubbornness. Others who have literally self-destructed through substance abuse, such as John Belushi, have also been given as examples of people in self-destruction.

I wondered how a fear of loss of control relates to destroying oneself. Then it occurred to me that if someone feels that order must be maintained at all costs, he does not feel it is safe to genuinely express his anger or share his pain. He turns his anger in on himself, increasing his pain, which he suffers silently. He may use alcohol,

---

[5]P. 39.
[6]P. 227.
[7]P. 154.

drugs, or food to dull it, which compounds his problem.[8] Or, he may continue to suffer silently, until his self-denial manifests as cancer or another disease. As his pain and anger grow, so does the apparent danger of losing control. He feels like he would explode and cause great damage if he ever let loose. It appears safer to implode and damage himself instead. Under those circumstances, it might look like life isn't worth living anyway, causing him to take daredevil risks. His only way out of this inexorable downward spiral is to find a safe place to express his feelings, perhaps with a therapist. He might affirm: My life is precious to me. I trust the free expression of my life.

Greed is the fear of not having enough, no matter how much one has. Greed does not usually arise universally; it tends to be fixated on a particular area(s), such as money, food, attention, love, and so forth. Actually, this isn't all that different from the other chief features; someone in impatience, for instance, isn't impatient under every circumstance, but only when his "buttons" are pushed. But greed, by its nature, attaches itself to a particular definable area, whereas the other chief features are more generalized.

People in greed carry a sense of a bottomless pit of emptiness; no matter how hard they try, they cannot fill it. For example, a person with greed for food never feels satiated, no matter how much he eats. (This is not always the dynamic in gluttony: someone else might stuff himself *past* satiation, perhaps because he is hedonistic and undisciplined. Incidentally, Michael has similarly differentiated between drunkards, who may simply be lazy and unwilling to deal with their lives, and alcoholics, who are physically intolerant of alcohol. These two are often lumped together nowadays.) A person with greed for experience may rush around, looking similar to someone in impatience, but his motivation is different—he is trying to fill the hole he feels rather than trying to avoid missing out. It is a subtle distinction, but in greed, although one can be ruthless in extreme cases, a person looks more voracious than testy (intolerance is the negative pole of impatience).

Those in greed are so busy trying to get more of whatever they feel they lack that they do not recognize and acknowledge what they already have. A useful affirmation for greed is: I recognize and enjoy the abundance of my life. I have enough.

---

[8]This is different than overindulging due to greed, a fear of not getting enough.

NO CHIEF FEATURE

I have channeled a few adults as having no chief feature. I do not find them to be "enlightened," in the sense of having arrived at spiritual mastery, but they usually seem to lack those "rough edges" that the chief feature imparts to the rest of us. They may have extinguished their chief feature, or they may have qualities of several of them, but not enough of any one to have it constitute a chief feature.

CHILDREN AND CHIEF FEATURES

Although we do not settle on a chief feature until around the age of twenty, we can show signs of a particular chief feature even in early childhood, not only because of the influences of others, but because of unresolved issues brought forward from past lifetimes.

> *If you have a child leaning toward a particular chief feature, you may not be able to help him erase it during his childhood—he may need adult capabilities and experiences to complete the lessons involved. Nonetheless, you can certainly give him tools with which to deal with it, so he can soften it and perhaps even eliminate it, at least later on.*
>
> *For example, if you have a child who is leaning heavily toward self-deprecation, there is much you can do to build his self-esteem, mainly by giving him plenty of encouragement and unqualified approval.*

Transforming Your Dragons—Turning Personality Fear Patterns into Personal Power by José Stevens (Bear & Company, 1994) is entirely devoted to chief features. I highly recommend it.

Chapter 24

BODY TYPES

	ORDINAL	NEUTRAL	CARDINAL
INSPIRATION	*LUNAR* + Luminous – Pallid		*SATURNIAN* + Rugged – Gaunt
Physical	Pale, "baby fat," round-faced[1]		Tall, strong bones, high forehead
Psychological	Calm, introspective, mathematical		Enduring, self- control, leadership
EXPRESSION	*JOVIAL* + Grand – Extravagant		*MERCURIAL* + Agile – Frenetic
Physical	Large, short, male baldness, wide-necked		Dark hair & eyes, slender, compact
Psychological	Magnanimous, knowledge- able, able to enjoy pleasure		Clever, quick, extroverted
ACTION	*VENUSIAN* + Voluptuous – Obese		*MARTIAL* + Wiry – Muscle-bound
Physical	Dark & thick hair, olive skin, wide hands		Reddish coloring, sinewy, broad
Psychological	Easygoing, sensual, loyal, nonjudgmental		Direct, decisive, volatile
ASSIMILATION		*SOLAR* + Radiant – Ethereal	
Physical		Delicate, slight, young-looking	
Psychological		Light-hearted, elegant, creative	

---

[1]These descriptions of the body types are necessarily quite limited. Although they may convey flavors, they should not be viewed as absolute. For example, not every lunar type has a round face, and as we will discuss later, each person has a combination of body type influences.

Body types are sets of physical and psychological traits stemming from the influences of the celestial bodies on our physical bodies. Above are the seven major body types; there are also three minor body-type influences: neptunian, uranian, and plutonian.[2]

Often, our body-type influences relate to our astrological chart, although there is not necessarily a direct correlation.[3] As in astrology, the energy of each celestial body is linked to mythological symbols. For example, Mars, the red planet, is named after the Roman god of war, and people with a martial body type tend to be feisty. Also, people with martial body-type influence tend to have reddish coloring.

The planetary influences have been used for years in general parlance to describe people. For instance, two dictionary definitions of *mercurial* are "having qualities of eloquence or ingenuity...attributed to the god Mercury or to the influence of the planet Mercury" and "characterized by rapid and unpredictable changeableness of mood." These also somewhat describe the mercurial body type. A saturnian person is prudent, sober, and perhaps sluggish. A jovial person, influenced by Jupiter, is convivial and merry. These qualities also relate to their respective body types.

Strictly speaking, body types are not an overleaf, but like the overleaves, they are chosen before the lifetime begins, although there must be adequate genetic raw material from which to fashion a particular body type. There are people with all body types within each ethnic group (although different groups emphasize different types), but if no one in a person's family has had, say, a saturnian body type for a few generations and his genes don't lend themselves to saturnian characteristics, it would be difficult for his essence to develop a saturnian body type.

Through one channel, Michael said that both one's body type and one's astrological chart are set more by the configuration of planets at the time of conception than at the time of birth, and that if one was born prematurely, one's astrological chart could be off. No mention was made of genetic influences. However, I have found that identical twins, who have the same moment of conception, do not necessarily have identical body types. I channeled Michael charts on a set of twins, and one was saturnian with a mercurial secondary, while the other was solar with a mercurial secondary. Saturnian and

---

[2]These are discussed in *Michael—The Basic Teachings* and *The Michael Handbook*.

[3]In fact, astrologers have told me that the whole Michael chart fits well with a person's astrological chart, although the connection is clearest with body types.

solar are both positive-charged and active, as will be discussed below, but look different. With another set of twins, one was mercurial with a lunar secondary, and the other was saturnian with jovial and mercurial secondaries. Coincidentally, both members of each set share mercurial influences in common, and the planet Mercury rules Gemini, "the twins." It would surprise me if twins did not have at least one body-type influence in common, but the soul builds the body it wants out of the raw material present, so there is flexibility. As the body ages, it can be increasingly imprinted by the soul, which is one reason identical twins tend to look more and more different as they get older.

The moment of conception indeed does set up certain influences, but essence controls the body type as it does the overleaves, and body type can be viewed as an overleaf in this sense, just as the body itself can be viewed as an overleaf. The planetary configurations (not just the sun sign) "pull forward" genetic raw material for essence to more easily select from—it can be more easily matched to the desires of the essence if the planetary influences are supportive.

Body-type attraction was referred to and discussed in general terms in the Yarbro books, but the specific body types were not mentioned. However, a recent client of one of the Yarbro channels showed me the blank role and overleaves chart she uses, and it included the seven types, with positive and negative poles.[4]

The book *Body Types* by Joel Friedlander is the only current book devoted to this subject. However, in 1900, a book on palmistry—*The Laws of Scientific Hand Reading* by William Benham—set

---

[4] I have adopted her terms for the poles, which are given at the beginning of this chapter, other than those for the jovial type. The term for the negative pole of jovial on her chart was *elephantine.* I don't use that term because, even though it is accurate—the dictionary partly defines it as "ponderous, heavy-footed"—it can seem demeaning to people sensitive about their weight. The term for the positive pole was *grandeur* rather than *grand;* I changed it so that all the poles would be adjectives—*grandeur* is a noun.

Her chart listed the five types named for planets as nouns, e.g., *mars* rather than *martial,* while retaining the adjectives *lunar* and *solar* rather than *moon* and *sun.* Again, for consistency, I use each term in its adjectival form.

A chart used by the Michael Educational Foundation in Orinda, California, also listed the five types named for planets as nouns. In addition, it employs some different terms for the poles: the positive pole of saturnian is given as *patriarchal,* and martial's is given as *endurance.* Several negative poles differ: *immature* for lunar, *vacuous* for venusian, *volatile* for martial, and *fragile* for solar.

out the seven types. Benham learned the material from Gypsies. Russian philosopher George Gurdjieff, who traveled extensively in the East collecting esoteric teachings early in this century, discussed body types in general terms. His pupil, Rodney Collin-Smith, wrote about the types in *The Theory of Celestial Influence* in 1954. Gurdjieff teacher Robert Burton elaborated on these writings beginning in the late Sixties. Friedlander was in Burton's group.[5]

The Michael and Gurdjieff teachings are "cousins" of sorts. In addition to body types, Gurdjieff taught about centers and chief features, using some terms that later became part of the Michael teachings. "Jessica Lansing" and others in her group were also members of Burton's group before she began channeling Michael. Therefore, Gurdjieff terminology was in her subconscious mind, although Michael used the material somewhat differently, and only in part. (I often find in my channeling that Michael uses the contents of my subconscious, but breaks them down to their primary components and uses them in new ways.)

The body types move in a progression from least developed, lunar, to most, jovial. This progression is in a circle, with jovial connecting back to lunar. Solar is outside the progression, so it is not numbered.

Each of the types has either a positive or negative charge (which is not the same as positive and negative poles). The positive types are more like the day: brighter, more optimistic, emphasizing the outer, and tending to overlook flaws. The negative types are more like the night: darker, more pessimistic, emphasizing the inner, and tending to notice what needs correction. Obviously, both kinds of charge are needed. The positive types are saturnian, jovial, venusian, and solar. The negative types are lunar, mercurial, and martial. It is easy to see why solar is positive, since the sun creates daylight, and lunar is negative, since the moon and the night are so closely connected. Solar types tend to be radiant and light-hearted, and lunar types tend to be sensitive and thoughtful. The traits of other positive types are, like solar, brighter—the jovial type, known for its mirth, is an obvious example. The traits of other negative types are, like lunar, darker—for example, the mercurial type can be given to sarcasm.

---

[5]Friedlander was an owner of Globe Press Books, a publisher of Gurdjieff books.

BODY-TYPE CIRCULAR PROGRESSION

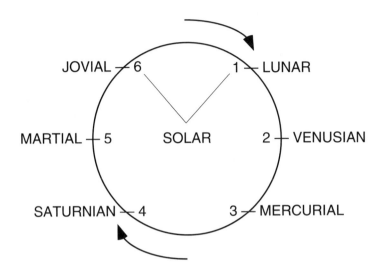

Each body type is also active or passive, but unlike positive and negative, it isn't either/or; there are degrees of activity and passivity. Body types wax and wane in this regard around the progression. The first body type, lunar, is the most passive. The second, venusian, is less passive. The third, mercurial, is active. The fourth, saturnian, is the most active. The fifth, martial, is again active, but less so than saturnian. The sixth, jovial, is passive, but less so than lunar, the first, which begins the progression anew. Solar, which, again, is not part of the progression, is also active, lightly or neutrally so: neither wound-up (mercurial), stolid (saturnian), nor explosive (martial).

Activity and passivity refer to whether the body's tendency is more "to do" or "to be." For instance, if someone has a totally free day with nothing he "has to" do, he is likely to do something athletic or take on a project if he has an active type, whereas someone with a passive type might choose to read quietly or watch a movie (although it's not cut-and-dried).

Active types easily muscle up with exercise; passive types don't. I know a woman with a saturnian type, and martial and mercurial secondaries—all active types. She's afraid to exercise because she gets so muscular. That would be great if she were a body builder, but she is an actress, and too much muscle could limit her ability to get the parts she wants. Active types also tend to be thinner, even without exercise, whereas passive types tend to be larger, softer, and rounder (although the active-type actress just mentioned is also large-breasted, which I assume is a genetic exception to her normal body-type influences). I know a man with a jovial type whom others often perceive as being too thin. I suspect that if he were a mercurial type, and had the same weight and frame, he would be perceived as being at his normal weight. The passive types are meant to have a little more "meat on their bones." Any body type can be fat or thin, but active bodies have a "boxer," less-round look even when they're fat.

The current ideal of beauty is a thin, tall saturnian type with a martial secondary. Bodies that are naturally heavier are out of fashion. It is unfortunate that our young soul society promotes the idea that everyone should look the same.[6] This attitude makes it more difficult to appreciate the beauty of each type.

Positive and active are both considered masculine traits—they are on the same "side" of their respective polarities. Saturnian, both positive and the most active of types, is considered the most masculine body type. Astrologically, Saturn is the father figure, meting out discipline. Negative and passive are both considered feminine traits. Since lunar is both negative and the most passive of types, it is considered the most feminine body type. This is not surprising, since the moon is a prevalent symbol of femininity, and women's bodies are particularly affected by the lunar cycle.[7] Lunar men and saturnian women are more likely to be homosexual or bisexual than when the reverse is true, although body type is only one of many factors influencing sexuality. (The percentage of lunar or saturnian influence and the secondary body-type influences determine how strong a factor the lunar or saturnian influence is.)

Both mercurial and martial are a blend of negative and active, so they are characterized by the apparent paradox of being active yet more internal. The opposite is true of jovial and venusian: they are passive yet more external. Venus, named for the goddess of love, is also a symbol of the feminine, but perhaps not as "purely" as the moon.

We each have a primary and secondary body type. People often have a tertiary and sometimes even a quaternary type as well. Virtually no one has only one body-type influence, although single body-type influences show up in cartoons and archetypes. For example,

---

[6]Here we can see evidence of the motto "Do it my way."

[7]As a man with a lunar body type, I have always been particularly sensitive to the full moon—I feel emotionally more full, and often have the greatest sense of well-being then. I think that this is unusual for men in general. Other Michael students have guessed me as having higher female energy than the fifty-three percent I do have, and my body type, along with childhood imprinting, is probably why.

Uncle Sam of U.S. Army recruitment posters is saturnian, and Disney's Snow White is solar. The proportion of a person's body-type influences can shift during his lifetime. For example, lunar accounts for fifty-four percent of my body's energy. My secondary is thirty-six percent martial, and my tertiary is ten percent venusian. My percentage of lunar is decreasing, and my martial is increasing. A few years ago, lunar accounted for fifty-six percent of my body's energy, and martial was thirty-four percent (the ten percent venusian has remained the same). Also, each body-type influence moves toward the next one in the progression—for example, lunar moves toward venusian—although that movement tends to be very slow and gradual. If I incarnate again, I might choose a venusian body type, since it's next in the progression. However, one's own body type occupies a single point on the progression, whereas the whole body type designation occupies a band of frequencies, like a color of the rainbow that spans the space between one frequency and another. A person can be lunar more toward jovial (which precedes it on the progression), or more toward venusian (which is probably true of me), just as green can be more toward yellow, or more toward blue.

We are usually most comfortable with types the same as or adjacent to our own on the progression (many married couples have adjacent types), and most excited by the type opposite our own, which is what is meant by *body-type attraction*. With opposites, one is positive and the other negative, and one is active and the other passive. The principle of body-type attraction relates to all relationships, not just sexual ones. The following chart shows the pairs of opposites. They also appear opposite to one another on the "Body-Type Circular Progression" diagram earlier in the chapter.

BODY-TYPE OPPOSITES

LUNAR	passive	negative
SATURNIAN	active	positive
JOVIAL	passive	positive
MERCURIAL	active	negative
VENUSIAN	passive	positive
MARTIAL	active	negative

Friedlander writes that solar, being outside the progression, "lacks the tensions of attraction and repulsion that inflame the other types."

That sounds like the neutral assimilation axis, upon which the solar type sits on the Michael chart, and the neutral role, scholar. It is interesting that the solar type is perceived as being androgynous rather than the ultimate masculine, despite its being both positive and active, like saturnian. The sun itself is a potent masculine symbol, but it is also suggestive of the neutral assimilation axis in that its light and heat interpenetrate everything in the solar system. The sun is the resource for the planets, just as the role of scholar is the resource of knowledge for the other roles. Since solar is active and positive like saturnian, we might think that it is also most attracted to lunar, the one type both passive and negative, but solar itself doesn't favor any of the other body types, again, because it is outside the progression. Friedlander writes that if someone's type is solar, his secondary type(s) determines his attractions.

Although both mercurial and martial are active and negative, they are different in their attractions because of their position in the progression. They receive different influences from their neighboring types: whereas mercurial is moving toward saturnian, which is more active, martial is moving toward jovial, which is passive. Venusian and jovial, which are both passive and positive, are likewise in different positions in the progression.

> *Saturnian, being the apex of masculinity, is at a pivot point. Mercurial has a quality of "building steam" toward it, whereas martial is "losing steam," or discharging energy. This makes mercurial more high-strung—it seeks opportunities to wind up—and martial more explosive—it seeks opportunities to wind down. Saturnian, having reached that apex, can "afford" to be utterly still.*
>
> *Similarly, lunar is at the apex of femininity. Jovial approaches that apex, so it is releasing itself into passivity, through the pleasures of company, among other things. Venusian, coming from passivity toward activity, is "gearing up" for it, taking in stimulation from martial, which wants to release it. In the opposite way, jovial releases stimulation to mercurial, which wants to absorb it. Lunar is not in motion in either direction; like Saturnian, it is still.*

As a result of this "stillness," both lunar and saturnian types tend to be calm and slow-moving, even though saturnian is an active type—it is calmly active. Both mercurials and martials are more obviously active and energetic, in different ways. Martials express their active energy in being feisty and strong. Mercurials, on the other hand, tend to be "zippy," lively people with fast metabolisms; they are often the kind of people who can eat anything and burn it up. However, that is, of course, not always true; it depends on many factors, such as health and secondary body-type influences. One mercurial I know has the nervousness of the negative pole, but not the liveliness and agility of the positive. He tends to be sluggish and put on weight because of a glandular dysfunction, and he also has a secondary body type of venusian, which is passive.

Body-type attraction is not the same as thinking that someone is beautiful or handsome, or even that someone is our "type." These reactions have more to do with conditioning. Our image of beauty may relate to what advertising and the media in general promote; our "type" may be someone who reminds us of one of our parents or an earlier lover. Body-type attraction is more subtle. It is our body's fascination with its opposite, which is partly a magnetic attraction between positive and negative, and between active and passive. Simply sitting next to someone with an opposite body type can excite or stimulate your body, even if he's not your type or of interest as a sexual partner. Body type attraction can also account for our being drawn sexually to someone who doesn't seem to be our "type" or conform to our image of "good-looking."[8] In addition, it can account for some of those "odd couple" relationships, such as a thin, wiry mercurial type in relationship with a large jovial type. If there is not some body-type attraction or at least body-type compatibility between two people in a romantic relationship, there are probably other elements of attraction between them, such as opposite male/female energy ratios, compatible overleaves, or close essence bonds.

Even though my body's energy is thirty-six percent martial, and I have the reddish hair and ruddy complexion of the martial type, the psychological profile of the martial type in *Body Types* doesn't fit me, whereas that of the lunar type is, in many ways, very apt; it explains things about me that are not explained elsewhere.[9] One reason that lunar seems so much more "me" is that some other elements of my Michael chart, such as intellectual centering, and some of my imprinting, emphasize its influence, whereas there is less that supports martial personality elements. Also, even though fifty-four percent is relatively low for one's primary body-type influence, it is still half again more than thirty-six percent. My ten percent venusian energy

---

[8]Essence connections such as agreements and karmas can also cause you to be attracted to people in surprising "packages."

[9]My first reaction upon reading that chapter was, "How terrible to have a lunar body type!" Upon reading the rest of the book, however, my reaction was, "How terrible to have *any* body type!" The descriptions tend to be fairly unflattering, in my view.

adds to the passivity of the lunar, so my body is sixty-four percent passive. The venusian energy is the only positive-charged body-type energy I have; both lunar and martial are negative, so my body is ninety percent negative, which is a significant factor in my life, influencing me to be more sensitive and internal.

Of course, even taken together, the lunar, martial, and venusian archetypes do not account for all my traits. Body types merely describe influences coming from the body. The rest of the Michael Reading chart describes influences from the personality and essence. Countless other factors beyond those considered on a Michael Reading chart, such as imprinting, numerology, and astrology, also play a part—we are marvelously complex beings! Essence and overleaf traits have more influence on a person than body type, especially in older souls and in people who are physically older. A sage with a lunar body type looks quite different from, say, a lunar-type server, who might be more stereotypically lunar. Friedlander's wife, Jill, an expert in "diagnosing" body types, felt that, because of my "sunny" disposition, I also have some solar influence, which did not agree with my channeling. I explained that being a sage essence, I'm naturally outgoing, and my lunar body type is a little bit like an actor being cast against type; sages, as mentioned, are the most social of the roles, whereas lunar is the least social of the body types. Mercurial, for example, is more natural for sages, since it facilitates communication and wit. I also have an idealist attitude, which tends toward optimism and brightness, whereas lunar is a negative type, and tends to notice the dark side more. Although that is definitely part of me—it's easy for me to notice flaws, and sometimes become bogged down in dealing with them—the fact of being an idealist and a sage predominates; I'm basically an upbeat person, albeit with a darker, lunar undercurrent.

When secondary body-type influences are strong, they can obscure the main one, at least at first glance, especially when they're opposite—opposite types can seem to cancel one another out. For example, jovial and mercurial are opposite. If someone is fifty-three percent jovial and forty-seven percent mercurial, it might be difficult to read his type; he won't stand out as being either passive or active, positive or negative. If someone has a strong saturnian secondary and is quite tall, we might guess saturnian as his main type, since his height is what strikes us about him first. (Although saturnians tend to be tall, a person can be tall with no saturnian influence; jovial and venusian influences can also make for tallness. Also, not all saturnians are tall—specific genetics still play a part—although shorter saturnians tend to look taller than they are because of their lanky build and prominent bone structure.)

According to Yarbro, task companions, when incarnate together, tend to choose the same body type, and essence twins tend to have opposite body types.

Body types are different from overleaves and roles in a few respects: Although seven main celestial influences are recognized (from the sun, the moon, and the five closest planets), there are also many other celestial influences that impact the body, whereas there are only seven roles, for instance; there are no other types of essence energies, only combinations of the seven. Also, a soul has only one role, and, in most cases, only one of each overleaf (although a person can slide to others), whereas a body type is dominant only because the body happens to have a higher percentage of its energy, not because the body *is* that type, in the way that a soul *is* an artisan (or whatever), despite other influences. Therefore, when I'm channeling a person's body type, and two types have almost equal influence, sometimes Michael pauses to discern which is slightly higher. That one is given as the body type, and the one that is slightly less in influence is given as the secondary type. If the types shift in influence, this could be reversed. It is not like an overleaf that is constant for the lifetime.

BODY TYPES ON THE MICHAEL CHART

On the chart at the beginning of this chapter, which uses the same arrangement as the Yarbro chart and the one in *The Michael Handbook*, cardinality and ordinality are assigned to the seven types according to whether they are active (cardinal) or passive (ordinal). This makes sense, since the Yarbro books gave the negative poles of cardinality and ordinality as activity and passivity. (The positive poles are lucidity and responsiveness.) They place opposite types, those that most attract each other, on the same axis. Lunar and saturnian, on the inspiration axis, are the quietest and most internal types. Jovial and mercurial, on the expression axis, are the most lively and communicative types. Venusian and martial, on the action axis, are the most sexual, and solar, on the neutral assimilation axis, is the most androgynous.

In *Michael—The Basic Teachings*, the authors use the same arrangement except that they switch jovial and mercurial, making jovial cardinal. I've also seen an arrangement that does not keep the pairs of opposites together, and places venusian on the inspiration axis, since Venus is the goddess of love in mythology, and venusian types tend to be nurturing. It might seem contradictory to put any passive body type on the action axis, as in the other arrangements. However,

Michael pointed out to me that putting the venusian type on the action axis is reasonable.

Venusians are doers, in their more passive ways—they certainly enjoy the fruits of the flesh, like the action axis roles do.

This is a reminder that *active,* as in active and passive, refers to something different than *action,* as in the action axis.

Part V

THE BIG PICTURE

Chapter 25

REINCARNATION

The concept of reincarnation is simply that our soul lives multiple lifetimes, gaining experience through them. It is not within the scope of this book to attempt to prove reincarnation; it is a "given" in the Michael teachings, which are of limited use without this idea. However, perhaps we can dispel some of the confusion around it.

For those who are skeptical about reincarnation, there are many books on the subject.[1] I myself have had vivid, emotionally charged recollections of many past lives, and have regressed others to remember some of theirs. In fact, I believe that almost anyone who is adequately open and relaxed can be guided to remember their past lives.

There is other evidence supporting reincarnation. For instance, there have been many documented cases of young children vividly describing places they had never been, and past events in accurate historical detail to which they had never been exposed. Also, an earlier version of the Bible contained references to reincarnation that were removed by the Church. Furthermore, a majority of people have some kind of belief in reincarnation, even a great number of Americans.

None of this is "hard" proof of reincarnation. One can always come up with other possible explanations, although I often find them to be convoluted. I doubt that anything involving the nonphysical can be proven conclusively to the satisfaction of those who rely solely on physical evidence. (Scientists are continually "proving" things that are later "unproved" anyway.)

If we have been reincarnating, it stands to reason that some part of our consciousness knows about it and can confirm it. In fact, some part of us knows the truth about everything we've experienced. Although intellectual exploration has its place—otherwise, why bother with books like this one?—the ultimate referee in debates about such things as reincarnation is our inner knowing. Aligning with that is part of maturing spiritually. Without inner knowing, we can argue "till the cows come home" and be no closer to resolving the issue.

Here are some comments by Michael on reincarnation:

---

[1]*Other Lives, Other Selves*, by Roger Woolger (Bantam 1988), is a fascinating book by a Jungian analyst about past life therapy.

You are now the sum of all you have ever been.

Each morning, you put on different clothing, but you are the same person you were the previous day. Perhaps certain things about you changed during your sleep, but there is continuity.

When you die, it is like going to sleep at night. Your time on the astral plane between lives is like your night's sleep. When you "awaken," you "put on" a new body (as well as new overleaves and life circumstances) rather than different clothing, but it is still you.

You may have limiting beliefs you have carried over a number of lifetimes. It is sometimes useful to know what went into forming them, but the point is to see and release them. Whatever ways help you do this are all to the good.

REINCARNATIONAL SELVES

Our astral self, which might be described as the outer "layer" of our essence, casts parts of itself into reincarnational selves in order to live on the physical plane, much the same way our spark cast a part of itself into our essence in order to exist in the dimensional universe. The reincarnational self is the foundation of our personality, what we start with, and what is left after death. It includes our overleaves and identity but without the temporal elements, such as our physical body and the problems of day-to-day life.

There has been some question as to whether reincarnational selves are reabsorbed back into the essence after the death of the body, or continue to have an independent existence. Apparently, the answer is "both." Each reincarnational self is like a subpersonality of the essence that continues to develop under the "umbrella" of the essence.

On the level of our personality, we spawn many subpersonalities. For example, when we were children, we developed what is later the subpersonality called "the child within." That part of self never ends. In childhood, it was who we were, but because we have grown, it is now just a part of who we are. If it was traumatized, it calls out for attention so that it can be healed. Once it is healed, it becomes integrated into the whole personality. It is not the focus of our personality anymore, because it doesn't need to be, but it keeps developing and doing its "job" of bringing wonder and playfulness into our lives.

The same is true of our reincarnational selves. When we lived those lives, they were who we were, but now, they are just a part of who we are on the level of our essence. Like the child within or other subpersonalities, those needing healing or resolution call out for our attention when we are in a position to offer it. In any lifetime, there is likely to be a handful of them clustered "around" us. Once we experience the necessary healing and resolution, they can integrate into our essence. In future lifetimes, we are likely to be less conscious of them. However, the fruits of their lessons become available to the whole self. They also continue to develop and grow, while remaining part of our essence, just as our "child within" can continue to develop and grow in us. Perhaps they can even be thought of as spinning off from our essence while remaining part of it, as though tethered to it by an infinitely stretchable string. In any case, they go on to become creators by expanding our essence, becoming creative aspects of it.

> *As your personality (or reincarnational self) integrates its lessons, your essence integrates your personality. Your essence and personality are organically linked, and integration is a gradual process. In some cases, personality elements from lifetimes thousands of years ago are still not integrated.*
>
> *The personality does not end at death, even by suicide. Once in a while, a complex personality with overleaves that severely abrade internally cannot "get it together" on the astral plane after death, and disassembles itself, usually with the essence's blessing. Probably the essence does not have enough experience for the personality to reconcile itself.*[2]

Our other reincarnational selves are both us and not us. One way of expressing this is that we "share essence" with them. There is a part of us, the personality, that has not lived before, but it is also true that our essence has spawned other personalities. We are connected to them through our essence. We could say that those who believe in reincarnation and those who don't are both right. In a sense, our essence fragments into reincarnational selves in the same way our entity fragments into essences, our cadre fragments into entities, and so forth. Although in one sense we are not our other reincarnational

---

[2]There is also what is called "astral suicide," in which the essence itself decides to cut short its grand cycle and "go back" to the Tao. This is rare, and would only be undertaken by a very troubled soul. If someone's Michael Reading chart says that he has, for instance, eleven and a half previous cycles, that indicates that a previous cycle was cut short in this way. Such an experience might result in an especially strong resolve to carry through this time, particularly if the aborted cycle was the one just before the current one.

selves, in another sense we are all that is contained within our essence, as well as within our entity, cadre, and so forth.

After death, the reincarnational self, in tandem with its essence, has the opportunity to review the previous lifetime and integrate as many of its lessons as possible. What it is not yet capable of resolving or willing to look at must wait for another reincarnational self to handle. Some issues, and most karmas, must be resolved on the physical plane. Obviously, the more we can resolve while living the life generating the issues, the better. A characteristic of being on the spiritual path is living consciously and deliberately "cleaning up after ourselves"—staying up to date on handling our issues and not generating karmic debts. This requires being willing to face facts about ourselves and grow.

After death, once the personality and essence have processed their previous lifetime on the physical plane as much as they can for the time being, the essence is free to birth more personalities, i.e., reincarnate. If the essence has not reincarnated, or if it has, but the previous lifetime's personality is not deeply engaged in the new incarnation, the personality is free to travel and take advantage of the resources of the astral plane. It can continue to grow and advance itself for as long as it wishes, until reintegrating into its essence.

The personality is not something apart from the essence, but the essence is capable of maintaining many personalities simultaneously, just as you are capable of maintaining many subpersonalities simultaneously, and they are developing even when you are not paying attention to them.

FROM LIFETIME TO LIFETIME

Do we surround ourselves with many of the same people from lifetime to lifetime?

Yes, and you also occasionally bring in new friends. Of course, it depends on the age of the soul. If you are quite young, just about everyone is new to you, at least in this cycle. Older souls tend to "run with the same crowd" from lifetime to lifetime, but the crowd is a large one. It varies widely from person to person, but you might have, for example, three hundred souls you "hang out" with a lot. This still gives you quite a bit of variety.

319

Even people we meet through our jobs, whom we wouldn't necessarily choose to have in our lives otherwise, may have past-life connections with us. Our issues with them may be continuing from past lives.

When clients feel strongly enough about someone to ask Michael if they have past-life connections with him, they usually do. If they don't, it is often a case of body-type attraction. Also, we occasionally run into friends from the astral plane or even from previous cycles with whom we have not yet shared a physical lifetime. As they say, there's a first time for everything. And we do sometimes make brand new friends.

Clients often ask about the nature of past-life connections with loved ones. There are often interesting dynamics to explore, but the relationships themselves are usually standard: mate, sibling, parent, child, friend, coworker, and so on. With someone who is particularly close, we are likely to have shared most of the above forms of relationship, and more, although there may be some souls with whom we like to specialize—for instance, there may be a soul with whom we like to have business relationships but with whom we rarely if ever have mate or family relationships.

When people ask Michael through me about their past lives, Michael reads the information from their energy, rather than looking it up in the akashic records. It is both easier and more practical. The past lives that impact our present life are like open documents on our desk, as opposed to those filed away; they are relatively accessible. Those "open" lifetimes are the very ones that relate to the important life issues about which a person is likely to ask Michael.

As with any other type of information retrieval, it is one thing to pick up raw data, and another to translate and interpret it accurately. Undoubtedly, even Michael occasionally makes at least minor errors when extemporaneously summarizing a lifetime from the psychic "pictures" in a person's energy. Usually, the particular details are relatively insignificant anyway; it is knowing the dynamics of the situation—the nature of the relationships, karmas, attitudes, emotions, and so forth—that can be most helpful.

In my experience, most of us have lived a series of mostly ordinary lifetimes. It is a bit of a joke in the New Age movement that sometimes many people claim to have been the same famous historical person, and it seems that nobody was ever a peasant. No doubt egotism occasionally plays a part in this, through unbridled imagination or through psychics and channels who tell clients what they want to hear. However, reality is complex, and it is possible that several claims to have been the same person are simply misunderstandings.

We might be read as having been a particular person because we really were. If an historical figure experienced a walk-in, or if more than one essence was sharing his body[3] (which is not common but is more common for those who have wide impact), more than one person can accurately claim to have been him.

We also may have been closely associated with that person in some way, and that association can be confused with actually having been that person, since his energy is in our aura. Here are some forms of association that can be misread in this way:

1. We may have been physically present with that person, as a friend, family member, student, even antagonist, or in some other form.

2. We may have been working with him energetically from the astral plane, as a spirit guide or as a member of a group supporting him or his task in some way.

3. We might have been that person, or the equivalent of that person, in a parallel universe.[4]

For instance, a person may have been Joan of Arc in a parallel universe but not in this one. The essence who incarnated as Joan of Arc in this universe might not have lived in that one, or may have had a different name and occupied a different historical role in it. He may also have been someone comparable to Joan of Arc in another universe who didn't exist in this one, giving him a special resonance with the person known as Joan of Arc in this universe. This sort of thing, however, is rare.

In general, when we are tuning in to past lives, we can't always be certain that we're picking up an experience from this universe—it might be from one that is presently on the same "track" as this one, but that wasn't on the same track in the past.

4. Someone spiritually close to us may have been that person.

For example, we can access the past lives of cycled-off entity mates and other nonphysical souls who are working intimately with us in this lifetime.

---

[3]See the subchapter "Combined Essence Energies" in Chapter Nine, "Roles."

[4]There are infinite parallel universes that are as real to themselves as our reality is to us. Through these "parallels," our essence experiences the full range of significant possibilities open to it with a particular life task and set of overleaves. See also Chapter Thirty, "Parallel Universes."

5. The historical figure may simply be an important archetype we relate to.

Some people attribute past-life memories to tapping into the cell memory (akashic record) of, say, a carrot we ate. In other words, the memory belongs to someone whose body died and decomposed. A cell of that body is now in the carrot, and we unlocked that memory. I find this idea convoluted. A similar idea is that memories of past lives derive from our genes—we are accessing the records of lives of our physical ancestors. But if that were true, why would someone remember one particular ancestor and not another? Why might someone remember an ancestor in the distant past but not several more recent ones? What makes more sense to me is that if we remember a past life, it was a past life in which we had at least some involvement. However, there is some truth in most ideas. Here, Michael comments on the cell memory theory:

> *Cell memory is not different from remembering one of your own past lives, because you create your body and store important memories in your cells. You do not remember past lives unrelated to you from eating a carrot, although it is possible to unlock the history of the cell of a carrot. It may correlate with a lifetime related to you and trigger a memory.*

On an essence level, we experience our lifetimes consecutively; in other words, lifetime forty-three follows lifetime forty-two. However, because our essence exists somewhat beyond time, time is elastic for it. Therefore, lifetime forty-three is not necessarily later in time, according to the calendar, than lifetime forty-two; it is possible to have what our essence considers to be our next lifetime in the past or in the same physical plane time frame. During our present era, with its population explosion and unprecedented changes, the Michael fragments I channel are aware of essences with as many as eight reincarnational selves living simultaneously.[5] Many of us have two or three. This is different than spinning off a parallel self, who has the same basic personality (including overleaves) and life task we do, but in a parallel universe. Reincarnational selves are in the same universe (and are on earth, in our case), but have different overleaves and life circumstances. Reincarnational selves living simultaneously

---

[5]Seth, as channeled by Jane Roberts, calls these simultaneous reincarnational selves "counterparts." I also understand that the new age author Dick Sutphen has written about one of his past-life selves that died eleven years after he was born.

are just like reincarnational selves who lived in the past except that they happen to be living now. Of course, if you request a Michael Reading chart, you will get your overleaves, not those of a reincarnational self.

If your essence has more than one reincarnational personality in this time frame, from its point of view it did not cast all of them at the "same time." It finished lifetime forty-two, for example, and then "bent" time a little to begin lifetime forty-three at about the same time lifetime forty-two began. This is not very difficult or disorienting, although reincarnational personality forty-three might subconsciously remember some of civilization's advances that had been available later in lifetime forty-two and be impatient for them to arrive. For your essence, it's like reading a novel written with consecutive chapters that take place in different locales but at the same time, so that readers can follow various characters.

More difficult, disorienting, and rare is incarnating in the past, in a time frame before an already-completed lifetime. This is usually only undertaken by more experienced or experimental essences. (Scholars especially enjoy this game, as well as anything else unusual.) For your essence, this might be something like reading the chapters of a novel out of order, or reading a novel in which the chronology is jumbled.

It is true that, from the vantage point of higher planes, all events are simultaneous. However, time is real on the physical plane, and also has some influence on the astral and causal planes.[6] Since it is the astral aspect of essence (astral self)[7] that directly incarnates, our essence is not completely outside time.

Even if we previously lived in the future and then incarnated backward in time, our vantage point in this lifetime is the same as in any other: all we can see are probabilities. Having lived in the future might help us tune in to the probabilities more strongly, making us more visionary of what is possible. However, we don't know which probabilities will manifest in this parallel universe; at any moment in any parallel universe, the future always consists only of various probabilities, not certainties, since each person has free will. If we remember an event from a past life in the calendar's future, we still cannot be certain that it will belong to this universe's future, just as

---

[6]See also Chapters Five and Six, "Time" and "Beyond Time," in my upcoming Summerjoy Michael book *Being in the World*.

[7]The term *soul* is sometimes used to refer specifically to this aspect of essence, rather than the whole of essence. See Chapter Twenty-Eight, "Aspects of Self."

we can't be certain that a past life we remember from the calendar's past belongs to this universe.

When our lifetimes are not in chronological order, it is not that we're jumping around on the physical plane, like someone in a time machine; it is that our essence is *experiencing* the lifetimes in non-chronological order. If, for example, someone is now fourth-level mature, his essence might have experienced being third-level mature in the year 2100—that lifetime contributed to his present level of consciousness, even if the specific memories that might arise from it cannot be assumed to be the future of this particular parallel universe.

In *Michael's People*,[8] Michael says, "No fragment is able to 'return' as its own grandparent." This is not a contradiction to the concept of having simultaneous or future reincarnational selves. If we are incarnate in more than one place in the same time frame, we almost always pick diverse locations. Since the purpose of incarnating is to expand our horizons, we don't want to duplicate experiences. It is probably impossible to meet another reincarnational self in the flesh. From the standpoint of the selves that preceded them, future selves do not exist except as probabilities, even though from their own standpoint, they are valid. Simultaneous selves occupy distinct realities or "sectors" of this universe, even though they are in the same time frame. This is a case of our essence "recycling" a universe, taking maximum advantage of its resources, practicing an "economy" that characterizes not only the cosmic design, but also all great art. Despite occupying distinct realities, we can communicate with our simultaneous (as well as future and past) reincarnational selves—for example, in meditation or in the dream state.

Theoretically, if we did meet another reincarnational self, he would probably seem like a close entity mate. His body could look quite different from ours, although we tend to look somewhat similar facially, especially around the eyes, from lifetime to lifetime.[9]

Despite the fact that lifetimes are consecutive, lifetime forty-three may be about entirely different lessons than lifetime forty-two. In our

---

[8]P. 79.

[9]I once had an intuitive "flash" that a new friend had been my grandmother's uncle, who had died in the Holocaust. I unpacked my grandmother's photograph of him, to which I had previously paid little attention, and was amazed at how much the uncle looked like my friend. My friend was blond and Scandinavian, but the face was very similar. When I mentioned this to him and showed him the photograph, he validated my intuition by saying that he had always felt he had chosen his present body partly out of a fear of dying in another holocaust.

present lifetime, we might be completing lessons related to lifetimes twenty-nine, thirty-two, thirty-six, and forty-one.

As mentioned, if we think that we have had past lives with someone, we probably have, unless our attraction is based only on body types. Here are some comments Michael made on differentiating body-type attraction from past-life and other essence connections.

> Body-type attraction is a relatively shallow type of attraction. It can be powerful and quite pleasing, but it is mostly limited to the physical level. So if you share a sense of emotional connection with someone, or a feeling that you deeply understand each other, or a sense of increased spiritual energy between you, as opposed to just physical attraction, you have some other kind of connection. If you are in the same entity, you usually feel like a comrade or sibling. If you are in another entity in the same cadre, you are likely to feel both similar and complementary to one another, on more levels than just the physical. You have not necessarily had significant past lives with everyone in your cadre, but if you are meeting someone in your cadre, there is a good chance that you have past-life connections of some kind, especially if you have a feeling of knowing him from somewhere, or if you find memories stimulated. If he is a member of your cadre but you have not had significant past-life connections, there is a feeling of relatedness but also a feeling of a blank slate between you. Of course, you can have significant past-life connections with someone not in your cadre.
>
> Often, when you first meet someone in this lifetime whom you have known in others, you have a sense that you are starting where you left off. If you immediately feel motherly toward him, for instance, and you are not a mother in this lifetime, you are probably continuing from a past life in which you were his mother or a mother figure. You might find yourself wondering why you want to take care of him, or feel so protective of him. Those feelings are likely to fade as you develop a relationship with him based on how things are in this lifetime.

BETWEEN LIFETIMES

I channeled that, on average, a person waits about seventy years after death before reincarnating. However, I understand that "Jessica Lansing" channeled the number as being about two hundred. I think that through me, Michael was referring to more recent times, when the growing population has created more opportunities for incarnation. Perhaps over the entire span of one's physical plane cycle, two hundred is the average. Whatever the case, the length of time between lifetimes varies considerably from person to person and depends on the particular circumstances. Generally, younger souls reincarnate more quickly, whereas older souls become increasingly specific in their needs and tend to take more time setting up their lifetimes. To the younger soul, almost any kind of experience can look interesting and worthwhile. The older soul wants to avoid repeating what it has already done and seeks the particular circumstances needed to repay karmas, complete monads, and otherwise grow. Also, older souls become increasingly comfortable with the astral interval and its fluidity, whereas younger souls can be threatened by it and often can't wait to get back into the structure of the physical plane. (Younger souls, like children, need more structure.)[10]

Being between lifetimes is like being an actor between acting jobs. Just as one actor can play many different parts, your essence expresses itself through many different personalities. No matter how varied they are, the nature of your essence shines through, just as you can usually recognize the actor behind his various roles.

Before reincarnating, we plan our upcoming lifetime. Once in a while, we take on too much.

Why would a soul take on circumstances that are more difficult than it can handle?

Inexperience, mainly. To make an analogy, a contractor building his first house lacks experience and may try to do things that look fine on paper but do not prove to work. Until souls have adequate practical experience on the physical plane, they may bite off more than they can chew. There are also souls who, upon death, rush into the next available body, without adequately examining what they are getting into. However, those who are willing to take advantage of their guides' advice make fewer such mistakes.
Also, events do not always happen as expected, and halfway into a lifetime, souls can find themselves in unforeseen circumstances that overwhelm them. That is part of the lessons

---

[10]See also Chapter Ten, "Death," in my upcoming Summerjoy Michael book, *Being in the World*, for further information about the astral interval.

of the physical plane. There is nothing wrong with that; you might say that it aids in keeping everyone on his toes. If you find yourself in a situation you cannot handle—in other words, that you cannot understand, process, and effectively respond to—you can sometimes leave it. Other times, you suffer the consequences. This accounts for a relatively small part of human experience. Most people are in circumstances about right for their level of skill, even if they are difficult.

Circumstances that cannot be handled are sometimes experienced to pay back karmas. You probably would not be very well equipped to handle being physically or mentally tortured, and it is not an experience that your soul would likely seek out deliberately for its growth, although there ultimately would be much growth resulting from such an ordeal. However, if you had subjected someone else to torture in a prior lifetime, your soul might choose to be in a circumstance in which that debt can be erased. Of course, not everyone who experiences torture is erasing a karmic debt—sometimes people are the unfortunate victim of karmic formation; they are in the "wrong place at the wrong time."

Although the repayment of karma can teach much, it goes under the heading of "growing through pain." The enlightened soul seeks to grow through joy, but everyone has done his share of growing through pain. You continue to do so to some extent until you learn not to.

The soul is not all-knowing. If it were, it would not embark on this journey. There is no all-knowing source anywhere. We are all participating in a book whose final chapter will never be written. We are eagerly waiting to see what happens next!

Between lifetimes and after completing the physical plane, there are informal "classes" and study groups of all kinds available.[11] There are also many opportunities for contemplation, rest, and healing. Some souls work closely with the physical plane as spirit guides or as "light workers," who work with the larger energy patterns of the planet to bring growth and healing. There are those who help nonphysical souls who are earthbound or otherwise stuck, and those who help souls plan their next lifetime more skillfully. And so on. Souls are also free to "waste their time" if they wish.

---

[11]*Journey of Souls—Case Studies of Life Between Lives* by Michael Newton, Ph.D. (Llewellyn, 1994), gives fascinating accounts of these study groups and other facets of our astral interval, gleaned from his clients under hypnosis.

Any time we are astral, whether between lifetimes, after finishing the physical plane, or during sleep or out-of-body experiences, we can visit the astral aspects of any place in the universe, although we tend to stay fairly close to home. For example, we might visit Venus to work on lessons on love, or for rest and relaxation; the Sun, to re-energize; or Mars or Mercury, for stimulation. Some people feel that they are not from earth and feel uncomfortable here. They may be picking up memories of recent travels to other places between lifetimes. To make an analogy, a New Yorker returning from six months in Tahiti might have trouble readjusting.

When we visit another part of the universe between lifetimes, we virtually always remain astral rather than physically incarnating on another planet. We do not want to form karmas (which would require being physical) or otherwise get deeply involved; it is like being an exchange student. Having karmas on more than one planet at the same time would be messy. Despite our lack of involvement, we can learn things or have experiences that contribute to our growth. Soul age only advances when we are on the physical plane, because soul age relates to our physical-plane perspective, but our other studies and explorations, including those on the astral plane of other planets, can support that advancement and be enriching in general.

In *Messages from Michael*,[12] Michael said, "We have told you that humans invariably reincarnate in human form, and this is a fact. As long as a species is planet-bound,[13] as you are, then their experience will be limited to the species into which all of the entity members are cast." Some people say that extraterrestrials are now incarnate on earth, walking among us, or even that they themselves are extraterrestrials, "not from this planet." A friend of mine was told by a channeled entity that this is his first lifetime on earth, that he is from another planet. I channeled him as being in my entity and this lifetime as being his 653rd on earth!—a very high number. I suspect that the other channeled entity was picking up on a part of him that is connected with another planet. We are all complex and have diverse connections; perhaps he is getting help from an astral essence from another planet, and some of that essence's energy is in his body, along with his own essence's energy. However, he looks like an earthling to me! The point is that while we're incarnate on earth, this is home. In a sense, none of us are strictly from this planet. Ultimately, we are all from the Tao, and most of us have had previous

---

[12]P. 270.

[13]A planet-bound species does not have the capability of traveling to another planet and living there.

cycles on other planets. Nevertheless, even if we began our current cycle elsewhere, we're here now.

According to my channeling, there are a few people who can more or less legitimately say that they are from another planet—they are like diplomats—but this can be problematic. For one thing, it can take a while to get used to a new planet, which is partly why there is a lengthy infant soul cycle. Someone from a planet that is significantly different from earth could be disoriented and make a lot of *faux pas*. If he formed karma with someone here, he might obligate himself to return for more lifetimes, and when would it end? He would have to "commute" between planets, juggling his obligations on both of them. It's complicated enough to deal with one sentient species! (The situation would be easier if he had already cycled off on the other planet.) So although anything is possible in the universe, you can see why such an arrangement is rare. In some New Age circles, being identified as an extraterrestrial, like being identified as a walk-in, has a certain cachet, but "aliens among us" are not necessarily wiser or more evolved than the garden-variety earthlings here, just as Englishmen are no better than Americans, although Americans tend to romanticize them. We are all eternal sparks of the Tao.

Some people who are attracted to the idea of not being from earth are in denial of their humanity; they have an unhealthy lack of acceptance of life's imperfections and human physicality, perhaps due to childhood or past-life trauma. Those on the spiritual path often feel out of step with the world. Since the world is not in harmony with the universe at the moment, this might be a sign of being more in step with the universe. But denying our humanity, although perhaps a temporarily useful survival mechanism, comes at great cost; it limits our ability to be where we are effectively and to enjoy our lives.

NUMBER OF PAST LIFETIMES

I no longer channel on my Michael Reading charts the number of past lifetimes a person has had. Although reincarnation is intrinsic to the Michael teachings, the number of lifetimes per se is not particularly important (although it is sometimes interesting).

When I was including it on charts, the lowest number of past lives I saw was fifteen, and the highest was 1735.[14] The average

---

[14]Michael said that the woman with 1735 past lives is a specialist in infant mortality! She is a server who, on an essence level, likes the experience of being born and then quickly dying. Perhaps she sees it as a means of service, giving parents an opportunity for intensive growth. If no essence is willing to incarnate in an unhealthy body that will probably die within days or weeks

number of past lives in my practice was perhaps around a hundred. Channeling in one of the Yarbro books stated that the average person spends seven lifetimes per soul age level, of which there are thirty-five, which suggests that the average person has two hundred forty-five lifetimes before cycling off. Simon Warwick-Smith and José Stevens stated in *The Michael Handbook* that it takes about three lifetimes to complete a level. Both sources agreed that it takes about two hundred years on the physical plane to complete a level, so the disagreement was about the average length of a lifetime. That obviously has been different during different eras. Also, different levels tend to take different amounts of time. A sixth level of any soul age, for example, usually takes far longer than a seventh.

The specific number of lifetimes has some significance.

Lifetimes group into clusters, *generally five per cluster. Five clusters gather into* greater clusters *of twenty-five lifetimes. Seven greater clusters gather into* segments *of 175 lifetimes. These have significance vibrationally, but there is no compulsion to complete a segment.*

Finishing five, twenty-five, or one hundred seventy-five lifetimes constitutes a completion apart from soul age. One might, for instance, do a cluster in China, or in various religious orders. It's like finishing a year of school: we have completed our course work, but that doesn't necessarily correlate with our process of inner learning, which is what soul age is about. Michael said "generally" five per cluster because lifetimes lasting less than about twenty years don't count toward a cluster.

Having a relatively high or low number of past lives is not meaningful of itself. A friend who is also seventh-level old has had forty-two past lives, and I've had five hundred forty-four. I see no substantial differences between us based on that; if anything, she is more "street smart" than I am. Someone with few lifetimes may be just as involved here as someone with many, but may spend proportionately more of his time "behind the scenes" on the astral plane. He may be active as a spirit guide, for instance, or as a member of one of the many groups that energetically support growth and healing on the physical plane. Some people work with nature in a deva-like form between lifetimes.

---

anyway, the body will probably be stillborn (although a body can live for a while after birth without an incarnate soul). If a body will probably survive longer than that, there is virtually always a soul willing to incarnate in it.

Fewer lifetimes may also indicate a less in-depth experience of the planet, like someone who chooses to read the abridged version of *War and Peace* instead of the full-length version. Such a soul might have a lot of interests in other parts of the universe.

Since we choose everything, having a lot of lifetimes is not necessarily an indication of being a "slow learner" or "not getting it right." Michael does not regard physical incarnation as a prison sentence to be made as short as possible, but as an opportunity as valid as any other. Certainly, many people do get stuck in limited, repetitive karmic patterns, but others come simply because of what they wish to accomplish.

I wrote earlier of repetitive numerical patterns in cadence positions on my Michael Reading charts. This also occurred with respect to the number of past lives. For a while, patterns combining ones, twos, threes, and fours, such as 123, 134, 224, and so on kept coming up. After a couple of years, the pattern changed so that the digits varied more, but the total number of lifetimes tended to be between sixty and ninety-nine. Sometimes, during a session of channeling charts, two or more of them listed the same number of lifetimes, or several formed a pattern, such as being in the nineties.

There were plenty of exceptions to these patterns, but their existence raised concerns in me that there was something wrong in my channeling. I would have expected more randomness in what came up. I have also experienced patterns with other information on the chart, such as a string of people with nonincarnate priest task companions, or with eleven previous cycles. (It was comforting when another channel complained to me that she was channeling a lot of charts with eleven previous cycles as well—I hadn't said anything to her about it.) When I asked Michael about patterns, they told me:

> *You do tend to magnetize people at certain times who share commonalities. The number of past lives enters into patterns. Those who have each completed one hundred eleven past lives, for example, have resonances and might be drawn to you in the same incoming wave.*

Numbers do have specific vibrations, and this being an orderly universe, it makes sense that certain vibrations would be attracted to me, and I to them, at certain times.

In any case, there's no way for me to validate numerical information—for instance, I can't tell how many past lifetimes a person has had from anything I can objectively measure or observe about him. However, since I am able to consistently validate many other items on the charts, I am less skeptical about those I can't.

Chapter 26

SENTIENCE

Everything in the universe has consciousness, in varying levels of complexity. There is consciousness both far less and far more complex than that of human beings. Even within humanity, there is a wide range of complexity. However, every human being is sentient.

Sentient consciousness is self-aware, and has the capacity to function intellectually, to make reasoned choices. On earth, humans are one sentient species. Dolphins and whales are another, and some apes are entering the beginning stages of sentience. As mentioned, nonsentient animals have hive souls, which are less complex than sentient souls.

Sparks of the Tao develop sentience over unfathomable eons of "time," through experience. Although the consciousness of a blade of grass largely springs from the grass itself, even a blade of grass has an animating spark that makes it possible for it to exist, and that spark, too, is evolving. When it is complete on earth, it may, on some other planet, animate a more-complex form of grass. As a life form, the blade of grass itself, like all creation, is also evolving and becoming capable of accommodating more complex consciousness. So while grass exists on earth, both its form and its animating spark evolve. The reason grass exists isn't simply to evolve—like everything else in the universe, it is an expression of the Tao's creativity—but it naturally evolves as a by-product of its existence.

The ability to make increasingly complex choices grows in increments. There is some point at which a species is capable of allowing sentience. It is slightly more complex than it was before it crossed that threshold, but it is definitely different, just as in a rainbow, the blue is distinctly different from the green, though they are adjacent on the spectrum. One difference in a species capable of sentience is that it is capable of functioning in the intellectual part of the intellectual center. In other words, it can reason.

At this point, the type of consciousness incarnating into the species can shift: a first-level infant sentient soul in its first lifetime can be born to an animal in which a hive soul is incarnate. Hive souls are not fundamentally different from sentient souls—all souls are sparks of the Tao at their core. However, sentient souls are more complex. Also, their collective organiza-

tion includes entities, cadres, and so forth, which only experience being completely reunited at the highest planes. The equivalent of this unity is experienced by hive souls on lower planes because of the lack of interceding subdivisions such as entities. Hive souls do not have extended experiences of higher planes, but they do touch into them relatively briefly. There is one cat hive soul, for example, for all cats; it is more complex than the dog hive soul, but less complex than any sentient cadre. The need for more levels of organization among sentient souls is a result of the greater specificity of function.

Some people think that cat behavior is more common and uniform than dog behavior.

Cats are a little more complex than dogs. This does not mean that they are necessarily more intelligent. Cats do have some predictable traits; however, their way of being is based more on their perceptions than that of dogs. They have more subtle understanding of their environment, and react to more subtle information. Dogs are more social and "outgoing," and therefore appear to be more spontaneous. The differences in cat behaviors are more subtle than in dog behaviors, but cat behaviors are not more common and uniform.

Consciousness does not simply arrive at sentience and remain static at a particular level of complexity. Consciousness is always evolving, becoming more complex. Sentient consciousness can become more sentient,[1] and some souls are more sentient than others. On the larger level, some cadres of souls (including human souls) are more sentient than others.

A soul rarely takes full advantage of its capacity for sentience in any given lifetime, but explores various "corners" of it over many lifetimes. To make an analogy, few human beings use more than three percent of their brain capacity at a time, and some use virtually none of it, but at least, the capacity is there. Although you may use only three percent at a time, you may use different three percents at different times in your life, in different activities. Over a lifetime, you may use a span of fifteen percent of your capacity.[2] Similarly, as a soul progresses, it explores more and more of its capacity for sentience.

---

[1] To be more sentient is to have a greater depth or complexity of sentient consciousness, of conscious awareness. Those with more previous cycles are generally more sentient.

[2] In *Michael's People* (p. 194), Michael describes the present human condition

Each person is a fragment of his entity, cadre, and so on. Every grouping has its own consciousness. On the physical plane, you are only aware of a small part of your entity's con- sciousness, for example. As it unifies on higher planes, you increasingly partake of the awareness of the whole, thereby exploring more of its total capacity for sentience. Since you will eventually experience reunification with everything, helping others evolve is ultimately in your self-interest.

The universe is full of beings whose level of complexity is equal to or greater than our own, but who are not planetary sentient souls; for example, the sun is made up of physical sun beings. Their bodies are made of gas and fire. They are not intellectual in the sense that sen- tient souls are, but they are intelligent. A planetary sentient is anchored to a particular planet, starting as a "creature of reason" on that planet's physical plane, and ascending through its higher planes until its consciousness is again fully focused in the Tao.

Michael compared sentients to actors on the stage. In a theatri- cal production, there are likely to be many more people behind the scenes than on stage. They design, paint, and build the sets; make the costumes; set and run the lights; advertise; sell the tickets; usher; not to mention writing and directing. Likewise, as mentioned, only about five percent of the Tao is cast as planetary sentients. There are plenty of other things to do. (Michael commented that those beings in the sun are analogous to backstage technicians who oper- ate stage lights!) However, those of us who do grand cycles as planetary sentients generally become "hooked" on it, and keep doing it, just as people can become hooked on acting in their community theater.

Only sentient souls can be described in terms of essence roles, casting, and so forth. In addition, overleaves and soul ages are only applicable to sentient souls when they are physically incarnate. Sun beings, devas, and other universal expressions of the Tao are playing different games, each with its own "rules" and procedures, based on what works in that situation. The training and development of an actor are quite different from those of a set designer. Similarly, those

---

as a "waking sleep." In other words, we rarely experience the full depth or complexity of consciousness available to us; our consciousness is rarely fully awake and operative in our lives. Theoretically, if we were fully awake, we would be able to take complete advantage of all our resources, both on the level of consciousness and on the level of the physical brain. As the New Age progresses and humanity opens to greater spiritual upliftment, individuals will find it easier to be more awake.

beings who design planets for the Tao, for instance, follow a different path from that of sentient souls.

Chapter 27

PLANES OF CREATION

The Tao has created many universes, or overall experiments. (I am not speaking here of parallel universes.)[1] Our universe is based in part on the law of seven. It permeates the Michael teachings and many other teachings, as well as being applicable to musical scales, colors of the rainbow, and so forth. Seven consists of two sets of three connected by one.

Twelve is another significant number in this universe, and it relates to seven. For example, the seven-note musical scale is a series of whole and half steps. It is drawn from the twelve-note chromatic scale, which is all half steps.

Apparently, other universes are based on different mathematical ideas. Some of our previous grand cycles may have been in other universes, especially if we have had a high number of them, since this universe is relatively young.

Michael brought up the topic of other universal schemes in relationship to the seven roles:

> *In this universe, the Tao fragments into the seven roles, like white light bent into the seven rainbow colors through the particular prism that this universe offers. A different universe might have a different prism that results in something that cannot be understood in this universe. Our system of seven is only one way a perfect whole can be differentiated.*

This universe has seven planes, or dimensions. (A diagram later in this chapter illustrates them.) Three are ordinal (concrete), three are cardinal (abstract), and one is neutral, providing connection. The most ordinal plane is the physical, which is concrete energy. Its position is mirrored by the most cardinal plane, the buddhaic, which is

---

[1] I read once—I think it was in an introduction to *The Urantia Book*—that this is the twelfth universe, and that after this one, the Tao will play a different game altogether rather than making universes. There are, no doubt, other ideas about it, or alternate ways of looking at it.

Michael found some agreement for the twelfth-universe theory, but said that validating it would require an enormous amount of research on their part. This illustrates that there are limits to Michael's knowledge, and a particular area of study might not be a priority for them. Without research, they must depend on hearsay or speculation, just as we would, although obviously, their sources, even for hearsay, are much greater than ours.

abstract energy. The astral plane (concrete emotion) is the middle ordinal plane. It is mirrored in position by the middle cardinal plane, the messianic (abstract emotion). The causal plane (concrete thought) is the highest ordinal plane.[2] It is mirrored in position by the lowest cardinal plane, the mental. This mirroring balances the universe. The higher planes are about pure energy, love, and truth; the lower planes are about manifesting them. The fulcrum of the balance is the neutral akashic plane. It connects all the others through the akashic or record-keeping aspect of each plane, which feed into it.[3]

There are etheric, nonsolid levels of the physical plane both lower and higher in frequency than our physical bodies. Some people with psychic skills can see them. The fact that they can be physically seen indicates that they are part of the physical plane.[4] We cannot physically see what is nonphysical, although we may translate our nonphysical perceptions into physical images. The etheric substance lower in vibration than the solid physical connects it with the Tao. This is the realm of devas, or nature spirits; it could be called the "lower physical plane." The etheric substance higher in vibration than the solid physical connects it with the astral; it is in the realm of what could be called the "upper physical plane." It is the domain of "ghosts," and some extraterrestrials. The ethereal life form of the "higher sentients" who lived on earth before the "fall of man" was also of the upper physical plane. What we consider solid substance, as well as other vibrations that we can directly perceive such as light and sound, exist in the "middle physical plane."

It might be more accurate to view the planes as being in a circle rather than a line. This is illustrated in the following diagram. Each spiral loop is a plane of creation. The six spiral loops that make one big loop, like a "Slinky" toy with the beginning and end connected, are the planes we experience in a progression. The loop in the middle is the akashic plane; it is not directly part of the progression because we do not actually have a cycle of experience there—it is a resource for the universe as a whole, and provides the Tao with a distillation of all that has been accomplished in this universe. The point of beginning ("Entrance") and end ("Exit") is in the Tao, the undimensional ground of all being—this is where we start and finish the game. The pattern filling each loop representing a plane matches that of the

---

[2]"Highest" here refers to frequency, or speed of vibration, not to any kind of hierarchy.

[3]We discussed the akashic records and plane in the subchapter "The Akashic Records" in Chapter One, "The Nature of Channeling."

[4]Some people consider the etheric substance connecting the solid physical with the astral plane as another plane, and leave out the akashic.

plane on the same axis; for example, both the astral and messianic planes are on the inspiration axis, and both are filled with a checkerboard design. The fill of the loop representing the akashic plane is a darker version of the neutral gray pattern that fills the circle representing the universe as a whole, signifying the akashic records that extend from the akashic plane and interpenetrate all the planes of existence. The akashic plane is directly accessible from the causal and mental planes, illustrated on the diagram with straight lines.

Although this model demonstrates the progression of sentient consciousness, it should not be construed as meaning that only the physical and buddhaic planes have direct contact with the Tao. The diagram illustrates this by showing the universe (the inner circle) as being contained within the Tao (the outer circle).

> *Since the Tao is the ground of all being, every plane has a direct connection with it. The Tao is inherent in any vibrational frequency; those on any plane can "arrive" at it "coming or going" through either increasing their frequency to "all frequency" or decreasing it to "no frequency."*
>
> *On the physical plane, by transcending the material illusions round about and entering into a space of no space and a time of no time, you experience the Tao. You can get there by descending through the earth vibration or ascending through the heaven vibration. The solid roles generally find the former to be easier. The fluid roles find the latter to be easier. However, any role can do both. This is available only when balance and nonattachment are achieved.*

Incidentally, Michael normally uses the word *Tao* in place of *God* (depending on the beliefs of those listening) because *God* is usually personified as a judgmental and hierarchical male figure. They may also use the word *God* to signify the overall consciousness of the manifest universe, as opposed to its source in the dimensionless Tao. In that case, we are each part of both the Tao and God. As microcosmic individuals, we are sparks or units of the Tao experiencing this universe as separate essences. God could be seen as the macrocosmic individual, the larger "chunk" of the Tao who, as a whole, inhabits this universe and experiences the overall expansion and lessons the Tao seeks.

THE TAO AND THE UNIVERSE

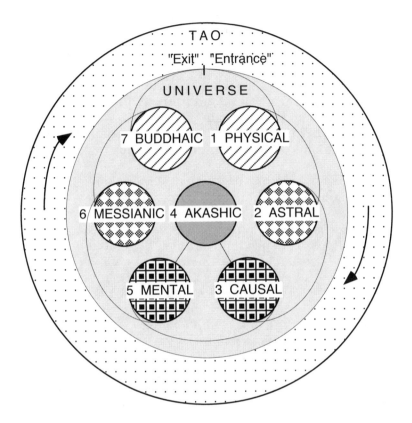

On every plane, those planes that are higher are experienced as resonances. Since the physical plane is first in the progression, only here do all the other planes resonate. (Just as the laws of physics dictate that musical overtones are always higher than the note sounding, only higher planes can be resonances.) However, on other planes, the resonances remaining are stronger. For example, Michael experiences strong resonances with the akashic plane, and works with it a lot. Also, these resonances may seem particularly faint on the physical plane because of our unnecessarily strong sense of separation from the whole.[5]

---

[5]This relates to the "waking sleep" of humanity, mentioned earlier. Humanity has taken young soul materialism and striving for independence to an extreme, resulting in a sense of loneliness and alienation—a majority of us no longer feel our connection to the bigger picture. Hopefully, that is changing.

We as individuals resonate with some planes more than others. For example, someone intellectually centered might have strong resonances with the causal and/or mental planes.

As mentioned, devas are etheric beings who are slower in vibration than the solid physical. Most sparks have a devic stage before committing to a sentient cycle on a planet in order to get a feel for that planet; once in a while, a spark may decide that that particular planet is not its "cup of tea." Devas are directly from the Tao—they have had no intervening experiences in the universe—and, as Michael put it through me, they wear "Tao-like clothing." They are caretakers of the physical kingdoms of the earth, the "wee people" of legend.

Regarding devas, how can a vibration slower than physical matter not result in something even more solid?

Solidity is a convenience of physical existence. It does not refer to the slowest possible speed of vibration, but only to what is slowest or most dense within the usual range of human perception. If something that was as hard and solid as it could be were to slow down in vibration, it would lose solidity, insofar as human perception is concerned, and become part of the unseen world, just like those things that vibrate faster than what is in the world of human perception.

To make an analogy, just as there are sounds that are higher than human beings can hear (but perhaps some animals can), there are also sounds too low for human perception—they are so low that they are not "low" anymore.

Before our devic stage, we have already tentatively planned our entity, role, frequency, and so forth. We are cast from the Tao "from below" the physical plane onto the lower physical plane as a deva. The devic stage is informal; we are done with it when we are ready to commit to a sentient cycle. Those in the same entity tend to work together as devas, although there is much fluidity in devic associations. When we complete our devic stage and commit to a sentient cycle, we gather together into our entity, and firm up our plans for our role and so forth. Usually, there are few changes, if any.[6] Then, we are cast "from above" as an essence, "landing" on the lower astral plane.

To cast means "to form in a mold," as in casting bronze. Being cast from the Tao could be seen as being made from the Tao's mold. It also means "to throw" and could be seen as the Tao

---

[6]Most common is a change of position within our cadence.

"throwing" or, more precisely, extending parts of itself into the dimensional universe, as you might extend your hand. (Essences do not actually leave the Tao, since all is included in the Tao, so it would be less accurate to think of the Tao as throwing essences out of itself into the universe, as though they were separate.)

At this point, our essence is fundamentally our role and casting. However, behind our essence is our spark, with all our experience in the Tao, in previous cycles, and in other universal activities.

Next, we plan our first lifetime, and begin incarnating. Usually, the first-cast essence of the cadre's first entity is also the first to incarnate.[7] Typically, most of the rest of the cadre follows soon after, according to a pattern based on casting.

How does this progressive casting tie in with time being simultaneous on a certain level?

This is an example of the progressive nature of structure unfurling itself against the structure of time; although it is not required that casting mesh with physical time, it is "elegant" and it works.

When you embark on something new, you usually feel excited anticipation about it. This is certainly true of your essence when you begin to incarnate. You usually have no hesitation about doing so. At this point, any and all experiences look interesting, so you dive in.

Through incarnating, the part of us coming "up" from our devic stage meets the part of us coming "down" through the higher planes. It is not that our spark is divided in half, but that it expresses itself from the Tao into the universe from both directions.

"Lower" and "higher" here do not connote better or worse. Both are needed for our wholeness. History, both personal and collective, could be seen as our attempt to merge these two aspects. Religious and spiritual people often revile the "lower" self, but clearly, it is essential, and comes from the Tao just as surely as the "higher." The

---

[7]Suppose that artisans are in the first position among the roles in the cadre's first entity. This essence would be an artisan in the first position of his cadence, which is first in its greater cadence, which is the first greater cadence of artisans in his entity. This casting pattern would be written as 1/1/1 under cadence on my Michael Reading chart. See also Chapter Eleven, "Cadences and Numbers."

lower self is wild, in the sense of being natural, not yet acculturated, but it is not innately destructive. (Devas, for instance, are known for sometimes being playfully mischievous.) There is no real joy in life until the higher and lower selves are integrated.

Parenthetically, just as we are cast from the Tao both from "above" and "below," there is energy that comes "up" from the earth, and energy that comes "down" through the higher planes, which could be called "heaven energy." We need both earth and heaven energies in our bodies, in balance, to be healthy.

When we are out of the physical body, we can visit the astral plane of other places in the universe. We can also visit higher planes, particularly those of earth.

> When your astral self goes traveling in higher planes, it is like channeling, in a sense, although the astral self cannot be said to be a vehicle. It speeds its vibration and goes into what is, for it, an altered state. It "visits" higher planes for its own education and inspiration, giving it a "preview of coming attractions" and reenergizing it for its work. However, it does not sustain such a sojourn for very long.

The astral self slows its vibration to incarnate. When a reincarnational self becomes a "ghost" after death, the astral self is being kept weighted down, abnormally dense, which is a burden to it once the lifetime is complete. This occurs either when the reincarnational self won't let go of the physical plane (or someone or something in it— sometimes addictions are involved[8]), or when someone else won't let go of the reincarnational self and the reincarnational self isn't strong enough to free itself.

Only on the physical plane are we divided between two planes, returning to the lower astral between lifetimes and often at night when we sleep. Apparently, that is because the physical plane "fell" in vibration. It is no longer light or quick enough to sustain a very high consciousness on its own. The lower astral plane had to become the seat of the essence for earth's physical plane. (On many other planets, the upper physical plane is the seat of the essence.) The New Age is ultimately about the physical plane becoming higher in vibration, which has many ramifications.

---

[8]Physical addictions such as those involving substance abuse can have emotional and psychological components that can continue after the body's death, even though, obviously, the body's cravings are no longer a factor.

There is an opening occurring between the physical plane and the higher planes. Originally, there was much more communication and ease of movement between them. Earth's physical plane is currently denser than it was intended to be. That makes it more difficult for those of higher planes to just "stop by for a visit." Slowing down our vibration requires a great deal of energy, because the drop in vibration is so great. This is why we use channels. Originally, channels were not necessary. Likewise, it is now difficult for human beings to speed up their vibration and visit higher planes while in their bodies. The earth is returning to a lighter density, which will make channeling unnecessary. Also, a lighter physical body will live longer and get sick less, if at all.

As part of this transformation, a new kind of physical body may be in the offing sometime in the next thousand years, but it is still on the "drawing board."

When we complete the physical plane, we "cycle off." Michael has emphasized that we cycle off not when we're perfect, according to some definition, but when we feel finished.[9]

Is it necessary to become like Buddha or Christ before you can cycle off?

Most people would not cycle off if they had to become as elevated as Buddha and Jesus. You do not have to achieve some concept of perfection; you just have to be finished. It is up to you to decide whether you are finished. If you have karmas or lessons that can only be completed on the physical plane, you will, at some point, feel drawn to come back.

Cycling off is the essence deciding that it is finished with school on the physical plane, and enrolling in postgraduate studies on the astral plane. All "schools" in the universe are work/study programs. You must do useful work at each step along the way to take advantage of the schooling. As you move along, your ability grows—you become more and more capable of expressing yourself effectively.

---

[9]John Friedlander, author of *The Practical Psychic*, told me that he sees a sort of "porch light" go on outside the aura when someone is ready to cycle off. This is literal "enlightenment."

We experience the greatest separation of our individual parts or aspects of self on the physical plane. On our journey through the higher planes back to the Tao, we experience increasing integration. We recombine with our entity, our entity recombines with our cadre, and so on, until we're totally recombined back into the Tao. Meanwhile, our various subpersonalities integrate into our personality, and our various reincarnational personalities integrate into our essence—it is a multilevel process. The consciousness of the individual parts gradually recedes, as the consciousness of the whole increases. Paradoxically, this enhances the individuality and effectiveness of the parts. As mentioned, it is like the evolution of organisms: as they develop, individual cells become more specialized, which allows them and the whole organism to function more effectively. The reunited individual members of the Michael entity, working together as a "team," are more sophisticated and individuated than they were as separate fragments on the physical plane, although the separation was useful at the time—it allowed a broader band of experience.

Also as mentioned, after our entity reunites on the upper astral plane, and our cadre reunites on the upper causal plane, we are no longer considered fragments. We move on to the cardinal planes. However, our individuality as specific points of consciousness remains on all planes, and even in the Tao, although it is experienced differently than on the physical plane. It is an individuality beyond our present comprehension.

By necessity, we interpret our perceptions of higher planes through the perceptions of the physical plane, since that is where we are. By the same token, when Michael is not being channeled, they see us energetically, almost as though we were causal ourselves.

We see the causal energy of physical-plane action. That is primarily how we know you. This energy is more real and prominent to us than your physical body. It provides much information to our direct vision, telling us what is fundamentally going on. However, we cannot read the New York Times, *for instance, unless we are being channeled.*

The causal plane is a plane of intellect; it has a medium of thought (expression axis) energy, whereas the physical plane has a medium of kinetic (action axis) energy, emphasizing movement and action. The astral plane has a medium of emotional (inspiration axis) energy, or content. The causal plane is here, where you are, like the other planes. You live in all of them, but do not see them, because they vibrate faster than the physical plane. You do not even see all the vibrations of the physical plane. At this moment, your body is being coursed with radio waves, but if you do not turn on a radio, you do not perceive their presence. When you access pure thought, you are accessing the causal plane.

Seth, as channeled by Jane Roberts, teaches that we create our reality from our beliefs. So our beliefs are the *cause* of our reality—they are the thoughts we have chosen to provide the framework of our life. And the causal plane is the plane of pure thought. So the name of the causal plane is apt. Incidentally, according to my channeling, Seth, as he was channeled by Jane Roberts, is a causal-plane entity, like Michael.

It is possible to channel a source from a plane (or level) lower than its true one. It is rather like interacting with a person manifesting lower than his true soul age. So one channel may be accessing Michael or Seth from the fourth level of the causal plane, while another may be tapping in at the sixth level of the astral plane. In the latter case, Michael would seem like an astral entity, which is neither better nor worse than manifesting as a causal entity—only different. Astral aspects of Michael would, for one thing, show more vestiges of human personality.

One could even access a source from a plane higher than its true one. For instance, one could channel the "future" or potential messianic plane resonance of Michael, in which case a more abstract, inspirational part of Michael would come through. However, since Michael predominantly engages with the late twentieth-century physical plane as a mid-causal entity, those higher-plane resonances would not seem fleshed out. Similarly, one could channel the future or potential causal-plane resonance of one's own essence or reunited entity.

The akashic plane is between the causal and mental planes, giving these two planes direct access to it, similar to the way we have direct access to the astral plane from the physical. (Other planes have indirect access to the akashic plane, since, as mentioned, it interpenetrates them through the akashic records generated on each plane.) It makes sense that the universe's "library" would be "sandwiched" by the two intellectual-axis planes—it's like locating a major research library between a university's main campus and graduate school. Though it is a band of frequency, like the other planes, we don't have a separate cycle of experience on the akashic plane.

Beyond the mid-astral plane, there is little fear, "negativity," or ego. These are mainly functions of the mortality and separateness of the physical body. Without bodies, there is not much to sustain fear.

That does not mean that everyone on higher planes is "perfect," or has the same capacity for light and understanding. It just means that the game is different. For one thing, it is less rigidly structured, just as college life is less rigidly structured than children's experiences in most elementary schools, because college students can handle a greater variety of choices. Still, there are challenges at every step.

Incidentally, the higher planes of earth are part of earth and are specific to it. They continue its purposes and lessons. The same is true of other planets.

The only perfection is the Tao. The Tao and the seven-plane universe are two parts of one thing, balancing each other. The Tao is in equilibrium, while the universe is in motion. The Tao can be "perfect," stable, and complete, because the universe is "imperfect," unstable, and incomplete. The universe expands the Tao. If the universe were also complete, there would be no room for growth and movement.

Chapter 28

LEVELS OF SELF

V arious metaphysical and spiritual teachings describe the levels of self differently, [1] and even when different teachings describe them in fundamentally the same way, there is no standard terminology. Words such as *soul* can mean different things.

In discussions when the distinction between them is not significant, Michael generally uses the words *soul* and *essence* interchangeably, and for the sake of consistency, I have adopted this policy, favoring *essence*, since it's such a characteristic Michael word.[2] Up to this point in this book, I have not made a distinction between them. However, technically, they are not identical. In Yarbro,[3] Michael said that the essence is the intrinsic *core* of the soul. Michael through me has stated that when speaking of essence, they mainly mean the abstract aspects of self resonating with the three cardinal planes. These could be called our buddhaic, messianic, and mental selves. Although the essence, as defined here, is in the dimensional universe rather than the Tao, which is undimensional, it is beyond time and space. It could be contrasted with the concrete aspects of self, those that resonate with the ordinal planes and are influenced by time. These could be called our physical, astral, and causal selves. Our ordinal levels of self could be viewed as clothing or expressing our cardinal levels, just as our essence itself clothes our spark, and our personality clothes our astral self. Our astral self, which has direct contact with our body and leaves our body at death and sometimes during sleep, could be specifically designated as our soul. It contains our reincarnational selves.

This delineation is supported by the following passage from *Messages from Michael:*[4] "What makes the agreements is your astral self...which is mostly in essence, and the vestiges of personalities. Agreements are not made by the essence."

Don Kollmar, the founder of Complete Self Attunement, an approach to meditation, differentiates the words *soul* and *essence*

---

[1]Buddhist and Vedantic texts, for example, contain detailed descriptions of the levels of self.

[2]I titled this book *The Journey of Your Soul* rather than *The Journey of Your Essence* since most people aren't familiar with the term *essence* used in this way.

[3]*Messages from Michael*, p. 36.

[4]*Messages from Michael*, p. 197.

similarly. He defines essence as the underlying truth of our being, or our pure presence, and the soul, which is created from essence, as its vehicle into the physical body. He says that the emergence of the essence transforms the personal self.

So perhaps the levels of self can be summarized and correlated with the planes with which they resonate:

LEVEL OF SELF	PLANE
Personality	Physical
Soul (astral self)	Astral
Causal self	Causal
Personal akashic records	Akashic
Essence	Mental
Essence	Messianic
Essence	Buddhaic
Spark	The Tao

The reason the terms *soul* and *essence* can usually be used interchangeably is that the soul is the part of essence with which our personality has direct contact. We cannot experience the abstract levels of our essence except through our soul.

From our point of view as a personality, our higher levels of self are potential rather than realized, since we have not yet lived them during this grand cycle, in the sense of focusing our consciousness in them. That will come after we cycle off the physical plane. For example, our causal self is the part of us that will be fully activated when our consciousness is focused on the causal plane. However, our progression through the planes is not a progression through physical time. It is linear in one sense, but it is also true that all levels of self exist simultaneously. It is the focus of our awareness that progresses.

> *You are now present on the other planes simultaneously with your current existence. However, they are not activated in relationship to you right now. They are just "there." These higher-plane aspects of self give you resonance and relationship with what is coming in your experience. To you right now, they are the unformed or potential parts of you, just as probabilities provide this function within the physical plane.*

Although we experience our nonphysical levels of self as potential, they are also functional in our lives. An acorn is a potential oak tree, but the oak tree could be seen as the essence of the acorn, guiding its development into the oak tree. When a baby is born, it is a potential adult. It has all the parts that it will have as an adult. In a sense, the adult is its essence, guiding its development so that it realizes its potential. When an essence is cast from the Tao, it is unrealized potential seeking realization. It guides its realization at every step, like the potential oak tree and adult. Although it has a basic design, it doesn't know exactly what it will look like until that realization is complete.

In our normal waking state, our sense of self is usually centered in our personality. When we're asleep, our sense of self reverts to being centered in our soul. Our soul can be quite active at night and often leaves the physical body. Sometimes our dreams are the personality's memories of those excursions, but we generally only remember a fraction of what we actually do in the dream state. A technique called "lucid dreaming" allows us to be "awake" in our dreams and deliberately guide them, effectively merging our personality and soul even as our body sleeps. People often wake up tired after lucid dreaming, since the personality isn't at rest, as well as after extensive unconscious out-of-body excursions, because the body isn't receiving the soul's undivided attention; energy is being expended rather than regenerated.

A client I don't know well but who is in my entity related an intense dream she had in which she told me that she felt sad. In her dream, I thought about this a little and then asked her to follow me. We walked up a hill in her hometown (in Germany). I showed her a beautiful new little house with red shingles. It immediately made her feel very happy. A few months after having the dream, she was back in her hometown. A friend offered to let her stay in her house over the summer. It turned out to be the house in the dream. She had a happy, creative summer there.

I assume that, although I don't remember the experience, her dream was a record of something that actually happened: I left my body to show her where she would be staying so as to help alleviate her sadness. Perhaps part of the reason I chose a body that requires a lot of sleep was to leave time for all this astral activity. (Sleep also facilitates creativity and mental/emotional processing.)

AURAS

The aura is a band of etheric substance surrounding our physical body that reflects our seven levels of self. It consists of seven layers of middle-physical substance vibrating a little more quickly than the physical body itself. It is at the fringes of human perception—some people can see it, although most people have lost the capability if they ever had it. (Young children can be especially adept at seeing auras, as well as nonphysical spirit guides, until adults convince them that such visions are imaginary and should be disregarded.) Our essence "shining through" our personality is like a "light bulb" lighting up the various colors and shapes of our aura. When false personality obscures essence, the aura reflects this with grayer colors; heavy blocks can show up as patches of black. The aura is constantly changing, reflecting the person's internal "climate," although its basic framework remains constant.[5] (We have discussed, for example, how artisans tend to have large, diffuse auras, and warriors tend to have compact, concentrated auras. An individual's aura also tends to have its own "look," in spite of being fluid.)

Barbara Brennan, author of *Hands of Light,* a book about spiritual healing, names the aura's seven levels as shown in the following chart, in which I correlate her terms with Michael's terms for the centers and planes. She psychically sees the first level as being closest to the physical body, and the seventh as the farthest.

THE AURA

LEVEL OF AURA		CENTER	PLANE
One	ETHERIC BODY	Physical	Physical
Two	EMOTIONAL BODY	Emotional	Astral
Three	MENTAL BODY	Intellectual	Causal
Four	ASTRAL BODY	Instinctive	Akashic
Five	ETHERIC TEMPLATE	Moving	Buddhaic
Six	CELESTIAL BODY	Higher Emotional	Messianic
Seven	KETHERIC TEMPLATE	Higher Intellectual	Mental

---

[5]This is hearsay, as I don't see the colors of auras. I do perceive energy "shapes" around people, if I "tune in" to them, that give me a sense of what's happening in their experience.

The levels of the aura have straightforward correlations with the planes and centers, except that Ms. Brennan orders them differently than the Michael teachings order the planes. In the Michael teachings, the lower planes *mirror* the higher. It is as though the middle, assimilation-axis plane, the akashic, were a mirror: the first plane corresponds with the seventh—both are kinetic, action-axis planes; the second corresponds with the sixth—both are emotional, inspiration-axis planes; and the third corresponds with the fifth—both are intellectual, expression-axis planes. In the aura, Brennan sees the lower levels of the aura as *paralleling* the higher. The first corresponds with the fifth, the second corresponds with the sixth, and the third corresponds with the seventh.

When we were exploring the correlations between the planes and roles, we saw that the universe is complex and practical, and does not always follow neat, consistent patterns. Even though the theme of seven is common, its application is "variations on a theme"—the order of kinetic, emotional, intellectual, and neutral qualities is not always the same. The aura itself is physical and relates specifically to how the seven levels of self impact the body. Naturally, the order in which these manifest is appropriate to the body's needs. The seventh level of the aura, which Ms. Brennan calls the *ketheric template*, correlates with the higher intellectual center, or what she calls the "divine mind." This is symbolic of the fact that the consciousness of the whole provides the "container" for our individual experience. We all share a structure made up of fundamental beliefs, such as in gravity and time, so that we can play the same game; as essences, we each agree to abide within this structure.

In the aura, the outermost layer corresponds with the foundational structure of consciousness that creates one's reality.

The three interior levels of the aura could be seen as representing the personality; the exterior three, the essence; and the middle (fourth) level, the astral self, which connects the personality and the essence.

Chapter 29

INFINITE AND TRANSCENDENTAL SOULS

An infinite soul is a representative of a reunited cadre from one of the three high planes. A transcendental soul is a representative of a fully reunited entity from the upper causal plane. An infinite soul brings the Tao directly to bear on the physical plane. When the infinite soul walked in through Jesus, it was a representative of a reunited messianic-plane cadre that channeled the Tao's energy inspirationally, since the messianic plane is the cardinal inspiration plane. Therefore, Jesus's teachings emphasized love.

An infinite soul incarnates in order to catalyze massive spiritual change in a civilization, generally during a shift from one average soul age to another. An incarnation of a transcendental soul usually precedes it in order to catalyze massive social change.

> When an infinite soul displaces a "garden-variety" soul on the physical plane, tremendous power is brought to bear. No infinite soul is incarnate now, nor will one probably incarnate in the next few years. The last incarnation of an infinite soul was through Jesus.

Messages from Michael[1] emphatically stated that there have only been four manifestations each of the transcendental and infinite souls. My channeling said that that should have read "in recorded history."

> Human beings have been incarnating on earth for a long time. Infinite and transcendental souls did not just start showing up in the last few thousand years.

Besides Jesus, the infinite souls came through Buddha, Krishna, and Lao-tzu. The transcendental souls came through Gandhi, Zoroaster, Mohammed, and Socrates. These incarnations are achieved when a highly accomplished seventh-level old soul "walks out" of his body and an infinite or transcendental soul simultaneously "walks in."[2] Because infinite soul energy, especially, is so intense, the human body cannot handle it for very long. For example, the actual incarna-

---

[1] P. 85.

[2] In a walk-in, the incarnate soul permanently leaves its body and another soul incarnates into it, assuming responsibility for the person's life.

tion of the infinite soul through Jesus occurred only thirty days before he completed his work. Before that, he was a seventh-level old king. However, no doubt Jesus built up to the walk-in gradually, increasingly blending his energy with that of the infinite soul. Also, the infinite soul was not unrelated to his own essence.

The infinite soul was like a higher or future aspect of the seventh-level-old king Jesus. It was completely aligned with his energies and was the exaltation of them, seamlessly raising his vibration immeasurably to shine a great light across the earth. In other words, it went in exactly the same direction as his own energies, only to a higher mathematical power. With the other infinite soul manifestations, that "line" was not so much in evidence; there was more of a shift, although there will always be some of that alignment with manifestations of the infinite soul.

The infinite soul could probably manifest a physical body rather than walking in to an already-existing body. However, things being as they are, walking in is the most sensible approach. Why do things the hard way?

Jesus incarnated when our Western civilization was changing from being predominantly baby soul to predominantly young. We are now in a similar transition, from young to mature.

An infinite soul will likely incarnate again within the next forty or fifty years through more than one individual, most likely three, one or more of them female. This will reveal and bring to bear different aspects of the infinite soul. However, nothing has been definitely decided yet. In fact, nothing in the universe is certain until it happens.

There is one person now living who is a possible vehicle for this incarnation, or so we hear. However, there will probably be as many as a hundred candidates "lined up" so that the Tao can see who is the most apropos when the time comes. It is like your making several mate agreements before your lifetime. You generally do not expect to mate with all of them. You line them up as possibilities. When it comes time to mate, you decide based on how things are then.

You will probably be able to recognize the infinite soul without much problem.

Some channels are getting information that certain living people are transcendental souls. Technically, if our entity still has fragments incarnating, we cannot be transcendental; the oldest soul age we can have on the physical plane is seventh-level old. According to my channeling, when people other than Gandhi, Zoroaster, Mohammed, and Socrates are channeled as being transcendental, it does not refer to a complete displacement of the originally incarnate soul through a walk-in, but usually to a shared energy. Although the essence originally occupying the body is still present and responsible for the life being lived, it is being assisted by an essence (or essences) from a fully cycled-off entity. This assistance can be "part-time," through unconscious or conscious channeling, or a "full-time" sharing of the body, in which case it would account for no more than about seventy-five percent of the person's life force. This collaboration both helps the incarnate essence achieve his life task, and helps the cycled-off entity achieve its purposes. It is a "win-win" arrangement.[3]

Some seventh-level old souls keep incarnating after they are fundamentally complete with the physical plane—they have tied up their essential loose ends here. They may have even cycled off and later decided to return, out of interest or a desire to assist others.[4] These people can develop resonances with the astral plane so that their perspective becomes a blend of seventh-level old and astral. Through the channel "Jessica Lansing," Michael referred to such people as "final-level old souls transcendent," as opposed to transcendental souls.

> *Those with much resonance with the lower astral plane see physical reality as being flexible, like astral reality. They become more oriented toward creating their own reality, and do it more quickly because of their resonance. Those with much resonance with the middle astral plane begin to have a more universal perspective. They also become more oriented toward combining energies with others, since that is a middle-astral focus.*

---

[3]In the subchapter "Combined Essence Energies" in Chapter Nine, "Roles," we discussed secondary essences in the body who are mainly from entities still incarnating, especially entity mates and essence twins. There is only transcendental energy if the person's "roommate" is from a cycled-off entity, of either the upper astral or causal plane. A true transcendental soul is a representative from an upper causal plane entity that is not only cycled-off but fully recombined. Michael is mid-causal.

[4]Being complete with the physical plane does not imply that a person has no further issues to work through. Some issues need to be worked through physically, such as most karmic debts to other people. Others, such as self-worth issues, may not require incarnation to fully clarify. We continue to learn and grow through our experiences on all the planes.

Resonances with the lower astral plane occur through the individual astral self. Resonances with the middle astral plane occur through cycled-off entity mates who are focused there and have begun the entity's process of recombining. The more cycled-off entity mates one has, the stronger the resonance with the middle astral plane one can have. These resonances are another reason someone may be channeled as being a transcendental soul. The information may come through as "first-level transcendental," or whatever, as a kind of shorthand, indicating resonances that can be asked about further.

Incidentally, this type of incomplete, sometimes misleading channeling occurs fairly often; it certainly has in my channeling. It may be due to inexperience: the channel may lack an adequately sophisticated vocabulary of concepts or the flexibility to transmit the complete picture. Also, Michael may simply not wish to take the time to explain a complex concept, particularly if they have already gone over it. (In addition, different channels may transmit the Michael teachings in different ways, with different terminologies.)

There will probably soon be a complete walk-in of a transcendental soul to prepare for the infinite soul.

This would probably occur through someone already working with transcendental energy. However, if transcendental energy has enough impact without a complete walk-in, there may not be a need for one.

Once reunited on higher planes, your entity or cadre may or may not choose to incarnate physically as a transcendental or infinite soul.

The need for infinite and transcendental souls on the physical plane in the way they have been known in history may be diminished as the physical plane reattains a greater connection with the higher planes.

Some people believe that the infinite soul, or Jesus in particular, is now incarnate.

The loving, inspirational vibration of the messianic plane is sometimes called Christ energy. When someone feels attuned to it, he or others may assume that must mean he is Jesus, which is not the case. The man who was incarnated as Jesus before the infinite soul manifestation is not incarnate, and does not intend to incarnate again, to our knowledge. He is now focused on the middle astral plane. Also, the infinite soul is not now incarnate through anyone else.

There are many people these days who are tapping in to higher energies, but the truly great rarely make claims. They allow their presence to make those claims for them.

In any case, you do not have to categorize the source of a teaching or energy to receive value from it.

I would have thought that Jesus was higher than mid-astral by now.

Jesus, as now experienced by those in this time frame who connect with him directly, is mid-astral simply because that is what works. His entity is recombining on the upper astral, but he works mostly with the physical plane from the mid-astral in order to give better access to those who are physical. Soon this will no longer be necessary.

I have heard many different, apparently conflicting channeled accounts of the death, or nondeath, of Jesus. Michael through JP Van Hulle said that Jesus's body was worn out from the intensity of the infinite soul, and died. Seth through Jane Roberts said that the crucifixion didn't literally happen to Jesus at all, but that there had been a stand-in—it was the enactment of the psychic drama that was essential. I have also heard confirmations of the Bible's report that his body ascended. I once read, and my channeling on the subject concurred, that Jesus did not die on the cross, but that rather than fully ascending the body (to the astral plane), the infinite soul walked out and the body was "recycled" since its vibration had been so raised and transformed—it was rematerialized in India. Another essence (not Jesus's) walked into it, and continued to teach through it for several hundred years.[5]

Most bodies are worn out at the end of the lifetime and it is better to dispose of them. This body had been regenerated, and thus could be used for transformational purposes in India.

It is possible that all the versions of the story are correct, that they occurred in parallel universes that were previously on different tracks, but now share the same one. This leads us to our next subject: parallel universes.

---

[5]There are people now living in India reported to have mastered their physical bodies and achieved physical immortality. For instance, one woman is said to have lived in the same village for four hundred years. See also my upcoming Summerjoy Michael book *Being in the World.*

Chapter 30

PARALLEL UNIVERSES

Just as there are seven "vertical" planes of existence "layered" on top of one another, there are infinite "horizontal" or "parallel" levels of existence "side by side," called parallel universes. The concept of parallel universes sounds like science fiction. In fact, many science fiction authors have tapped into universal truths through the free play of their imagination. According to Michael, as well as some other channeled teachers, our particular experience of reality is but one of countless realities that our wholeness is experiencing. We know ourselves as having a particular identity, address, body, job, set of parents, friends, and so forth. However, there are infinite parallel "us"s whose experiences range from being very similar except in a few details, to almost unrecognizable as being us.

The constants among our various parallel selves include our essence (including role, male/female energy ratio, and so on), overleaves, basic life task, and approximate time frame. (Our parallel selves are different from our reincarnational selves, which have different overleaves, life tasks, and overall circumstances, and usually different time frames.) Other characteristics usually predominate, but not exclusively. For example, we are either male or female in most of our parallels. We are often working in the same field, such as the arts or business, in many of them. At least one of our parents is our parent in most of them, and both parents may be the same in many of them.[1] Although we may look quite different in some of our parallels, our basic appearance and primary body type is usually the same in most of them. However, events of our parallel lives may vary a great deal. Here's why:

Whenever we reach a significant crossroads in life, where the choice we make will affect everything that follows, our essence wants to experience all the significant probabilities. Suppose there are three major alternatives. If we choose the first in the majority of our parallels in which this choice comes up, there will be added pressure on those aspects of us who have not yet chosen to go with the second or third. Let's say that at least one parallel self goes with the second alternative, but none choose the third. We will then "spin off" a parallel

---

[1]The essence of the parent with whom we have a child agreement will generally be one of our parents in most of the universes in which we incarnate. However, if that essence doesn't have children in some universes, or it otherwise doesn't work out, we might make different arrangements in them.

universe where we choose the third one. That universe has the same past as the one that spun it off, but moves in a different direction from that point forward. Of course, other people are also constantly spinning off parallels. We spin off ours in concert with them.

We can picture an incarnate essence as the center of a sphere, and each parallel life as extending in a line from the center to the periphery. Just as an infinite number of lines can be contained in a sphere, we have an infinite number of parallel selves. A certain part of that sphere can be considered to contain "main trunk" lives, those that are more central to the essence's purposes in incarnating; the rest of it contains "fringe" lives, more peripheral or experimental for the essence. As hard to believe as it may be, each of our parallel selves is as real to itself as we are to ourselves. It is not that this is the "primary" one and all others are parallel to it—there is no one parallel life that is primary, no one parallel self that is the "real" one. The parallel universe you experience as you read these words is just one of an infinite number. All our parallel selves are real, are part of the total reality of who we are. When you also take into account our reincarnational selves and the whole of our essence, our present experience of self accounts for only about one twelve-thousandth of our total self, according to Michael.[2]

Not only do parallel universes spin off, but when two or more universes have become essentially the same, they recombine; they merge onto the same track. We feel it when that happens—it's an odd time when something seems different; things look slightly rearranged or in different places—but we usually do not consciously identify the shift. So there is a continual expansion and contraction.

Each parallel universe keeps an integrity of movement. It is like Highway #212 that might, for a few miles, merge into #487, but then again take a track of its own. It is more complex than this, but still, each parallel has its own history.

The universe in which you are reading these words currently shares a "track" with several others, not all of which were on this track, say, two hundred years ago and not all of which will share this track two hundred years hence. Even though they were essentially the same when they recombined, they do not have exactly the same history. That is partly why there are conflicting accounts of past events.

---

[2]Although there are infinite parallel selves, there are many factors shared in common among parallels, especially among those on the "main trunk." That is why Michael didn't say that our present experience of self accounts for an infinitesimally small fraction of our totality.

You have access to the pasts of all universes on your present track. If one of them moves onto a different track, it will take its past with it, and that past will fade from your awareness.

By definition, at any crossroads there is more than one possible outcome. For example, there may be a time when the world situation could lead to either nuclear holocaust or a breakthrough in establishing world peace. At least one of our parallel selves will experience each outcome, and other parallel selves will experience other probabilities. Sometimes a parallel self is at least subliminally aware of the possible outcomes and chooses, in collaboration with our essence, to associate with a particular one; it may choose, for instance, to experience the future in which there is a breakthrough in establishing world peace. The more spiritually advanced a parallel self is, the more skillful he is in thus "creating his own reality."

The parallel selves of others who have shared your universe may choose different outcomes than the one you choose, and hence, no longer share your universe with you.

Individual tracks are superimposed over collective tracks. Your essence is constantly "deciding" which part of itself will experience which collective reality, and is continually "rearranging" itself accordingly, but its work is seamless and unapparent to you—this is not something of much relevance on the level of personality.

That doesn't mean that people suddenly disappear from our lives—we may continue to see them; it just means that we share our universe with the particular parallel selves of others who wish or need to experience the same collective reality. At least one parallel self of all those incarnate within a "band" of universes experiences each of its significant alternate realities.

An individual essence is present in only a portion or "band," narrow or wide, of a planet's parallels, and chooses one that concentrates his experiences where he wants them. For example, if experiencing nuclear holocaust will not be very growthful for him, he can choose a band where that is not a likely main-trunk outcome.

As mentioned, every parallel universe maintains its integrity; in other words, there is a through line maintained for every individual and collective parallel, but individual and collective parallels are constantly shifting in relationship to one another, because of individual free will. The mass consciousness of a collective parallel universe (for example, one parallel universe of the earth as a whole) also has its own gestalt and free will. It is not merely the sum of all the individual parallels it contains.

As also mentioned, sometimes lifetimes we remember in past-life regression are not from this universe.

If you need to work on an issue that you also dealt with in a particular past life, but in a parallel universe, you might "pull in" that lifetime during past-life regression, just as you might pull in a past life from your own universe. This could help you gain more insight and bring to bear the healing power of your current level of consciousness on a greater part of your whole-ness. Probably less then ten percent of the past lives you might remember in regression are from parallel universes, and all presently occupy the same track as your own universe.

Parallel universes provide the means for our essence to experience all its possibilities, and therefore its wholeness, on the physical plane. To our essence, these various parallels are not separate, although they seem separate to our personality. On higher planes, our essence continues to experience all its possibilities without apparently sepa-rate parallel universes, since it is only the solid nature of the physical plane that creates the illusion of separate parallel realities.

Here are some further comments by Michael on parallel uni-verses:

You affect your other parallels, so if you have a particularly worthwhile growth experience in one parallel, you might in-crease the percentage of your parallel selves who are availing themselves of that experience, wherever that is convenient and possible. However, it will not become a very high percentage— no one specific activity dominates all your parallels, because your essence wants to explore all sides of your life. Someone who is, say, a superstar in this parallel universe may have such superstardom in perhaps a maximum of ten or fifteen per-cent of his parallels.

If the earth is destroyed from nuclear war in a parallel uni-verse, what does that do to us in this universe?

If you are affected, the effect would probably be subtle. You might find that your resolve to prevent nuclear war strengthens if a parallel self experienced nuclear destruction. Incidentally, you will probably not have a nuclear holocaust in this universe.

Was the earth destroyed in a parallel universe in 1986?

Yes, in about five of them. Earth has been destroyed many times in other parallel universes, in various ways.

Each parallel universe has its own past, and therefore its own akashic records.

Déjà vu may be a memory of having met in a past life, or of an out-of-body "rehearsal" for the current event, such as a meeting. Often, however, it is an awareness that you just had the same meeting in a parallel universe that is slightly ahead of this one.

Would artisans, being so fluid, have more access to their parallel selves than the other roles?

All have the same access. Artisans might tend to take advantage of it more, which is important for them, being so creative.

This discussion may sound wholly theoretical. However, it can be useful as well as broadening to be aware of our parallel existences. Knowing what we are doing in some of them can give us added perspective. Also, we are probably doing in a parallel what we can't get to in this universe, if it is important. Understanding that can help us relax and enjoy what we are doing, rather than worrying about the things we are not doing. (That should not be used as an excuse for not doing what we'd rather be doing now. If we'd rather be doing something, that may be an impulse from our essence to do it.) In addition, we can draw on the expertise of our parallel selves.[3]

We can learn about our parallel selves within, through meditation, for example, or from a channeled source or a psychic. We can also access the experience and knowledge of our parallel selves, just as we can with our reincarnational selves. Again, meditation can be helpful, but the key is simply holding the intention to access that knowledge and experience, and deliberately opening to it.

---

[3]See also Chapter Four, "Multiple Aspects of Self," in my upcoming Summerjoy Michael book, *Being in the World.*

Epilogue

THE UNIQUENESS OF WHO WE ARE

T he Michael teachings are an excellent model for describing the framework through which we express ourselves. However, they do not define who we are, which is unique and beyond classification. If we have an attitude of spiritualist, for instance, we are merely using it for this lifetime. In our Michael teachings shorthand, we may say that we're a spiritualist, but that's not really who we are; we are far greater than that. Similarly, we are not a server, if that is our role, but a spark playing the role of server for a cycle. Although each role tends to emphasize certain inner qualities, there are infinite ways to play a role, and unlimited depth we can bring to it, as any actor knows.

We may bring to our role a remarkable communion with plants or animals, or an original, joyful sense of humor. We may have an ability to be there for others, or a gift for bringing beauty into every aspect of life. We may have indomitable courage in working through limitations, or an uncompromising willingness to see the truth about ourselves.

Our consciousness has evolved uniquely over eons, and everything we have experienced has contributed to that evolution. Not only are we unique combinations of role, frequency, casting, and so forth (in addition to overleaves, karmas, agreements, imprinting, and the like); we came to this cycle already unique. We had evolved our own viewpoints, interests, talents, and qualities in our previous cycles, not to mention during our nonsentient activities. Beyond even that, our spark was unique from the moment of its beginning, born of unique cosmic circumstances. If no two snowflakes are alike, how much more is this true of two sparks of the Tao?

It is easy to write someone off: "What can you expect of a young warrior in aggression mode?" for example. If we think we already know someone because we know his role, overleaves, or any other fact about him, we are like those who mistake actors for the parts they play. We miss the real person. We might say that the part is two-dimensional, whereas the actor is three-dimensional. We are far greater than the sum of our "Michael parts." To know someone, we must experience him, and that knowing will not exceed our self-knowledge—we cannot know someone else to a greater depth than that to which we know ourselves.

All true teachings expand awareness, not limit it. The Michael teachings can make us aware of our probable strengths and weaknesses, and give us tools for going beyond where we are. Their classifications do not pigeonhole us. We might say that the Michael teachings are like a catalog of opportunities, not a law book. The universe is complex, and exceptions to the rule abound, so rigid interpretations of any teaching can be misleading; the words *always* and *never* rarely apply. Having free will, we create our own reality, and virtually everything is "negotiable."

Although we are each unique, we *are* the same in this: we have all learned many things, we all have much to learn, and we are all perfect as we are. Starting here, with love, respect, and openness, we can begin to know the endless, ever-changing yet changeless uniqueness of who we are.

APPENDIXES

INTERVIEW WITH FORMER
MESSAGES GROUP MEMBER

I met Susan, a mature scholar (honorary warrior, in my terminology), when she attended a lecture I channeled at a NewLife expo. She was a member of the original Michael group for eight months in the middle 1970's. In fact, she lived in Jessica Lansing's house for five of those months with her husband at the time, James. I was delighted to meet her, since, like many fans of the Yarbro books, I have had several questions about the *Messages* group. With her permission, I am sharing some notes from our discussions. As elsewhere in this book, I have changed the names of those involved to protect their privacy. ("Jessica Lansing" is already a pseudonym.)

Susan and James were first invited to the group by Ellen, Susan's aunt, after James had asked her about Transcendental Meditation. Years later, after Jessica had stopped channeling, Ellen hosted a Michael group at which her daughter, Connie, channeled Michael. Since leaving the Michael group, Susan's main connection with Michael has been through having sessions with Connie when she returns to the Bay Area to visit. Also, James, with whom Susan is still in contact, later married into Jessica's family, and has maintained a connection with Jessica over the years.

At the time of Susan's involvement, there were about forty people, including children, in the group. The other Yarbro book channels, such as Milly, and Yarbro herself, were not part of this group, and Jessica was the only channel. During this period, the group was considering starting a commune or a school. Many members of the group were upscale and older, and were discussing having each person contribute a large sum of money to buy land for a commune, which was not possible for the younger and less affluent members like Susan, who was twenty-one. An old warrior in the group, Joseph, became something of a leader/catalyst, and suggested that rather than waiting until they moved onto a piece of land, they start a commune with what they had at the time. Jessica and her husband had a large, fine home in the suburban hills near a northern California city, and invited Susan and James to move in with them. Joseph and his wife and child lived in a truck that they parked nearby. Other group members usually joined them for dinner, and people were around most of the time, which became demanding on Jessica. The group often met twice a week and spent weekends together, with marathon channeling sessions—up to five hours, although Jessica was not channeling straight through. Because she used the Ouija board, time was required to piece together the answers, since usually no one person got all the words; this allowed her to rest. The group also worked with meditation and past-life regression during those weekend gatherings.

Then, Joseph proposed that rather than remaining tied down to jobs they didn't like in order to pay rent and so forth, they adopt a transient lifestyle. Fourteen of them, including children and teenagers, went to Iowa, built a boat out of used barrels, and floated down the Missouri and Mississippi Rivers to New Orleans. They were all under twenty-five, except Joseph, who was about forty. Now, many years and two boats later, a group of about ten people remains together and continues to live on a boat, currently in a large city. Three of them were in the Michael group (one was a teenager at the time). They support themselves by playing Dixieland music and painting signs. (The Sixties live!)

One reason Susan, Joseph, and the others left the Michael group was that they felt that, on the whole, it was getting bogged down in relatively obscure information and detail, rather than doing the work of seeing their own negative poles and actually applying the teachings to their lives.[1] However, Susan said that Michael never expressed impatience about this or about anything else. Although they would comment on useful work a person might do, or suggest a change of focus in a question someone was asking, all energy connected with them was positive and loving. That is consistent with my experience with Michael.

Jessica and others in the group had studied Gurdjieff before channeling Michael, and Susan feels that this influenced the choices of terminology that came through her channeling. (The Gurdjieff teachings contain extensive information about centers and chief features, for example.) Many in the group also had traditional religious affiliations. At first, it was difficult for the group to come to grips with the idea of intelligent life that isn't physical. It was also difficult for Jessica to accept her abilities. The only other channeled information

---

[1]Before the second printing of this book, I was able to correspond with Jessica about the original group. She felt that a main reason Joseph left was that he was more interested in Gurdjieff than in Michael. I was also surprised to learn that his departure with several others in effect ended the group. She channeled several special sessions from 1976-1978. After that, she did a handful of sessions until 1981, when she stopped channeling entirely, due to other interests and demands on her time, although she continued to use the teachings in her life. The Yarbro books imply one continuous group; however, other channels she had introduced to the material formed new groups with new members, and at least one of these provided material for Yarbro's later books.

they were aware of at the time was the Edgar Cayce material, and the Seth books by Jane Roberts, which were just coming out. Because everything was so new to everyone, it took a long time for Michael to get each basic idea across. Group members would ask repeatedly, "What do you mean by...?" Generally, Michael did not present complete discourses on individual elements of the Michael teachings. Instead, the information came out as a by-product of other, often personal information, so it could take weeks of sessions to get a reasonably complete picture of, say, modes. By the time Susan joined the group, material on roles, goals, modes, attitudes, chief features, and soul ages had already been channeled, but questions being asked would bring forth new information about, say, power mode. So the information was constantly growing and being refined.

At a session, four or five people, as fast as they could, would write down the letters as they were called out. Some of the group members got quite good at it after a while, and would only miss a few words. Some of them met later to type up a transcript for those who had not been present, and to provide a record for those who had been, in time for the next meeting. Evidently, this procedure continued for as long as the Ouija board was used, and it was those transcripts that Quinn Yarbro used, in part, for writing *Messages from Michael.*

When a new person came into the group, Michael might ask the group to guess the person's role, goal, mode, attitude, and chief feature. Let's say that the "vote" was "scholar, growth, observation, spiritualist, and arrogance." Michael might simply say "right," rather than going through each item separately. Later, the person, when self-validating, might discover that one or two of those items didn't fit, that the blanket "right" did not seem one hundred percent applicable. I have had the same experience, and I now insist that Michael go through each point separately with me when I ask them to validate something. This also indicates that, despite the impression given in the books, Jessica did not always get completely accurate information. Susan agreed that the Yarbro books contained the best and most impressive of the material. Although the only inaccuracies she remembers were minor and concerned Michael information, the group did not scrutinize any of the material a great deal—they didn't know enough about it at the time to question it. Much of the sense in Susan and her friends that some Michael information was not correct came later, after having lived with the material for a while. If someone questioned Michael at the time about recently given information that didn't feel right, sometimes Michael would say that it had come through incorrectly the first time.

Another factor Susan feels may have affected accuracy was how much Jessica was "out of the way." When Jessica would begin, she was mostly conscious; she might have sipped a drink (nonalcoholic) between answers, for example. Susan felt that if there had been a consensus beforehand about someone's role, for instance, Jessica was sometimes unduly influenced by that. However, as she continued with the channeling, she would become "out of it" and hence, "out of the way." She would "come to" at the end, not remembering what had happened. So some of her channeling was in trance, and some was not. Although Susan implied that Jessica's trance channeling may have been more accurate, her accuracy in general seemed quite high.

Another corroboration of my experience is that the channeling seemed to be more accurate when the group was focused on it rather than talking amongst themselves, for instance.

Susan doesn't remember any specific type of material that Jessica couldn't get, but sometimes she would say, "Nothing is happening. I'm not getting anything." Susan also recalled that Michael never gave "bad news," something I can also corroborate.

It was exciting to meet someone who had participated in the group that was responsible for bringing forth the foundation of the Michael teachings as we know them today.

Appendix B

MICHAEL STUDENTS SHARE

As a result of my work with Michael, I have met many wonderful people. For me, this is the greatest reward of channeling, other than the contact with Michael itself.

I asked some of them to write about their experiences with the Michael teachings, as well as with sessions and other Michael students. Here are excerpts from their replies:

The Michael channeling has shown me how gentle and purposeful the universe really is, rather than consisting of an exclusive view where one dogma or teaching is "the truth." The Michael work brings me acceptance and understanding where before there was a lot of judgment and intolerance.

I find the group sessions to be physically vitalizing, intellectually stimulating, and full of love and compassion. Sitting in front and looking directly at the channel gives me a feel for causal-plane energy, and what my everyday life could be like if I maintained a clear vibration.

Discovering the Michael teachings was a turning point in my life. They gave me a framework on which everything I knew fit neatly into place. I'm constantly learning more and, as of yet, it still holds it all together beautifully.

The people in the Michael group are, to me, not just friends but family. Some I see only once a month or less, some quite frequently. All of them have that feel that says, "We are connected in a special way."

I consider Michael old friends. I feel so grateful to reacquaint with them. I have transcribed all my channeling sessions and frequently re-read them, always finding more insight.

I have begun channeling a fragment of the Michael entity. However, he refers to himself as "Samuel," explaining when we first made contact that I took Michael too seriously. He appeared to me looking like Mr. Clean. I never laughed so hard in my life![1]

---

[1]When a person first begins channeling a collective entity such as Michael, one fragment generally comes through; others may be added as the channel opens.

I am so glad a teacher like this is available to me. I honestly never expected it in this lifetime. I feel infinitely challenged and no longer bereft that my parents were not quite up to guiding me in what I would like to accomplish. Experience has gotten much more interesting. I feel like a child who has just discovered the world outside.

My chief feature is impatience. No wonder I want unlimited sessions with Michael, right now! And you know what? I'm a warrior, so I'm going to get them!

I had been passing through, or perhaps more precisely, had been run down by, my fourth internal (midlife) monad, when Michael came into my life. They brought profound understandings about who I am, my direction, and at my very first "Michael Speaks" meeting, true love! So drastically and dramatically has all changed for the better, I hardly recognize this experience as my own.

Michael doesn't solve my problems, but I don't feel stupid or wrong for having them. In "Michael Speaks" sessions, they treat everyone's questions with respect. No matter how strange an idea or question may seem, Michael makes it sound normal. They don't put up with any nonsense, but the manner in which they do this is so gentle that no one feels chastised. They don't get defensive, and consequently, no one else does either. Just to witness this quality of communication is valuable to me.

I had been involved with the Michael teachings through books for a few years before a friend informed me of a Michael channel in New York City. Finally, a chance to experience a Michael meeting, complete with information, joy, other "Michael people," and heavy causal energy! It's all that and more.

Michael answered my agonizing questions of "Who am I?" and "Is there a God?" I've learned so much from the books, and I keep learning more and more from the meetings. The energy at them is intense, and I feel it for days afterward. There's a new happiness in my life. I'm more tolerant because I understand myself and other people a lot better.

Recently, I started channeling a king fragment of the Michael entity. I hope to learn more, love more, and help Michael help others. The whole Michael experience is enlightening, and fun, too.

At my first "Michael Speaks," Michael's response to a question of mine was gentle and penetratingly personal. More importantly, there was an energy of communion. The group creates an environment where one can share and exchange ideas without judgment, but with support for the journey of each person.

Learning that artisans can experience difficulty adapting to the physical plane gave me the perspective to express more compassion toward myself while working to become more grounded.

I read Messages from Michael *ten years ago and viewed the information as an excellent tool. However, I lost interest after a while due to being unable to identify the role and overleaves of myself and others with any certainty. When I heard about Shepherd and had my Michael chart channeled, self-understanding began to dawn: I'm not strange or unmotivated. I am simply a typical sixth-level old scholar doing what sixth-level old scholars do!*

As I shared my new-found enthusiasm with others, they too became interested in the Michael material and called Shepherd. Pretty soon, we were all comparing notes, so starting a Michael discussion group (in New Jersey) *seems exactly the thing to do!*

I had been looking for a job since September. By the following February, my midlife crisis had just about peaked. I had been to many psychic readers and channels in search of in-depth counseling. Unfortunately, my success and satisfaction with them had not been too good. They kept predicting that I would have a job in my field of expertise within weeks or months. In the meantime, I was still unemployed and depressed. My belief in myself, God, and spiritual counselors was at its lowest level. When I ran across Shepherd's advertisement, I felt I had nothing to lose.

A marked change took place in my life after my first session with Michael, and I often replayed the tape of it. It helped me to focus attention on my problems and needs, and offered direction for attaining goals. The meditation at the end of it provided me with energies when I was about to undertake a difficult project, such as going on a job interview or taking an exam. I had been very uneasy about making a career change. However, Michael helped me gain a sense of security and strength. Today, I am loving every minute of my new career and feel confident about my future.

The first thing I noticed after my initial session with Michael was that my whole intuitive side had been reinforced and expanded. My "antennae" had been sensitized and lengthened, and I developed greater access to information from the inside. In fact, the word "expansion" best describes the overall effect of Michael sessions on my life. As Michael put it so well, they are a part of my "spiritual fitness program."

I do not write from the point of view of a diehard Michael fan. As a matter of fact, I haven't yet had a private session. Why, then, do I go to the "Michael Speaks"? Quite simply put, to have access to the words, which when spoken have a beautiful quality.

I have always found the teachings of any of the unseen guides to have a profound influence on my life. Whenever I take the time to realize that such incredible beings exist, I feel like a teenager with one huge crush on the high school football star. The very thought of having the opportunity to physically participate with one of them brings tears of joy to my eyes.

How my life's path will change is dependent on the impact I allow these words to have. It is only recently that I have accepted that I do indeed create all my reality, and what a wonderfully perplexing responsibility that is. My closet of stumbling blocks is yet to be cleaned out, but of this much I am sure: the New York "Michael Speaks" is one more gift of the intricate, magnificent miracle called life.

Michael and I are old friends—of that I am sure. Meeting up with them again a year ago ended a long search that covered much ground on this planet. Their wise and loving words have been like a beacon splashing lights and colors on all the dark spots I carried around— spaces for missing pieces. Now they are filling in nicely and I am growing, exponentially at times!

Probably the single, most exciting lesson I have relearned is that there is no good or bad, just choice. After years and years of uncertain, fear-ridden decisions, and tons of guilt dressed in nun's habits, I feel such a relief. There is no hell, purgatory, or limbo! Life can actually be a joy. It is permitted!

COMMENTS FROM CLIENT LETTERS

In the preceding comments, people wrote in response to my request to discuss their experiences with Michael and their teachings. As you saw, many comments focused on the "Michael Speaks" lectures. The following are excerpts from unsolicited client letters that were written mostly following private sessions:

Though it has been a few days since our session, I still think of little else. When Michael came through, it felt like a strong breeze, though I know nothing in the room moved. Yet throughout, I could feel your presence, and was in awe of the energy that was your own. How appropriate that the next day was Thanksgiving. You have a wonderful gift that I am grateful and honored to have shared.

Thank you for being such a kind and gracious guide on my first journey into my being. You and Michael have planted a seed that no foul weather can uproot or destroy. I know that the path to growth will not be easy, but from now on I will realize that the "shit" I go through is really fertilizer for growing a wiser, more loving me.

The reading was a blockbuster (literally) and everyone I've shared it with has been very much impressed.

I just wanted to pen a note to say what a pleasure it was to meet you and how much I appreciated your loving assiduousness and friendly hospitality. The results of the channeling are invaluable to me: a help, a challenge, an encouragement, and a swift kick in the right direction. Thanks again.

The Michael teachings have been of the greatest importance to me. Having the overview of the whole universe and of my personality specifically has been so liberating. I've spent most of my life trying to make myself conform to other people's ideals (and feeling extremely strange for not accomplishing it), and the teachings have helped me understand and be more accepting of myself and everyone else. I've seen this same thing happen to virtually everyone who has gotten his Michael Reading chart from you and has read about the teachings. I love it. I thank you eternally for your work.

Michael and you always make things so clear and make my way clear before me. They also have a way of saying things I couldn't hear from anyone else.

My channeling session with you and Michael was one of my most enlightening experiences to date. The information gained and the atmosphere created have taken me to yet another level of awareness. It is the reunion of kindred souls that signposts our progress. My meeting you is one more great example of this.

I want to thank you for all the good work you do. The "Michael Speaks" was a truly beautiful evening and a testimony to your abilities as a channel. I am truly grateful for the opportunity to be part of such a wonderful community.

I'm still drawing so much usable information and enrichment from your last two "Michael Speaks" sessions. I've lost twelve pounds and am still at it, and I've been able to sustain an overall feeling of joy and peace with myself for several months now, much of which I can attribute directly to the Michael work.

When Michael answered my question at the "Michael Speaks," it was all I could do to keep from melting through the floor because the heat coming from you was intense, and the energy unreal. The lady sitting next to me noticed it, too, without me mentioning it first.

It was immensely important for my life that I have met you. Ever since you helped me learn to channel, I've known that I'm on my path. I know I will be able to do whatever I came to do this time. And, of course, what I have learned from Michael! Through them I was able to shift a lot of fears and learned how important energies are. Earlier in my life I would have freaked out about my present situation; now, there is a lightness and a lot of trust in me. I know it's a lesson that I will solve....I'm blessed.

This past year has been an utterly amazing time of growth for me, and the Michael work has played a major part in that.

The Michael Readings you channeled on my children were very informative and eye-opening for me. They shed light on their behaviors that helped me immensely. Thanks so much, Shepherd. I feel that you're performing a really invaluable service for people.

That evening of channeling with you was an all-time high! I'll remember that as a sendoff into a new world for me.

Michael and you were so helpful and on target, as always. The reading has helped me get unstuck. Thank you!

The energy work you and Michael did with me marked the end of months of leg cramps—they later reappeared briefly after lots of physical stress but weren't as severe.

My love and thanks go out to you and Michael for the last batch of charts you did for me. How I wish I had had the charts of my parents for the last forty years. I visited them a couple of weeks ago, and by keeping their overleaves, etc., in mind, our visit was totally free of a long list of habitual conflicts that have eroded our relationships for many years.

After having read the Michael books, I did not at all expect the great warmth I felt and saw coming through during our session. It was quite wonderful.

I was really impressed by my session with you. I've been very up for the past two days. My house is calm and everything with my friend is smoother than before, like about ten bricks were removed from both of us. Michael was reading just about everything I was thinking. It was a little scary, but the whole thing meant a lot to me. I think I'm ready to start trying a little more trust in my life. I had about fifteen questions, but as it turns out, everything I really wanted to know and then some was answered. The whole thing was rather amazing and I still feel like things are shifting around for the better. I can't stress enough how much this has affected me. I've been sleeping and eating better also. I thank you and thank Michael. The work you guys do is really important, in ways I'm not even sure I fully understand yet.

Appendix D1—Humor

MESSAGES FROM BOB

[Please note that this is the beginning of Appendix D, Humor.]

I'm sure that many of you have had the experience of saying that you're into Michael channeling, and getting a reply something like, "Yeah, me too! The archangel Michael, right?" Then you must explain, "No, this is the entity Michael, consisting of 1050 souls on the causal plane."

"Well, the archangel Michael is the one who came as Jesus."

"Is that so? Then why didn't he keep *that* name?"

This is all very confusing—the name *Michael* seems to be as common on higher planes as it is on the physical plane—so I suggested to Michael that they change their name. They agreed that it was worth considering.

A simple route would be to go with "Mike"—"I like Mike" could be our slogan, and we could have buttons printed—but I favor something different altogether.

Since, like all of us, Michael has both male and female energies, perhaps we should think about some female names. Michael consists of kings and warriors, so someone suggested "Brunhilda." My mini-encyclopedia of baby names says it means an "armor-wearing maiden who goes into battle." (A dictionary defines Brunhild (without the *a*) as "a queen in the *Nibelungenlied*.") It has possibilities. I also like "Ethel," which means "of regal bearing." Since Michael is a collective entity, they could have more than one name. "Lucy" means "will bring much illumination and knowledge." So one could channel "Lucy and Ethel." Or two channels could team up, one channeling Lucy, the other, Ethel. However, although it's perfectly socially acceptable for a woman to channel an entity with a male name (such as J.Z. Knight channeling Ramtha), a man channeling an entity with a female name would not be taken seriously in our society by many people. Since channeling needs all the positive public relations it can get, perhaps a male name would be more practical for the time being.

How about "Gary," or "Fred"? Who do you know who channels Fred? The Michael Educational Foundation (in Orinda, California) could then be called "The Fred Educational Foundation," or Fred Ed for short. The only trouble with "Fred" is that I already have both a spirit guide and a father named Fred. If a causal entity, spirit guide, and father all answered when I said "Fred," it would be confusing for me. However, that's not your problem, and I still feel that "Fred" should be given due consideration.

My favorite, though, is "Bob." It's short, and sounds pleasant and approachable:

"I channel Bob."

"Bob who?"

"Just Bob."

"Who's Bob?"

"Bob is a friendly, easygoing causal-plane entity made up of kings and warriors who give practical information on things like relationships and parallel universes."

Now I know that some of you would prefer something more spiritual-sounding, something Indian (either kind), or at least Biblical, but let's face it: most of the Biblical names have been taken, except for some obscure ones in the Begats. The East Indian names are long, and the Native American ones are hard to spell. No, I'll take "Bob"—good ol' Bob, your causal friend, and mine.

DIAL–A–MICHAEL
An Advertisement
[*From a late-night infomercial*]

Announcer: You know the scenario. It's been a rough day: Your significant other walked out on you....

Alice: *Oh, Jim! Jim! Please don't go! I'll do anything to keep you! Anything!*

Jim: *It's too late, Alice! I'm in love with Ralph.* [Jim closes the door behind him. Alice hurls dishes against the wall, and then collapses in tears.]

Alice: [Anguished] *Maybe I should I have had that sex-change operation.*

Announcer: You lost your job...

Boss: *Sorry, Alice, but with the market the way it is, we have to downsize. Brain surgeons with law degrees are a dime a dozen today, and those discount operations are killing us.*

Alice: [Later] *What does this mean? Is this the opportunity I've been waiting for to attend The Wilford Beauty Academy?*

Announcer: And astral fragments are trying to take over your body...

Astral fragment: *Ha! ha! ha! ha! ha!*

Alice: *I said get away, Attila!! Get away! You can't have it!*

Announcer: You desperately need a channeling session, but it's 3 a.m. and your channel is vacationing in the Caribbean anyway.

Sound familiar? If it's happened once, it's happened a thousand times—but <u>NO MORE</u>!!

DIAL-A-MICHAEL TO THE RESCUE!

YES, NOW YOU CAN SPEAK WITH YOUR FAVORITE CAUSAL ENTITY TWENTY-FOUR HOURS A DAY, SEVEN DAYS A WEEK! Michael, the entity of the stars, is personally available to YOU whenever you need them. Our well-trained staff of courteous Michael channels is standing by. Just dial

1-900-MICHAEL

Michael: You see, Alice, Jim and Ralph are essence twins, and have been mates in many past lives, so even with a sex-change operation, you could not come between them. They met at this time because you and Jim are now complete with your sex karma, and it's time for you to move on.

Alice: So this is my life plan unfolding?

Michael: Precisely!

Alice: What a relief!

Michael: And there's more good news. Jim's essence thought it would be fun to die in California's next earthquake, which is coming up this February. The plan is for you and Ralph, who is your task companion, to reconnect at the funeral to provide mutual support. You'll fall in love, marry on March twenty-second at 2:30 p.m., and eventually have thirteen children. And Jim will be your first daughter.

Alice: Hmm. That's very interesting.

Michael: About your former boss...he's a first-level infant slave in rejection, repression, stagnation, retardation, aggression, and power. He's in the instinctive part of the instinctive center, a cynic and skeptic in arrogance, self-destruction, greed, martyrdom, and stubbornness.

Alice: No wonder he was so difficult to work with!

Michael: Also, he was completing an agreement he made with you before this lifetime began to fire you when your midlife monad began so that you could confront your childhood imprinting. You see, Alice, by becoming a brain surgeon and an entertainment lawyer, you were unconsciously trying to fulfill your mother's ambition of becoming an actress on "General Hospital." Now you are free to find your true destiny.

Alice: You mean, becoming a cosmetologist?

Michael: Yes! You've wanted to do this ever since your lifetime as Cleopatra.

Alice: I was Cleopatra?

Michael: That's basically correct, and you really got into the cosmetics.

Alice: Wow! Now I understand why, when I was little, I was always wrapping my pets in gauze bandages and putting them in boxes.

Michael: Right. Now, regarding those pesky astral fragments trying to take over your body—you have to learn to set boundaries. Every woman has the right to say no to a man, whether he's incarnate or not. You were once Attila's sex slave, and you've got to make it clear to him that your relationship has changed.

Alice: Oh, Dial-A-Michael, how can I ever thank you? You've saved my life once again!

Michael: It's nothing Alice. Glad we could be of assistance.

Announcer: If your life is falling apart, or if you just have questions about *your* relationships, career, or possession by evil forces, dial now! Your call will be listed discreetly on your phone bill as Sex Karma Enterprises. Only $3.95/minute.

HOW I *REALLY* BEGAN CHANNELING

When people ask me how I began channeling, "how I knew I had this gift," they usually expect to hear something cosmic such as "Michael appeared to me in my kitchen.[1] They spoke to me out of the flame of my range and told me that it was my destiny to channel them," or something like that. However, the truth is actually much more down-to-earth.

One day, I was reading a magazine, and in the back was an ad for Famous Channelers' School (FCS). FCS offers a home-study course taught by world-renowned channels such as Maureen Johnson (who channels Millard Fillmore), Stephen (who channels a fifty-thousand-year-old Atlantean fashion designer, El Elan), and Lester Dumkowski (who channels extraterrestrials from the Great Green Cheese Brotherhood). I had never thought much about channeling, but they offered a free evaluation of your channeling talent. I thought, "What the heck!" and decided to give it a try. After all, I had nothing to lose.

The test simply consisted of drawing a picture of a dog they were *thinking of.* I tuned in to the Famous Channelers' School, and an image of a miniature poodle popped into my mind—I didn't know why—so I drew it and sent it off. A few weeks later, when I had all but forgotten about the test, the results came in the mail. To my surprise, they had been thinking of a miniature poodle! They said I had a natural gift for channeling, and offered me a special deal on their course—just $499.95. So I decided to enroll.

The first entity I channeled was Alfred E. Neuman, which was interesting, in light of the fact that I had seen the ad for the school in *Mad Magazine.* I found his energy and insight quite healing, but after a while, "What, me worry?" was just not specific enough advice. I decided to look for another entity. It was *then* that Michael appeared to me in my kitchen, that very evening, while I was cooking dinner. They spoke to me out of the flame of the left rear burner of my Kenmore range. It was a miracle, because that burner had not been working, and now, flames were leaping four feet in the air! It was especially impressive because I had an electric range. After that, the whole thing broke down and I had to junk it. Anyway, Michael told me that we had agreements for me to channel them and for them to assist me

---

[1]There's a famous story about how J.Z. Knight first made contact with Ramtha in her kitchen.

in my spiritual growth. They said that Alfred's task was just to get me ready.

What was really interesting is that I had almost ordered in Chinese food that night, and something told me to heat up a can of pork and beans instead. I guess it was just my spiritual destiny. Anyway, I've been channeling Michael ever since.

Appendix D4—Humor

"BASICALLY"
[*A letter to* The Michael Connection[1]]

Dear Editor,

I was channeling the other day and got some really interesting material. I thought that the "Letters to the Editor" column would be a good place to share it. Basically, Michael has asked that the Michael community refrain from using the word *basically* throughout the entire mature soul cycle on earth. The basic reason for this is that throughout the end of the young soul cycle, it was used in almost every sentence. Michael feels, basically, that if it's used anymore, it will aggravate the basic mature soul tendency toward mental illness. In other words, it will drive everyone nuts.

So basically, Michael is asking that if we feel the need to use the word *basically*, we go to the positive pole of scholar and get out our thesaurus where we'll find words such as "fundamentally," "mainly," "primarily," and "principally," or better yet, go cold turkey and just say what we basically have to say without filler.

Basically yours,

Shepherd Hoodwin

---

[1]This is an in-joke if you haven't been exposed to the Michael community that *The Michael Connection* represented, but I think you'll get the idea.

THE MICHAEL HOME
FOR VERY OLD SOULS
An Advertisement[1]

---

[1]Some background: As with everything else in the Michael teachings, each soul age has pitfalls as well as strengths. Old souls sometimes have problems "getting their act together" relative to physical survival.

DO YOU SOMETIMES FORGET
WHAT PLANE YOU'RE ON?

"Why doesn't that table fly when I will it to?"

OR EVEN WHAT PLANET THIS IS?

"Boy! Those Venus women sure have big—*oops!*"

MAYBE IT'S TIME TO JOIN
THE HAPPY FOLKS AT

THE MICHAEL HOME FOR VERY OLD SOULS

Yes, you can retire in the comfort and peace you deserve! After six million years on the physical plane, live out your golden years free from those irritating younger souls who still believe THAT TIME AND SPACE ARE REAL!!! (God love 'em.)

At The Michael Home for Very Old Souls, you'll live among flowers and trees, birds and bees, in genteel poverty, your every need filled by our highly trained staff. You will feast on sumptuous meals of salad, soyburgers, wheatgrass juice, potato chips, and Coke. After a hard day of reading, watching videos, taking walks, and hot-tubbing, you will be free to spend your evenings relaxing with like-minded friends, discussing the meaning of life and other people's kinky sex. Once a week (or whenever they get around to it), other old souls even more impoverished than you will clean your room and do your laundry, releasing you from the drudgery of physical-plane existence, freeing you to advance spiritually through meditation, chanting, and washing dishes (not actually dirty dishes, of course).

Yes, the senility of very-old-souldom can actually be fun, and not just for old kings such as Old King Cole. You too can be merry, even if you're an old scholar or priest with abrading overleaves such as cynic, acceptance, and heavy self-dep sliding to exalted arrogance! To learn more, call 1-800-OLD-SOUL now!! for your <u>free</u> all-black-and-white photocopied brochure. (Ask about our fabulous out-of-body field trips!)

IDENTICAL COUSINS

I was flipping the dial on my TV last night, and came across a documentary in black and white about two cousins who are identical.[1] I was astounded by it. Of course, I know that sisters or brothers can be identical, especially if they are born at the same time, but I didn't know that cousins could be identical. There have been many studies done of identical twin siblings, but as far as I know, this is the first study of identical cousins. It was fascinating. For instance, one of them adores the minuet, while the other likes to rock and roll and sometimes even lose control. Not only are their different temperaments interesting, in light of the fact that they are identical, but it is especially intriguing that one of them loves the minuet, since practically no one has danced it in over two hundred years. Could she actually be a past-life self of her cousin?

The whole thing got me to thinking: I have a big family, and I don't know all my relatives. Maybe *I* have an identical cousin somewhere. If that's the case, I'd really like to meet him. It would be so much fun. We could dress alike, and no one would know who was who. Maybe he even channels Michael!

Then my skeptical side kicked in. After all, I wasn't born yesterday. How is it genetically possible for cousins to be identical? With brothers or sisters, the egg splits. Could it be that an egg can split a generation or more back, and be passed genetically *through* siblings, so that when they have children, they both get the same egg? After mulling this over, I decided to ask Michael about it.

They said that no, the identical cousin phenomenon does not result from splitting eggs. It occurs when two parallel universes try to merge, but are not quite similar enough. In the example cited in the documentary, had the two universes involved fully merged, it would have resulted in a schizophrenic personality—you can imagine the chaos if someone tried to minuet and rock and roll at the same time. The universe, being orderly, provides for such contingencies through the rare phenomenon of identical cousins.

I also saw a fascinating program about a man whose uncle is apparently from Mars.[2] However, Michael said that although he has a

---

[1] "The Patty Duke Show," in the 1960's, starred Patty Duke as identical twin cousins, one of them reserved and European, the other a "normal" American teenager. It is now in reruns on cable television.

[2] "My Favorite Martian," also in reruns, featured Ray Walston as a Martian

martial body type, he is actually from Mercury. Anyway, I am thankful for the resources that television provides to expand our awareness.

---

masquerading as "Uncle Martin."

SUPPLEMENTAL MICHAEL READING

	INSPIRATION		EXPRESSION		ACTION		ASSIMILATION
ROLE	Server	Priest	Artisan	Sage	Warrior	King	Scholar
ROLL	Raisin Pumpernickel	Cinnamon	Poppy Seed	Bagel	Hard	Onion	Dinner
GOAL	Floss	Lose 10 Lbs.	Pay Off Visa	Floss	Go to Health Club	Get Out of Jacuzzi	Set Clock on VCR
À LA MODE	Butter Pecan	Chocolate Fudge Swirl	Rice Dream	Bubble Gum	Rocky Road	Rum Raisin	Vanilla
ATTI-TUDE	Get Out of My Face	Don't You Wish	You Must Be on Drugs	I'm Okay—You're Psychotic	Yo	Read My Lips	Get a Life
CENTER	Rockefeller		Lincoln		World Trade		
–FLOOR	1	2	3	4	5	6	7

BODY TYPE	Too Fat	Too Fat	Too Fat	Too Fat	Too Fat	Too Thin	Too Fat
BEST FEATURE	Incandescent Complexion	Beautiful Eyes	Gorgeous Hair	Great Smile	Big—Fixated on ———	Amazing Legs	Nice Personality
DWARF	Bashful	Happy	Sleepy	Sneezy	Dopey	Grumpy	Doc
SAMURAI	Ichi	Ni	San	Shi	Go	Roku	Hishi
SOUL AGE	1 2 3 4 5	6	7 Infantile	Childish	Stunted	Immature	Senile

ABOUT THE AUTHOR

Shepherd Hoodwin arrived on earth about eighty thousand years ago in a spaceship similar to the one Superman used to come from Krypton, only a little larger. He, too, was fleeing an exploding planet, his in the Sirius solar system. His spaceship splashed down off the coast of Africa, where local tribes greeted him as a god. Needless to say, that first lifetime on earth was quite pleasant, and he reincarnated into one of those tribes for his second earth lifetime as well.

During his young-soul cycle, Shepherd had several lifetimes as prominent politicians in Atlantis. After Atlantis sank (while he was off on business in Tibet) Shepherd turned to serious spiritual pursuits in lifetimes as high priests, shamans, and erotic dancers.

Shepherd's most notable past life was as Jesus's younger brother, Joe, Jr. of Nazareth (called "Little Joe"), who, ironically, was thought of at the time as the spiritual one in the family. To quote from the recently discovered *Absene Gospels,* "Joe, Jr. wenteth to temple everyday while his older brother was out with the boys in the wilderness—God knoweth what they were doing there. But Joe, Jr. idolized his brother and died tragically the summer after his Bar Mitzvah when he literally tried to walketh in his footsteps: he attempted to walketh on the water, and drowned. How sad that he didn't knoweth the secret of Jesus's flotation sandals, designed to save ferry money!"

According to Michael, in three parallel universes, Joe, Jr. survived and became the first sage infinite soul rather than his big brother (Jesus instead opened J&J Construction with John the Beloved). As the infinite soul, Joe, Jr. decided to bring massive spiritual transformation by putting on a musical for Pontius Pilate rather than being crucified. It was called *Joseph and the Amazing Technicolor Dream.* Judas was especially good in the Bette Davis role (of course, women weren't allowed to perform in musicals in those days). This was Judas's true calling, and it gave him a constructive outlet for some of his Millennial angst and bitchiness (he'd always been upset that Jesus liked John best).

In more recent lifetimes, Shepherd has been a pirate, several monks, and was tortured by the Inquisition! He also had several lifetimes as an agricultural engineer (formerly called "peasant"). He coauthored two brilliant bestsellers, the Bible and the *Kamasutra.* In a simultaneous past life in a parallel universe, he was Steve Lawrence, who popularized the song, "I've Got to Be Me" and had many other hits with his lovely wife and essence twin, Edie Gormé. He is also Robert Redford in several parallel universes.

In this present lifetime, likely his last (but not least), Shepherd is an international sex symbol, known the world around as "Flabio." He is on the faculty of California's Hunks State University at Malibu; his recently published papers include "Why Long, Dangly Earrings Make the Wrong Statement" and "Tattoos: How to Choose the Right Skull and Crossbones for Your Build." Despite the high price of fame (including having his expensive clothes ripped off whenever he leaves home), Shepherd takes quite seriously his responsibility to humanity.

Shepherd has also achieved international distinction for his numerous artistic accomplishments, including Oscar-winning screenplays, Pulitzer Prize-winning books, and Platinum Records—not in *this* universe, of course; that was in several parallel universes. In this universe, he hasn't gotten much done yet, but he intends to very soon.

In this lifetime in this universe, Shepherd was born in Chicago, Illinois on October 15, 1954, at 8:18 a.m. (for all you astrologers out there), but everyone guesses him to be twenty-eight. He attributes his youthful good looks to clean, healthy living and stunted emotional development. Incidentally, several astrologers have predicted that Shepherd would write musicals, since he's got the sun in the morning and the moon at night. He has naturally curly red hair, and a B.M. from the University of Oregon.[1] He is the lead singer for Sage Bleedthrough. Shepherd's many philanthropic activities include the Homeless Flossing Project, which he co-founded after learning that a shocking 87% of all homeless people don't floss regularly.

Shepherd makes his home in Laguna Beach, California with his "significant other," who happens to be a cat. Known as the "Michael Channel to the Stars," Shepherd has offered his expert advice to celebrities such as Chi-Chi LaRue and Eartha Quake. He has channeled internationally, from Santa Ana to Burbank. Shepherd is the creator of the popular personal growth workshop, "Potty-Training Your Inner Child," and is the author of *Do-It-Yourself Near-Death Experiences—How to Die on the Operating Table and Come Back to Life in Ten Easy Steps.* He has also published three volumes of memoirs, beginning with *Life in the Right-Turn Only Lane,* followed by *Men Are from Mars, Shepherd is from Sirius.* In his latest, *Struck in the Head and Knocked Unconscious BY THE LIGHT!,* Shepherd tells the moving story of his Near-Life Experience (NLE) in which he momentarily came into his body until he heard a voice calling him back.

Shepherd Hoodwin has met Shirley MacLaine's dentist.

---

[1]B.M. stands for Bachelor of Music.

BIBLIOGRAPHY

NOTE: All in-print Michael and Summerjoy Press books can be ordered through any bookstore or from Summerjoy Press, http://summerjoy.com, 31423 S Coast Hwy #84, Laguna Beach CA 92651-6998, 877-SUMMERJoy (877-786-6375). Volume discounts on Summerjoy Press books are available from the publisher, as is information about upcoming Summerjoy books and cassettes, and private sessions and workshops with Shepherd Hoodwin.

BODY TYPES—*The Enneagram of Essence Types*
by Joel Friedlander, Samuel Weiser, Inc., 1993.
Although body types are part of the Michael teachings, most of the details on them have come from Gurdjieff students. This fascinating book is the most comprehensive resource on them.

CELEBRITIES—*The Complete Michael Database*
by Emily Baumbach, Causalworks, 1996.
Celebrities contains a brief overview of the Michael teachings, and overleaves, etc. on about twelve hundred celebrities and historical figures channeled by the author and others.

CONCORDANCE TO THE MICHAEL TEACHINGS—*Index to All 21 Published Books on the Michael Teachings*
by Barbara Taylor, Rainbows & Miracles etc., 1996.
Here is a spiral-bound reference for finding where particular topics are covered within the library of Michael and related books.

EARTH TO TAO—*Michael's Guide to Healing and Spiritual Growth*
by José Stevens, Bear & Company, 1994.
This is the conclusion of a three-part series, which includes *The Michael Handbook* and *Tao to Earth*. It also stands on its own as an overview of new age techniques as seen by Michael. Developing self-acceptance and working with chakras are among the subjects covered.

LOVING FROM YOUR SOUL—*Creating Powerful Relationships*
by Shepherd Hoodwin, Summerjoy Press, 1995.
This is the first in the Summerjoy Michael series of books containing Michael's insights on a wide range of topics of general interest. It explores the nature of love itself as well as practical matters of relationships. It does not contain technical material about the Michael teachings, but expands on many of the topics in *The Journey of Your Soul*.

MEDITATIONS FOR SELF-DISCOVERY—*Guided Journeys for Communicating with Your Inner Self*
by Shepherd Hoodwin, Summerjoy Press, 1995.

This is a collection of forty-five vivid, often pastoral, guided imagery meditations channeled from my essence (higher self), one of the first in book form that can be read to oneself or others. Teachers and group leaders would find it particularly useful. It includes blank pages for journaling.

MESSAGES FROM MICHAEL, MORE MESSAGES FROM MICHAEL, MICHAEL'S PEOPLE, and MICHAEL FOR THE MILLENNIUM
by Chelsea Quinn Yarbro, Berkley Books, 1983, 1986, 1988, and 1995.

These contain channeling that is the foundation of the Michael teachings. Some readers find it easier to begin with one of the introductory books by other authors, and some take to these immediately. At this writing, the second and third books are at least temporarily out of print.

THE MICHAEL GAME
Various authors, Warwick Press, 1988.

This has articles by several authors on fascinating subjects such as whales and dolphins, planes of existence, and walk-ins.

THE MICHAEL HANDBOOK
by José Stevens and Simon Warwick-Smith, Warwick Press, 1990.

The *Handbook* is a detailed reference of and introduction to the basics of the Michael system. This is a good choice for someone looking for a lot of information presented in an organized manner.

THE MICHAEL INTERVIEWS—Practical Wisdom from an Enlightened Perspective, Volume 1: MICHAEL ON MICHAEL—Channeled Conversation with a Non-Physical Entity (VIDEO)
by Fred Wymore, Dream Traveller Productions (P.O. Box 691, Zephyr Cove, NV 89448), 1998.

Writer/director/producer Wymore interviews Michael through channels Emily Baumbach, Alma Perez, Aaron Christeaan, JP Van Hulle, José Stevens and Kay Kamala.Upcoming titles include *Michael on the Millennium* and *Michael on Self-Actualization.*

MICHAEL'S GEMSTONE DICTIONARY
by Judithann David and JP Van Hulle, Affinity Press, 1990.

This is a unique, comprehensive guide including more than one thousand gems and minerals, relating their metaphysical properties and how they can be used with the Michael teachings.

MICHAEL—THE BASIC TEACHINGS
by Aaron Christeaan, JP Van Hulle, and M.C. Clark, Michael Educational Foundation, 1988.

The Basic Teachings provides a lucid overview, with helpful charts and illustrations, for those who are looking for a "happy medium" between the simpler and more complex books.

OPENING TO HEALING ENERGY
by Shepherd Hoodwin, Summerjoy Press, slated for Spring, 2000.

Second in the Summerjoy Michael series, it explores the nature of healing. See http://summerjoy.com/UpcomingBooksIndex.html for sample chapters from this and other upcoming Summerjoy Michael books. (*Growing Through Joy*, third in the series, is slated for Fall, 2000.)

THE PERSONALITY PUZZLE
by José Stevens and JP Van Hulle, Affinity Press, 1990.

This book describes the personality in terms of the Michael teachings without referring to Michael or channeling. One of its unique features is several photographs of anonymous people, giving Michael information about them, which offers readers a sense of what various energies look like. It also discusses certain combinations of overleaves.

SEARCHING FOR LIGHT—*Michael's Information for a Time of Change*
by Carol Heideman, Twelve Star Publishing, 1994.

This contains information and tools for dealing with the changes occurring on earth in this era.

TAO TO EARTH—*Michael's Guide to Relationships and Growth*
by José Stevens, Bear & Company, 1994.

Tao to Earth is a good follow-up to the *Michael Handbook* or *Michael—The Basic Teachings*. Topics include prosperity, karma, and intimate relationships.

TRANSFORMING YOUR DRAGONS—*Turning Personality Fear Patterns into Personal Power*
by José Stevens, Bear & Company, 1994.

This contains by far the most in-depth treatment of chief features anywhere in the Michael literature. It is an excellent tool for growth.

UPCOMING CHANGES—*Prophecy & Pragmatism for the Late Nineties*
by Joya Pope, Emerald Wave, 1995.

Here is a look at what's on the horizon, country by country, based in part on each nation's average soul age.

THE WORLD ACCORDING TO MICHAEL
by Joya Pope, Emerald Wave, 1999.

This delightful introduction to the Michael teachings is accessible to anyone with curiosity about the universe. It is appropriate to give to a friend or relative who is not particularly metaphysically inclined.

GLOSSARY

Abrading overleaves: Overleaves that tend to clash, especially in their negative poles, either internally or with other people.

Acceptance: The second most common of the seven goals. Its positive pole is *agape*, or unconditional love, which is also the highest goal in general for all sentient consciousness; its negative pole is *ingratiation*. It is used for lifetimes emphasizing love and tolerance.

Action axis: One of the four axes, or universal qualities, upon which the roles and overleaves lie. The action axis relates to doing in the outer world.

Agape: A state of unconditional love for everything. This is considered the ultimate goal of all sentient evolution. (Usually pronounced *ah*-guh-pay.)

Aggression: One of the seven modes. Its positive pole is *dynamism*; its negative pole is *belligerence*. In aggression mode, one releases one's energy vigorously.

Agreement: A plan made between two souls, usually before incarnating, to work together on the physical plane in a particular way. There are many kinds of agreements, including to help one another in a variety of ways or to have a particular kind of relationship, such as that of mate or parent/child.

Akashic plane: The central, neutral plane of creation that interconnects the other six. The distilled knowledge of the universe is recorded there.

Akashic records: The records generated of everything that happens in the universe as it occurs. The appearance is that all matter and energy have a sort of built-in digital recording device, storing its entire history in a photographic code, but the records are actually windows into the past. The records show events exactly as they were experienced, so the information in them begins raw—it is not clarified, understood, and assimilated until a consciousness takes responsibility for doing so. Once it is fully assimilated, it is stored on the akashic plane.

Arrogance: One of the seven chief features. Its positive pole is *pride*; its negative pole is *vanity*. It is a fear of being judged or of vulnerability.

Artisan: One of the seven essence roles. Its positive pole is *creation*; its negative pole is *artifice* or *self-deception*. Artisans seek originality.

Assimilation axis: One of the four axes, or universal qualities, upon which the roles and overleaves lie. The assimilation axis is neutral; it provides objectivity and a resource for the other axes.

Astral plane: The second plane of creation. Its medium is concrete emotional energy. It is where consciousness is focused between lifetimes and after completing the physical plane.

Attitude: One of the overleaves. The attitude is a person's primary slant on life. The seven attitudes are *stoic, spiritualist, skeptic, idealist, cynic, realist,* and *pragmatist.*

Aura: A band of etheric substance surrounding the physical body that reflects the seven levels of self. It consists of seven layers of middle-physical plane substance vibrating a little more quickly than the physical body itself.

Baby soul: Someone in the second of the five main physical-plane soul ages. The baby soul cycle emphasizes lessons about working with the structure of civilization.

Body type: Physical and psychological traits resulting from the influence of the celestial bodies upon a person's physical body. Everyone has a primary body type, and from one to three secondary body-type influences. The seven main body types are *lunar, saturnian, jovial, mercurial, venusian, martial,* and *solar.* A person can also have *neptunian, uranian,* and *plutonian* influences.

Buddhaic plane: The highest plane of creation. Its medium is pure or abstract kinetic energy. Essences experience the buddhaic plane just before fully refocusing their awareness in the Tao. The infinite soul who incarnated as Buddha taught from this plane.

Cadence: A permanent grouping of seven essences. A *primary cadence* consists of seven essences of the same role; it is the smallest "building block" of the entity. An essence's numerical position within his cadence, and his cadence's position within his greater cadence, significantly influence how he directs his energies. (See also "Greater Cadences" and "Casting.")

Cadre: A unit consisting of seven entities. (See also "Entity.")

Cardinal: Relating to the large or general picture; catalytic. Its positive pole is *lucid*; its negative pole is *active.* (See also "Ordinal.")

Casting: The Tao's expression into the dimensional universe, as in "fragments cast from the Tao," and the order of it, as in "first-cast warrior in the entity." A person's casting is his position within his entity (see "Entity"), or commonly, just his primary cadence position (see "Cadence").

Causal plane: The third plane of creation. Its medium is concrete intellectual energy. It is Michael's plane of existence.

Caution: The second most common of the seven modes. Its positive pole is *deliberation*; its negative pole is *phobia.* In caution mode, one releases one's energy carefully.

Center: One of the overleaves. People have seven centers that each process and store a different aspect of experience: *emotional, higher emotional, intellectual, higher intellectual, physical, moving,* and *instinctive.* A person's primary center is the part of self from which he dominantly experiences life and responds to stimuli—either the emotional, intellectual, physical, or moving center (or rarely, the instinctive center). The part of center is where his secondary responses originate. The higher intellectual and higher emotional centers are rarely if ever dominant in most people's experience.

Channeling: The act of allowing an intelligence not in human form to express through oneself.

Chakra: An energy center in the body. There are seven main chakras.

Chief feature: One of the overleaves; also called "chief obstacle." The chief feature is the focus of a person's fears and illusions. A person can also have a secondary chief feature. The seven chief features are *self-deprecation, arrogance, self-destruction, greed, martyrdom, impatience,* and *stubbornness.*

Chief obstacle: (See "Chief feature.")

Cording: The act of establishing a cord of connection with another person that draws energy from him.

Cycle: (See "Grand cycle.")

Cycle off: To finish incarnating on the physical plane for this grand cycle.

Cynic: One of the seven attitudes. Its positive pole is *contradiction;* its negative pole is *denigration.* Cynics view the world in terms of what isn't, or what won't work.

Devas: Nature spirits or "elementals" who take care of the earth "behind the scenes." They work with the mineral, plant, and animal kingdoms, as well as with larger elements, such as the oceans, clouds, and mountains.

Discarnate: Not incarnate; not in a physical body.

Discrimination: One of the least common of the seven goals; called "rejection" in Yarbro. Its positive pole is *sophistication;* its negative pole is *prejudice.* It is used for lifetimes emphasizing critical faculties.

Dominance: One of the seven goals. Its positive pole is *leadership;* its negative pole is *dictatorship.* It is used for lifetimes that emphasize "winning" and helping others win.

Emotional center: One of the seven centers. Its positive pole is *sensibility;* its negative pole is *sentimentality.* (See also "Center.")

Energy: The fundamental substance of everything in the universe. The nonphysical factors of life are energetic in nature. Energy is characterized by vibration and the impulse to move.

Entity: In this book, usually refers to a "spiritual family" of about one thousand souls. Michael is the name of one entity. *Entity* is also used as in "channeled entity," meaning a channeled consciousness of any kind, but generally a discarnate astral plane soul.

Essence: Soul, or "higher" self, as opposed to the outer personality, or "lower" self. It generally refers to all nonphysical levels of self, including the astral and causal selves, as well as those that resonate with the three highest planes, although it can be used to refer only to the latter.

Essence contact: Occurs when the personality makes a direct connection with either its own essence or the essence of another person. Essence contact is necessary in order for spiritual growth to occur. It can be a powerful and life-changing experience, or relatively mild.

Essence mate: An essence who was your essence twin during a previous grand cycle.

Essence role: (See "Role.")

Essence twin: Another essence one teams up with in the beginning of a grand cycle to "reflect" oneself; also known as "twin soul" or "twin flame." It is the closest bond an essence can have. (See also "Grand cycle.")

Expression axis: One of the four axes, or universal qualities, upon which the roles and overleaves lie. The expression axis relates to bringing the inner world into the outer.

Extraterrestrial: A sentient soul based on a planet other than earth who is visiting earth either physically or astrally, usually in order to study it and/or to assist in the changes occurring here.

False personality: False ego; the part of self motivated by fear.

Flow: One of the seven goals; called "stagnation" in Yarbro, also known as "relaxation" and "equilibrium." Its positive pole is *suspension* or *free-flowing*; its negative pole is *inertia*. It is used for lifetimes of rest or of learning to let go.

Fragment: Individual essence, or soul. The term conveys that each person is a fragment of the whole, and particularly, a fragment of his entity, with which he will recombine when he has completed all his lifetimes on the physical plane.

Frequency: Rate of vibration of the soul on a scale of one to one hundred. It gives the essence its "consistency." Slow frequencies feel more solid, medium frequencies feel more liquid, and fast frequencies feel more gaseous.

Goal: One of the overleaves. The goal is a person's primary motivator. The seven goals are *reevaluation, growth, discrimination, acceptance, submission, dominance,* and *flow.*

Grand cycle: A cycle of experience that begins when the essence is cast from the Tao. It includes physical-plane incarnations and subsequent progression through the higher planes. It is complete when the essence is fully reabsorbed back into the Tao.

Greater cadence: A unit of seven primary cadences. (See "Cadence.")

Greed: One of the seven chief features. Its positive pole is *egotism*; its negative pole is *voracity*. It is a fear of lack or want, usually fixated on something particular such as money, food, sex, or attention.

Growth: The most common of the seven goals. Its positive pole is *comprehension*; its negative pole is *confusion*. It is used for lifetimes emphasizing learning new things. People in growth seek stimulation.

Heart link: A bond formed through life experience that does not end when the lifetime is completed. It can be forged regardless of cadre by any intense sharing, from being an exemplary parent or child, to saving someone's life.

Higher center: The *higher intellectual, higher emotional,* or *moving* center. These are inner pathways to truth, love, and pure energy, potently accessed most often during moments of great intensity, bringing transcendent, revelatory experiences. (See also "Center.")

Higher emotional center: One of the seven centers. Its positive pole is *empathy;* its negative pole is *intuition.* (See also "Higher center" and "Center.")

Higher intellectual center: One of the seven centers. Its positive pole is *integration;* its negative pole is *telepathy.* (See also "Higher center" and "Center.")

Idealist: One of the seven attitudes. Its positive pole is *coalescence;* its negative pole is *abstraction.* Idealists view the world in terms of how it could be changed for the better.

Impatience: One of the seven chief features. Its positive pole is *audacity;* its negative pole is *intolerance.* It is a fear of missing out.

Imprinting: Conditioning by outer influences such as parents, education, or society in general.

Incarnate: Living in a physical body, as in *incarnate soul.*

Infant soul: Someone in the first of the five main physical-plane soul ages. The infant soul cycle emphasizes lessons about survival.

Infinite soul: An incarnate representative of a reunited cadre who brings the Tao to bear through one of the three high planes, e.g., Jesus, who manifested the infinite soul from the messianic plane during the last thirty days of his life. The infinite soul is a catalyst for the spiritual transformation of humanity.

Inspiration axis: One of the four axes, or universal qualities, upon which the roles and overleaves lie. The inspiration axis relates to the inner world.

Instinctive center: One of the seven centers. Its positive pole is *atomic;* its negative pole is *anatomic.* (See also "Center.")

Intellectual center: One of the seven centers. Its positive pole is *thought;* its negative pole is *reason.* (See also "Center.")

Jovial: One of the seven primary body types. Its positive pole is *grand;* its negative pole is *extravagant.* Jovial types tend to be full-bodied, maternal, and extroverted.

Karma: A major violation of another person that limits his choices, resulting in a compelling debt.

King: One of the seven essence roles. Its positive pole is *mastery,* which kings seek; its negative pole is *tyranny.*

Level: (See "Soul age level.")

Life plan: The overall blueprint for one's life. The soul designs its life plan before incarnating. It includes life task(s), overleaves, and agreements with other souls to be guides, parents, children, etc., to help complete monads, karmas, and to otherwise help each other.

Life quadrant: A person's position in the life quadrate. In each lifetime, people specialize in one of four possible primary contributions to each group of which they are part: the *love* position initiates; the *knowledge* position provides information; the *power* position moves the group to act; and the *support* position holds the group together.

Life task: The "centerpiece" of one's life plan; the most important thing the soul wants to accomplish. There can be more than one.

Lunar: One of the seven primary body types. Its positive pole is *luminous*; its negative pole is *pallid.* Lunar types tend to have pale skin, round faces, and "baby fat." They tend to be slow to react, and to excel at abstract thought.

Male/female energy ratio: The ratio between male (focused) and female (creative) energy in a particular essence. For example, an essence may have a male/female energy ratio of thirty-five/sixty-five— thirty-five percent male energy and sixty-five percent female energy. Male energy emphasizes doing; it moves into the outer world. Female energy emphasizes being; it moves inward.

Martial: One of the seven primary body types. Its positive pole is *wiry*; its negative pole is *muscle-bound.* Martial types tend to have reddish hair and skin, and muscled bodies. They tend to be feisty and active.

Martyrdom: One of the seven chief features. Its positive pole is *selflessness*; its negative pole is *mortification.* It is caused by a fear of being unworthy.

Mature soul: Someone in the fourth of the five main physical-plane soul ages. The mature soul cycle emphasizes lessons about relationships, emotions, and the inner world.

Maya: Fear-driven illusion or false belief, particularly on the essence level (as opposed to false personality). It is a Hindu term referring to the transitory, illusory appearance of the physical world that obscures the spiritual reality from which it originates.

Medium: A channel who specializes in communication with people who have died, as opposed to one who works with higher or more abstract sources.

Mental plane: The fifth plane of creation. Its medium is abstract intellectual energy, emphasizing truth. The infinite soul who incarnated as Lao-tzu taught from this plane.

Mercurial: One of the seven primary body types. Its positive pole is *agile*; its negative pole is *frenetic.* Mercurial types tend to have dark hair and eyes, and compact bodies. They tend to be energetic and good communicators.

Messianic plane: The sixth plane of creation. Its medium is abstract emotional energy, emphasizing love. The infinite soul who incarnated as Jesus taught from this plane.

Michael: A group of 1050 souls who individually completed a series of lifetimes on the physical plane and who now work together and teach from the causal plane, partly through channels.

Midlife monad: Midlife crisis; an approximately two-year period around the age of thirty-five (although it can occur anywhere from ages twenty-five to forty-five) in which a person's genuine role, over-leaves, and life path emerge wherever they were obscured by what he was conditioned to be. Those who do not successfully complete the midlife monad tend to remain stuck in their restrictive imprinting.

Mode: One of the overleaves. The mode is a person's primary way of operating. The seven modes are *reserve, passion, caution, power, perseverance, aggression,* and *observation.*

Monad: An essential physical-plane experience.

Moving center: One of the seven centers. Its positive pole is *enduring;* its negative pole is *energetic.* (See also "Center.")

Negative pole: (See "Poles.")

Nine needs: These are qualities of life experience that provide satisfaction: *security, adventure, freedom, expansion, power, expression, acceptance, communion,* and *exchange.* For each person, three are primary, and are listed in priority order. For example, one person's needs might be exchange, power, and freedom.

Observation: The most common of the seven modes. Its positive pole is *clarity;* its negative pole is *surveillance.* In observation mode, one releases one's energy neutrally.

Old soul: Someone in the fifth of the five main physical-plane soul ages. The old soul cycle emphasizes lessons about perspective.

Ordinal: Relating to the small or specific picture; receptive. Its positive pole is *responsive;* its negative pole is *passive.* (See also "Cardinal.")

Overleaves: Personality traits that "overlay" the essence. They are usually chosen before a lifetime begins in order to facilitate the purposes of that lifetime, and operate for that lifetime only. They include the *goal, mode, attitude, center,* and *chief feature.*

Parallel universe: An alternative reality similar to this one in which a person makes different critical choices, and goes in different directions as a result.

Passion: One of the seven modes. Its positive pole is *self-actualization;* its negative pole is *identification.* In passion mode, one releases one's energy boundlessly, downward and outward.

Perseverance: One of the seven modes. Its positive pole is *persistence;* its negative pole is *immutability.* In perseverance, one releases one's energy steadfastly.

Physical center: One of the seven centers. Its positive pole is *amoral;* its negative pole is *erotic.* (See also "Center.")

Physical plane: The densest of the seven planes; where we presently reside.

Planes of creation: *Physical, astral, causal, akashic, mental, messianic,* and *buddhaic.* Just as there are seven colors in the rainbow and seven tones in a musical scale, each with a different vibratory rate, there are seven levels of being on the spectrum of creation. The slowest speed of vibration occurs on the physical plane; the fastest, on the buddhaic plane. From the buddhaic plane, energy returns to its source, the Tao.

Poles: Two aspects of an energy. The *positive pole* is an energy's true or love-based manifestation. The *negative pole* is the distortion or constriction of that energy by fear.

Positive pole: (See "Poles.")

Power: One of the seven modes. Its positive pole is *authority*; its negative pole is *oppression*. In power mode, one releases one's energy strongly.

Pragmatist: One of the seven attitudes. Its positive pole is *practicality*; its negative pole is *dogmatism*. Pragmatists see the world in terms of what works best or most efficiently.

Previous cycle: A grand cycle completed by an individual spark before its present one on earth. (See "Grand cycle.")

Priest: One of the seven essence roles. Its positive pole is *compassion*; its negative pole is *zeal*. Priests seek the higher good.

Probabilities: The range of potential future events. At any given moment, a possible future event can be described as having a certain percentage probability, e.g., a thirty-seven percent probability. As people continue to exercise their free will and make choices, that percentage can change.

Quadrate: A configuration of four souls who work together over many lifetimes; also known as "quadrant," although technically, a quadrant is one quarter of a quadrate. The positions of a quadrate are *love, knowledge, power,* and *support* (or *compassion*). The first and third positions are strongest.

Realist: One of the seven attitudes. Its positive pole is *perception*; its negative pole is *supposition*. Realists view the world in terms of what is; they focus on a situation's objective facts.

Reevaluation: The least common of the seven goals; called "retardation" in Yarbro. Its positive pole is *atavism* or *simplicity*; its negative pole is *withdrawal*. It is used for lifetimes spent processing past experiences.

Reincarnation: The idea that the soul lives multiple lifetimes, gaining experience through them.

Reincarnational self: A past-life, simultaneous, or potential-future self; another personality spawned by one's essence.

Rejection: (See "Discrimination.")

Repression: (See "Reserve.")

Reserve: One of the seven modes; called "repression" in Yarbro. Its positive pole is *restraint*; its negative pole is *inhibition*. In reserve mode, one draws one's energy inward and upward, in a contained manner.

Retardation: (See "Reevaluation.")

Role: One of the seven types of essences: *server, priest, artisan, sage, warrior, king,* and *scholar*. Everyone has a particular role. It defines the individual's way of being or fundamental style, not his worldly position.

Sage: One of the seven essence roles. Its positive pole is *expression*; its negative pole is *oration*. Sages seek insight.

Saturnian: One of the seven primary body types. Its positive pole is *rugged*; its negative pole is *gaunt*. Saturnian types tend to have a prominent bone structure and be tall. Psychologically, they tend to be steady, enduring, and paternal.

Scholar: One of the seven essence roles. Its positive pole is *knowledge*, which scholars seek; its negative pole is *theory*.

Self-deprecation: One of the seven chief features. Its positive pole is *humility*; its negative pole is *abasement*. It is a fear of being inadequate.

Self-destruction: One of the seven chief features. Its positive pole is *sacrifice*; its negative pole is *immolation*. It is a fear of losing control.

Sentient: Self-aware, choice-making consciousness. Humans and cetaceans (dolphins and whales) are the two sentient species on earth.

Sextant: A configuration of six souls who work together over many lifetimes. The positions of a sextant are *love, knowledge, power, support* (or *compassion*), *eccentric*, and *integrator*. The first and fourth positions are strongest.

Server: One of the seven essence roles; called "slave" in Yarbro. Its positive pole is *service*; its negative pole is *bondage*. Servers seek the common good.

Skeptic: One of the seven attitudes. Its positive pole is *investigation*; its negative pole is *suspicion*. Skeptics view the world with doubt.

Slave: (See "Server.")

Sliding: Temporarily moving to another overleaf. Neutral (assimilation axis) overleaves can slide to all others. Overleaves on the three other axes can slide only to their "partners" on the axis. For example, dominance can slide to submission, and vice versa.

Solar: One of the seven primary body types. Its positive pole is *radiant*; its negative pole is *ethereal*. Solar types tend to have slight, delicate bodies. They tend to be charismatic, childlike, and cheerful.

Soul age: The soul's stage of development relative to the physical plane. The five main physical-plane soul ages are *infant, baby, young, mature,* and *old*. (See also "Transcendental soul" and "Infinite soul.") Each soul age is divided into seven levels. (See "Soul age level.")

Soul age level: One of seven subdivisions of soul age, e.g., a person might be described as being "fifth-level young."

Spirit guide: Nonphysical souls who support a person's growth, help him complete his life tasks, and in general provide the spiritual assistance he needs. Many people are spirit guides to others when they are not incarnate.

Spiritual path: A way of living that emphasizes the growth of conscious awareness, particularly relative to the expression of agape, or unconditional love. (See also "Agape.")

Spiritualist: One of the seven attitudes. Its positive pole is *verification*; its negative pole is *faith*. Spiritualists view the world in terms of its possibilities.

Stagnation: (See "Flow.")

Stoic: One of the seven attitudes. Its positive pole is *tranquility*; its negative pole is *resignation*. Stoics view the world with serenity, feeling that outer events aren't of primary importance.

Stubbornness: One of the seven chief features. Its positive pole is *determination*; its negative pole is *obstinacy*. It is a fear of change.

Submission: One of the seven goals. Its positive pole is *devotion*; its negative pole is *subservience*. It is used for lifetimes that emphasize supporting a greater cause.

Support circle: A configuration containing twelve positions that offer the various kinds of support that each individual needs, making one's journey through life easier. The positions are *love, knowledge, compassion, mentor, beauty, child, humor, discipline, anchor, healer, enlightenment,* and *muse.*

Tao: The All That Is. It usually refers to the dimensionless ground of being rather than to its expression in the manifest universe's seven planes of creation (see "Planes of Creation"). (Pronounced *dow.*)

Task companion: An essence one teams up with in the beginning of a grand cycle (or during the infant soul cycle) to help with each lifetime's life task, either by having the complement of one's life task on the physical plane, or by being a spirit guide. It is the second-closest bond an essence can have, after that of essence twin. However, an essence twin relationship is inward-looking, whereas a task companion relationship is outward-looking.

Task mate: An essence who was one's task companion during a previous grand cycle.

Transcendental soul: The incarnation of a representative of a reunited entity, e.g., Gandhi. The transcendental soul is a catalyst for social transformation.

Venusian: One of the seven primary body types. Its positive pole is *voluptuous*; its negative pole is *obese*. Venusian types tend to have olive skin, dark hair, and rounded bodies. They tend to be sensuous, warm, and easygoing.

Warrior: One of the seven essence roles. Its positive pole is *persuasion*; its negative pole is *coercion*. Warriors seek challenge.

Young soul: Someone in the third of the five main physical-plane soul ages. The young soul cycle emphasizes lessons about worldly success.

INDEX

Q

R

S

ABOUT THE AUTHOR

SHEPHERD HOODWIN is a Laguna Beach, California channel, intuitive, workshop leader, and teacher. He also does past-life therapy, counseling, and channeling coaching (teaching others to channel). He has been channeling Michael since 1986.

He is the author of several articles on the Michael teachings, and seven books, including *Meditations for Self-Discovery—Guided Journeys for Communicating with Your Inner Self* and *Loving from Your Soul—Creating Powerful Relationships.*

His next book is *Opening to Healing Energy.* Other upcoming books include *Growing Through Joy, Being in the World,* and a fairy tale, *Sabina and the Angels' Golden Crystals.* He is also writing a collection of new age humor.

He is a graduate of the University of Oregon in Music Education, and is a songwriter, singer, and actor. He is currently writing a musical.

In terms of the Michael teachings, Shepherd is an old sage with sixteen previous grand cycles. He is in Cadre Three/Entity Two, with 5/4/3 casting, a sage essence twin, a goal of acceptance, a mode of observation sliding to passion and perseverance, an attitude of idealist, a chief feature of impatience, and a secondary chief feature of arrogance. He is in the emotional part of the intellectual center. His body type is primarily lunar, accounting for fifty-four percent of his body energy, and secondarily martial (thirty-six percent) and venusian (ten percent). His male/female energy ratio is forty-seven/fifty-three percent, and his frequency is sixty-four.

He can be contacted at shepherd@summerjoy.com or Summerjoy Press, 31423 S Coast Hwy #84, Laguna Beach CA 92651-6998, 949-499-3197, 877-SUMMERJoy (877-786-6375), http://summerjoy.com.